TIGERS
OF THE RAJ

TIGERS
OF THE RAJ

Pages from the Shikar Diaries – 1894 to 1949
of Colonel Burton, Sportsman and Conservationist

Edited by Jacqueline Toovey

ALAN SUTTON
1987

ALAN SUTTON PUBLISHING
BRUNSWICK ROAD · GLOUCESTER

First published 1987
Copyright © D.J. & J.W. Toovey 1987

British Library Cataloguing in Publication Data

Burton, Richard W.
  Tigers of the Raj : the Shikar diaries of
R.W. Burton, 1894–1949.
  1. Big game hunting—India
  I. Title   II. Toovey, D.J.
  799.2'6'0924   SK235

  ISBN 0-86299-335-0

Jacket: Painting by Martin Latham.
Photographs: Front, R.W. Burton's Ford car being ferried across
the Godavery river, 1928. Back, Drop-nets out on Vambanad Lake.

Typesetting and origination by
Alan Sutton Publishing Limited
Printed in Great Britain by
The Guernsey Press Company Ltd,
Guernsey, Channel Islands.

The family would like to dedicate this book to the memory of Colonel Burton's wife, Hilda, and their two daughters, Phyllis and Stella, who shared some of these adventures with him.

ACKNOWLEDGEMENTS

I would like to thank the Bombay Natural History Society for their permission to use extracts from the Articles written by Colonel Burton for publication in their Journal. I have also received encouragement and support from Colonel Burton's descendants, and particularly my own family who have lived with the 'Diary' over the several years it has taken to bring the book to completion. I would especially like to thank Colonel Burton's daughter, Mrs. Stella Malcolm for her interest throughout and for providing some of the earlier illustrations, my husband John for his constant support, and my son Richard, whose interest in the life of his great grandfather and whose helpful criticism and comments made the book come together when I occasionally despaired. Finally, I would like to thank Simon Kingston, and all those who have helped and encouraged me in the preparation of this book.

CONTENTS

'A Father's Advice to his Son'

If a sportsman true you'd be,
Listen carefully to me.

Never, never let your gun
Pointed be at anyone;
That it may unloaded be
Matters not the least to me.

When a hedge or fence you cross,
Though of time it cause a loss,
From your gun the cartridge take,
For the greater safety's sake.

If 'twixt you and neighbouring gun
Birds may fly or beasts may run,
Let this maxim e'er be thine:
Follow not across the line.

Stops and beaters oft unseen
Lurk behind some leafy screen;
Calm and steady always be:
Never shoot where you can't see.

Keep your place and silent be:
Game can hear and game can see:
Don't be greedy, better spared
Is a pheasant, than one shared.

You may kill or you may miss,
But at all times think of this:
All the pheasants ever bred
Won't repay for one man dead.

Commander Mark Beaufoy
from 'Game Pie',
by Eric Parker, 1925.

INTRODUCTION

COLONEL R.W. BURTON

'I think of the interest and unending enjoyment there is in the mere living of the jungle life, and it is this, more than the shikar, which forms the main attraction to those who like myself retain a desire to journey in wild places until advancing years inexorably call a halt.'   RWB.

Colonel Burton's shikar diaries were kept, together with his personal papers and a large number of photographs, in the black tin trunk which had accompanied him as he travelled throughout India. Amongst his papers, were many technical notes, letters and comments on conservation in India, and notes on a comprehensive Bibliography completed for the Bombay Natural History Society.

Richard Burton was a Cantonment Magistrate in India for fifty years. In his spare time, a sportsman and hunter of big game, he later became an active conservationist. His Shikar Diaries, begun in 1894 and continued until 1948, describe his many adventures from the mountain isolation of Kashmir to the arid plains of the Deccan and the jungle covered hills of Southern India. Colonel Burton was an acknowledged authority on big game hunting in India. In his travels throughout the country he acquired a broad knowledge of its wildlife. Sitting quietly in his tent writing up the events of the day in his diary, he recorded a lively picture of his surroundings. As he grew older, his love of fishing took him to unknown places like the Laccadive Islands, and sea fishing off the Western Coast of India, as well as to the unexplored lands of Northern Burma. His wife was not really interested in this outdoor life, and showed a great deal of patience as she accompanied her husband from one jungle camp to another, but she was able occasionally to escape to civilisation by staying with friends or with her married daughter.

Using the material from his diaries, Colonel Burton wrote a number of travel and adventure tales for publication, initially in the *Magazine of the Indian State Railways*, and later in the *Journal of the Bombay Natural History Society*. He also wrote knowledgeable articles such as those on 'The Indian Wild Dog' and 'The Linaloe Tree', for the Society's Journal. He had no academic training as a naturalist, but possessed an awareness of detail and a keen sense of observation. Some men, such as Jim Corbett in his books, made much of the heroics of hunting tigers, but these books were written from memory as adventure stories, also Corbett knew little of India outside the Kumaon Hills. Many hunters have a natural awareness of the need for conservation, but most were not deeply involved. Burton's concern drove him to positive action against the combination of apathy and vested interests which existed at that time. The cause of conservation was not popular amongst the majority and it was left to a few who had vision and energy to help the Bombay Natural History Society in its struggle for recognition of this cause.

Many sportsmen, especially planters, hunted and fished only on their own Estates. Because of his financial circumstances, Burton had to 'shikar on a shoe-string' and this brought him into closer contact with the country and its people than those who, with wealth and position, chose to shikar for reasons of prestige. Casual shooting for small game and birds, such as duck or snipe, was fairly common in the area around and within riding distance of the Regimental Barracks or Cantonment.

In the 19th century and earlier, big-game hunting was a very popular way for the Indian Princes to demonstrate hospitality and wealth to visiting dignitaries. In the British Army in India many officers, and especially those who had any ability for shooting, were expected to 'try for a tiger'. They developed a style of shikar without the ceremony of the Indian Princes, which was the casual arranging of beats, and limited by what a young officer could afford. The higher ranks, and those with money, embarked on more extensive hunting and shooting trips.

In most parts of India there was strict observance of game laws, which consisted of a close season for hunting certain animals and birds, a permit system whereby a licence was issued listing the animals which could be shot, and the appointment of a Game Watcher or Forester who kept a record of all the animals killed. The jungle was divided into shooting blocks which were booked for a month and restricted the sportsman to a particular area. There were also parts of the country which belonged to the Indian States, for which permission to shikar had to be obtained from the Head of the State, and this was often refused. Some of the Indian States had policies of conservation and most of them had restrictions of some sort, which were often based on religious beliefs. All this, together with the limited range of the guns used at this time, controlled the game without any danger of eliminating it.

By 1946, the destruction of the jungle – the animals' real environment, the increased effectiveness of guns, and the encroachment of the human population into the wilderness was a more disturbing factor in keeping a true balance of nature. His awareness of this led Colonel Burton to take a positive role in pressing for an immediate and effective conservation policy for India. Salim Ali, President of the Bombay Natural History Society and an ornithologist of world-wide repute, wrote to Oryx in 1960 when Editor of the Society's Journal, '. . . that he wished to make it widely known, the strongest voice within his Society was that of Lieut. Col. Burton', and added that '. . . it was largely Burton's missionary zeal for conservation which made the Bombay Natural History Society take up the cause in good earnest; and it was because of his and the Society's ceaseless demand for action, through the Press, radio, lectures, and the Journal, that the Government of India constituted the Indian Board for Wild Life.'

One of the first results from the constitution of the Board of Control in 1952 was the publication of *The Preservation of Wild Life in India – A Compilation* by Colonel Burton, which listed all the important articles contributed to the Journal on the subject of wild life preservation. In 1948 Burton had also published a brochure *Preservation of Wild Life – India's Vanishing Asset*, which was circulated widely to those in authority, in an effort to arouse official concern.

The diary entries relate to his adventures hunting and fishing. Much of the appeal of a diary is in the variety of information it contains. It is also an instant record of events which could otherwise be lost to memory, as well as a record of the personal thoughts of the writer. The diaries were hard to decipher being written in pencil and cramped onto the page; but often so exciting to read that it was impossible to put them down.

Extracts from Col. Burton's diaries and some of his articles, have been put together with a selection from the large number of his photographs, to give a lively picture of his adventures in the rural areas of India at that particular time in its history. Some sketches by his daughter Phyllis have also been included. This book has been compiled as much as possible using Colonel Burton's own words. The spelling of Indian names and words is as Colonel Burton wrote them, and sometimes varies within the text.

JACQUELINE TOOVEY

INDIA

1894
TO
1903

Chapter 1

FAMILY

'My dearest Dick,' wrote Georgiana Burton to her son in August 1921, 'I hope you are enjoying Kashmir, for which you were to start on June 30th. I can only say of your three days in the jungle – Growling panthers close by – dreadful risks! Wild elephants which you did not see – pray be careful!' and she ended her letter – 'I beg of you to take care of yourself and never to forget what a valuable life yours is, your ever loving mother, my dear dear Dick, G. Burton.'

Richard was born in Madras on 5th November 1868, the sixth son and seventh child of Georgiana and Edmond Burton. Commissioned from Sandhurst in 1889, to the 1st Battalion of the Lancashire Fusiliers, he was transferred in 1890 to the 2nd Battalion XX Regiment, stationed at Ahmadnagar, India. He was posted to the Indian Army in December 1890 at Belgaum, and after having spent two months in Burma, moved to the Hyderabad Contingent of the 5th Madras Infantry at Aurangabad in 1891.

By 1890, Richard's parents had returned to England and were living at Whitehaven, Cumberland. In 1902 he received the news of his father's death, but was unable to get leave to go back to England. Indeed, in all his thirty four years' service, he took a total of only four years' leave out of India, and most of that was sick leave. He wrote regularly to his mother giving her all the news from India, and she sent him letters always on the first day of each month. In one of these, after having received from him a vivid account of hunting in the jungle, she wrote – '. . . I enjoyed very much reading your journal, but my usual desire – no dangerous beasts, tigers, bears.'

'Dangerous beasts' were not likely to prevent Richard from embarking on numerous adventures. His love of shikar was certainly inherited from his father, who was a noted big game hunter and had published two books based on his life and hunting experiences in India. Writing as early as 1857, General E.F. Burton expressed the unconventional view that the tiger should not be shot to complete extinction, but that a balance should be found within the environment between the needs of the people and the acceptance of wildlife. The following extract is from one of his books:–

'The man-eater should, of course, be followed up to the death, but the ordinary tiger, if kept to a moderate number, does more good than harm. No doubt he lifts many cattle, but he also kills an enormous number of deer and hog, which would otherwise overrun and destroy the crops; indeed I have known land surrendered and villages abandoned on this very account.'

In 1890 when Richard Burton first joined his Regiment in India, the large number of tigers living in the jungle resulted in a large number of tigers shot, since at that time conservation was not considered important. Burton notes that General Gerard, when shooting in the Chanda district in May 1890, shot eleven tigers, bringing his personal bag of tiger to two hundred and twenty seven!

The Northern cities of Calcutta, Delhi, and the hill station of Simla, were well known to the British Raj as these were the seats of Government, but many British subjects made their homes in India, often over several generations, and were spread over the whole of the Continent, from North to South, and East to West. Richard Burton's parents lived in Madras on the Eastern coast. In spite of the harshness of its climate, India was a fascinating country for many Europeans. In one of his books General Burton gives the following graphic account of the monsoon weather in Madras, and the storms which swept along the Eastern coast.

'At no season of the year is the climate of Madras very pleasant. The heat is great, the atmosphere close and steamy, but tempered in the afternoon by the cooling sea breeze. At its first sighing gusts all the heavy cane blinds are drawn up and the grateful wind enters the rooms, stirring the chandelier drops with a tinkling sound from which they are not inaptly designated the 'joy bells'.

'When the north-east monsoon arrives, and heavy clouds mount up tier upon tier, wind-driven over the darkened sky, and when rain falls, first in heavy drops and then in rushing torrents, the roadside ditches run fast with reddened water swirling along under a buoyant covering of leaves, sticks and straws accumulated during many months of dry hot weather. When the thick coating of red dust is washed from the reviving shrubs and trees, then does Madras enjoy, for a while, a purer, cooler climate.

'Croaking frogs squat on the margin of every puddle. Snakes, driven from their hiding places by the flooding rain, crawl into the huts. Scorpions and centipedes also invade the huts, and hosts of less noxious insects creep, hop and fly over the moistened plain. Winged white ants, bursting from their deep-seated nests, especially swarm, the flickering flight of their gauzy wings glitters in the occasional sun-gleams. Hundreds of beetles, great and small, drone and whirr in every open room and flop on floors and tables, lying with feebly scrabbling legs on their sharded backs. These are mostly inoffensive, but two species, commonly called 'green bugs' though one of them is a russet brown, are disgusting in smell and if touched, or worse, crushed on one's person, emit a most nauseous odour. Every damp coppice and every little swamp is alive with fireflies, their green light sparkling like living emeralds among the leaves.

'A cyclone on the Coromandel coast is a terrible exhibition of the power of the winds and waves. With the moaning gusts of wind preceded by drenching rain, and ragged drifts of cloud flying before the storm, the full fury of the hurricane rushes up, seeming to blend the leaden sea and dull grey vapour, the drifting rain and salt biting spray, in one bewildering mass of confusion. Tortured trees groan and twist. Grass roofs, torn from their supporting walls, rise in the air, and career like huge bats over the plain. All animal life, human and quadruped, seeks shelter, and many wretched birds are whipped to death by the lashing branches of trees in which they have taken refuge. Such ships as have not slipped and put to sea strain furiously, high pitching at their anchors, and occasionally are driven broadside on to the fatal beach.'

In spite of the strangeness of the country, General Burton enjoyed living in India. As an officer in the Madras Staff Corps he travelled throughout Southern India, and arranged shikar trips whenever possible. In 1857 he married his cousin Georgiana Burton, who had travelled out from England. At that time the Suez Canal had not been built, which made the journey to India extremely difficult and tedious. She often told her children how she came across the Eastern Desert from Cairo to Suez riding on a camel. She was one of a large family, with eight brothers and eight sisters. Her eldest brother Edmond was an outstanding athlete, an Oxford Blue, a champion oarsman unbeaten on the river, and one of the fastest amateur sprint runners in England. He also won the first Grand National Steeple-lechase when it was held at Market Harborough in 1860 and again in 1861, and was a founding member of the Grand National Hunt Steeplechase Committee.

Georgiana was escorted to Madras by two of her brothers, Henry and Francis, who were serving in different Regiments in India. Later that year, Francis was in the forces fighting for the relief of Lucknow and was mentioned in Despatches. Knowing that his brother Henry was among those trapped in the Residency, it must have been with the greatest courage and determination he fought his way through the streets of the city. Following so soon after the massacre at Cawnpore, the besieged garrison at Lucknow held out through the long hot summer and prayed that the relieving forces would soon reach and break through the rebel ranks of sepoys.

Georgiana and Edmond Burton had nine sons and three daughters, all born in India. As was common with many families of this size, all their sons followed their father's profession and went into the Army and all of them served in the Indian Army except for Geoffrey, their youngest son. He was a brilliant sportsman, like his uncle, but his life was tragically ended when in 1893 he drowned off the coast of Norfolk whilst saving his sister from drowning. He was only nineteen at the time, and still a cadet at Sandhurst.

A strict attention to detail was instilled into the family by their parents, and this is very noticeable in Richard's diary entries. In 1920, Georgiana wrote to her son – 'Your name is Richard Watkins Burton, please, so your last signature is not correct. There is another Richard Burton belonging to our family who is my cousin's son. . . You should in every letter you write sign your whole name – and not merely a part of your name. . .' But, she welcomed the letters giving her news from India and which enclosed extracts from the Shikar Diaries, and she wrote later – 'I have told you before how much I enjoyed reading your diary, and read it several times – in spite of the writing not being as beautiful as mine!!' Her love and affection show through the strictness of her upbringing as she ends her letter – 'Give my love to Hilda and to my two dear grand-daughters. I will write to you again on October 1st. Again, I impress upon you not to risk your valuable life by hunting dangerous beasts. Your ever loving mother, G. Burton.'

Her anxiety was understandable. She had seen four of her nine sons die before her. In 1905, Aubrey, who was a year younger than Richard, died after a riding accident in India when he was only thirty four years old. Her second son, Gerard, who was Commandant of the 54th Sikhs, died a year later, and her beloved Robert, the second youngest, died in 1918 of pneumonia whilst on active service in Mesopotamia. Richard was now the youngest of her surviving sons; another of her sons, Reginald, was also a keen big game hunter and author like his father. Her three daughters were artistic, and the eldest, Clara, drew the illustrations for her father's books.

Richard outlived all his brothers and sisters, except for his sister Jo, with whom

4

5

CHAPTER
I

1
The house in Secunderabad
where Richard W. Burton was
born, 5 November 1868

2 & 3
Colonel Burton's two
daughters, Phyllis and Stella

4
The wedding of Lieutenant
R.W. Burton to Hilda Stuart
in Bangalore, 19 June 1895

5
'Paddy', a Kerry Blue terrier,
given to Richard Burton in
1894 following the death of his
previous owner, M.F.A.
Sexton, from wounds inflicted
by a tigress

6
Mrs Hilda Burton with
Phyllis, 1899

3

he corresponded regularly. He was never particularly concerned about old age, and when in his ninety third year he heard of the death of a former friend and comrade, remarked – 'He died? How extraordinary! What did he die of?' However, this must have registered to some extent, as the following year he wrote out his own Obituary, since, he said, there was no longer anyone left who could write it correctly.

He was elected one of the first members of the Bombay Natural History Society, on 23rd March 1893. Two years later he married Hilda Stuart, the daughter of Charles Alexander Stuart I.C.S. Madras, at St. Mark's Church, Bangalore, and by 1900 they had two daughters, Phyllis and Stella. In 1903 he was thrown from a horse and the broken leg which resulted meant three years' convalescence in England, and a final shortening of the leg by four inches. This meant a withdrawal from active service, but he returned to India in 1906 as a Cantonment Magistrate and Superintendent of Railway Police. When he broke his other leg many years later this four inch difference was reduced to three and a half inches! He served both in the Deccan and the Central Provinces and for many years in the Himalayas. He retired in 1923, and was then able to hunt and fish as much as his income permitted.

Colonel Burton later became an active member of the Advisory Committee of the Bombay Natural History Society and his ceaseless efforts in support of the Society were instrumental in creating the constitution of the Indian Board for Wildlife. He and his wife moved to England in 1953, where he lived quietly until he died in 1963, aged ninety five.

The Diaries begin in 1889. On leaving Sandhurst, Burton joined the Regiment at Maryhill Barracks as 2nd Lieutenant. He spent eight months in Scotland before being posted out to India. With some of the other young officers of the Regiment he often went out shooting for duck and snipe, usually to Possil Loch which was nearby, and the diary entries record some of these days.

DIARY

Scotland – April 1889. Possil Loch was twenty minutes walk from Maryhill Barracks. It was a swamp on the site of a disused coal mine, and most dangerous to shoot on being in many parts a quaking bog. I several times fell through the surface and was once saved only by my gun which I placed crosswise and so supported myself, afterwards crawling out crocodile fashion to firmer soil. I used to wear high waders – waist high – and recollect very well getting them full of icy cold water, having gone into a hole over my waist, and having to get rid of the water by doing a gymnastic straight arm balance with my toes up against a thorn bush and so let the water run out on my head and shoulders. I got Tallents to go with me one day, but after a venture on the bog he decided the edge of it was safer for him, being a family man.

I made the acquaintance of a poaching labourer one day by his small spaniel bitch taking to him a snipe which I had shot. I used afterwards always to call for his dog on my way to the loch. His cottage was the farther side of a canal and the dog used to swim over to me when I called it. She was a splendid little dog, A.1. retriever, and most obedient EXCEPT WHEN HUNGRY! First time I took her out she ate, feathers and all, several snipe which I shot. I discovered this was pure HUNGER, and on future occasions always gave her a good meal of biscuits. 'Nell' was her name and I heard of her death not long after I got out to India.

I had a rough punt made in the Regimental workshop which I used for the deep water and for crossing from one side to another. I kept no record of my bag, but used to get five or six snipe on most days. I shot a few duck also; once by moonlight out of the punt.

Chapter 2

AURANGABAD AND RAICHUR

'No doubt to learn to forget is as necessary as to learn to remember, but memories of what we have seen and experienced in the way of sport do not come within that category, so let us to our memories.'

JOURNAL _____

It is some small consolation to look over the old diaries and recall those times before the advent of the motor car, when we were young and enjoying all that life in a military station had to give. Not too much to do, with plenty of leisure for sport and shikar. No work on Thursdays, except the rifle range, and that was not all the year round. Weekends during the cold weather were frequently spent out of the station. Anything up to fifteen miles was the limit and we would ride out to be at the meeting place by early morning. Those chilly star-lit rides gave an exhilarating and adventurous feeling. There would be the deep solemn note of a horned owl, the pack-gathering call of prowling jackals, the staccato bark of the fox, and the croak of a pond heron returning from its nightly feed in the marshy lagoon by the river. Then would come the dawn, the song of birds, the call of peafowl, partridge and quail, and the screech of parrots flighting to the crops.

A favourite place from Aurangabad was the plateau between the fortress of Daulatabad and the Caves of Ellora. There, beating the jungly slopes and ravines with a line of men, we would enjoy varied sport with grey partridge, quail and painted sandgrouse, and the few small ponds were stalked for common teal which might be found there. Since that time, archaeology has become an established care in Indian States, so these caves, as also those at Ajanta which were neglected and wholly uncared for during many centuries, are now tidied up, restored and made attractive for visitors.

On 30 April 1890 Richard Burton left Glasgow on board HMS Euphrates bound for Bombay. His first posting was to Ahmadnagar to the 2nd Battalion XX Regiment. Five months later he was sent on detachment duty to Kirkee, where, in the Captain's absence, he commanded the Regiment on the occasion of an inspection by Lord Roberts, Commander-in-Chief India. Sport was a popular activity for the young unmarried officers of the Regiment; the main activities being polo, golf, fishing, hunting and shooting. Large numbers of wildfowl were attracted to the 'tanks' which served as a reservoir or water supply to the area and it was here that Burton liked to go out shooting whenever he had the opportunity, frequently wading up to his arms in the water with his belt of cartridges wrapped safe and dry around his topee. Careful and detailed records were kept of these shoots.

In December 1890, Burton joined the 23rd Madras Infantry at Belgaum, and four months later went with the Regiment to Mandalay. In July that year he went by steamer up the Irrawaddy to visit his brother Ged (Henry Gerard Burton) who was Commandant of the Mogaung Levy, Burma Military Police at Bhamo. Before 1891 the country beyond the Confluence of the Upper Irrawaddy was completely unknown save for one expedition in 1884. By 1930, when Burton visited Burma again, there was a motorable road and a railway had been built as far as Myitkyina. Previous to the advent of the railway the greater part of the stretch of country between Mogaung and Myitkyina was without human habitation. In an article written in 1930 for the Indian State Railways magazine Burton commented –

JOURNAL ————————————————————————————————————

Travellers passing through the district in 1891 were obliged to light fires round their camps at night to protect the transport animals from the depredations of tigers. Now the railway passes through this tract, which has been constituted a Game Sanctuary. I have vivid recollections of the First Defile, and of the river rising twenty feet in one night, and of the multitudes of winged insects; I had to dine under mosquito netting on deck. White ants were swept up in bucketfulls and the whole river was white with them. I recollect also a dust storm on 'the shore' near the river. I was riding and had to stand still for twenty minutes; couldn't see the ponies ears while I was sitting in the saddle.

He contracted fever at Mandalay, but when things were beginning to look bleak, was fortunate to receive a transfer to the 5th Infantry Hyderabad Contingent stationed at Aurangabad. Here his health immediately began to improve and by October he was sufficiently recovered to go hunting again with his beloved dogs. With one or two friends he rode out into the open country after foxes, hares and jackal. The thrill for Burton was in the fast, reckless riding and being out with his dogs.

JOURNAL ————————————————————————————————————

That early morning meeting of Master and pack! What a pleasure it used to be. Each dog had its own distinctive manner of expressing delight. 'Bob' staunch and solid quietly wagged his tail; 'Pup' showed her pearly teeth in a delighted grin; old 'Nelly', 'Bob's' inseparable companion pranced about like a puppy. So the memory runs back bringing to mind dogs big and small, and of various breeds. 'Stag' a Persian hound, and 'Prince' an Australian, formed the first nucleus of the Bobbery Pack, with 'Jupiter' a country bred greyhound, 'Jingo' and 'Sloe'. Dogs, alas, are often shortlived in this country of so many speedy and fatal ailments to man and beast.

I recall one memorable morning when, with a friend, we galloped after a jack over the top of a rocky hill, across several stone quarries, and down a steep jungly slope on the other side. We failed to get the hounds to see him and had to abandon the chase. As we walked back a mile or so to where we had started, I was astonished at the places we had galloped over, and yet could not attempt to cross at a walk. At one place my pony had tried to stop at a perpendicular drop in the sheet rock, but being unable to do so had been obliged to drop some four or five feet onto a slippery surface down which he slithered for some yards before regaining his equilibrium, when he was again urged on his mad career. Ginger was indeed a gallant beast, and a great handful on such occasions.

The best and most pleasant time of year for this sport is during the early part of the rains before the grass gets high and the cover too thick. The fresh feel of the air and a tinge of green all over the countryside is an extraordinary relief after the heat of the previous three or four months. Myriads of flying white ants issue from termite mounds, providing a ready feast for foxes and jackals, which I have found to have their stomachs distended with this easily gorged meal. It was my custom always to hold an autopsy of the stomach contents and at that season the jackals were found to be in the habit of eating various fruits besides the many lizards, rats, mice, and small birds which were more easily come by.

Wolves were not uncommon, and when riding out to camp one morning, my only weapon the cleaning rod of a gun, I sighted two of these marauders and gave chase on my pony. The animals had recently fed heavily, having probably killed an antelope, so I actually ran them to a standstill and prodded the big male wolf with the end of the rod. Leaving the pair exhausted in a pool of water I rode back to camp for a spear, but on my return the wolves had gone. Our bobbery pack dogs never ran into wolves, and the only time they came up with them, turned tail before the raised bristles and great threatening teeth.

During the cold weather the counter attraction of shooting gave the hunted animals a well-earned respite. Among the hills adjacent to Aurangabad were valleys in which we had good days in quest of painted partridge, peafowl and duck, besides the usual grey partridge and hares; but we quickly realised that feathered game cannot stand being shot as well as preyed upon by its natural enemies, so confined our shoots to about two days only at any one spot during the season.

In the level country we had many pleasant mornings after common sand grouse, first waiting for them at their drinking places, and then following up the packs in the surrounding country, where we encircled them until they rose with that rapid disconcerting 'jump off' which gives them several yards start of the uplifted gun.

Burton was an exceptionally good rifle shot and the choice of gun was very important, particularly since this might mean the difference between life and death. Early in his career he bought and sold several different types of gun. At Deolali Musketry School, using the Martini Heavy, he was an easy first on the range at the shorter distances and with some effort maintained the lead at the longer ranges. However, in 1893 he had to go into Madras Ophthalmic Hospital for treatment of an opaque cornea of his left eye and granular lids.

DIARY ——————————————————————————————

I never recovered complete definition of sight. At near view I couldn't see foresight of the rifle clearly; so learnt to shoot from my left shoulder with rifle both on the range and in jungle; a very useful accomplishment, as, for quick shots using a big foresight, I am quite all right from right shoulder.

Shot with a new gun made to order by J & W Talley, London. It was a 'Ubique' shot and ball gun. A very good shot gun, but not accurate with ball; took 6 drs. black powder. Sold it at end of year to a tea planter in Assam who was very pleased with it and killed buffalo with it. In January 1893 I sold for Rs.100 the twelve-bore gun by Edwinson C. Green of Cheltenham which my father gave me on my coming out to India. With this gun I shot very well indeed. In March 1894, got a twelve-bore Paradox gun made to order for me by Holland & Holland: used it during shooting trip April–May 1894; and eventually sold it in September 1895, when hard up in Madras

General Hospital for Rs.500. I gave £42 for it. After this bought a twelve-bore shot gun by Jeffery from my brother R.G.B, sold it in 1896.

From 30th October to 8th November 1891, I was employed with Morris in bringing up to date the map of the country between Aurangabad and the Godavery River. Our work was sent to Calcutta and a map printed for use at the Camp of Exercise.

On the march to Raichur 1892–3. We started from Aurangabad with cholera in the Regiment, but shook it off after a few marches. M.F.A. Sexton caught us up some way out; he was Adjutant, I was Quarter Master. He brought with him from Ireland a splendid old Irish Terrier 'Paddy'. First thing Paddy did was to lay hold of Jock, the clumber, and split his skin across top of the skull. Took many stitches to sew it up. He was a great fighter but the gentlest of dogs with people and children. When Sexton died I kept Paddy. He (Paddy) died in 1897 at Raichur.

As well as shooting, there were many opportunities for fishing either at Raichur or Hyderabad. He went out usually with his friends Sexton, Andain and Fagan, to the Beema or Kistna Rivers or to one of the tanks. The first mahseer caught in the Kistna River was 35lb. hooked by Sexton in April 1893. Andain's mahseer of 36lb. held the record over a period of five years, and Burton came close to these with a mahseer of 34lb. Burton's eldest brother, Charley was stationed at Madras and joined him on several fishing trips.

DIARY ——————————————————————————————————————

30.12.93. Beema River, Yadgiri. 1 mahseer – 26lb. This fish is the same that broke me on the 23rd. C.W.W.B. with me on the second occasion, the 7ft. Berthon boat nearly swamped when playing the fish as I put my weight back and so the stern, with the weighty C.W.W. went under water! Photo of this fish hangs in the verandah of Harcourt's bungalow.

Raichur. The 5th Infantry Hyderabad Contingent was at Raichur from January 1893 to November 1897; and again in 1903. The whole of that time I was either Quartermaster (until June 1894) or Adjutant. Had it not been for the Kistna River, seven miles distant, it would have been a worse place 'penal settlement' than it was. That fine bird, the demoiselle crane, used to frequent the sandbanks in the river bed and feed in the jowari fields, where we used to stalk the wary birds with small success. Duck and teal were found in small packs along the river.

JOURNAL ——————————————————————————————————————

The Kistna was a great standby and many were the fine mahseer we captured by means of a 16ft. fly rod. The heaviest taken was 42lbs. Blank days were also not infrequent! There are quicksands in the river and care has to be taken when wading in certain places. Few things are more terrifying than to be bogged down in a quicksand, but this was the experience of several of us when riding about that country. The unfortunate pony would be extracted with staring coat, and dripping with sweat. One officer when crossing a sandy nala, cantered into a quicksand while two villagers squatting under a tree on the opposite side offered no assistance, but quickly vanished from the scene, leaving the officer and his nag to do the best they could in almost hopeless circumstances. Fortunately he managed to struggle out, and obtained help before the pony went below; that most terrifying mishap might easily have been a tragedy. Such apathy on the part of the native cultivator is born of the universal dread in India of being mixed up with any affair which might lead to contact with the police and the Courts. In this case they would have let horse and man disappear beneath the surface and never said a word.

The ponies we owned as Subaltern's hacks were usually not above 13.3, which was polo height in the nineties. Horses have wonderful eyesight at night and seldom did our nags put a foot wrong, however rough the track, but once riding home from the river with Andain, by moonlight, I turned a complete somersault, pony and all, into a Sendi (thorny aloe) bush.

DIARY _____

I got with difficulty into the saddle as my thigh muscles were pierced by many spikes, twenty seven spikes between hip and knee of my left leg: all except two were taken out same evening by Mahoney, Assistant Surgeon. One came out some three weeks later and did no harm; one was so deeply embedded over top of my knee that Mahoney could not remove it, he bent his forceps in the attempt. Of course he should have at once cut down and removed it. Was laid up with this for many weeks. Thorn was cut out in June by Surgeon Captain Carr White at Bangalore. I was in splints for weeks with the result that knee became rigid. Eventually had to go to Madras General Hospital where knee was forcibly bent under chloroform two days running. Later Maitland took over the case and cured me by passive movement and massage. Had to sell my twelve-bore Paradox to pay expenses and was incapacitated from all sport until 19.11.95. The remainder of my time at Raichur I used a borrowed gun, lent me by Harcourt. He was always a most kind and good friend to me and December 1898 were the last days' shooting I had with him.

In 1894 there was never any doubt in the minds of the community that reducing the number of tigers which roamed in the jungle the country would make a safer and better place to live. Tigers bred quite freely and there was no indication that these would ever become a threatened species. For a young officer there was also the excitement and the challenge of danger. So it was with the certain knowledge that they would encounter tigers during their march through the jungle that Burton and Sexton set out from Raichur in April 1894. They were joined at Kazipet by Lieut. Brewster, and then marched to Kotajpur, a distance of fifty two miles which took seven days. They halted at Nagarum to collect supplies before crossing the Godavery river into British Territory.

JOURNAL _____

In many parts of the land the tiger-infested jungles of former years have been pushed back by the needs of an increasing population, yet there are parts of the country where India is still as it was half a century ago, and in such a locality was my entry to tiger shooting.

The transport of our camp kit was by pack bullock and it took us more than a week's marching to arrive at our first camp. Two days later we had our first tiger beat. It was the tigress which slew the tethered buffalo, as we saw later by the fang marks in the neck, for the teeth of the tiger were several sizes larger. He had probably joined in the ready made feast during his night's wanderings, and of the 'kill' there was scarcely anything left.

I have a very clear recollection of that, my first tiger beat. There was the assembly of the beaters at the camp, the sorting out of the small boys and the unfit. Then there was the drawing of lots by means of dry grass for the posting of the guns – longest, furthest, – the whispered instruction to the men posted behind the machan, and then followed a long wait in a leafless tree under a scorching sun, for it was mid-April and very hot. The bleached boughs and trunks of deciduous trees afford no shade, in and about the roots of trees are drifts of forest debris which are dry as tinder and crackle underfoot, and the large dry teak leaves go off like pistol shots. At such a season the tiger likes to lie among the feathery green tamarisk bushes in the river beds where he can repose on wet mud, or partly submerged in water, to keep off the ever-pestering flies.

Although the heat produces nearly overpowering drowsiness, the insistence of eye-flies prevents any chance of falling asleep. At this mid-day hour, except for the strident shrill of the cicadas, there is in the forest a silence almost greater than that at midnight. No birds twitter, no insects fly or chirp, all nature seems faint under the intolerable glare; only the salamander-like lizards are abroad. The barrels of one's weapon are too hot to hold, so rest upon a convenient bough. There are pulls at the water bottle and mopping of brow: it seems a long wait.

An hour passed, and then I heard a shot fired by the head shikari as a signal for the beat to begin. A renewal of shouts and rattling of sticks set every living thing in the forest on the move; first to appear were the peafowl and the junglefowl, some of them detecting me with their sharp eyes. Several jackals came slinking by and a pair of mongoose pattered over the dry leaves; small birds fluttered from tree to tree, and the plum-necked paraquets – 'live emeralds in the sun' – came screeching past. Soon the form of the tiger is viewed through the vista of bamboos and tree trunks. He looks huge; small chance has anything borne down by that massive form, gripped by those terrible jaws. His ruff stands out white on either side of his neck. The placing of the first shot is everything. With a grunt the great brute bounds forward, but then comes the welcome call from Abdul, 'girgaya, margaya' – 'he is fallen, he is dead'.

Two wild shots came in quick succession from B.'s twelve-bore rifle on the right, and I saw the tigress escaping with long bounds through the trees, the trunks flashing past her striped hide like the posts of a paling. Descending from our trees we met together. It appeared that the tiger and three cubs had broken on the right. The cubs were the size of mastiffs and allowed to pass; the big tiger following behind them lay where fired at. The tigress had stood in a nala before S., whose bullet, aimed at her head through a bunch of leaves, found a home in an unsuspected sturdy bough. The tiger measured 9ft. 1in.

All beats are not so simple, but mostly they are. It is only when a bad or hasty initial shot is made that danger arises and tragedy can befall; most such happenings can be traced to some error, some hastiness or mistake, and seldom to mischance. There is the Law of Karma – every action must have its result.

All sportsmen who pursue dangerous game have, sooner or later, to follow up a wounded animal. It is very important to make sure that your weapon is loaded! Also cartridges should never be carried loose in a pocket. When S. climbed into his tree, all but three of his cartridges fell out of his pocket. He did not know this until firing his third shot.

Do not part with your rifle when out shooting! Carry it yourself. This advice seems as unnecessary as that to 'make sure you are loaded', but it is often neglected to the undoing of the careless sportsman.

After crossing the Godavery River, they marched south. Several stops were made on the journey to camp, usually for a few days at a time, and on 10th May they arrived at Cherla.

11th May 1894.   Kill at Keshupur: two beats. First blank; second a tigress broke to Brewster who wounded her slightly in bottom of girth merely cutting the skin. She broke away between him and Sexton towards the village then came back at a gallop – luckily under Sexton's tree, who broke her spine by a fine shot, and finished her with two more shots; one breaking thigh and other in shoulder. She was very savage and as she was heading for the beaters would doubtless have scragged someone.

25th. Kill at Keshupur. First beat, she broke to me at a gallop – clean miss both barrels over her back at about twenty yards. Shankri's mistake in putting cloth too much forward and too near me, or she might have come at a walk. Second beat broke to Sexton who made a very fine shot at about seventy yards and hit her at point of right shoulder. He called out that he had knocked her over and that she had gone back out of his sight. We decided to reconnoitre at once, and to do so without any natives. We followed the tracks for about twenty yards, when she suddenly showed herself with a growl, but sat down at once without giving a chance. Brewster climbed into a tree while Sexton and I were ready in case of a charge: he had NO FIELD GLASSES, neither had any of us, he could not see her so came down again.

We now decided to wait two hours and then walk her up. We tried to get her to move by putting the beat in motion, but with no result. Of course we did not press the beat and let them merely make a tremendous din without advancing too far. At 4.30 we took with us two trackers, also Samand Singh with a Martini Carbine and Gulyar Singh with a hog spear. We had gone about sixty yards from place where she was first hit when she got up with a grunt and came straight for us. The jungle was fairly thick – a number of small saplings, but clear for the last fifteen yards. The line was as under and she was heading for Gulyar Singh.

.	.	.	.	.	.	.
Burton	Brewster	Gulyar Singh	Tracker	Samand Singh	Tracker	Sexton

Sexton could see her coming most of the way, and he headed her as she came, but his rifle would not, or did not go off: he then appears to have brought his rifle down and again sighted her when she was clear of the jungle, but still his rifle did not go off. Brewster and I did not see her to shoot at until she was about fifteen yards off. Brewster fired and in doing so stepped in front of me and prevented me from getting in a shot. I just had time to swing my gun over his head and take a snap shot behind the line, hitting the tigress in the shoulder (the bullet travelling forward to the neck and breaking the spine, and stopping against the skin on the further side), as she was actually in the air in front of Sexton who was staggering back a little. She came with a rush – not any great leaps. She got him by the upper left arm in her mouth, and one forepaw on his head and the other on his left hand, and knocked him over backwards.

We rushed up and forced her jaw open and released his arm. Tigress was gasping and I fired my left barrel into her head. She was practically dead already; dead indeed when she bit Sexton one can say. Sexton was very white and faint from shock. He could have got out of way of the beast if he had jumped to one side, and if he had done so there would have been no accident as the tigress would have fallen dead; but he knew trackers had bolted and thought she would get one of them. We laid Sexton against a tree and I at once syringed the wounds out with a strong solution of carbolic acid, and then cauterised them with caustic and bound them up.

I examined the tigress and found that Sexton's first shot had caught her on point of right shoulder and with proper penetration would have travelled forward to heart and lungs. His rifle was .500 by Reilly: rolled case: 5 drs. CTH black powder: 340 grain hollow point copper capped Eley bullet. The bullet having no sufficient base had split up and merely made a flesh wound about three inches deep, as I found by probing with my fore finger. Brewster's rifle was a similar one. (NO HEAVY RIFLE HANDY). His twelve-bore was not to be found when we started to follow up as the bearer of it had gone off for a drink or something of the kind.

The tigress had several spear thrusts from Gulyar Singh; all given uselessly as the tigress lay gasping; but excusable under the circumstances; and a bullet in shoulder from Samand Singh. I opened Sexton's rifle and found right barrel with a fired case in it, and left barrel with a loaded case; no sign of misfire (RIFLE NOT RELOADED). My belief is that if Sexton had hit her as she came she might have turned off and gone to his right. Samand Singh says his shot turned her slightly. The whole business was result of using Eley's .340 grain light bullet. Both trackers bolted immediately the tigress showed and perhaps that made her charge more. (It was found later that the fired case had three indentations and this showed that rifle had not been reloaded after the shot which wounded the tigress.)

The wounds Sexton received were: six fang holes right through upper arm, missing the bone and main artery and making twelve holes, highest right under arm pit. One claw wound on forehead above left eye and down to the bone. Another behind and little above left ear. Deep claw wound on left fore finger exposing bone. Having carried him to camp we made all arrangements to move him as fast as possible to Yellandu, and sent off my servant on his horse to let the Doctor there know we were coming.

We started 4 a.m. Saturday 26 May, and got to Dermapooram, a small village six miles from Yellandu, at about 11 o/c on 28 May. Here we halted as it was very hot and Sexton seemed not able to stand any more, and Brewster rode in for the Doctor. The previous evening Sexton had had high fever, and he complained of great heat in his feet. They felt stone cold; and of course this was the end though we did not recognise it. I rubbed his feet for him and it seemed to afford him relief. He did not in the least suspect he was dying, and said he wanted to be taken to Bolarum and not to Raichur. He was in great pain for the last half hour. He was conscious throughout and up to the very last, and his last words were 'Burton, what is it? I can't see'. I was bathing his feet and went to his side and he said 'Burton, hold me up'. I did so, and almost immediately heard the death rattle in his throat, and he threw out his right arm as if pointing at something and died in my arms.

This was about two o'clock in the afternoon. Brewster rode up, with the Station Master of Yellandu, a few minutes afterwards. We carried the body into Yellandu and he was buried next morning. Later on I sent up a stonemason from Raichur and had a protecting granite wall built. A tombstone subscribed for by the Regiment and others who knew him was also erected. All was in good order when I saw it in 1903, and again in 1912.

I

4

CHAPTERS
2/3

1
R.W. Burton (seated right)
with 'Jock', other dogs and
horses

2
Camping when out on shikar

3
R.W. Burton with his dogs,
'John Pigeon', 'Jack', 'Dinah',
'Bob' and 'Nellie' and his pony

4
Richard W. Burton,,
Hyderabad Contingent.

Sketches by Col. Burton's
daughter Phyllis

Chapter 3

JUNGLE MEMORIES

JOURNAL

Many treasured objects were collected over the years, such as snakes and lizards; among the snakes was one which I lifted from my pen tray when feeling for a pencil in the dark. Snakes were seen almost every day, cobras and daboias being numerous, sometimes my horse's legs used to be struck at, but never with success on the part of the snake. Whenever there was a chance of getting at these deadly reptiles I used to dismount and kill them. I have seen a man walking before me along a forest path in the dim light of early dawn leap high in the air and so escape the vicious strike of a cobra; and the same thing was done by one of my dogs when out hunting, which executed a second wriggle in the air and so avoided the wicked lunge made at him.

It was rare to have a dog bitten, for instinct seems to warn them not to tackle, but a fox terrier belonging to a friend was bitten in long grass and died twenty minutes after, and my faithful friend 'Pigeon' died twenty hours after being bitten while hunting among some rocks. The former snake was doubtless a cobra and the latter probably a Russels viper or daboia.

One day I saw a snake (python molurus) swimming across a well, and throwing a stone at it broke its back. I got it out, and seeing that it had recently swallowed something, cut it open and released a frog, which showing signs of life I placed it in the irrigation channel of the well and it soon recovered and hopped off.

The dreaded Hamadryad is fortunately not often encountered. Pythons of the larger variety, which attain in India a length of upwards of twenty feet are occasionally seen and are fairly common in the Himalayan terai. In those extensively tangled forests you may meet with almost anything, especially when wandering about on an elephant.

In 1898 Burton was stationed at Bolarum, and in March that year he planned a trip with Goodfellow to the jungles in the Chanda District. It took them two days to reach Warora Railway Station, arriving there at 2 a.m. on 22nd. A journey of twenty eight miles by bullock tonga brought them to Chanda, and here they re-organised their provisions before moving on into the jungle. On reaching the river Werda they discovered that the reels had been left behind at Chanda, so Burton had to improvise and put together a makeshift with shoemaker's thread and a cotton reel.

On 29th March they passed through Dhumera village near the banks of the river and saw a cow dying of wounds inflicted by a tiger two days earlier. Tigers and panthers were generally hunted either in a beat, from a tree, or by sitting up in a machan or hide tied in a tree near the tiger's kill; often this was just an ordinary chair with branches to screen it. Many hours could be spent waiting for a tiger or panther which might or might not return, and it was perhaps then that Burton began to develop an understanding and appreciation of the sounds and signs of the jungle.

31st March. Sat up till 8.0 p.m. There were many quail of different kinds feeding at edge of the tank, a covey of twenty quail passed under my tree. A panther came and sat under G.'s tree, but of course he let him go, thinking tiger was in the beat. Some peafowl chicks passed by me, very early for young birds.

A kill in bed of the nala one mile down stream, said to be by a tigress. I found that kill is by a panther but a tigress did the eating! Sat up over the kill which unfortunately had to be dragged 60 yards as the tree nearby was full of red ants. I found in the morning that a panther and cub had promenaded up and down to within 10 yards of the kill, apparently all night judging by the marks in the sand, but had been afraid to venture close.

Wella. We had breakfast and then crossed the river in dugouts. The beat began at twelve o'clock and a tiger came past me in an open space 60 yards away. I took careful aim with the twelve-bore rifle and missed. Tiger went on walking. Disgraceful performance! My only excuse is that I never used the rifle before; it was lent to me. We had another beat after tracking the tiger for some way. Goodfellow, who was going on ahead, put up a she bear with two cubs and had to shoot her as she went for the men with him. One cub was killed as it clung to its mother's back. We caught the other cub and took it back to camp. 'Tiger', our cross-bred bull terrier, was taught not to touch it. Little bear is very savage! and won't eat. We gave it a tub to cool its head.

It was at Gundapili that my little bear got away before daybreak one morning. I heard the rattle of his chain and got a man, the Sikh bhisti, and went after him. We tracked him by his chain dragging in the sand a long way down the nala until at last he turned into the jungle. We heard a melancholy howl and went towards the place. Little bear charged with a roar like a big bear. Out went the lantern, dropped by the Sikh, and the next thing was, little bear was silhouetted against the sky at the top of a tree! I sent to camp for a rope as the only way to get at him would be to climb the tree, hitch rope to the butt end of branch the bear was on, judge the drop and let the branch fall to the ground after cutting it off. The bhisti refused to attempt the task, so up I had to climb in my pyjamas.

All fell out (including the bear!) as arranged, but when he landed on the ground the bhisti and another man were afraid to handle him, so I had to come rapidly down and fall on the little beast, get him by the scruff of his neck and his pants – by which I mean the long hair at his rump, and take him back to camp.

The fate of my little bear was the sad one such pets mostly come by. It was in 1900, I think, I met a Major Wood; we were dining at his home at Secunderabad and the skin of a small bear, half grown or a little more, was on the floor. This was my little bear which had become big and playful and frightened children and people, and so had been shot at Hingoli when about a year old.

14th April. Kill by a tiger four miles away at Loha. We saw the tiger prowling around and then he went at a gallop towards Goodfellow and passed him at a walk 15 yards away. Goodfellow missed him! We followed up, down a very thick ravine, and a small bear came out below us. Goodfellow took careful aim – there was no report. Our eyes met, HE WAS NOT LOADED, and we were following up a possibly wounded tiger!

Crocodiles were numerous in the Beema river. One of them twelve feet in length, contained bangles, tresses of hair, and nose rings. Once, a tigress wanting to drag her kill across a stream was baulked by a mugger which met her at the water's edge twice again she tried to cross but was forced to retreat and managed finally to cross higher up the nala.

Talai. Very seedy, did nothing, rotten camp, no shade. Shot a mugger in the evening with .303, at 80 yards. Killed it dead as it turned toes up and sank slowly.

22nd April. Stayed in to look after patients. Pertab Singh better, Sarfary Khan much the same, Syce better, Goodfellow sick in the night. Atma Singh and Tarmur Singh went to look at the kills.

Fever spread rapidly through the camp. They had moved on to Inkatapur, ten miles across the Pranhita River. 'A good place', Burton remarked, 'but too many mosquitos'. On the last day of April, Burton also became ill and was forced to return home.

DIARY _____

30th April to 5th May. Damarincha. Fever 105° at night and 104° in the morning until the night of 5th, when quinine arrived. I took 18 grs. at once and 24 grs. in the morning. I was very weak, couldn't walk or ride. All the quinine had been used up in treating the men, so none was available when I got sick. I improvised a dooly out of my bed, and left on the evening of 7th for Sironcha. I arrived on night of 10th, good going, and found my carts there which had also gone on the 7th. The dak bungalow was in a bad state. I left my little bear with Goodfellow. He went to Goornagur for three days, and saw lots of buffalo, also bison and sambur.

7th May. I met General M.G. Gerard in the evening on the road near the Mess. His manner was very curious. I discovered there was no end of a row on. He went to Sirpulla after us. The D.C. Chanda reported that BURTON had shot a tiger and cub in the forest reserve. Turned out it was Goodfellow, and his shikaris had used my name! The end of it was, Goodfellow's leave was stopped. I had not done anything so the General couldn't get at me, but he never forgave me. Goodfellow shot five tigers, after he left me, on his way back to Chanda working along the Werda River.

In 1899, Burton was shooting for panther and small game in the area around Bolarum, and in April 1900 he arranged a trip with Maj. H.G.C. Swayne, R.E., and W.E. Pye, 5th Infantry H.C., to go to Kasamudrum on the N.G.S. Railway, an area for which Swayne had obtained a pass.

DIARY _____

13th April. We arrived at Kasamudrum 1.30 a.m. and walked to camp two miles from the station. We found the shikaris had put our camp on wrong side of the railway, so gave orders to march straight to Katrapully, four miles north and arrived there 7.30 a.m. Maj. Swayne sat in a cart all the way. The shikaris would show us nothing and appeared very obstructive.

14th. The jungle is very dry and there are few tracks. No news of game, and Swayne decided to go back to Bolarum. The shikaris seem now inclined to show us game and say that a panther killed a goat near Appanpully and that there are two bears which drink every night at the well near Dumasay. Drew lots with Pye as to which of us should sit up for the panther and which over the well at Dumasay.

Pye won and sat up all night. I went in bullock cart to spend the night at Dumasay. Got there 8 p.m. and was told that bears had already tried to get to the well, but had been frightened by the men who were putting a screen ready. At 10.30 p.m. two bears came. One went down to the water and I took careful aim with taped sights and fired: a fearful noise, and thought I had bagged him. He scrambled out of the well and was met by the other bear at the top and fought him and then they both went off. Got out and looked, and found no bear and no blood, and came to the conclusion I must have missed.

17th. Got up at 2.30 a.m. to go to the hill south of the railway line. Was standing talking to the shikari when there was a tremendous uproar of bears fighting about eighty yards away among some rocks. We could see nothing from below so I got to top of the hill and heard the bears breathing heavily. Pye had seen a bear coming to the hill and he no doubt had a squabble with another one on entering the cave.

Evening. Beat a bear out of the hill. Trusting to local shikaris I allowed myself to be posted by them, with result that the bear broke so I only got a very hurried glimpse of him and no time to put in a shot. Ran after him but couldn't catch him up. Great recriminations among the shikaris as to whose fault I was wrongly placed. One must trust to them to know which way the animals run on hills they have often seen beaten. It seems that Pye also saw the bear and that it was turned from him by a man near him waving his hands to show it was coming! As if Pye couldn't see that for himself! Home to camp very disgusted.

In 1900 Burton received the bronze medal of the Royal Humane Society for attempting the rescue of a fellow officer, Lt. Fagan, from drowning. Lt. Fagan had only recently arrived with his Regiment from Mominbad and, with a group of friends, had gone out duck shooting to one of the tanks. A sowar belonging to the H.C. had jumped into the water to retrieve a duck and immediately appeared to be in difficulties. The following extract from The Deccan Times, *December 28th 1900, gives an account of what happened.*

'. . .*Seeing the man in danger, both Capt. Burton and Lieut. Fagan took off their coats and boots to swim to the man's rescue. Lieut. Fagan, who was nearest to the man, was in the water first, but before he could reach the place where the native was struggling to disentangle himself from the weeds, the man had sunk.*

Capt. Burton, as he was entering the water, saw Lieut. Fagan apparently trying to dive and before he had swum a couple of strokes, Lieut. Fagan called out – 'Help!' As Capt. Burton got close to him, Lieut. Fagan cried out – 'keep your legs up, the weeds are very bad'. Capt. Burton told him to grasp his hand and commenced to swim away pulling him along about a boat's length. Suddenly Lieut. Fagan, who had been holding tight, opened his hand, let go and sank instantly. Capt. Burton, getting into difficulties with the weeds himself, and finding that Lieut. Fagan had disappeared, turned on his back and floated to the shore by using only his hands.

There were five other men of the 1st Lancers present, but all on the other side of the tank. Lance Duffadar Abdul Rahman Khan (who was devoted to Lieut. Fagan and had been several times big game shooting with him) made efforts to get into the water, but was prevented from doing so by Capt. Burton. A raft was at once made by Capt. Burton and a search party was sent on it into the tank, but all attempts to recover the bodies for six hours proved fruitless.

Capt. Burton is of the opinion that Lieut. Fagan let go of his hand purposely, knowing that he could not be saved, as his legs were so tied together, and that the last thought of this gallant officer was to avoid, so far as it lay with him, bringing his comrade to grief as well as himself. The caution to keep his legs up and the letting go of the hand, were the saving of Capt. Burton's life. Lieut. Fagan was a popular young officer, a sportsman of the first rank, distinguished as a cricketer and polo player. He entered the service as 2nd Lieut. in the Worcestershire Regiment in 1892, and was transferred to 1st Lancers H.C. in 1896.'

DIARY _____

May to August 1901. Working for Law Exam: also too much Court Work to be able to go out with dogs or do any shikar at all.

28th September. Poor old 'Bob' died today, had been sick for two days. A fine old poligar hound, who had been hunting for nine years. Given to me in 1898 by Tom Bridges, R.H.A., and formerly belonged to A.N. Fagan when he was at Nagpur. There are no better dogs than the poligar which come from the Poligar country in South India, good feet, not too fast, stand the heat, splendid staying power and the best of constitutions.

October 1901. Found at Liquor Shop, four hundred yards east of Target Rock and killed at Boenpilli Ridges, fifteen minutes hard galloping, 'The Phantom Fox'! A good two miles run. This is the same fox run and lost on nine or ten different occasions. I must have been twenty miles after him all together. A good run on Ginger. Ginger was an arab, 14 h.h., bought from Bombay Stables for Rs.600. Fiery, fast, and a splendid fencer, I sold him at Bolarum for Rs.700. I ought to have raced him, he would certainly have won steeplechases.

At Yadgiri one morning I killed a cobra 6ft. 1in. I saw one of the beaters hit at him with a stick as he was disappearing into a white ant heap. I got hold of his tail with my left hand and after sundry 'cracks' of his bones and much hissing and disturbance, he came out with a jerk and expanded his hood in my face, but a back hander from a stick in my right hand knocked him out and he was soon slain.

By 1901, Burton was married with two children, and hunting and fishing trips became less frequent; also expenses were high. One entry at this time reads – 'Invested in Rs.10/8 of toys for the babies (Phyllis and Tiny).' His family is not often mentioned in the diaries, as these were kept as 'shikar' (hunting and fishing) records. His wife Hilda, when she is mentioned, is referred to as 'wife' or 'H.G.', but a chink occasionally shows through this reserve when he writes about his young family. One Christmas the whole family embarked on a trip into the jungles near Jalalpur.

DIARY _____

We left Secunderabad on morning of 22nd December, and reached Masaipett Station 9 a.m. I put wife and Phyllis and Tiny into a bullock cart and arrived at halfway camp at Eltooty 4 p.m. A long weary journey as the cartmen took the wrong road. On next morning to Jalalpur. As the dogs were going off at night to Masaipett Station with the carts a panther made a bold attempt to seize one of them, but was beaten off by the chaprasis and cartmen. I sat up two whole nights, but no panther. Very nice country, the hills to the east very jungly. This is a place to visit again. Phyllis got ill, probably from too rich food, her throat and lips bad. She was asked in the train on the way home what the wheels were saying and replied, after a little listening to the rumble of them, 'My dear daddy, give me a dolly'! and so as the wheels said, so she received.

There were more exciting expeditions into the jungle with his friends in search of tigers and bears. There was no place on these trips for the faint-hearted, and in March 1902, he planned a trip with Maj. A.H. Block R.A. into the Nalla Mallai Hills.

DIARY _____

15th March. With much difficulty I got away from the office at 5 o/c and home in time to have tea and be at Secunderabad Station at 6.30 p.m. I met Block there and we got to Bezwada next morning. Off to Chelama on 17th, and found shikaris there with the kit. There were no pack bullocks here, so shoved all the kit into the train and went on to Gazenpully. We put up in the Forest Bungalow close to the railway station. After breakfast next morning I was off on foot to Brokapur, five miles, to get the bullocks, a blazing hot walk, and walked home in the evening.

18th. 7 a.m. went to see the kill. Back to the bungalow and after having breakfast returned to the machan at 11 a.m. and sat up till 6.30 p.m. The hottest time I ever had, a very badly made machan, no rest for my back. From sitting still so long my posterior was paralysed and felt numb for some days. I saw four jungle cock, two mongoose, three spur fowl, also some kind of crested hawk which made a continuous attack on the kill. He attacked its chest and finding that no good tried the ribs. The body of the kill was much swollen by the heat and, if he had got through, the gas would have blown him up! Finally he got to where he should have begun, the rump, and there he stayed and fed heartily. The jungle appeared to go to sleep at intervals and then wake up again.

19th. After some delay got off at 6.45 a.m. Found the kill had been dragged away and had been taken up a steep bank twenty five feet high. We followed on and Block smelled it 60 yards or so further on. I had a cold in my nose so I couldn't smell it! We saw what we thought was a rock; we were crawling on hands and knees through thorny bushes and a network of creepers and thorns, I had the twelve-bore with s.s.g. We went on and the rock turned out to be the kill, and the tigress must have been watching us all along from behind it, as at about twenty feet she got up with a growl and made off. A good deal of the kill was eaten. There was no place for a machan and I decided to leave this animal alone and not waste time trying to get it as my leave is so short. I had looked carefully for several minutes with my glasses but never made out the kill or saw anything of the tigress – an instance of how difficult it is to make out anything motionless in thick jungle.

Set off for Bareini, a distance of twelve miles. There is a splendid avenue of old trees here, must be about a hundred years old. It leads to Mahamundy Pag, which Block, who was here at Christmas, says is a very pretty place – perennial spring. We walked on and found tracks of tiger on the road. Arrived at a pool of water near Chelama at 11.30 and rested there. About a mile short of Bareini, Block and I separated, he taking the path to the left and I to the right, and walked back to camp, arriving there at 6.0. I am out of condition as a result of long hours of office work and all riding, no walking, and am very tired and footsore. Glad to get dinner and go to bed.

A few days later, a tiger killed a buffalo and left it by the roadside on the edge of some bamboo jungle. Burton selected two trees one on either side of the kill where he and Block could sit and wait. Cloth had to be used extensively in this beat as they could only afford twenty beaters. Burton was sitting in the tree to the left of the kill and hearing the monkeys call in front of him was expecting the tiger to appear front left. A sudden movement caught his eye to the right and the tiger with two bounds was up the steep nala bank 25 yards away and making off through the bamboo jungle. Chucking his rifle over to take quick aim from his left shoulder, he fired, and felt certain he had hit. Abdul, who had been placed up a tree behind, shouted that the tiger was down and that it was dead.

Burton's ability to shoot from left or right shoulder, learned in the early days at Musketry school in Deolali, once again proved a very useful skill. The bullet had penetrated 10in. behind the right shoulder and exit was at left shoulder, having gone through heart and lungs. Block had found himself in an awkward position in the fork of a tree, so that when the tiger paraded past him earlier at a walk, he had been unable to take proper aim. When later he saw the tiger as it bounded up the bank, he fired at the exact moment when Burton also fired. Block's bullet, however, passed through the animal's stomach and would not have killed.

DIARY ———————————————————————————————

25th. Up at 4.30 a.m., off at daylight. Block had a very bad night on account of the mosquitos, but they did not trouble me at all. Soon after leaving camp I saw a green pigeon fly off a nest and found a fledgeling in it. The bad points of this jungle are: no shady trees except in the nalas, red ants everywhere, the ground so stony that it is almost impossible to walk quietly. I kept well up the hillside and worked west of the nala, then climbed a devil of a mountain in order to get to the higher reaches of the east nala, then climbed down to a lovely waterfall and lay up. Lunch was chocolate and ginger biscuits. These upper pools hold none of the 3 and 4 oz. fish of which the lower pools are full. I had no idea there would be so much water or would have brought my rods and tackle. The upper pool was very deep and clear. A 30ft. slope of sheet rock led to another pool.

I was much annoyed on getting to camp to find the tiger's skin going wrong in parts – the tail, neck, and one whisker. He was not properly skinned. I did the head and feet myself and left the cleaning up to my servant and camp people, and they scamped it. I treated the parts where the hair was slipping with pure carbolic.

26th. Said goodbye to Block and started off for Bareini, where I put up at the forest bungalow. At Gazenpully I met Battie, Forest Officer, and he says that November is the best time for sambur at Bareini. He got a 39in. stag after Block and Gunther were here at Christmas.

I arrived at Secunderabad on evening of 28th, and had to meet the Viceroy (Lord Curzon) at Hyderabad Station next morning at 9 a.m. Levee at the Residency on evening of 29th March.

15th April. I went to see the Lungur procession at Hyderabad, the Viceroy was present. Was out with my dogs on Sunday, 14th April.

16th April. Knocked down with high fever while at the office and this turned out to be enteric coupled with malaria and, subsequently, with pneumonia. I was forty two days in bed, and then went to Kodai Kanal for a month to convalesce. Back to work again on 22nd July, as fit as ever. I made a great collection of butterflies at Kodai – also killed a number of *barilius futensis*, on zulu and black gnat, just in the lake. Sent the butterfly collection to the Bombay Natural History Society.

Chapter 4

ADVENTURES IN THE DECCAN

In February 1903, Hilda Burton and her two daughters, Phyllis and Stella, sailed from Bombay on 'Plassey' for a visit home to England. Burton spent much of the next two months with W.E. Pye, fishing, mainly in the Kistna river. The largest fish they caught on these trips was one of 23lbs, although many larger fish were hooked and lost. They often saw otters in the river, and once watched a fish eagle strike and carry off a small fish.

DIARY

Raichur, 26th February. Evening went down to Gangihalli, rotten water and we had to 'porter' the boat a lot. Missed our ponies owing to coolies not keeping in touch with us, and had to walk home ten miles across country as we missed the road in the dark. High crops and hot work. Marched by the stars, Sirius mostly, and made a good line. Got home 9.45 p.m., very thirsty.

12th March. Kistna River. Trolled up the big pool with no result. 3½ inch gold and silver spoon 2oz. weight. At 11.30 I hooked a whopper; he bent out one of the end triangle hooks and got off, top treble came up ornamented with a belly scale. Ten minutes later I hooked a fish bigger than any I have ever seen before, I put him down at 40lbs, Pye says 50lbs. He was firmly hooked and was off for a record run and had taken out ten yards line when all went slack, end treble twisted off. Pye said he must be the same fish, but he was not, as he was very black and the other was golden brown and not so big. One hook of the top treble was also broken. Awful luck! (Note: the steel links and stouter trebles of the present (1933) day would have obviated all these losses.RB.)

14th. Kistna River. We were aroused at daylight by large flocks of coolun flying over us. Jowari birds (Pastor) in THOUSANDS roost on trees on the island in the river. During the day hooked two turtles; one straightened out a heavy treble hook, another, while we were away, was hooked on rod and played by the Transport Driver and lost by wire breaking. Shot a white necked stork which was very good eating. Found two freshly killed small carp in him, both had been seized by the tail and swallowed whole.

8th to 20th April 1903. No fishing owing to the Regiment being suddenly moved to Aurangabad, but I returned to Secunderabad as Superintendent of Railway Police and Railway Magistrate on 7th May 1903. Hence the following.

May 1903. Basar. Prospected Godavery for fishing; quite useless, now or at any time; too sandy and flat. Dirty from storm and very little water. Bought a nice little Banjara bitch, eight rupees, three quarter bred. These dogs hunt by sight and scent and are fast and courageous. Those of pure breed can seldom be procured as their owners will not readily part with them.

17th May. Beyond Moul Ali with Gage, each of us with .310 sharpshooter. Got on to a hyaena and ran him over two miles, hell for leather! I loaded rifle early in the run, but couldn't get within thirty yards at any time. Gage's waler got right on to him once, but his rifle not loaded, his horse pulling too hard, and lost him in the scrub.

24th June. A dead elephant at Panther Rock. Went with Gage to see if any visitors to it, but found nothing.

As Superintendent of Railway Police, Burton had to travel a great deal through the Deccan, the country between the Tapti and Tungabadra rivers, either on the HGVR or the NGSR. It was the end of the hot weather in July 1903 and he had occasional opportunities for small game shooting.

JOURNAL ——————————————————————————————————
In some localities blackbuck and bustard are found in wide open spaces where they are very difficult to approach, and that is all to the good in the way of true sport; but much of this class of game, in the plains of India, is in highly cultivated country, and it is very disturbing to one's peace of mind to wonder, after firing a shot with a small bore high velocity weapon, whether some innocent cultivator or stray cow has not received the bullet, perhaps a mile away, intended for the buck which was the target aimed at. Such unfortunate occurrences were not unknown even before the small bore and long range, so it is better for this and other considerations to have a .310 or a .300 both of which used to be favoured by sportsmen in former years. Having been unable for some years to enjoy sport of this kind, a weapon had to be obtained and so my choice fell upon the .310, also it was cheap at the time and light to carry.

The monsoon was daily threatening, and a few scanty showers, precursors of the deluge about to arrive, had caused a tinge of green to appear over the land. In the far distance, where the dim outline of the Western Ghats was visible, heavy rain was falling as was seen by the columns of dark, almost black, shadows depending perpendicularly from the clouds on the horizon. A warning that the few days sport in prospect might be interrupted by the onset of the annual rains. The morning was bright and fine and we started for the hills to the north east of Nagarsole. We saw a lot of antelope, about sixty does and two or three buck. It came on to rain heavily for an hour, but the thirsty soil absorbed most of the moisture. A solitary bustard was seen, striding about on a knoll and I stalked him to about seventy yards away. He spotted me and wasn't going to wait till I could exchange the gun for a rifle so I fired both barrels at him, no result and off he went. I marked him down and tried to get a shot with .310, but he was too cute and only gave me a flying shot as he was rising – a miss.

DIARY ——————————————————————————————————
6th July. Nagarsole, same place as yesterday. Any amount of sandgrouse, lots of antelope, spotted a good buck near some nalas, made excellent stalk and got him at 60 yards. Horns 19in., not quite black.

The white neck of a cock bustard caught my eye about half a mile distant, and three others near him. A detour under cover of a fold in the ground allowed a nearer approach, and a long crawl on hands and knees and sometimes on elbows and stomach, all through wet plough, land brought me exhausted and unseen to the shelter of a bush not more than ninety yards from the nearest bird. As a sitting position was slowly gained the long white neck appeared peering this way and that to see what strange beast it could be sitting near the bush, for the keen eyes had spotted the movement! and the inquisitive bird actually paced slowly to within seventy yards

without having been able to make me out. I sat like a stone as the least movement
would be fatal. I thought it was time to shoot and – missed him! Can't make out how I
did so, I must have shot UNDER him.

7th. Grand country, just like the English downs. No doubt there are bustard here
all the year round. Walked to Tarur Station, thinking it nearer, and must have walked
quite eighteen miles. Shot two sandgrouse; saw two herds of antelope, not less than
eighty or ninety does in one herd, did not go after these herds as I have shot enough
buck for one trip.

25th July. Mudkhel. It rained all day. I started at 10.15 with umbrella. Went one
mile in front of the station to low jungle covered hills. Put up a chinkara and missed
two shots at him. I was very shaky owing to the heavy going. The whole country a
large sticky pudding with slippery boulders for currants! At least 2lbs of mud to each
foot all day. Saw a few painted sandgrouse and five or six hares. In the evening I shot
a small buck as food for the men, also one pigeon.

*Only two weeks after this diary entry, when walking in the same area he com-
ments: 'Very hot, and whole country looks as if it had not rained for weeks.' News
was brought to him here of a tiger which had been killing cattle in the district. The
villagers begged him to shoot it and a special permit was obtained to do so.*

JOURNAL ————————————————————————————

An Official of the railway staff saw the fresh tracks of the tiger and sent news to me,
adding that the villagers were loud in their complaints against this beast.

A tree was selected in which to sit when the beat took place. This was on the left
bank of the river and commanded the only place where the tiger was likely to break, as
a thick patch of reeds and bushes extended here across the bed of the stream. There
had been no rain for some days, so there was only a little water trickling over the
rocks, and there seemed no reason to think that the tiger would refuse to face this
small open space which could be crossed in two or three bounds leading to the safety
of the thick jungle.

The tiger appeared under the steep bank of the hill on the opposite side of the river.
There was a clear view of him as he stalked slowly along, the sun glistening on his
glossy side, now in the shade, now passing through the reeds. There was no fear of his
getting out of the beat as the 'stops' were Banjaras, and picked men. He looked very
big, but by his tracks we knew he was of ordinary size. The beat had closed in and
blocked the exit down stream. The tiger had turned into the belt of reeds and it was
expected that his great head would peer out of the cover a few yards away. The beaters
were now making much noise, but nothing moved. With a signal to the beat the noise
and efforts were redoubled but to no effect; so all the men except those in trees, were
collected at a safe place and a personal investigation made.

The piece of cover down to the water was ringed and no tracks leading out of it
could be found. The tiger would not be driven across the river, so there was nothing
for it but to let him have his own way in the matter, and drive him down the right
bank. I made my way round quietly through the reeds to a sapling, the only possible
stance, and swarming up it stood on a branch the thickness of my thumb, with one
foot on top of the other and secured my position not six feet above the reeds with the
aid of a thin rope round my waist. There was a tremendous uproar by the beat; not a
move by T.P. Then some more venturesome ones started to beat through the reeds
and he was at last roused and let loose a very fine roar and came crashing and dashing

through mud and water passing almost straight under my tree, but inside the reeds which were about six feet high. I had not much time for aim, but he was very close. Landed him with a .500 express 480 grain bullet three inches to left of spine and dropped him flat.

I put him on a litter of poles and took him to the line and so to the Railway Station by the Trolly. Truly a very peculiar tiger. I can't imagine why he would not face the few feet of open towards my first machan with thick jungle and safety beyond. It was very lucky there was no accident. All the time the men were talking, smoking, and sitting in open places and along the edge of the reeds.

The tiger measured 9ft. between curves. I hadn't time to weigh him and only got through the worst part of skinning by dark and finished by lamp light. I found a square piece of stone, evidently used as a missile from a gun, embedded under the skin above the near hind foot. Not much of a missile to fire at a tiger!

DIARY _____

16.8.03. Kondapilli. It rained hard until 9 o'clock. The whole country is more or less under water. I started at 10 o'clock to go up the hill, with a village shikari as guide. He says there are many sambur on the hill, about eight hundred, also tiger, bears, several panthers, and at the foot of the hill to the north are many chital, pig galore, porcupines, in fact almost everything, and all in great numbers. I watched the village people playing a curious game. All the people who have nothing else to do (about half the population of Kundapilli today) collect at an open place and divide into two bodies – this attained by one side wearing rags and the other nothing. Two cocoanuts are provided one from each side and a strong man, the two I saw were all muscle and must have been at the job a great deal, throws it perpendicularly into the air with a swinging motion from between his feet. Whichever side breaks a cocoanut first collars the other one, and so on, until perhaps a hundred have been broken. I forgot to ask who pays. One black one was broken while I was looking on and I was told it had been thrown up three hundred and fifty times. Rather a monotonous game; nice and restful for the crowd and rare good exercise for the throwers.

Weekends were spent, whenever possible, hunting and shooting in the area around the cantonment for small game. It was relatively easy to take the train out to one of the small stations and shoot in the area near the railway. There were many herds of black buck, and chinkara, the ubiquitous foxes and jackals, also many peafowl, sandgrouse, and pigeon and sometimes white-necked storks. The occasional excursions in the pouring rain often resulted in an attack of fever.

DIARY _____

13th September. With Morris. Got off train at mile 246 and each took one side of ridge to Muri. Very hot indeed. On the move until 6 p.m. and rather tired, especially not having had any sport.

14th. Muri. Woke up at 5.30 to find it raining; got worse and worse and ended up in a tremendous storm, torrents of rain, till 12 o'clock. Muri tank burst about 11 o'clock and was empty in a few minutes. Fairly fine now, 2 o'clock, but ground must be fearfully heavy and train goes at 5.15, so not worth while going out. All the animals will be in the jungle. Still raining a little; an unfortunate two days. Very seedy.

18th. Jalna. It rained heavily last night and lucky I left when I did as it hasn't stopped raining since. A most unlucky week of bad weather and disgraceful shooting on my part. Fact is that the .310 requires most careful shooting; the slightest difference in the amount of foresight taken makes large errors. I hope to do better now I know and realize this. What it is to have a slender purse and not the best of weapons; not that the best of weapons will do any better if not held straight! I have now missed four chink in succession.

1st October. Nalwar. Took eight men and beat the whole country. Scarcely any game at all, heard two or three peacock call. The jungle away from the hills is all cleared and the land under cultivation now; very different from what it was eight years ago. Petta tank full.

One day in October I went for a day's fishing with G.M. Morris and Subadur Major Ibrahum Baig. We caught about a dozen fish of about 1 lb. each, all labeo calbaru. The Subadur and a friend of his gave us a splendid tiffin. Morris politely ate 'pan supari' to his undoing, as he had to retire to get rid of his repast. I saw him get 'sea-green' colour and knew what was impending!

15th October. Gave away the dogs today – Pup and Bijli to Gage; Nelly, Dinah and Jack to Lloyd. This as I intended to take a year's leave home, the first for fourteen years. On 12th December while riding in the Lines, I broke my left thigh and didn't ride again for six years.

Detailed records were kept of every shoot between the years 1894 and 1912; the number of guns, the location, date, and content of the bag. This was mostly snipe, teal, duck, quail and partridge. Mixed in with the shikar records were personal notes on some of his colleagues who joined him on the shoots, and who did not survive the harshness and stress of life in India.

DIARY ───

Oswald, with whom I was duck shooting in 1892 at Aurangabad, was killed by a fall at Polo on the Secunderabad Parade Ground some years later. His wife died of cholera at Aurangabad after a few hours illness only in October 1892, and is buried in the Cemetery there. Mrs. Welchman, wife of E.S.G. Welchman, also died of cholera shortly after at Roza near Ellora Caves. The Regiment (5th Infantry, Hyderabad Contingent) lost one Subadur and several men. We moved to the Bidur Camp of Exercise en route for Raichur and the cholera left us on the march after Karlah.

On 16th December 1912, P. Roscoe Allen, Superintending Engineer, Irrigation, died at Bellary. In 1902 he lent me his D.B. .577 rifle when I went with A.H. Block to the Nallamallai Hills for ten days, and again in 1912/13 when I went to Jeypore, Vizagapatam. His death was the result of a gun accident. Looking out of a window with the loaded shot gun by his side, his fox terrier jumped up and the gun went off and killed him instantly.

It was early in November 1903 that Dalgleish, 1st Lancers, Hyderabad Contingent, committed suicide by cutting his throat with a razor in the 1st Class carriage of the Mail Train, when it was running between Lingumpully Station and Begumpett Station on the Wadi – Hyderabad Line. Temporary insanity. This was a few days after I had handed over the appointment of Railway Magistrate to Crawford, or I should have had the sad duty of holding the inquest.

Some young officers, like A.E. Wardrop (later, General Sir Alexander Wardrop) with whom he corresponded until 1924, continued in the Army to reach the top of their careers. He was to become Q.M.G. and G.O.C-in-C. Northern Command in

India, and died in 1961. Others, remained lifelong friends. Mr. and Mrs. Gage returned to live in England, but Burton visited them in 1927 and again in 1932 when he was in England.

DIARY _____

August 1927. Took the opportunity to go to Marnhull, Dorset, to see Gage and his wife, old Hyderabad friends, and their son Douglas; very pleasant stay indeed. Went one day with them to shoot rabbits, dogs 'Bob' cocker and 'Bing' springer, very keen. 'Bob' caught three rabbits in the hedges and one in the open, pounced on it like my 'Binkie' used to do with the Himalayan pheasants.

SHIKAR
FOR
A
CANTONMENT
MAGISTRATE
1903
TO
1914

Chapter 5

SPORT IS LIMITED TO FISHING

DIARY
Aurangabad. I was to have left Bombay on 23rd December 1903, but broke my left thigh bone on evening of 12th December, Saturday. Riding Andain's horse in the lines he got stung by a horse fly and took charge for a short distance and, getting foul of a tree in a narrow lane between the lines of sepoy huts, I was thrown. Simple fracture, ten weeks in bed to look forward to. I have not been out of India for fourteen years, having landed in Bombay in April 1890.

The fracture failed to mend and it was decided he should return to England for surgery. In London he contacted Sister Agnes who was in control of the King Edward VII Hospital for Officers, and made arrangements to go in for an operation. Sir Alfred Fripp operated on 6th April to wire the bones together and this was successful. The bones were quite straight from above and sideways. While he was there King Edward VII visited the Hospital and enquired about his accident. Sister Agnes, who ran the hospital with unrivalled energy and efficiency, introduced him with the words – 'This, your Majesty, is another case of mismanagement from India!'

On 29th June he was moved to Osborne Convalescent Hospital for Officers on the Isle of Wight. Unfortunately, he was allowed to walk, with sticks, too soon after the operation, and this resulted in a bending of the bone. He was ordered to do nothing that would put a further strain on the leg, and by the end of the year there had been no further movement, but a side view X-ray showed the bone was now bent forward as well as sideways.

In February 1905 Burton went to visit his brother Aubrey, who was in the National Hospital for Paralysis in London. Aubrey had been thrown from a horse at Ahmadnager, India, and suffered a dislocated spine and fracture of 8th dorsal vertebra. He was only six stone and very emaciated and the verdict of Sir Victor Horsley the spinal surgeon was that there was no hope, and never had been since the time of the accident. Aubrey was perhaps the closest to Richard of all his brothers. He was nearest to him in age being just two years younger and had been best man at his wedding in 1895. Aubrey died on 14.3.05. aged thirty four, leaving a widow and small daughter.

In April 1905, Burton was able to walk with two sticks and was instructed to use a tricycle to strengthen his leg muscles.

DIARY
26.8.05. Took a toss off tricycle while turning on an uneven road in the woods, no damage. Tricycle turned over when almost stationary, came down on left hip. On

30th, went over Carisbrook Castle with Phyllis and Tiny. One day the King and Queen (Edward VII and Alexandra) came to Osborne and Phyllis and Tiny waved their handkerchiefs, and the Queen waved hers in return. Saw fireworks and illuminations of the French and English fleets off Cowes.

However, there was again movement at the seat of fracture and on 4th November he writes –

Almost unbearable pain when putting weight on leg; mostly in knee. Walked four steps without pain on 14th, but that night leg began to hurt and next day a very severe attack of neuritis set in. Hypodermic injections of morphia every day until Saturday 21st. Out of bed on 26th, very helpless; leg had been quite immovable all this time.

23rd November: Can walk again, with thin cane, a few steps at a time, as on 14th October, but leg much less muscular than it was then and weaker and more helpless in many ways. X-ray shows nothing new and doctors positive that bone is now rigid.

Although now permanently crippled, Burton was saved from half pay on the understanding that he could return to India to enter the Cantonment Magistrates Department. This was obtained by means of a letter from Sir Alfred Fripp, also one from Colonel Thornhill, but principally from the kind efforts of Sister Agnes. He left London on 19th January 1906 and landed at Bombay on 9th February.

The final shortening of the leg was by four inches, due to the cutting off of ends of bone at the time of the operation, and to the bending at the seat of fracture. Although troublesome, he writes that by 1924 his leg was good enough for all purposes of hill and plains shikar. In February 1906 he received a letter from the India Office to the effect that final refusal was given as to any injury pension or compensation. He comments –

I was on Military Duty, and 'on duty' at the time of accident, but they hold 'the nature of the duty was not such as to increase risk of accident': that might safely be said ninety nine times out of every hundred. Others I know of got pension and actual cause of injury not traceable!'

DIARY ⎯⎯
11.2.06. Joined Regiment at Aurangabad. Leg fairly well now, but muscles not so free. I have to persistently keep up my knee bending exercises and use of tricycle purchased at Bombay helps me to keep it on the bend.

On his return to India, Burton stayed for a while with his brother R.G. Burton 94th Russel's Infantry at Poona. He was still crippled but was determined to stay active. Fishing was the only sport he could engage in and he had to have someone with him at all times since he couldn't yet walk easily. In March 1906 he made arrangements to go to a place called Dehu on the Indravani River. There were temples here and an escort was necessary to avoid trouble.

JOURNAL ————————————————————————————————————

After a short hour's run on the train we alighted at a small wayside station, bundled our kit with our men into one bullock cart, seated ourselves on a pile of straw in another, and rattled and jolted towards our destination. Three miles of good road, and one of no road at all, brought us to the river, where we saw a large pool fringed with trees about 1000 yards long and 150 yards broad, stretching out before us.

A woman seated at the water's edge had a large basket full of ground nuts 'mom-pullee' and threw a handful into the water. There was a surging and boiling as some fifty or sixty monsters tumbled and walloped over one another in their eagerness to seize the nuts. Nearly all the carp species will take a spoon, so supported on my unsteady pins, while my friend enticed the fish along with nuts, I soon managed to drop the spoon in front of a 'boil' indicating a good fish. Eighty yards of line was off the reel almost before one could realise what had happened, but the 16ft. Castle Connel rod was equal to the occasion, and after some thirty minutes exciting play the fish was brought under control. The stubborn struggles of the monster were of no avail and at last he was tired out, led to a shelving shore, and lifted out by the gills. He took the spring balance down to it's limit of 40lbs, so we may safely say that he was a good forty.

A change to gut cast was made and other fish were hooked and landed, and some were hooked and lost.

JOURNAL ————————————————————————————————————

Taking my turn with the rod, I was soon in contact and thirty yards was off the reel before an attempt could be made to stop the rush. Then there followed those disconcerting jags and short runs which indicate a lightly hooked fish and every moment was one of suspense. However, by careful handling, he also was brought to the bank, the hook coming away as soon as the line was slackened. 12lbs he weighed and was all the colours of the rainbow, most lovely to look on; but our Muhammadan attendants did not consider his beauty, they were calculating the number of seers of meat they would be able to get off his bones.

It was two o'clock and very hot, and the fish had all stopped feeding. Nothing disturbed the placid surface of the water except the heads of turtles slowly thrust up to take air and as slowly withdrawn. Even the black and white kingfishers had struck work to sit gasping in the leafy shade of the trees. All nature slept, so we did likewise after a belated breakfast, in the shadow of a large pipal tree. A few days later cholera swept the country and I have never again had the opportunity to visit that wonderful pool.

Burton used the tricycle as much as possible. As well as being the cheapest way for getting about, it was good exercise for his leg and he would journey up to ten miles

*on it, to reach different fishing grounds. There were occasional accidents. On the
way back from the Baircha tank after a day fishing –*

Riding tricycle back in dark, but with a lamp, right wheel hit a big boulder as I was
coming down hill at 11 or 12 m.p.h. Tremendous purler; landed on road on bend of
my thigh at the fracture, much pain and couldn't walk. Lifted into a dog cart which
was fortunately at hand and drove home. Up and about again after two days and none
the worse; tricycle most fortunately very little damaged. (Note: At Bombay in 1918, I
was X-rayed and photo showed that probably as a result of this fall, the 'twist' of silver
wire which joined bone together had broken off and travelled quite half an inch from
its proper position.)

12th August 1906. Across Kanar river where it falls into a deep ravine over a fall
eighty feet high near Mari. Had breakfast and then went down to the river at bottom
of a tremendous gorge, thickly wooded, quite eight hundred feet deep and half a
mile wide at top and one hundred yards or so wide at the bottom, widening as it
goes. A few peafowl were calling in the gorge, also some painted partridge; the
water was very clear. Lang got two small mahseer in the rapids further down, no
one else got anything. I did the climb down and up successfully. A splendid view
down the gorge from the tents. I saw a mugger about 6ft. in the first big pool.
Plumbed the water in one place to be over 18ft. It is probably 25ft. close to the
perpendicular rock.

*As his leg grew stronger he tackled more adventurous excursions. With friends, he
went several times from Mhow to the River Kanar, usually in a tonga or bullock
carts, sometimes on an elephant, and it frequently rained. On 24th August they
tried a trip further afield. Leaving in the evening in a bullock cart and tonga they
unfortunately lost their way in the dark, but eventually came across a rough track
which brought them to Dhobgatta, their destination, by the following afternoon. The
river here was thick with mud as it had been raining continuously, even the small
stream at the junction with the 200ft. waterfall was muddy. The total catch for the
trip was a few small olive carp.*

We camped at the gate of a ruined fort where the road descends the ghat
to Dhobgatta. Two recesses in a gateway were very handy for shelter. Did not
pitch the tent; carts gave enough shelter for the men, and gateway for ourselves.
Very hot and steamy and my leg felt it had done quite enough. Heavy storms inland all morning bode no good for our return journey to Mhow. Left 2.15 p.m.
on 27th and reached river at 2.0 a.m. and found it in flood. The guide said we
could not cross, so waited for three hours and eventually crossed the river and
to Tillor by 6.0 a.m. I finally arrived at 12 o/c in tonga and the carts got in at
4.30 p.m. Bullock men and bullocks did splendid work. It took us twenty and a
half hours to get out and twenty two hours to return. Not a trip to be done again
without camels for transport, and camels or elephants to ride – (but not in wet
weather!).

16th September. To Baircha tank in mule tonga four-in-hand. A tremendous storm
of rain came on. I sat patiently through it in the boat under an umbrella, and just as

the rain stopped the worm was taken by a big murrel, 8lbs. Good fun with 9ft. trout rod and fine gut. Gut nearly frayed through by his teeth.

30th. Mhow. Has rained almost without stopping for four days. My dressing room flooded with six inches of water. Next day to Kanar River; fished in rain and caught three buttu fish. No use attempting to fish now as river in full flood, so plodded back to Simrol on elephant much disgusted.

One fishing trip with Major Smith, on the Narbada river, ended in near disaster when the canvas boat they were in took in water and started to sink. They managed to swim until they reached a footing on a ridge of rocks, and a large boat by the bridge which had seen them came down to their rescue. All their rods and tackle, and Smith's haversack and boots, were lost. This was a financial disaster for Burton, since his income was low, and fishing was the only sport which he could enjoy until his leg grew stronger.

DIARY _____

My Castle Connell rod by Farlow, which I have had for thirteen years – a great loss to me. Also 'Ogden' 9ft. 'Multum in Parvo' Trout Rod. Meanwhile must sell my gun and buy new rods and reels.

Nowgong Cantonment – Orrcha State. 1907–1912. In 1907 Burton moved to Nowgong. Throughout July, August and September he had many attempts at fishing on the Dassan river, but although some mahseer, carp and tengra were caught, the river was too muddy for good sport. In September 1908 he was invited with his wife Hilda to the Charkhari Guest House as guests of the Maharaja. Here there were three tanks close together and a large tank some distance away. Rohu, perrun, murrel and carp of many kinds could be found in these, and the prize catch on this occasion was a perrun of 23lb.

There was little opportunity for fishing again until 1912, when he was at Meerut. Here he was able to cycle out to the Ganges Canal with his brother Charlie. They several times caught mahseer, but none above 8lbs.

JOURNAL _____

I got leave through the Political Agent's Office to shoot for four days west of the Dassan River in Orrcha State, and left Nowgong on 24th on an elephant lent to me by W.E. Jardine. I used the elephant as my leg, which was not yet too strong, and in the infrequent intervals of the old mahout's asthmatic cough, saw many interesting things. A couple of young chital stags, horns in velvet having a pushing match; a wild cat on a hare she had just caught; an imperial eagle attempting to annex a peafowl. The ber fruit and the fruit of the pipal trees were ripe and attracted many birds, also monkeys and lungoors.

DIARY _____

26th January 1907. On elephant to Ramsagar. A lot of teal. Got into boat, and as they would not readily leave the tank – all mud, no cover – I had good sport and got twelve teal with fifteen cartridges. All except one single shot and with that shot got two birds.

2

1

CHAPTER
5

1
'R.W.B.' recovering from his
leg injury on the Isle of Wight
with Phyllis and Stella

2
The Cantonment Committee,
Nowgong, 15 July 1908

3
A few Nowgong notabilities,
1908

4
A Magistrate's clerk,
Nowgong, 1908

5
Sketch of the bear hunting
from Col. Burton's diary

5

On to Daljam, two tanks close together and both packed with duck and teal and some sixty geese; must be some three thousand birds.

27th. Started 7.30 a.m. and got six teal only; most of the birds at once left for the other tank. Weeds awful and could scarcely move the boat along, so the stray teal, of which a good many refused to go away, were pretty safe as I could not get near them at any price. Went off to other tank and at once on the way spotted where the line of flight lay handy, and sending a man to rouse up the birds got seven splendid nuktas in a very few minutes: twenty duck and teal by 9 a.m. and two snipe. On to Dhumera, a big tank; some awful weeds and no getting through them. Very high wind, so boat difficult to manage and shoot out of at same time. Back to Chedari, and on way to camp saw about two thousand birds.

Nowgong. March 1907. A report came from a village twelve miles north that a boy had been killed and eaten by a panther. The same panther had, a month earlier, killed and eaten a woman of the village. On 17th March a woman was grabbed by the head near the village while sleeping, but the beast let go. Two days later a goat was killed in a savage onslaught with the top of the head almost bitten off. Burton had a pit dug as a hide, and a cart placed over the top and covered with thorns. A goat was left and not touched for three days. On the fourth day Burton sat up in the pit to wait.

DIARY _____

At 3 a.m. I heard a stone clink on the hill side and very soon afterwards the beast came with a rush and seized the goat. Moon had gone down. Fired a barrel with meade's shell (twelve-bore) and almost immediately after the left barrel with s.s.g. At daylight found that the beast was a female hyaena, with meade's shell in back of head and on into body. The hyaena was a big one, and the usual beastly smell, awful beast indeed.

Rode into Nowgong on tricycle on 25th and examined the woman's head; two fang holes and sundry scratches, no claw wounds, and little doubt that she was attacked by a hyaena. If no such seizures during next month or so may be pretty sure I shot the right beast. Have kept skull of hyaena and gave skin to so-called shikari, who knows nothing of big game shooting.

29th March. Out on elephant to Basar, Orrcha State. Camped under a mohwa tree. Found a nightjar's egg laid on ground, no sign of any nest. A great year for mohwa. Told Sk. Badulla he should get people to cut off the branches attacked by the parasite (Coranthus) locally known as 'banda' – a bunch of green leaves growing on the branches; many trees are doomed, but a number could be saved. Out after chink, but no luck, and so back to Cantonment the next day after a most unsuccessful and disastrous shoot, as my man broke stock of shot gun the first day and I dropped .500 rifle from my tree during a beat the second day and smashed the stock of that. Rifle just purchased, very cheap, for R.70/-

9th June 1907. At 12.30 a.m. on Lighasi elephant to Palchra. Slept comfortably as I had rigged up a full length bed on the pad. Panther had killed a calf that night. I sat up over the kill which had been dragged from the village into some thin jungle below the hill. My shelter was rather conspicuous, but there was no tree large enough to support a machan, and to sit on the ground for panthers over a kill is ordinarily quite safe. At 6.50 when quite light, I heard panther sniffing all round my shelter, and was expecting her to go on to the kill. Suddenly her head appeared looking in at my loophole! I instinctively moved my arm to take hold of the rifle, she saw the movement and bounded off. I had given the panther credit for seeing more than she had and whistled up the men. As the man came up she was coming back but seeing him she cleared off with a growl.

To Orchha State for ten days. June 1908. 6th. Up at 3 a.m. and at banks of Dassan river by daylight. Stalked through thick undergrowth for three hours, and had fleeting glimpses of chital only. This is the jungle which the whole country talks of as full of sambur and chital! Up at 4.30 on 7th and off to Palchra to beat the big hill near the village. A long and weary trudge home, as the old elephant being rather blind missed his way, and branched off to Bola; a two hour difference. Saw a sambur, about 38in., but couldn't shoot as had no permit.

12th. News by Nanwa, forest guard, of a panther in a cave; also of a calf killed by panther near Gora village. Set off on elephant at 2 o/c. Got to the hill at 3.30, very hot. After careful stalk in socks, found a pig and a peacock in the cave. Slew the pig, old boar but not large. What Nanwa had seen, and described as a panther, was the spots on the peacock's tail! In fact he must have just glimpsed the tail in the shadow; concluded it was a panther, and not returned to take another look to make sure. Much trouble for nothing. There were nilgae and chital in the jungles, but I never came within certain shot of them.

On 27th June 1908, he went to the Jhin Jhin jungles with Gardner, an uneventful two days. It was hot and muggy and their clothes were permanently wet through. On other trips to Palchra in January and February 1909 he stalked and shot some black buck and also a sambur stag with 36in. horns, as well as some snipe and duck. He used the elephant on these trips, but his leg was strong enough now to do a fair bit of walking.

In March 1909, Burton went to Meerut as Cantonment Magistrate and did scarcely any shikar. In October 1911, he was sent to Delhi to get all conservancy arrangements ready for the Troops for the Coronation Durbar and stayed there – clearing up, until January 1912.

In December 1911, Burton was joined by his nephew Hugh, son of C.W.W.B., on a shoot over the sandhills at Bahandurgang. They shot eight chinkara and five buck of which there were large numbers all over the country, and other small game such as hares and partridge. In April 1912, he went with Stirling on a hunting trip to Amoot, fourteen miles from Nazihabad Junction. The game in these forests was mainly chital and nilgae.

DIARY
22nd. Storm in the night. Stirling went south; I went north. Saw nothing except some pig which came to inspect me when I was resting under a tree near some water. Heard a peafowl squawking in great distress, ran on and saw a large eagle attacking her. Hid behind a tree to watch, but nothing further happened after the first round. The peahen was much dishevelled, wings hanging down and many feathers pulled out. The eagle kept her in sight by flying from tree to tree; I waited but did not see a second attack. Screeches of the peafowl sent a herd of chital off at a gallop.

24 April. Made our way to Nazihabad and back to Meerut by the night train. Total bag: two chital – 23in., 31in.: two blue bull: one hyaena.

Two months later he paid another visit to this jungle, this time on his own. From Meerut he took the train via Saharumpur to arrive at Nazihabad 1.30 a.m. Here he slept on the platform and left for Mohanwala at 5.0 a.m.

DIARY _____

10th June. Monday. Out alone at 2.30 p.m. Stalked two small stags. A tremendous thunderstorm rolled up and I got wet through and made for camp. 6 p.m. out again, heard a stag roaring and got close to him, but could not see his horns, so did not shoot, and the herd took alarm and cleared out. Later shot a stag, horns 31½in.

11th. Another thunderstorm, torrents of rain. Cool when starting out but soon became very hot. Came across excited crows at the edge of thick jungle and fresh tracks of a panther. No kill. The heat terrific except in the shade.

12th. Saw two jungle cock having a fight, also saw a hawk catch a small bird and it got free after being carried 20 yards and flew back to same tree, and its captor after it and both sat, apparently best of friends! Saw a green insect never seen before; jumped like a frog and had a horny head to it; size about two inches long; all bright green. Evening: did a short round – saw nothing: sat up over goat till 8 o/c, no sign of panther. Have now sat up and wasted sufficient time for shikari not to be able to say 'No panther because sahib wouldn't take trouble' – So I shall get one of the two stags which roar every evening, I hope.

When out stalking chital or nilgae, there was always the danger of coming unexpectedly on a panther, which might certainly attack a man. Walking through the jungle one evening, having sent the cooly back to camp, Burton heard a noise close by that sounded like a pig grunting, and noticed a pig leaving the cover. Then, as he paused, he saw in a jungle clearing a panther sitting in the open space. With a steady standing shot he killed it instantly. As he fired there was a movement in the grass close to him and a second panther got up and slipped away down the nala. This was a male panther, which Burton remarks was just as well, since had it been a female it would probably have gone for him. He visited this jungle again in November 1912, before going to Jeypore.

JOURNAL _____

There was a good deal of fairly open desert-like country with scattered clumps of scrub jungle, mostly tamarisk, thorn and euphorbia, ugly and without shade. On camel back it was possible to see and be seen, but by careful manoeuvring we managed to scan the open spaces from behind the taller thorn bushes. Desert foxes were seen, also hares and houbara, a fine bird of the bustard species. The number of rats was extraordinary, there must be millions of them, for the whole country is honeycombed with their burrows. Jerboa rats they are, graceful animals with a long tail at the end of which is a tuft of hair; with short forelegs and long hind ones they have the appearance of miniature kangaroos. One morning a black cobra was seen in the compound, so I sallied out in pyjamas and killed it by tapping it on the tail with a cane and cutting it down when it sat up to take notice.

I moved four hundred miles to the south east to a small forest block on the outskirts of the Terai jungles. My nose must have been in good working order for one morning I smelt a panther and walked up to his lair in the long grass by scent alone. He heard me coming and slipped away. Every night I hear the rasping calls of the panthers in the forest. There were many cobras about this jungle; all those I saw being of the light coloured variety. The cousin of my shikari, while gathering honey one day, came across a tiger. He ran off in fright, was bitten by a snake, and died in two hours. 'It was written; it was his fate' – was the comment of Abdul Rahmon on the occurrence.

Chapter 6

THE JUNGLES OF JEYPORE, TIGERS AND BEARS

JOURNAL

In December I was at Yellandu, some eleven hundred miles further south. Having purchased ponies and local supplies, I set off on a ten days march. After some days I reached the Godavery River. This caused great delay. The carts had to be unloaded and the crossing of the mile wide sandy river took seven hours. Bullock carts vary much in different parts of India. Here the wheels were 5ft.6in. in diameter, and the centre of gravity being high the loaded carts upset too easily on a rough track. This happened several times and caused much delay.

After having crossed the Saveri river I camped in the evening at the village of Koigonda, the inhabitants of which are Khonds. The language is a very musical one with a high intonation. All the people speak Telegu, a few know a little Hindustani. The hair is worn long and tied into a bun high up on the right side of the head. This is secured with a very grand silver hairpin. Then there are silver earings and a silver chain hanging from the top of one ear down to the shoulder; that completes the dress above the waist. Below, we have a scanty breech clout into which, on the right buttock is stuck a stout reaping hook; add bow and three arrows and all is complete. When nearing game, and with the bow ready for action, two arrows are hung by the barb on the bun (in that matter I can never qualify as a Khond!), and one of these can very quickly be taken in place of the expended arrow. The arrow blades are six inches long and razor sharp on both edges. All game, including bison, is slain with these; for birds the shafts have a round knob in place of a blade.

The huts and villages are very clean and tidy. I had a Muhammadan shikari named Jamal with me who spoke Telegu, and two local shikaris, Jogi and Singaru. The forest is mostly small teak with big evergreen trees, such as mango, jamun and gular, in the nalas. Everywhere are palm trees of a stunted variety. The subsoil is mostly rock and loose stones, and the spear grass is bad. It was a treat to see the lithe and silent progress of my Khond shikaris; such eyes for tracks and for the slightest movement. Sometimes the air was very still and yet a frond of a palm would begin to move quietly and rhythmically backwards and forwards, while all the others remained motionless.

All the tigers of this Jeypore country are potential man-eaters and readily take a man if they meet him after dark. It was therefore with a slight feeling of nervousness that I came along the road under the hill in the darkness, following a long day in the jungles. Jogi and Singaru kept close to heel and when we made out the form of the buffalo quietly eating his grass by the side of the path, we all chattered with relief from the strain.

News came of a big tiger which had recently killed several people along the Poteru river to the north, so I decided to move camp to Lachipeta. My kit was carried by the people in string nets slung at either end of 6ft. springy bamboos, about 30lbs in each net. The walk through the forests to Lachipeta was most interesting. The bird life was different from the jungles of the Godavery River. Here were many scarlet minivets, ground thrushes, parrots I had not seen before, green imperial pigeon, and many other birds new to me. The climate was delightfully cool and the grass being nowhere more than waist high, and mostly knee high with many open spaces, the walking was not too fatiguing to a damaged leg. Climbing to the top of a hill through bamboos and undergrowth, I obtained a fine prospect of the country. In every direction was a sea of forest, relieved from monotony by low clumps of hills, the dark winding lines of giant trees marking the course of the larger streams. Twenty or so miles away to the south east a range of hills, clad in purple on the lower and nearer slopes and melting into blue as they receded, display to my longing eyes the wild tracts of the Rampa and Golconda country in the Eastern Ghats.

The tiger killed a buffalo on the very night of my arrival at Lachipeta. I sat up for him in the machan, and with the moon at full took one shot. He went off into the jungle; I felt the bullet was well placed but heard no expiring moans. I heard the flute like call of four-horn antelope and the belling of the sambur, and it seemed as if the tiger had moved some distance. I woke in the early hours to hear the pattering and murmuring of the dew dripping off the teak leaves. Then the sun mounted higher and dispersed the mists; a crow flapped through the trees, a chattering flight of parrakeets swept in a green bow across an open space, and a whistle from the direction of camp announced the arrival of Jamal.

The tracks were followed up and the tiger was found fifty yards from where fired at, having evidently died within a very few minutes. He was very large and would have measured 10ft. between pegs if measured immediately after death. This was the tiger which had killed five people within the past three months. His left upper canine tooth was broken off short and had a deep cavity full of maggots which looked very painful. A bullet was found embedded in the muscles of the lower jaw on the same side, behind the last molar. It seemed to be the base of a .500 hollow point bullet – a most dangerous form of projectile to use. His toothache accounted for his having eaten so little of his kill, only one hind leg in 24 hours. No doubt he was waiting for it to get soft. I left the kill in the hope of attracting the other big tiger which was in the district. It was this tiger who had elicited the alarm calls which worried me during the night, but he seemed to have wandered off elsewhere.

At Gorukunta I tracked and shot a huge buffalo. As I unloaded my weapon I received a stab in my left Achilles tendon, the sensation being just as if I had been struck with a red hot iron. I did not think anything of it at the time, for some of the large jungle hornets can give one an almost similar sensation, but before long the foot swelled up and the boot had to be taken off. Being unable to bend my knee beyond a right angle, owing to an injury in 1903, I was unable to examine the spot, but my servant said there were two little black dots, so I knew what had occurred. There was nothing to be done but bathe the foot in hot water to reduce the swelling. Fever came on and my temperature rose to 103°, but beyond that no other symptoms supervened. Later on, with the aid of a book on snakes, I concluded that it was a Bamboo snake which had bitten me, a poisonous but non-lethal variety.

It was with eager interest that I neared Kondakamberu situated at the junction of the Machkund and Gurupreo rivers. The junction pool is a grand one, and the mahseer fishing should be splendid when the water is warmer. The bird life is wonderful, and indeed this valley must have few equals in the country. There was one drawback which did not affect me or my followers at the present season, and that is the fever. I gathered it is a very unhealthy place from April to November. The people had the appearance of being malarial, and all of them even the tiny babies take opium. On one morning, when about a couple of miles from camp, my village shikari began to feverishly search his scanty clothing and soon announced in a hysterical way that he had forgotten his opium and could not go on. It was evident that he could not do without this drug so I let him go back to camp.

On the first day after arrival I saw two herds of bison, also sambur and chital. One of the herd bulls was a fine animal with amber coloured horns having beautifully polished black tips to them. By the side of a path the shikari pointed out a bush and said that a month previously a tiger had killed and eaten his brother at that place. Twenty five years earlier tigers were a menace, man-eaters the rule rather than the exception. People fled the villages; whole tracts were depopulated. In 1884, a number of old police carbines were distributed among the hill men of Golconda but these were used against the deer tribe and bison on salt licks; the latter were slain in such numbers that it was reported – 'the whole country is dotted over with bison bones'. In the months of April and May there are several beats for game when all the able bodied male population goes into jungle and slays everything to be found! No wonder game is getting scarce!

One day I was out from dawn to dark and came home along the valley of the clear stream. One sees so much bird and animal life: large yellow and black squirrels are plentiful; lungoors and monkeys everywhere; and green pigeon, jungle fowl, red spur fowl, and peafowl in great numbers. On one sand bank I saw the tracks of all the game animals of these parts; tiger, panther, bear, buffalo, bison, swamp deer, sambur, chital, four-horn antelope; also hyaena and pig and all the smaller animals such as otters, cats and mongoose. All these had not been there during the same day or night, but the tracks were there – old and new; and there were also crocodiles sunning themselves near the water's edge.

Soon I moved camp to Jamnai, seven miles up the Gurupreo. Near that place was a bull bison well known to the villagers, who very much wanted him killed as he had taken to frequenting a glade in which was a palmyra palm they tapped for liquor. For several days I tracked him but he always eluded me. He crossed the river and I did the same – in my bath tub, as the water was very cold and I dreaded a return of that awful neuritis of eight years ago. I searched daily for the big bull but the shikaris were unable to keep to his tracks in the hilly country at that season.

On 24th December the weather suddenly became warmer and at once fish in large numbers appeared in the river. I decided to return to the level country for more tiger shikar and had a day at the river when I caught a few mahseer, but to do the water justice a boat was essential. On 27th I regretfully left that delectable valley and marched for three days in the direction of Udgiri to a place in the forest far from any village. Here, on 7th January, I tracked and shot a large bull buffalo, 2001 lbs.

DIARY _____

7.1.1913. A day indeed! Off with the village shikari at day-break. When the sun rose he scraped a piece of ground clear of grass and did a lengthy poojah, praying for success in the day's shikar. At 8.30 coming out of jungle into open space suddenly saw enormous horns facing our way at about 100yds. Slipped off pony, took eight-bore Paradox and advanced to battle. In and out of deep nala and tried to perform a flanking movement. Signs of uneasiness on part of the colossus who had seen us all right and was three quarters on to me, so fearing a stampede, in which case no shot at all, I took him at fifty yards aiming low – I couldn't see very clearly on account of the grass, but enough to make sure of a good shot. He retreated into some small tree jungle, and almost at once we found him looking back at us. Got within thirty yards and took a careful shot. On receiving the bullet he whisked round, in spite of his lameness, and advanced a few paces, snorting defiance, and presenting a most formidable appearance and looking like mischief. I could not see the bottom of his girth and aimed low hoping to get behind foreleg – and did. In a couple of seconds over he went. Four shots; the first two well placed, the third rather high and had merely cut a long groove in the skin and stuck in the massive bones of the shoulder. The movement of the shoulder at once forced the bullet out of the bone as I cut it out just under the skin where it went in; an illustration of the uselessness even with heaviest weapon of hitting these big beasts anywhere but the right spot. The fourth shot was through the lungs low down, exactly where the first was intended to be. The two holes not ten inches apart, but the angle made the difference. The bull fell within 120yds of where he stood when first shot was fired. Bull had only four teeth; the other four – three on one side and one on other seem to have disappeared a long time ago. After 7th January I went towards Sileru river, and on the way there shot another buffalo, heavier by a good deal than the first one.

6th February. Kill by big tiger near Udgiri dragged about 350 yards. Tiger nosed round the kill about 7.30, but didn't touch it although he must have been very close to it. Perhaps not hungry and only satisfying himself that it was there. Men very late coming for me and couldn't understand why, whistled several times. Was sitting waiting when up trots a panther looking highly pleased at finding a ready made breakfast! Took him in chest at forty yards. He fell at once and saw his tail twitching but couldn't see body because of leaves. 6ft.7in.: tail 3ft.: weight 72lbs. Plenty of fat on him but he was built like a greyhound and evidently hadn't had a square meal for some time. All the panthers of these parts said to be of this small size, and the tigers seem all to be extra big. Cause of delay of the men was that while they were waiting for an answer to their whistle (which I did not hear), Tom Puss appeared and made an advance on my pony! Pony snorted and T.P. seeing the men kept to edge of the jungle. (But it is likely he heard the shot at the panther and so turned aside.)

12th. Moving tomorrow to Poreh, eight miles north. Bad luck indeed not to have got this tiger; he has a bad record. Last rains he chased a herdsman out grazing cattle but the yells of the man and yelps of three village dogs scared him off. A month later he killed the same man when he was again out with the cattle. He also killed one of three men who were going to draw toddy. On 30th December, when I was marching from Girganpili to Pulmetta, he killed the son of the Patel of Udgiri, a boy of sixteen. The boy was with two others grazing cattle and the tiger ignored the cattle and caught this boy who was among them. The two other boys and the cattle ran off to the village and the villagers drove the tiger off. He had eaten one leg and half one side of the body. They buried the remains in the path and I passed the grave each day I went to machan. I was not told of all this until yesterday. It seems now possible that the tiger saw me that first evening. I removed the leaves over loop hole on first hearing him and he may have looked up, when standing almost over the kill as I think he must have been.

Curious that the people of villages below Girganpili all carry bow and arrow; while scarcely ever saw bow and arrow beyond there. The Khonds eat any offal; didn't despise a bit of goat which had lain in jungle from night of 5th to night of 7th. Very high meat indeed. They chew much tobacco of their own growing, and in consequence can beat anyone at expectorating: not safe to be either side of a Khond! (Rajputs of Janucar also eat food killed by panther as late as twenty four hours after it is killed.)

Between Kurti and Poreh I passed over the bund of a fair sized tank which was under construction, and I stopped to enquire about it. A man came forward who to my surprise talked Hindustani. He stated with some pride that he had learnt Hindustani when a convict in the Andaman Islands! It transpired that he had been concerned in the Rampa Rebellion of 1879 and had been transported. Six years ago he was released, after twenty seven years in Andamans, and having brought away with him Rs.400, earned while a convict, was making this tank as a provision for his family, which will live in affluence from proceeds of cultivation below the bund. He said that six convicts were released and four died shortly after return to their villages. He and the other survivor were very ill for a year or more suffering from severe fever and inability to take any nourishment other than milk.

15th February. Moved camp to Dhuranupili, eight miles, with hopes of a tiger there and also swamp deer. Started at 7 a.m. to beat out bears at Rock 721. In 1900, Percy Smith of H.C. Cavalry shot five bears in twenty minutes at these rocks. His companion got enteric fever and had to be taken back to Rajahmundy (he died there); and that is how Percy Smith only had fifteen days shooting. He told me the heat was very great; and it is worse in May.

Bear's entrances were A and C. When two bears were roused at B, they ran round and went in at A, instead of going in at B. For a long time efforts were made to get them to break at C, but without result, and I had given up hopes of getting a shot and decided to put machan in a tree and try for a shot at dusk or in early morning; when a village shikari said that a Sahib had once shot a bear in the space D by making a ladder and getting on top of one of the high rocks. I told them to show me the place and they went to entrance A. There a shikari, Kundaswamy, looked round the corner and between where two high rocks came close together saw a bear and beckoned to me. I at once saw that the shot was an easy and safe one, and sitting down on a hog back rock, below which were smaller rocks and boulders, screwed myself into position and taking steady aim at the bear's neck, about twenty five to thirty feet away, pulled the trigger. (See plate section)

On the report a hairy beast uprose at my feet, probably had an eye on me all the time, and seized my right ankle. Another moment it got my right thigh above the knee, and then was over me. At this moment I could have shot her in the stomach, I was lying back in order to get rifle up, and instinctively did not fire thinking – in a flash – of the result if the beast were to drop wounded on top of me. She grabbed my head as she scrambled over me and, I think, closed jaws twice – rapidly, but am not sure. I heard the bones crack, but felt no pain at all, and thought all was up. Next second I found myself standing up and holding up my cheek which had fallen on my shoulder; and then unloading my rifle for fear of an accident when the natives got hold of it. Shikaris came running up with the usual lamentations of 'Sahib margaya' and got roundly sworn at and Jamal, head shikari, told to take his cocked shot gun from pointing in my direction and unload it. I put my rifle up so as to see along the sights and found right eye quite uninjured.

The bear had run round the rocks and gone in again at C, no tracks of blood. The one I shot at was a male: this one was a female as two cubs about the size of spaniels were running about below after she went for me; and as no cubs were with the two bears which were put up at the commencement there were doubtless three big bears at least in among the rocks.

There was a great deal of bleeding from my face and head wound, and I got off the rocks and sat under a tree and had a leafy screen made to protect me from the sun. Hat was undamaged, but had unfortunately fallen over on my leaning back from sitting position or it would have very likely saved my head; chin strap was not down. (Note. Always put down chin strap of topee when after bears, tiger, panther: it may save the head. Did save Sexton's head to a large extent, but as his chin strap was not down the hat was knocked off and he got claw wounds in head.)

Water bottle fortunately full of boiled water, so put in some permanganate of potash crystals and got shikari to hold up scalp flap and pour into the wound: then held open cheek flap and did same to that and bandaged up. Found three holes about ankle and six above knee, some pretty extensive and running one into another. Syringed out with permanganate and tied up. No pain, no faintness, no nothing. Told men to go and see if bear shot was dead. They said it could not be seen. Probably had not dared to look. I left it at that, as it would obviously not be possible to get it out. It must have been killed on the spot – not likely to have missed it.

Owing to moving of camp, things were a bit scattered and it took some time for the machan to arrive. When it came I had to show how it should be fixed up as a dooly and see that it was properly done; three poles were cut and brought before I was satisfied. Moved off to camp, but before doing so gave full instructions to Head Shikari as to what was to be done with kit etc. Arrived at camp, gave all wounds another dose of permanganate and put on fresh bandages. Wrote a couple of letters in case of accidents – erysipelas, blood poisoning, tetanus, all possible and unpleasant contingencies. Told Abdul Guffon what clothes and provisions to take along, and at about 4.30 started for Malkangiri. Before I left Shikari Kundaswamy had succeeded in getting comfortably drunk and came and asked how he was to get his share of reward for animals killed. Thought, of course, that I was going to die and that it was a good thing to get hold of cash as soon as possible. Took Abdul Guffon and one syce with me and thought I had soups and milk and clothes as explained to Abdul Guffon. About 7 o/c the syce had to be left in the jungle, drunk, with four coolies to look after him.

Got to the Malkangiri Dispensary, twenty six miles, at day-break and found that no clothes or milk or soups had come. Abdul Guffon had merely told the shikari to bring along the boxes in which the things were, instead of sorting out what was wanted and packing into one box. Fortunately I had personally made sure that the box containing medicine and cash was with me. Found that I had only just got to Dispensary in time to catch the Hospital Assistant, who was packed up and going off on transfer to Vizagapatam. He began to sew me up etc. at 9 o/c, using my camp bed as operating table, and finished in about two hours. Ten stitches to scalp wound was the first business and this was painful – very. I relieved my feelings by a few good yells: needles were not over sharp and had to be pushed and pulled with forceps. When all was over the Hospital Assistant said 'You have borne it very well Sir, I have met worse screamers than you'.

Sewing up of face, which I had rather dreaded, did not hurt at all. Nerves were numb from the tearing and shock and I was able to take a gallery seat and supervise the job with aid of my looking glass and see my phiz grow shapely once more, under the really skilful hands of the Hospital Assistant. Some forty stitches were put into the face. All wounds were washed out with perchloryde solution and whole job was done in proper surgical manner. Scalp wound was ten inches long, and caused by bruin's teeth slipping on the skull instead of penetrating. Face wound consisted of tearing open the face from centre of upper lip to top of right ear, the tear going under the nose, which was partly detached and up the cheek to under the eye. Another tooth had penetrated into corner of eye, outside eyelid, against the nose and joined the other tear and a single tear continued upwards to outer corner of right eye and then to top of ear. Practically whole of molar bone was torn off, being entirely detached from the skull. To anticipate – it was found in Secunderabad hospital not possible to save the bone, which was removed and so caused lower eyelid to drop a quarter of an inch and also left outer side of eye very much puckered up, and much exposed to chance of injury from any blow or knock.

The Hospital Assistant went on in the evening in his bullock cart. I waited for box of milk and soups etc. until 4 a.m. on 17th and as these had not turned up had to go on. Caught up the Hospital Assistant twelve miles out and got wounds dressed. He went on and next morning I followed and caught him up again. Got wounds dressed and pushed on, starting at 3 p.m. for Jeypore, thirty two miles: which I reached the next day 19th February at 4 p.m. At Jeypore went to the Civil Dispensary and got wounds dressed by the Hospital Assistant. Had greatest difficulty in getting any coolies to take me on. The Amin full of promises but obviously meaning to do nothing. Chanced to hear of a Mr. Harrison, Post Master General, having just come in on tour and wrote a note to him and he came and saw me, and eventually I was able to start at 3 a.m. and got to Koraput, fourteen miles, at 9 a.m. the next day. (Reported the Amin to the Collector when I got to Secunderabad.)

At Koraput found most kind Missionary and his wife who took me into their house and looked after me. Mr. and Mrs. Weber of the Schleswig Holstein Mission. Military Assistant Surgeon (McArthur) in charge of Police Reserve Hospital dressed wounds and at 6 p.m. I moved on taking along, in another dooly, the Hospital Assistant of the Civil Dispensary at Koraput. Went thirty miles and got wounds dressed in the Military Works Rest House on 21st. Moved on and got to Salur at 1 a.m. on 22nd. Mr. Weber had sent a telegram to a Missionary there to expect me and to arrange a conveyance to Bobbili Railway Station. Arranged to start at 5 a.m. to catch train at 8.

The drive was an interesting one and might also have been disastrous. He told me to get into the trap – an American spider wheel buggy (4 wheels) while he held the horses head as the syce was new to the animal; the proper syce having been sent to jail for theft, the day before. I took the reins and the Padre climbed in over the back seat as the horse mustn't know he is in the trap. Then we started. Before we had gone 100yds the crupper broke and had to be mended with a piece off one of my leg bandages as no string available. The Padre apologised for the mush up saying 'We missionaries cannot afford good harness'. He had told me the history of the horse – a fine chestnut five years old and about 15½ hh. It had been in a bad trap accident six months before, bolted and smashed trap to pieces and so had been bought cheap. Was now being re-broken and was very nervous. I prayed that the reins were stronger than the crupper and hoped for the best.

Jibbing appeared the principal trouble. We stopped at every turn through the salubrious town of Salur, and on each occasion the Padre had to soothe and pacify the nervous nag and start him by leading him at a run and then jump in and climb over behind. Syce had to do the same. Some forty jibs and gallops – he always went at a gallop after a jib, took us to the Station, fourteen miles, with twenty minutes to spare. On the platform I saw the fat Rajah of Bobbili who had not even troubled to answer the Padre's wire appealing for loan of a motor car. Padre had done his best and didn't want to land me in a ditch by the road.

Got to Vizagapatam by 12 o/c and was there met by Major Illingdon, I.M.S. Civil Surgeon, who dressed wounds and started me off by 5 o/c Mail to Secunderabad, which I reached at 6 p.m. next day, 23rd, getting wounds dressed at 6 a.m. at Bezwada (a hateful pig of an Assistant Surgeon of the local hospital) and between Kazipet and Secunderabad by a very excellent Hospital Assistant of Nizam's Railway. A Captain of I.M.S. met me at Bhangir and at Secunderabad a motor (and several kind friends) met me and took me to Station Hospital where everything was done for me. Major Porter R.A.M.C, to whom all gratitude, operated on the 25th and made an excellent job of me, and kind Sisters looked after me till 17th March when I left for Bombay. Scalp wound was healed when I got to Secunderabad and leg bites just healing up. Face was in a bad state.

At Ergudium I saw timber being floated down the river. It was said to take three months for a log to be floated from the Sal forests near Jeypore to the storage place at Koonta where the logs are put on to barges which take them to Rajahmundy. The contractor for the timber has an arrangement by which he pays Rs.3 for each log delivered at Koonta: and this work is done by the men of two villages only: both are close to Ergudium.

I did not see a single snake (did not SEE the one which bit me on 7th January 1913) during the whole time I was in Jeypore territory. One night I heard a snake in my bath tub and heard him get out and climb about the legs of my X-pattern camp bed, but was too sleepy to trouble about him. Tracks of wild dogs only seen once, near Koigaon. Tracks of wild cats in most nalas. I heard the diabolical shrieks of the owl, species unknown, and which is called in Ceylon the 'Devil bird'. It was on the night of 5th January at Pulmetta that I heard it. Curious that it should have been only on that occasion out of the many times I sat up at night. It may be that the bird is uncommon or perhaps silent except in the breeding season. A horrid and unearthly sound it is.

This ends the diary for 1913; with exception of list of stores and sundries, medicines etc. Total expenses – from Meerut on 29 October up to Montgomery, at Mohanwali and to Jeypore, and back to Bombay on 18th March – Rs. 2950. This spread over the five months comes to Rs.600 a month: but there was a good deal of extra expense in connection with the accident and under ordinary circumstances the out of pocket expenses should have been Rs.250 less. It may be taken, as I have found before also, that Rs.500 a month will enable one to shoot in comfort.

A shooting trip to Jeypore is probably as cheap as it can be anywhere in India. From Yellandu Station to Koigaon only cost Rs.51/- and I had five carts and three ponies. Ponies gram not included. I did not know that kulthi was procurable in Jeypore, so took gram with me and it was an unnecessary expense to carry this about. There is a colony of Pathans at Koonta and they could supply anything in reason. It is not necessary to take in any rice for camp followers. Tobacco should be taken and also any luxuries in way of condiments – pepper, assaforetida. Salt is obtainable.

Absolutely necessary to have two Jeypore durbar peons attached to the camp; three if possible. They collect coolies, get supplies, etc. With their services all is easy; and without them things would be most difficult and uncomfortable. Their pay is small, 4/- a month. So a tip of 5/- a month is much appreciated by them. I found it a good plan to form depots of surplus stores as I went along. Lachipeta and Pulmetta are convenient. About thirty five coolies ordinarily sufficed to move camp. This closes the diary of Cold Weather Shoot of 1912/13: a delightful memory in spite of sudden ending.

Chapter 7

CHAKRATA, IN THE JUNGLES OF THE HIMALAYAS

Almost throughout the length and breadth of India the panther, or leopard, is to be found in suitable localities. Every hill station has several of these animals within its area, and owners of dogs should keep their pets chained up when the sun has set and the short twilight is merging into the darkness of night. Dogs have been snatched from verandahs, and a panther has been known to carry off a dog being led along the road on a chain. In one instance a bull terrier was taken from beneath the camp bed on which his master was sleeping, the less conspicuous Irish terrier asleep on a chair close by having escaped notice.

The panther is a ruthless and wanton slayer on occasion. I have known one of these beasts of the lower Himalayas to enter the lower storey of a house, commonly used as a sheep pen, and kill thirty three of the flock in one night. On another occasion eleven sheep strayed and were not found before darkness set in. All were killed, the carcasses being dragged into a hollow and tumbled one on top of the other in a pitiable heap.

The ordinary twelve-bore shot gun is the ideal weapon for panther, but let us hope there will be no wounded panthers. Many have been the fatal maulings and accidents, for these beasts are indomitable antagonists. A final warning: make very sure the beast is dead before approaching it. A young sportsman of my acquaintance tested signs of life by pulling a tail and was immediately thoroughly scraped down with claws and severely bitten by the apparently defunct panther.

2nd April 1915. Goat tied up below the house killed last night. Neck bitten through and body taken below into thick jungle. Sat up that evening but he did not return. Very wary panther and same as defeated me on 19th May last year: and again on 13th September and on 15th September.

6th May. Goat again extracted from pen. Had much difficulty in finding the goat. Panther had carried it clean off down the hill, across a nala, and up the other side and down a spur and had left scarcely any sign at all to track it by. Had not disembowelled the goat until he had taken it all this distance, over quarter of a mile. Made machan and sat up. Horrid hail storm came on at 5 o/c. Sat for four hours: no panther. He is no doubt the same panther which killed the village pig at Magroli ten days ago and which he carried quarter of a mile and hid at foot of an oak tree, and never turned up, though I sat till 10.30.

28th July. At last. The old and cute is slain. On night of 25 July, panther came to the cage below the house and made great efforts to get at the goat inside. He got through two layers of half inch netting and then gave up in disgust having left one whisker sticking in the wire. He had torn a hole about 18in. × 15in. oval in shape:

but the third layer of wire defeated him. He must have been much annoyed as there were many scratchings on the path all the way up the hill.

I slept in the hut all night 26th: he did not return. Next morning, news was brought that a large calf had been killed. Sent Kidaru to investigate and arranged to have a machan over the kill. I sat like a stone till 7.25 when panther suddenly appeared. His body was up hill so I let him come down a bit then took him at point of shoulder with .375. At the shot he fell backwards and then went off down hill. After a minute I heard a coughing grunt about eighty yards off; whistled up the men and followed the tracks. Hunted about till dusk but could not find him.

Next morning learnt he had been found a hundred yards or so from where we left off last evening. When disturbed by the men on his tracks he went over the next spur, two hundred yards ahead, and then into some thick cover. He might be anywhere in a mile of very thick jungle; thorny scrub; young rhododendron, so decided to work along the hillside following the small path along which panther had been going. Sent two men over to opposite spur to watch the hillside; and another two men up a big tree a little way ahead. Then I started along the path with three men just behind throwing stones down hill and two men up hill throwing stones twenty yards in front of me. After going about thirty yards the men above came on the panther lying down and shouted to me that they had found him.

He went like a flash down the hill just as if he had never been wounded! As his tail disappeared I sent a second bullet after him. Followed on at once and found him fifty yards or so away; very steep hillside, and bushes and creepers very thick. Got to him by sitting and sliding down, and at last after much peeping and peering, made him out. Had to move to one side to see his head and shoulder and blew him up at twenty feet with .375 which shot knocked him a few feet down the hill. He was probably dead and not needing the last shot.

As well as panthers there were large numbers of sloth bears in the mountain jungles, and these were considered a danger by the local people. One big and heavy bear of 387 lb., which Burton had killed with one shot through the back of the neck, was found to have a sixteen-bore spherical bullet stuck in the shoulder and another slug in the jaw, both fairly recent wounds.

DIARY _____

Nadh. Went to inspect the nala below the olive wood with view to arranging a beat; met a bear coming down the nala. I didn't see it being just then in difficulties with a fallen log and slippery stones. Chaprassi saw it but it was up the bank and out of sight by time I got turned round. Three days later had thirty men out and beat the wood in which the bear was on the 16th. Shot one gooral before the beat began when I was on way to my post. Standing shot, 200yds: 62lbs. In the beat saw two serow, two musk deer, three gooral, one kakur, one small bear. Had three flying shots at a gooral at 200 yds and missed. He was going down the hill side like a race horse. Also had two shots at the bear as it went down the nala directly below me: had my legs held, and fired perpendicularly down, about 100yds it was. Everything came at a furious gallop as the men made such a din. They are afraid to beat silently when there is a bear expected. Saw a covey of chukar near Nadh village. Forest Ranger says six bears were seen one day a week ago along the Nadh–Mundali Road in the evening.

I left Chakrata on 20th October and four days later reached Thadiar. Right knee very much swollen, it has now been like this for five months since slight slip coming down Karambu hill on 15 June. As other knee only bends to a right angle, I am a bit too stiff-kneed for hill climbing, but manage to get about.

On to Deota, a stiff climb, and I rode all the way. Wife walked half way and did the rest in a dandi; thick jungle all round. Many deodar trees stripped by bears which do this damage during winter and spring.

27th October. Nothing in morning as village shikari turned up late; one Sher Singh of Gokul. Shot a couple of koklas and a woodcock. In evening went to the precipice two miles away on the Kulni Road. Saw a small male thar and was, of course, begged to slay it. Saw more moonal and koklas and a bear strolling along on ridge two miles away.

On the crags and spurs of this jungle there were thar as well as bears, but it was difficult for Burton to climb these steep precipices. One evening when out walking they passed within ten feet of a bear below the path in the undergrowth: the noise of the stream had probably drowned their footsteps. There were terrified shouts from Kidaru who was following behind, of 'Bhalu, Bhalu'; but, as Burton turned to look back, the bear slipped away uttering a few grunts. It hadn't heard them approach or seen them until they walked by.

Burton was joined on 13th November by his nephew Hugh. Although the Pabar River was crystal clear, they didn't have much success fishing. They climbed the cliffs on the right bank of the river in search of gooral. According to the Diary entries, Burton found his nephew much too excitable and impetuous in his desire to shoot at gooral whenever he saw them instead of taking the time to make a nearer approach and so being certain to kill and not wound.

DIARY _____

19th November. To the place where bear seen yesterday. Forest Guard took us up a fearfully steep boundary line. At top of it saw boughs of oak shaking. Hugh went straight up the line, I went to one side. Hugh had two shots at the small bear which came down the trunk backwards and peered at him round the bole of it – missed. Next he fired at the big bear as she came down the trunk head foremost: both misses. .280 Ross and he was too excited. A bad business for him if he had brought the bear down on top of him. Hill at an angle of forty five degrees; I tried to tell him not to stand under but he paid no heed.

Soon after we saw the bears on the opposite slope as they had gone down the hill and round the nala. Hugh opened fire at 500yds or more, and went eighteen inches over her back. Several other shots went somewhere near her. Went on up the hill, Hugh in front. He saw gooral and fired two shots .280 and missed. On the way down hill he went to see if he had killed his bear, I didn't go as no use! Some time later heard two shots and later five more. He had been firing at gooral. After I left him I heard langurs swearing at panther; couldn't get near, the jungle too noisy. Panther cleared out, as I heard kakur barking at him further up the hill.

20th. To Talra Tach Bungalow, splendid view from there and also from near Chajpur Rock (10800ft.). Came down about 2500 feet: very steep, and struck path five miles from Bungalow. Saw a great many moonal. Hugh had more shots than I, (I had only two) and all were no doubt behind their tails. Moonal travel faster than they seem to, being very big birds.

One day they spotted a thar high up on the cliffs. Hugh had first shot and missed, then Burton fired twice and the thar was hit. As it was late in the evening they waited until next day before going to retrieve the body. In the morning two of the shikaris went up as it was a difficult climb over the cliffs and impossible for Burton. They had to skin and cut up on the spot: the skin was brought back and the meat thrown down the precipice. They were able to retrieve all of this except for one leg which the vultures had found before the men could get there.

DIARY _____

Lakhwa   25th December 1915. Went to look at Jumna. Water very clear and saw lot of small mahseer cruising about. Too cold to fish with any chance of success.

30th. Heard yesterday evening that a bear had been seen in fields below Bansa village. Got there at 9 o/c. No beaters had turned up. Cold morning: time very short as I had to get back to breakfast and Riot Case fixed for hearing at 11 o/c. So Chatram and two chaprassis started to beat the upper part of two nalas before beaters turned up, five of them only. Third nala was beaten down to the bottom, and I told them to go back and beat the centre nala. They beat the first one instead! Scarcely any cover in it, and didn't seem any chance of a bear. When the men had got about half way down I saw it was 10.45, so decided to stop and get home quickly; late already. Gave .375 to Kidaru to hold, and took twelve-bore in hand and unloaded it, when the bear emerged out of the ravine to walk across the bare open spur thirty yards away to go into the other ravine. Before I could get rifle he was into cover and up to the top by the time three men got there to head him off. Ratti, Dillu and Chatram made a great demonstration but he broke through. Dillu was cutting a stick off a bush when the bear uprose by the bush and Dillu hurled himself yards down the hill, as it seemed to us, over the bear's head. The bear was away, alas! I had ten minutes before said to Kidaru when beat of third nala was finishing, that one should never say a beat was empty until all the men out of the cover and beat over, and last man out of last bush. Had I waited one minute longer I would have got him. It was impatience to get back to try the Riot Case which cost me this bear.

1916. January. Got to Kalsi on 24th and stayed there for four weeks. No fishing, fish not to be seen. Shot several jungle cock and some peafowl. Rotten place Kalsi. Shot by Thornhill and Prince. They never spared a hen bird.

Burton had a low opinion of 'sportsmen' who fired recklessly and at random at jungle animals. Two of his colleagues went out after a bear which had been raiding the crops, and one of them borrowed Burton's .375. He expended ten cartridges, and the other fired fifteen shots, –'and so they slew the bear!' wrote Burton, 'many holes in the skin.'

Panthers were constantly roaming the jungles, sometimes killing the wild deer, but more often the cows and sheep of the villagers. Once a calf was taken from the verandah of the bungalow. The Afghans who were sleeping near heard the grunts of the panther, but these animals are very wily and once disturbed seldom return to the kill. Burton had to fit in shikar trips with his official duties and was not always free to go hunting.

DIARY _____

One day Sabbal Singh of Muidar bought me a panther skin to claim a reward. Female: full grown, old, small. He hit it in hind leg as it was after langurs near his village. Then it took cover and he and his brother and other villagers beat it out. It

2

1

3

CHAPTER
7

charged his brother, a lad of twenty, who knocked it down as it was springing on him by a whack on side of head with his hatchet. The cut was about six inches long and bit deep into the skull.

August. News of a bear on the open hillside beyond the Kailana rifle range. I had several cases in Court and could not get away till past 1 o/c. Sent on men with rifle and lucky I did. Got there by 2.30. Bear had not moved but a minute later yells and shouts told me he was making up the nala below me. Cartridge bag and rifle were with Kidaru. I went down the hill towards the nala and sent a man flying off to meet Kidaru. Got the rifle just as the bear appeared far below. Put in a clip of cartridges and put up the 200 yds leaf; and as the bear stopped for a second after climbing up a steep rock in the nala, took careful sight from left shoulder at top of his back. At the shot he reared up and fell and never moved again. Acclamations from the crowd. An old man going down towards the bear with me asked me – he had evidently pondered this prodigious fluke – where I had aimed. I told him, and we found the bullet there. It was three inches to left of spine behind the shoulder and was found stuck in armpit on opposite side.

Male 5ft. 4in.: Girth 50in., neck 30in. forearm 17in. Perfect teeth. Weight 309 lbs.

Received copy of confidential report. All very good: but, in India, no reports, good ones at any rate, have any useful purpose. The rule, laid down, for C.M.'s Dept. is 'promotion to higher grades BY SELECTION'. No C.M. ever yet been 'selected'. All go up in rotation, and in front of me are men notorious as bad officers. Doctor's remark in confidential report, furnished by me, 'not fit for active service: left leg four inches short: result of an accident: unable to close right eye: result of an accident'. I couldn't, and doctor wouldn't, say I was 'fit for active service', but if any chance of employment comes I can show that I am pretty fit from a common sense point of view. At present Government of India won't allow any C.M.'s, or anyone else to 'volunteer'.

27 October. Climbed to top of Karamba (10025ft.). Splendid view of hundreds of miles of snows. Took photo of a group of men and women of Mandi State, also of beater 'Pearl of Price' (100/-) of Rampur State. All the snows – a line of some three hundred miles or more lit up in rosy glow by the setting sun.

November. Talra Tach. Saw about a hundred moonal altogether. Very hard to get at them. Signs of snow coming along. Had a bridge of sleepers and a felled tree made across the Pabar River and so up to the big tahr cliff. Took off boots and went along in my socks. Saw a female tahr only. On 19th marched to Thadiar and met wife and Tiny on the way.

To Sandra: Place horribly cold; awful wind from the snows and in the morning there was one inch of ice in the basin. On 12th December to Chakrata. Minimum temperature at Deobar last night six degrees F. Heard that minimum temperature at Mundali was six degrees below zero. During December 1916 there was no shikar.

THE
MOUNTAINS
AND
FOOTHILLS
OF
THE
HIMALAYAS
1914
TO
1924

Chapter 8

THREE MONTHS UP THE VALLEY OF THE SUTLEJ

From March 1914 to March 1917, Burton had been Cantonment Magistrate at Chakrata, but in April 1917, during the years of the First World War, he was appointed O/C Troops on Transport to and from Bombay, until April 1919, when he took over charge at Bareilly as Cantonment Magistrate. In 1920 he was able to take three months' holiday, and planned a trip up the valley of the Sutlej River in the Himalayas as far as the boundary with Tibet. No diary exists for this expedition, but he wrote a series of articles for the Bombay Natural History Society Journal, describing his travels, from which the following extracts have been taken.

JOURNAL
The advent of the hot weather in 1920 was heralded by frequent dust storms, increasing heat, and the monotonous insistent note of the 'copper-smith' on the topmost bough of his favourite tree. These annual annoyances were somewhat, softened by thoughts of the coming three months in the hills; and on 26th April I was on the Punjab Mail en route to Dehra Dun. It was a good thing I had taken this train in preference to the Allahabad–Dehra Dun Express, which leaving my station that night at a later hour, ran into a goods train in the early hours of the morning. Many third class passengers were killed as they could not escape from the splintered woodwork of the overturned and blazing carriages.

The change of climate on arrival at Dehra Dun was very marked, the fresh feeling in the air being quite different to the close and oppressive heat of the plains cantonment. Soon after leaving the suburbs of the city I noticed a sign-board reading 'To Arcadia'. It is the name of a tea estate and was doubtless Arcadia to the people who established themselves there in years gone by. The roadside hedges were bright with dog-roses, and the leafy avenue of tun trees afforded pleasing shade. The river Asan, crossed by a substantial bridge was quite dry, and the mighty Jumna was running clear but somewhat low. After leaving the river the road begins a gradual ascent, winding through forests and later along bare and rocky hillsides, and we arrive after a journey of sixty miles at the military cantonment of Chakrata. Only five years ago in 1915, this easy journey by motor car was performed in jolting and nerve racking tongas, taking two full days to accomplish a distance now covered in five hours. It was hot when we arrived at noon, but by evening warm clothing was necessary.

Next day was spent sorting, packing and making ready for an early start in the morning. The road is about six feet in width and winds along a high ridge, affording far reaching views down the steep and wooded hillsides over the valleys of both the Tons and Jumna rivers. All along the path were banks of wild violets. Snow was still lying in sheltered spots; and where the path wound through forests of fir trees such as morinda, spruce and deodar, it was quite cold. The air was crisp and clear, a change indeed from the dreariness and dust of the shimmering plains dimly visible in the far distance. At the eighth mile the path passing along the southern slopes of the Peak of Karamba crosses over to the north side, and affords a magnificent view of hundreds of miles of snowy ranges. The last three miles were all down hill to the Forest Department Rest House at Mundali. It was close to this Rest House that a famous man-eating tigress was killed in 1887 in a most exciting and dramatic way, after having terrorised the countryside for some thirteen years.

On April 30th a start was made by seven o'clock. A gradual ascent of three miles and then several miles of level path and a steep descent led to Tewni. It was pleasant to be greeted on arrival at Tewni by a Siana (Headman) with a gift of freshly caught fish and a jar of honey and to know that these people remembered the work undertaken in their interests during the three years this sub-division was in my charge. The Tons river, a snow-fed torrent, was roaring down as of old, its waters reflecting the same beautiful play of colours – dark blue, light blue, dark and light green, topaz in its many hues, and creamy white. Until my return three months later I was seldom out of the sound of running water.

Arakot Forest Rest House, eight miles from Tewni and situated on the right bank of the Pabar River, was reached next day. The path followed the river all the way. Wild roses were in abundance, and the lovely crimson petals of a variety of erythrina gave vivid splashes of colour to the scenery. It was good to see old haunts, and the familiar faces of village people; all vivid reminders of the three years so happily passed in these beautiful hills.

The next day's march of about eight miles was also along the banks of the river as far as Hatkoti. Here the river bed is level and the valley wider. I carried with me a bunch of lovely deep red roses gathered from a gorgeous profusion growing on the walls near Hatkoti school. Each of the baggage coolies had a rose stuck in his cap. A shade of green was appearing on the slopes of the hills, but they were practically bare of trees. As one gets away from the Jaunsar–Bawar and the influence of the Forest Department, the deforestation of the hillsides is very noticeable.

Roru is in Bashahr and here is the tahsil for the southern portion of that State. The distance from Roru to Soongri, a dak bungalow on the Hindustan–Tibet Road, is fourteen miles. Almost every foot of the way is up hill, the last eight miles being very steep. The rise in elevation is over 5,000 feet. I walked the whole distance and was glad of some tea on my arrival. The pony 'Motee', a white hill pony of the sturdy Rampur breed, was led behind me all the many hundred miles of this trip, but it was comforting to know that he was at hand should at any time the flesh become weaker than the spirit. The path passed through deodar plantations and some cultivated land; we met some shepherds returning with their sheep and goats to the upland grazing grounds after having passed the winter months in the pastures of the lower valleys. The dogs with these people were very friendly, wagging their tails and allowing their heads to be patted.

A day's halt was made at Soongri, which is sixty six miles from Simla, and the bungalow is at an elevation of 8750ft. The temperature was not much above 60 degrees at any time during the day. The path passes through fragrant forests of fir, and from now onwards the violets, wild flowers and flowering creepers were a source of the greatest pleasure. From Soongri to Bahli is twelve miles, but a short cut over a very steep and rocky path strewn with pine needles takes off some of this. Half way down the hill I heard the loud barking of a kakur. The noise came nearer and there soon appeared a wild looking man of Kunawar who was taking sheep back to their summer grazing lands. He was the 'kakur' and his imitation of the cry of barking deer was to my ear, absolutely accurate. I envied him this accomplishment, and vain efforts were made to acquire the trick of voice which he uttered with such ease. He had acquired this art in order to frighten his sheep and keep them on the move.

The next day's march was shortened to five or six miles by use of a rocky goat track which descended steeply through fields of terraced cultivation. News of tahr twelve miles up the Darkari Valley induced me to make a three days excursion in that direction. With an early start on May 8th, two shikaris were provided at short notice by the lambardar, and that evening we saw three tahr on the face of a precipice in the further valley. Having dined off army rations, stewed figs and chupattis, sleep under an overhanging ledge of rock was not long in coming. At day-break next morning we moved to another camping place; but I soon realised that the proper ground for tahr at this season was much further on, up the precipitous slopes of the Marrarle Hill, and that I could not afford the time to go in search of them.

A heavy thunderstorm came on next day, and rain early in the evening quickly changed to snow. I woke during the night very thirsty as the sausages for dinner were uncommonly salt. Having emptied the water bottle I was glad to eat some snow off the kit bag which was protecting my feet. One of the shikaris under the rock near me groaned and grunted all night, poor fellow, in a most distressing manner. The four coolies, however, were jolly as crickets. They had no bedding, and just stuck it out round a fire under the wide-spreading branches of a deodar tree. Whenever I woke up they could be heard laughing and cracking jokes. Indeed these hill men are much to be admired for their endurance. It is difficult to imagine more depressing circumstances than the spending of a night in a gloomy forest in a snow and rain storm at an elevation of near 11,000ft. I reached Tacklech that evening, the last six miles having been somewhat painful owing to rheumatism in the left knee.

Burton continued through the hills and valleys of the Himalayas to Wangtu, passing through Sarahan, Taranda, and Nichar. Around him was the glorious panorama of snow topped mountains, the recent heavy snowstorm having brought the snow line quite low down. The gloomy gorges of the Sutlej river below, and the deep ravines, contrasted with the snowy peaks of the country of Spiti, where some of the mountain tops were shrouded in mist. Burton then came to a more frequented part of the Hindustan/Tibet road, and here encountered many different people, some of them bound for the Shipki Pass and the wilds of Tibet.

JOURNAL

Owing to the traffic on the road and the day being sunny the march of fifteen miles did not seem so long. On this day I met the Conservator of Forests and learned that my shooting pass was on its way to me, the number of each description of animal being limited to one ibex, one snow bear, three tahr, three gooral, two serow and three burhel. If a snow bear should be notified as a sheep killer then another might be shot. Almost at the moment of my meeting with the Forest Department party, an accident had happened to the cooly entrusted with the departmental medicine chest. He had sat heavily on the road parapet, with his back to the steep hillside, and this giving way he and his load went clattering down the precipitous declivity. He looked as if he needed some of the few remaining contents of the much damaged stock of medicines.

At Nichar Post Office a packet of letters was waiting, and from there it was three miles on to Wangtu Bungalow. The descent was steep, and a terrific wind of the biting and penetrating variety was howling down the narrow gorge of the river, reminding me of the Tons Valley in December. The shelter of the bungalow and comfort of a blazing wood fire were very welcome. That day was the last of the great storm which had swept over the Himalayas for many hundreds of miles.

The jurisdiction of the tahsil of Roru meets that of Chini at Wangtu. Here the Tibet road crosses the river by a modern suspension bridge, and a track leads on to the head of the valley into Spiti. This is the route to Hanle and Ladak by way of the formidable Parang La, a pass 18,300 ft. high and much dreaded by all who have to make their way across it. Wangtu is a place so obviously suitable for a bridge that there has probably been one here from time immemorial. There was a wooden bridge here in 1817 which was destroyed by the Gurkhas in 1819 and afterwards replaced by a rope bridge. This bridge marks the ancient boundary between Bashahr and Tibet. The Tibetan influence makes itself felt in the frequency among the people of Tibetan names, but in this part of the Sutlej valley the language is Kunawari.

At Urni, a chaprassi from the Chini tahsil met me with a change of coolies. From the river bed the road winds zig-zag fashion up the steep hillside and in several places overhangs the precipitous slopes, being supported by means of buttressed planks. The country called the 'dry zone' had now been entered. Beyond Wangtu there is little rain, the several ranges of mountains holding back the surcharged clouds of the monsoons of India and causing them to discharge their torrential rain against the western slopes. Any rains which reach the valley are only in the shape of English 'April showers', falling gently and at intervals. The hillsides were less heavily wooded, and the air was perfumed with the scent of many aromatic shrubs and grasses.

The following days march of fourteen miles to Chini was a fairy easy one. The scenery was magnificent. In one place the road had slipped into the Sutlej several thousand feet below. The winter at Chini is severe but the spring and autumn months provide a perfect climate. Here I met Captain and Mrs. Mortimer who were most kind and helpful in every way, and told me much of their life in this out of the way place.

The town of Chini is very picturesque lying as it does on the level slopes of the widening valley and overshadowed by the perpetual snows of Castle Rock. The valley is well wooded, deodar and walnut trees being in abundance. In August the whole valley is yellow with ripe apricots and the luxuriant vineyards near the river produce the finest grapes. The climate is well suited to fruit growing, peaches, pears, plums, apricots, apples are all in abundance, as well as two hundred gooseberry bushes the produce of which sold in Simla paid the wages of a mali for a whole year. At Chini, warm clothing necessary for my servant and two Chakrata coolies, was made up by a local tailor from homespun cloth purchased in a neighbouring village, and a large blanket made of pure wool purchased for nine rupees has been in constant use.

The local shikari told me that owing to the lateness of the spring there was yet no grass, and no game to be found; so my hopes were doomed to disappointment. There was nothing to be done but take the road for Jangi and the Ashang Gad. After a march of fifteen miles, a change of coolies was made. The road was broken in many places, and it was a marvel to see 'Motee' cross like a skipping goat over the most impassable looking rocks. There were some fine precipices, and at one place there had been a great disintegration from the heights above, as could be seen by the immense number of huge rocks and boulders strewn over the slopes of the hill. The last two miles to Jangi afforded a change of scenery, deodar trees amidst deep mould and a broadening valley. Beyond Jangi could be seen almost bare hillsides, the few trees were mostly the Pencil Cedar, a kind of juniper.

I had now been twenty six days on the road and no game in sight, so a letter was despatched to India asking for a month's extension of leave. My plans were made to bring me back to Jangi to meet the reply to my letter and act as seemed best in the days remaining to me. We left Jangi on 23rd May for Rupa, the highest village in the valley of the Thanim River. The road became worse and worse and in many places the track was only fit for goats. The descent to the Thanim bridge was along the face of an immense precipice. On the hill near Kanam we saw the first monastery of this part of the country. Our way led us up the left bank of the Thanim River to the small village of Shiasu. Here direct postal arrangements had to cease as I could no longer receive letters from the mail runners.

The ten miles journey next day took us to camp at Chamiong. Just as we left Shiasu tremendous reverberations were heard and masses of the precipice were seen to be falling into the river bed. A colossal snow bridge, caused by an avalanche from the heights above was seen to be blocking the river. We crossed and recrossed the many shallow streams into which the river had been diverted on its way through the valley. Some of the women now met with had a distinctly Mongolian type of face, indicating the closeness of the neighbouring people of Tibet. Many earings are worn, in one instance eleven were counted on either side, but they are attached to the hair above the ears, and not to the ears themselves, an arrangement that seems eminently sensible. The earrings are strung on a piece of plaited wool and this is fastened to the hair.

In Rupa village deep banks of snow were still to be seen along the lanes and between the houses. Here I met an old shikari, Ramdass by name, rather beyond work, but he arranged for two young men to accompany my camp to do the shikar work. This settled he promptly extracted two rupees from me for the village deity.

On May 27th, the shikaris having got outside an enormous heap of chupattis, an early start was made. A long steady climb took us to the top of the side valley. Tracks in the snow were observed, but the ibex had evidently moved further up the main valley. The day before something had made me suspect that this excursion up the hill was mainly to discover how I could get over the ground, a natural enough desire as it is not usual for these people to see a sportsman with the obviously lame leg with which I am afflicted. My suspicions were confirmed as old Ramdass spoke to the two men in their own dialect and admitted on my asking him that they wanted to find out how much hill climbing I would be able to do. Bad weather during the night brought the snow line a thousand feet lower, although this soon disappeared. Dotted about the terraced fields were many apricot trees just coming into blossom, tiny pale pink flowers were struggling to be seen.

Next day camp was moved about seven miles up river. The river was rapid, roaring turbulently from under the several snow bridges which had to be crossed. As we progressed the snow bridge became almost continuous, but it was not safe to trust to it, and goat paths along the hillside had to be followed. On the opposite side of the river, about three hundred yards up near a shale slope, a female ibex was standing, a vigilant sentry on behalf of the herd on the other side of the spur. This shale slope was pointed out as the place where, a few days before, a man from Rupa had been found dead, killed by a stone hurtling from above; and within a few minutes we were to have a realistic demonstration as to how death had called him.

The sun was now well up and old Ramdass advised no delay. Turning a bed in the river we came to a shale slope similar to that we had just seen which had to be crossed. About half our party had got to the other side and I was some way across, the tiffin cooly with basket on his back a few paces behind me, when a warning shout was heard. Looking up, the dust was seen flying in half a dozen places not far from the sky line some two thousand feet above. Then appeared boulders, black specks against the blue, bounding down with leaps of hundreds of yards at a time. Almost immediately they were upon us, big as a man's head and whizzing past with dreadful force and velocity. One could but keep quiet, lying face up hill to afford as small a mark as possible, but ready to endeavour to shift a bit to one side or the other. That is what I did, but the cooly remained standing. The first few stones spared us; then there was a crash and down went the cooly, basket and all, hurled fifty feet by the impact of a rugged rock. I was hastening to him when he picked himself up and we both went on as fast as we could, to be again halted by a further discharge of aerial artillery, but reached the further side in safety. The snow was now melting fast and stones came down at more frequent intervals.

The damage to the contents of the lunch basket was found to be considerable. Glass bottles broken and contents all mixed together. The cooly had a fortunate escape; his back was half turned towards the hill and the stone caught the upper corner of the basket. Camp was soon reached and a site for the tents was selected under a great overhanging rock. The Chakrata coolies were very apprehensive as to the immense rock balanced above their heads. I think they were not happy in their minds until we left this camp, overshadowed by the mighty mass of stone which certainly had the appearance of requiring little provocation to descend upon us. In front of the camp was a roaring torrent fed by the melting snows from the mountains dividing Kunawar from Spiti. The evening light glowed in the sky as we settled down for the night, and luminous banks of burning crimson clouds hung over the summits of the snow-topped mountains.

At 4 a.m. on May 30th the first day's shikar was commenced by an expedition up the main valley. Some climbing over precipitous rocks with many a precarious hold above the raging stream below, opened out to better ground along the right bank of the river. About two miles from camp eight ibex were sighted. We followed the herd until they came to a precipice which would force the animals down towards the river. The distance was about three hundred yards and I was that day, for the first and last time, using the .280 Ross Rifle which had been borrowed from a friend as a second weapon to my old .375. No dust flew to the shot, and the buck galloped a few yards and disappeared behind some rocks. The remainder of the herd were carefully counted across an open space and the big buck was not among them, therefore he must be hit. Two men were sent up the valley to cross by the first available snow bridge, watching them I envied the ease and speed with which they moved.

They found the buck lying where he had disappeared, and four more shots at a distance of four hundred yards brought him rolling down the hill towards the river. I threw a rope across and the men fastened this to the body in order to haul it through the rushing torrent of the icy stream. This saved much trouble, but was very nearly lost, as the weight of the body was almost more than old Ramdass and I could manage. Three shots were through the body, one of these through the shoulder. After this experience of the .280 rifle I decided never to use it again; the .375 would have killed the animal at the first shot. The last day of May was spent in camp, seeing to the ibex skin, doing odd jobs of mending, and making preparations for a four days' bivouac further up the river.

The dawn of the first of June disclosed a cloudy sky and snow falling on the higher hills. An early start was made with three of the hill men and one of the Chakrata coolies. We went far up the valley and, turning up a side ravine to within the snow line, the men settled themselves down in the ruins of a last year's shepherds hut. My own bedding was laid out at an angle between two low stone walls which kept off the wind, while a green waterproof sheet rigged up overhead furnished sufficient shelter for ordinary weather. On the whole the camp was a good one, and fortunately there was no mist or snow. The hills around were very rugged, but wearing the woven grass shoes brought from Chakrata I could go over any sort of ground in safety.

The first day's excursion was over difficult country, steps having to be cut in several places over the steep slopes of frozen snow. There were no tracks in the snow and no grass had yet appeared, so it was certain that there were no ibex beyond that point, and we decided to return to the main camp. On the way some wild onion was found, also two kinds of rhubarb, the variety with the smooth leaves being less bitter than that with the crinkly leaf; but both of these, with plenty of sugar, formed an acceptable addition to the camp fare.

Although they found the tracks of snow bear and snow leopard they never saw these animals. They came across the remains of a large ibex with horns measuring 42in. which had been killed by a snow leopard. After several days spent tracking, there were no further signs of bharal and they decided to move into another valley.

JOURNAL ——

The bharal of the Himalayas is distinct from all other wild sheep, and is a link between the sheep and the goats. Its horn has a surface which is almost smooth and the horn of the ram has a peculiar S-like curvature. They are also distinctive in colour, and there is a clear black stripe running along the flanks to divide the fawn of the back from the white of the belly. In summer the bharal is found as high as 16,000ft. and in winter they seldom descend below 10,000ft., and are generally found not far from the snow line.

At midday three bharal rams were sighted in a wide valley. Almost as we saw them the cries of a cattle herd far below caused them to begin to travel up hill. The leading ram rose several times on his hind legs and butted at the second one, on one occasion making a leap of about fifteen feet downward, which the youngster wisely let pass. After five minutes it became evident that the animals intended to cross over, high up on the same spur that we were on. We followed as fast as possible, the shikari in front of me by a couple of hundred yards. He gained the crest and at once frantically beckoned to me to hurry up! Doing my best I arrived very breathless and panting to see two of the bharal disappear round the next spur, probably for good, as the next sight of them would be at long range. The big ram was standing in the little valley a hundred yards away gazing up at the ridge. No time was to be lost, but I was in no condition to shoot straight. The wobbling .375 sent a bullet under his chest and he scampered out of sight in the track of his companions.

There was now time to gain breath, judge distance, and make ready for the long shot which would be necessary. Two of the rams soon appeared making their way up the rocky spur, then the third ram which stood fortunately, and fell to a shot at 350 yards. He slithered down a shale slope until checked by a large stone. Lying there, his colour blending with the shale, he was invisible to the naked eye, an instance of how marvellously wild animals can suit their environment. To get to the fallen ram took some time, there being much bad and difficult ground to negotiate, and we then made our way back to camp.

Next morning the sky was clear and on all sides nothing but snow was to be seen. The mountains extended in all directions, range after range, peak after peak. No wind, not even a distant sound, disturbed the silence. Valley after valley was searched without success; and it was decided to retrace the upward journey and try for bharal in the neighbourhood of Charong. Camp was to be struck in the morning, and so we passed a second night under the glorious canopy of the starlit heavens.

The coolies arrived at seven o'clock, and we reached Suinam by two in the afternoon. The shikaris were pleased with ten rupees each as pay and two rupees eight annas for animals shot. They asked me to come again, and were eager to take me further afield, so perhaps I overpaid them. The return journey showed that much had changed since I came through. The poplar trees were now in leaf, the snow bridges fast disappearing, and people were busy in the fields. It was very hot toiling up the hill from the iron bridge to the Benang Pass.

On arrival at Jangi on 15th June, the unwelcome news was received that no extension of leave could be given, as I was being transferred to another Cantonment; so next day I set off for Charong, crossing the Sutlej by the 'jhula'. This is a substantial affair of galvanised rope wire, the means of crossing being a wooden seat hung on the main rope and pulled backwards and forwards from either side. The cooly Gangaram, a man of timorous nature, was unashamedly terrified at having to be swung in mid-air over the roaring river! I had him tied in as a matter of wise precaution.

Leaving the main river the path returned up the Tadoung Gad and wound up the hillsides through fir forests, before descending to the bed of the nala and from there for two miles was mostly a scramble over the boulders in the bed of the stream. At one spot there was a great waterfall, many hundreds of feet in height, thundering down the perpendicular cliffs. There was a large volume of water from the melting snow rushing down the rocky stream; but it was a mere trickle compared to what it would become as the summer progressed.

The local shikari, Durjan, was about to go over the border to Tibet on a trading expedition, but was induced to remain for three days; and on 19th June camp was moved to a ravine about seven miles from Charong. At day-break the following morning I went several miles up the bed of the river. There were many bharal scattered about and it was interesting to watch them. At about 9.30 they began to move upwards to the snow line to lie up for the day. Higher and higher we climbed to attain a ridge well within the snow line. Nothing is more fascinating than to roam along the crest of the higher ranges in mighty mountains, the whole country below seems to be yours, and yet you feel what a very very insignificant creature you are! The desolation is relieved only by the shrill call of the chukor and the majestic sailing of the lammergeyer in the brilliant blue of the sky.

We carefully wound our way along the slopes of the mountains for several miles, thoroughly searching four large valleys and gradually descending to finally arrive at a magnificent grazing ground of wide undulating grass downs. At one place the snow bridge, by which a crossing was imperative, had given way, leaving a wide and gaping fissure over the icy torrent below. This had to be jumped and it was a relief to be safely across. Further on we passed the snout of a small glacier, the twenty foot thickness of ice being a deep emerald green where it was sharp cut and overhanging the bank of the stream. Camp was gained just as the last rose tints of the setting sun faded from the fleecy clouds surmounting the perpetual snows. The elevation attained this day, one of the most exhausting I have ever experienced was well over 15,000 feet.

Perseverance is often rewarded. The intention was to set off next day to look up some of the animals seen previously. Standing at the door of the tent just after day-break,

Durjan drew my attention to an animal far up the hillside above the camp. The field glasses showed three rams of which one possessed a good head, for the fine sweep of his horns was silhouetted against the sky as he stood on the brow of the hill. In a few minutes the animals disappeared from sight.

When we arrived at the top, a distance of about 1,200 yards, all likely ground was searched in vain, and the shikari went back to try and pick up the tracks. Having proceeded only sixty yards up the slope, the man whistled and pointed. Two bharal were just topping a ridge about one hundred and twenty yards away, they were among rocks and difficult to define. With my field glasses I saw that one of them was the big ram. He was gazing in my direction and only his chest and part of one shoulder were visible. The shot quickly taken was fortunately a good one, the bullet striking the point of the shoulder and making its exit behind the shoulder on the opposite side. The ram fell dead in his tracks and his smaller companion fled clattering down the hill. The horns taped 26½in.   The cooly with us carried the animal on his back up a steep slope on which I had to go, in places, on all fours! He carried the load down to the camp without any difficulty, which was a pretty good performance as the beast weighed 140lbs. Durjan assured me that this head was the best that he had ever seen shot.

On June 22nd camp was moved to Kuno, the shikari coming with me as he was eager to catch up the people with whom he was going to Tibet. His way was over the Sholarong Pass, six marches, all the way being over the rough bed of the stream. The snow fall at Charong is heavy in the winter months and the people cannot leave the village. A great store of firewood has to be collected and all grain has to be ground by hand as the frozen water mills cannot be worked. The principal occupation through the winter is weaving cloth and knitting. At Kuno there was no further news of the snow leopard; days were precious, so it was decided to make for Pangi without delay.

Camp was struck about nine o'clock, after the tents had dried, and the march to Lamber was accomplished by evening. Because of the recent rain and the rapid melting of the snows, the river was now more noisy and turbulent. The water was of a light coffee colour instead of the lovely green and blue hues seen on the upward journey. Many people from all parts of the country were met journeying to the Ramrichka temple, at which an annual fair was to be held during the next few days. Gangaram was once more in a great funk at having to cross the Sutlej, now far more formidable in appearance than on the sixteenth of the month. He tied himself in like a piece of luggage and, seeing the state of his nerves, the merry damsel at the winch kept him dangling in mid-air over the raging flood. Shouting with glee she pulled him backwards and forwards in tantalising fashion before winding him in to the safety of the landing platform. One cannot imagine a woman of the plains doing that!

The walk to Rorung was a very pleasant one, much of the way being under the welcome shade of walnut and apricot trees. Extensive vineyards with the prospect of many luscious bunches of grapes were seen. At day-break on July 1st, I went up the valley north of Pangi to bivouac at a camping place the people called Ting Ting. The elevation was about 13,000 feet. The hillsides were now becoming carpeted with flowers of many varieties. Purple iris, buttercups, daisies, pimpernels, forget-me-nots, and many other small flowers, wherever I went, and the clover was ankle deep.

Below and to either side, lush grass land sloped down to the fir forests, which were parted by the silver streak of the rivulet hastening to add its waters to the mighty river far down in the valley. The lofty range behind camp stood out boldly, its high turreted rocks and rough peaks forming fantastic shapes against the sky line. The sunset on the snows was magnificent, and just as the last lingering rose tint faded out of the sky, the great round orb of the full moon appeared over the edge of the mountain and flooded the scene with its soft luminance. The stars at that altitude appeared twice as large and brilliant as at lower elevations.

Next day we move on to Chini. Now, there was much vegetation; many flowers, huge white and yellow flowers like daisies but three inches in diameter, splendid pink and yellow roses. The fruit was not yet ripe, but cherries, gooseberries, asparagus and several other vegetables were brought to me from the Salvation Army Mission garden, and formed a very welcome change of diet. After passing Chini the influence of Buddhism becomes more and more marked; and Hinduism fades off gradually into the Buddhism of Tibet. Lamas in red and in yellow robes are to be seen, and the 'mani' walls strewn with stone and slate tablets bearing the words 'Om Mani Padme Hum' and lamaist gateways are commonly met with.

The dress of the women of Kunawar is a blanket, worn as a coat and skirt, the spare stuff being folded behind and falling from the waist. This one piece costume is held up by a rope of goat's hair passed round the waist. In some cases a woollen coat or bodice is also worn, and this style of dress is well suited to the climate. The men's coats are very loosely made with large sleeves, and are long, down to or below the knees. Trousers are of a coarse material. All the people carry a blanket and a goat's hair rope at all times. When not in use the blanket is rolled up round the waist. Much of the population emigrate in the winter to the lower valleys taking the sheep and goats with them.

The weather was now much warmer, so the fourteen miles to Urni on July 5th seemed long and tiring. 'Motee' was requisitioned to carry me some miles of the way, the first time he had been ridden since the march from Darangati to Sarahan, since there was now no need to keep in training for the strenuous mountain work. When passing Rogi, news was brought of a villager having that morning fallen off the 'jhula' by which the crossing of the Sutlej was effected. He was instantly swept away in the roaring flood and can have lived but a few brief moments in those icy waters. Gangaram's reception of the news indicated that he felt he had not been so foolish as was thought, at the time of his timorous crossing on the way to and from Rupa.

At Urni the house flies were very bad. They nearly ate me, and my tea, and even after dark did not let me have dinner in peace. Flies are always a great plague at staging bungalows and near villages in the hills during the summer months. When crossing the river at Wangtu the increase in the volume of water was very marked, and it was difficult to make oneself heard above the noise of the rushing torrent.

The views on the way to Taranda and Sarahan were wonderful beyond description. Everything was clear and fresh. Jewelled butterflies flitted in sun and shade and the distant hillsides were shrouded in a lovely blue and purple haze. The road was now thronged by mules, ponies and bullocks, taking food supplies to the many hundreds of sawmen and wood cutters working in the forest. All the forests of Bashahr and Kunawar are under long lease to the Imperial Forest Department. Many of the animals met with were bleeding at the nostril owing to the leeches which infest the lower hills at this season of the year; but for the most part the beasts looked fit and well fed. The men with them were banjaras, but not recognisable as being of the same race as the much finer looking gypsies of the Deccan. There is a very busy grain trade to the higher valleys, and the herds which take grain to Tibet return with wool and other produce. Mules carrying grain charged a rate of Rs.4/8/ a maund, while the slower travelling bullocks carrying the same weight the same distance charged just Rs.3/10/ a maund.

The roar of the Sutlej was now but faintly heard; and the descent from the comparatively cool temperature at Gaora to the heat of the valley at Rampur was somewhat unpleasant.

The Guest House where I stayed is some little distance down stream from the town and not far from the river bank; however I was very glad to leave the steamy heat of the Rampur Valley and get to Bahli. An early start was made on account of the heat and three out of four miles along the river was accomplished before the rays of the sun reached the valley. The transport consisted of five mules and four coolies.

The Pabar River was in heavy flood and stranded against a rock in mid-stream was the carcass of a huge buffalo, his very large horns conspicuous against the flood. The people along the valley complained to me of the damage done by sambur to their crops. On July 19th we got to Kathyan – Motee and I! In former days I had always hoped for a panther at this place, but without success. An entry in the Visitor's Book dated October 22, 1918, recorded that an Official on tour had shot a panther from the west bedroom window; so perhaps 'Judy' and two other dogs taken by panthers close to the bungalow in June 1914, were avenged.

At Mandali that night, there was a heavy thunderstorm. The clouds grew black, lightning flashed along the crest of the hills, peals of thunder reverberated among the woods, small rivulets soon became rushing torrents. In the morning it was fine, but there was a thick mist almost all the way along the ridge. I got to Chakrata on the afternoon of July 21st just in time to avoid another soaking. The coolies with the kit, however, got caught and this was the last march, and the only occasion on which the baggage had got wet!

CHAPTERS
8/9

1
R.W. Burton with his Bareilly
staff on his retirement as a
Cantonment Magistrate, 1922

2
The village of Lakhwar

3
A group of hill people near
Kalsi

4
The Sardar river above
Barmdeo

5
Elephants in Gond swamp,
Kheri, 1920

6
Another of R.W. Burton's
dogs 'Simba' at Pahlgam,
Kashmir, 1921

Chapter 9

ADVENTURES IN THE PUNJAB AND RETIREMENT

JOURNAL

1920. Kala Chitta Range – Punjab. Early in December 1920 I was able to take a few days' leave from Bareilly Cantonment for a coveted shoot in the Kala Chitta Range. We passed the ancient city of Taxila, now under archaeological excavation, and came to a small wayside station which was near to my shooting ground. I was greeted by the news that on the previous evening, dacoits had raided the station, and the station buildings were completely gutted. The Assistant was seated amidst the charred remains of furniture busily ticking away at his telegraph instrument. The dacoits having gathered up everything of value to themselves had heaped up the furniture, drenched it with kerosene oil and set fire to it. The place was full of police and I was taken to a small bungalow some three hundred yards away where I was to spend the night.

One of the gang had entered this bungalow, occupied that afternoon by an Indian Official who was travelling on transfer with his family. The young ruffian, who was said to be only about eighteen years of age, entered into amicable conversation with the official and enquired casually if a pistol was carried. The reply being in the negative he promptly produced his own weapon. Having obtained a large sum of money, and all the ornaments of the women, he brutally shot the unfortunate man and made his way back to his companions. All this took place in broad daylight. The blood of the victim was fresh on the whitewashed walls, the plaster of which was scarred by bullets. Fortunate for me that I had not arrived twenty four hours earlier; weapons in locked cases are not of much use against the sudden appearance of a determined ruffian armed with a revolver. This gang was not brought to book on this occasion, but met with just deserts at a later period in consequence of further murderous outrages in the Attock District.

Next day an early start was made, and camp was pitched at the foot of the Kala Chitta Hills. The following morning I was joined by two shikaris, father and son, and we were soon working along the slopes of the rocky scrub-covered hills. Soon after day-break, a hissing sort of whistle, the alarm note of the urial, drew our attention to a couple of rams who moved quickly up hill. After that first view of game until leaving the hills at four in the afternoon, we were seldom out of sight of sheep. Most of these, of course, were ewes, and we must have seen over a hundred animals.

About twelve o'clock a halt for 'lunch' was made. Packing up was nearly done when the old shikari hastily signalled to me. A number of urial were coming up the slope from the valley below and would soon top the ridge to our side. Almost before the rifle could be got ready the first comers arrived amid much clattering of stones. Several sheep appeared, paused to stare, and then dashed off up the ravine. Then came a ram with horns of massive appearance. He halted exactly where the other animals had paused and a quickly sighted right shoulder shot at 120 yards dropped him where he stood. This was a somewhat fortunate shot as my right eye is not in top class, but for very quick shooting it must needs be trusted. This was to be the best head of the trip and the owner of it was named 'Itifak' on account of his chance appearance on the scene. The horns presented an almost perfect circle, the tips touching the hair of the cheek bones, and measured 34½ in. All day I had been feeling chilled by the wind in spite of warm clothing, and a rising temperature and aching legs warned me to be off to camp, where suitable treatment enabled me to shake off the threatened attack of fever.

Next morning a bitterly cold wind was blowing from the north, but all my aches and pains had gone, so a start was made by seven o'clock. We saw nothing all morning except one small ram and some ewes, probably most of the animals were sheltering among the bushes and in the ravines. The keen-eyed shikari drew my attention to a white speck far up the hill. Viewed through the telescope he was lying down facing towards me, his horns forming a perfect circle. We recrossed the ravine to make our way up the reverse side of the spur. I had just selected a place on the steep hillside on which to sit, when a clatter of stones announced an animal travelling at speed. He crossed the nala out of sight, going fast, but halted in an open space on the opposite side of the valley; a fatal pause. A good and quick shot from the left shoulder took him at two hundred yards through his right shoulder. Stone dead, he slithered down the slope until coming to a stop by a small shrub. So much was he dead that he could not be hallaled. He proved to be a very old animal, several teeth gone, and his beard was quite white. Horns thirty one inches only, they seemed bigger than that. 'Dada' (grandfather) was the quite appropriate name given to him by the men.

A long climb took us to a high ridge, on the other side of which was a deep and precipitous ravine. Some sheep now came into view, and two rams branched off by themselves and lay down, out of shot, under a thorny tree. After about an hour, the two rams started to move and came quietly on. Foolishly becoming nervous as to the distance, which owing to the deep and wide ravine was not easy to judge, I put up the 200 yards leaf and twice went over the back of the larger one of the pair. He turned uphill and the third shot, aimed much lower, got him through the body, and a fourth shot through the neck. The man up the hill came leaping down at such a pace as only these hill men can venture on such ground, his garments flying and his knife glittering in the rays of the setting sun. Reaching the ram he called out that it was dead.

'Hallal karo, Hallal karo' yelled the three men with me, and this was done amid great reverberating shouts of 'Allaho Akbar' from our side. This patriarch also had an almost wholly white beard. His horns were 32 in., being very symmetrical and massive. The tips were worn and not broken. He was ironically named the 'Sipah Salah' on account of his having taken up a strategic position with his 'Adjutant General' in attendance. We were far afield, camp was not reached until dark and the unfortunate 'Sipah Salah' was pronounced by the village mullah to be unlawful meat as he had no breath in him when hallaled. This was certainly the case as his neck was broken, although if blood flows that should suffice; but the strict Muhammadans of this part of the country will not allow any latitude in this matter. This mullah had a fine voice and it was most impressive to hear his call to prayers ringing out over the country side in the early hours of the day. This long day's work over, the knife-edged rocks and rough stony hills completely finished the new rope soles with which the shoot was commenced. I took to the 'chapli' of the country after this, and also in the Salt Range where the going is even worse than in the Kala Chitta Hills.

On the last morning, the fifth day of the shoot, a fox was seen – not good, but later on a jackal crossed our path and this counteracted the former malign influence. A stone thrown down the hillside moved some animals which had been lying up unseen on our side of the ravine. One ram appeared to have a good head and the shot travelled forward to the chest and he only moved a few yards. This time the meat was 'lawful'. An old beast he was, turning grey as to beard, but not a patriarch. His horns were very much broken at the tips and also at the bend, probably in fighting and, as he was evidently something of a bruiser, they named him 'Pahlwan'.

My trusty .375, when held straight shoots straight, and is as merciful a weapon to use as one could wish, for it is a very rare thing for any animal to get away after being hit: also the trajectory is not so flat as to eliminate the judging of distance, as do so many high velocity small bores, to the detriment of sport. Four heads had been obtained, enough indeed, and no more could be shot. The old shikari who had hunted urial of these hills for thirty years, told me he only once saw a head of 36in. and that was in 1918. Protection appears to have come into force about twenty years ago, and to have been much needed as urial were becoming scarce. The men said that a good deal of poaching went on in some parts but that the forest guards were powerless in the matter. That can be readily imagined as the people of these parts are not of the most law-abiding in the land.

The old shikari accompanied me back to the railway station as he was suffering from raging toothache, and I was taking him to a doctor to extract the offending tooth. On the way, a chinkara with horns 11in. in length afforded a somewhat difficult stalk which ended in a successful shot at about 180 yards; a few others were seen, all of them very wild. The blackened ruins of the railway station were gained by sundown.

When Burton visited this country again in November 1923, he judged there to be more than a thousand urial in the area. He shot a male and female for the Bombay Natural History Society Museum, and writes — 'Ewe not hallaled and will make a good specimen; plenty of meat for all and sundry. So ends the urial shikar at this place as no use shooting more animals than are wanted.'

From Bareilly, Burton was transferred in March 1922 to Ranikhet, and from here it was possible to reach the jungles at the foothills of the Himalayas by means of one of the smaller railway lines.

JOURNAL _____

One Christmas week a short holiday outing was made from a wayside railway station on the Kathgodam Branch Line. The bag was a mixed one; duck, teal, peafowl, partridge, hares and green pigeon.

There are swamp deer east of the Kathgodam Line, but none to the west of it, and that is the western limit of the species. The swamp partridge also is not found west of the Tanakpur Line; at least I have never seen it there, or heard the peculiar hoarse cry of 'kya kya' from which it derives its familiar name. All these sub-montane forests teem with most interesting bird and insect life. At the commencement of the rainy season the innumerable winged and crawling insects, many of which inflict painful bites, make life unbearable to man and beast. Many of the tigers migrate to the hills, and there some of them take up permanent residence, to become man-eaters in numerous cases, as game is scarce and most of the livestock is driven to the plains during the winter months.

Tigers are much more silent animals than panthers. On most evenings the sawing grunt of the panther will be heard, but only occasionally does one hear the voice of the tiger. A grand sound it is, and awe-inspiring when close at hand. Lungoors, sambur, chital, and kakur respond to it with their alarm cries and thus betray themselves to the more deadly human hunter.

There was one day a curious happening. A chital stag dropped to a facing shot at about a hundred yards and apparently stone dead. Walking up to him, the rifle was laid down in order to use the tape measure. Suddenly signs of life were noticed and I seized one of the horns. There was a wound in the neck close to the skull and this was evidently a mere graze; the animal had in fact been creased in the style of the old backwoodsmen of Fennimore Cooper. Very soon I was being dragged around and soon losing my footing was forced to quit hold of the horn. The stag went off somewhat groggily for a few paces but before the rifle could be used he was fast recovering and was soon out of sight. He was never seen again, and would probably have been none the worse for his adventure.

One frequently finds chital grazing with cattle and both sambur and chital are to be looked for where there are lungoors feeding on fruit-bearing trees. Panthers know this and are often disturbed from a tree of the fig species by the sportsman wandering through the forest. When 'still hunting', one makes frequent halts to listen to the jungle sounds and catch any movement there may be such as a twitching ear or tail, or the shaking of a branch or shrub.

There is much that is of interest regarding these age-long forests and their flora and fauna, and the habits and customs of the people of the few inhabited areas: for it is not only the pursuit of animals and birds which exercise that irresistible attraction which draws one to the jungle life.

In 1923, Burton reached retirement age. Over the next six years, he and his wife had no fixed home, but lived 'on the move'. Some of their possessions were put into store, some sold, and the rest packed onto bullock carts or trains and taken with them. Camping in those days, although basic, retained an attempt at civilisation. They took table and chairs, camp beds, and of course a bath tub; except for short 'bivouac' excursions from the main camp when they took minimum gear and only what could be easily carried.

DIARY ──

I made over charge on 5th March 1923 to Mr. S.S. Nehru I.C.S. and left Ranikhet on the morning of 6th March: thus commencing eight months continued leave on full average salary pending my retirement from the service on 5th November 1923, on attaining the age of fifty five. On the afternoon of 5th March some of the Indian Residents of Bijnor and Cantonment gave me a Farewell Party in the Officer's Mess: Alma Barracks: at which there was much eulogistic speechifying.

Wife and I and three dogs, 'Judy', 'Molly' and 'Simba', left by Motor Ferry and caught the train at Kattigadam, 2 p.m. Molly and Simba sat on resin tins and got well 'stuck', especially Simba's nice yellow curls. Judy sat at our feet in front. In spite of Q.M.G.'s office having received my leave application six months ago, orders for the necessary transfers to effect my relief were not issued until 27th February, and then by letter. It was only by means of two frantic telegrams that I managed to escape to my long earned rest after thirty four years service. We stayed at Lucknow until evening of 14th March, Phyllis' wedding to Capt. C.W. Toovey, M.C. 82nd Punjabis: now 5th Battn. 1st Punjab Regiment.

I had a hurried three hours at Bareilly taking kit to Cantonment to be stored, collecting my rifles, and then to get potatoes, onions, sugar, and to the market for meat and veg, and a hurried breakfast at the railway station. Train got to Ramnagar 8.30 p.m. and we slept the night in the carriage, getting out at 4 o'clock as the train went back at 5.0 a.m.

After the wedding of his eldest daughter, Burton with his wife Hilda and their younger daughter, left for six weeks fishing in the Ramnagar jungles near the Ramganga and Kosi rivers. Following the train journey there was a two day trek up and down hill on rough roads until they arrived at Sarapduli. For this they hired an elephant to help with the transport of kit.

DIARY _____

18th March. Arrived at Sarapduli F.B.: which is situated close to the Ramganga. A small bungalow, two rooms, two bathrooms, one dressing room, and pantry. The verandah facing north towards the river. It is still quite cool in daytime in the shade, and cold at night.

The elephant, came to us at Sultan: a female with excellent paces. Cost of feed of elephant and mahout and two attendants is Rs.57 for fifteen days. The country is very hilly and we will probably not need the elephant very much, but it will be useful in many ways and for the march back to Nashan F.B. in the Chilkiar block. It was good sambur ground and next morning I had a steady shot at a sambur with fair horns. Meat was needed for the camp, and the elephant was sent to fetch it, so it wasn't long before she was put to good use.

20th. Tiny and I were up and off on elephant at day-break. Did a round in long grass and jungle near the river. Lucky we went to look at the kill as we found the two men sent to see and report, going yelling up the nala. It is difficult to shikar without reliable people. I don't think old Chandan Singh is of much use; he doesn't know more of tracks and tracking than I do.

24th. Saturday. Off on elephant at 4.30 a.m. with wife and Tiny and reached the parao soon after day-break. Shot a kakur within thirty yards of the parao; left shoulder with .375, and back to Sarapduli by 11 a.m. Found this excellent elephant is recalled for the Collector of Bejawar and another sent in its place; a young lady of eighteen summers from Burma and only under training for two or three months. She is very fast, and has most comfortable paces. Her old mahout says she cost Rs.4800 at the big elephant fair down country. It remains to be seen whether I will be able to take a steady shot off her; rather doubtful. Did a long round through the forest until dark and saw only sambur and no good stag.

31st. White goat killed by panther not far from camp. I did not have the carcass uncovered before sitting in machan and when it was cleared of leaves at sundown, saw with my glasses no marks of teeth on neck and didn't like the look of it at all. Investigated and came to conclusion that poor goat was killed by a jackal, and that was the only animal which came to it: one large male jackal. Fool of a shikari must have had suspicions and never said a word. This is the great Chandan Singh, so renowned all around Ranikhet. Felt rather seedy yesterday and today.

7th April. River Kosi. Went fishing with Tiny, one 'tug' from a small fish when using fly spoon: no offers when using dead bait. Tiny got one mahseer.

10th. As I write, shikari comes back to say the tigress came in the night and has removed the skeleton of the big buffalo which was killed about the 4th and also the bones of the buffalo killed on night of 8th. The 'fearful' shikari had not even dared to follow up the skeleton a few yards. It was in quite thin undergrowth. Sat up two evenings but no result. The jungle had been disturbed by a lot of hill goats being grazed through it, and these probably shifted the tigress.

14th. Sat up in evening a little later than normal and not completely settled down, when I saw tiger show for a second some eighty yards in front of me. In a few minutes he came sloping along in the open up the shallow sandy nala running along edge of the jungle. Took him at forty yards to my right front, and he fell over to the shot and rushed with loud grunts into the undergrowth. Whistled up the two men and putting old shikari up in my chair began cautious approach. Sent a man up the tree where he should have been able to see the beast, but as usual he could see nothing – they never can. Then peeping and peering saw a bit of hide; beckoned to the man for a stone and heaved one in – no movement. Tom Puss was dead. Old shikari much excited and yelled 'ek golee maro'! ('killed with one shot' (ed.)) Found first shot exactly where aimed: centre of off shoulder and exit not half way down opposite flank. Excellent shot.

Length – along curves 8ft. 11in.: between pegs 8ft. 5in. – Weight 250lbs. A reward for perseverance; sixth evening of sitting in chair.

We had the Terai Bhabur elephant from Mohan to Ramnagar and glad of it. The mahout said Wyndham, Commander of Naini Tal, had wounded a tiger at the place where I was after them. He has a dozen or more elephants. The Governor of U.P. (Sir William Morris) came on 19th 'to shoot at Mohan and Sarapduli'. Arrived Bareilly 18th and did four days strenuous sorting and packing for Kashmir. Bareilly quite cool at night and no need for punkahs during the day.

Chapter 10

IN THE MOUNTAINS OF KASHMIR

The best time to visit Kashmir is in the summer. The intense cold of the winter months has given way to warmer, sunny days, and the heavy snowfall covering the lower mountain slopes has been replaced by grass and wild flowers. So it was in April, the beginning of spring, when Colonel Burton, with his wife and younger daughter, left Bareilly to spend six months in the Himalayas in and around Srinagar. They arrived by train at Rawalpindi at 2.30 a.m. on 24th April, and having sorted their belongings drove on via Uri to Srinagar by car, arriving there on 25th. Their kit was sent separately by lorry and arrived at Srinagar two days later.

Burton had planned several jaunts into the mountain ranges, moving from one camp to another, sometimes on his own and sometimes with his daughter Stella, who was affectionately known as Tiny. His wife Hilda preferred to stay in the more inhabited places such as Srinagar and Sonamarg, either on a houseboat or at base camp, rather than in a tent halfway up a mountain.

As soon as the kit arrived and had been sorted, Burton and Stella left on an expedition into the mountains beyond Islamabad and the Wadhwan valley. They were able to make use of the motor lorry which was cheaper, quicker, and more comfortable than four or five tongas would have been, and it conveyed all their kit, as well as themselves and the shikari, cook and three camp coolies. On 1st May they left Islamabad with twelve pack ponies and one riding pony to take them to Maltigun not far from the Margan Pass. Burton was searching for red bear and ibex which could be found in this part of the Himalayas. At Maltigun they sorted out the stores and left one month's provisions in two kiltas, and having discharged the ponies, they marched on to camp that night at the foot of the Pass.

DIARY

4th May. Up at 3.30 a.m. and off at 5.15 and reached the top of the Pass (elevation 11,119ft.) at 7 o'clock, the last mile over snow. Then down over snow for three miles and had breakfast at 9.30. Got to Inshin by quite a good path, rather steep the last two miles. Camped on left bank of the Wadhwan River which is a lovely greenish colour and very rapid.

Camp in Wadhwan Valley at entrance to Busmen Nala, Kashmir. 6th May 1923. It has clouded over and threatened to rain the last three evenings. All things considered I decided to go at once to Sukney. We arrived there at 3 o'clock and pitched camp among some rocks with a small stream of spring water just behind the tents. Twelve coolies at 15as. each. Temperature at Inshin was 44° at 7 a.m.

11th. Up at 4 a.m. and off at 4.30. After two hours climb we found last night's tracks of a fairly large bear. Spring is advancing rapidly now. Many flowers are beginning to appear and the hillsides getting green. Small patches of snow are fast disappearing; and rock rabbits and marmots are emerging from their long winter sleep. Took a photo of the view down the valley from camp.

12th. A storm came up in the night, so today's expedition did not come off. As soon as weather clears it will be as well to bivouac in a cave which I saw about three miles up the valley, near the bear tracks, and so be able to watch early and late. In the evening Tiny and I went up the river for a mile and a half; crossing the Wadhwan River by the bridge above the village, where it has a double span resting in the centre on a rock. We made our way along the river bank for the most part, to a place under a steep bank where we had seen a lagoon of deep blue water.

13th May. Tiny has been saying that there isn't much for the Diary to relate, but NOW there is plenty of material.

We were in bed and asleep early, when suddenly at about 11.30 the tent came down on top of us. I was roused by a great weight falling on me forcing my head into the pillow. I called out to Tiny who got clear with a struggle, and she pushed at the bulge which was on me and this shifted the weight of snow. I felt half suffocated, but found a way over the edge of the bed, a very low camp cot, and was able to get out. The back pole and ridge pole of the tent had both snapped at the joint and the tent had collapsed with a foot of snow on it. It was lucky that the front pole held, otherwise we might have fared far worse. 'Molly' (the airedale daughter of 'Judy') was safe enough between the two beds.

My yells from under the snow before I got clear failed to arouse any of the servants in their tents close by. I got hold of matches and lantern and went to the tent of the shikari and roused him. The snow was falling heavily and their tents would also have come down in time, no doubt. The shikari woke up with a frightened 'ow! ow!' I think he thought I was a bear. However, he proved capable and resourceful and sent to the village for help. Soon a number of men came with snow spades and cleared the snow from the tent, some poles were brought and with these and two or three of the spades the tent was made habitable for the night. All night every half hour the tent had to be scraped clear of snow.

In the morning the snow abated and we packed up our kit and made our way through two feet of snow to the village where a room in a house was placed at the disposal of ourselves and servants. The whole country is snowed under, a very different scene to yesterday. Our room is the upper storey of a wooden house. Sheep and cattle occupy the ground floor, as we know by noses and ears. The space is about 16ft. by 13ft. with an entrance way which has a fire place on one side and a store room on the other. The floors and walls are well 'leeped' with cow dung. The ceiling of rough beams is black with smoke.

There is one window in the west wall, 2ft. 6in. × 2ft. It has two frames; one of board when no light or air is required, the other has the skin of a young calf stretched over it. It makes quite a good window for the purpose of giving light, but one cannot see through it. Farm implements, butter churns etc. are round about the room. We were warm enough at night as the door was closed. There was plenty of ventilation by means of the fireplace apparently, as it did not seem very stuffy. The fowls, our future dinners, were a nuisance, starting to crow at 4 a.m. They must be banished this evening. Our host is quite a genial fellow and will doubtless expect much 'baksheesh'.

Quite forgot until now to note about the cuckoo. I heard it for the first time this year at Ramnagar (near Mohan) on 14th April: then near Islamabad on 1st May: and on the morning of 11th May far up among the birch trees where there was nothing but snow, the cuckoo was busily calling.

15th. Tiny and I both had our baths last night, and yesterday Tiny went up to have a look at the camp. The tents were covered with snow, but were dry as to floors. It snowed heavily again during the night, but the sky is clear this morning. The tent is torn in several places, and will require patching; fortunately I have with me, as usual, needles, twine etc. for such emergencies. We went to the bridge up stream and saw the volume of water in the river much diminished. Soon the river will be full again with the result of the thaw now beginning. This morning there was a wonderful blue sky, not a cloud to be seen.

The Ramzan fast will end on Friday 18th, and I shall have to provide a sheep for our people, and the owner of this house. The poles are all repaired now and practically as good as before; the ridge pole better. We were saved from complete collapse of the tent by the socket of the front pole join being thick iron and not as the ridge and back pole joins.

18th May. The Ramzan. Gave the Camp a sheep Rs.14, couldn't get a decent one for less, and stayed in camp. Weather is still threatening and the sky overcast. I hear that the two sportsmen who were in the Apun nala are now at Busmen and have as yet shot nothing at either place. They came to see us in the afternoon and we gave them tea. Their shikaris evidently want to try down in the warmer parts of Kishtwar.

20th. Up at 3.30 and off at 4 a.m. Very hard work ploughing through the fresh snow still overlying the old snow. I was pretty well cooked, and shirked following the shikari through the thick snow, so kept where I could to the grass slopes. Went to tea in the afternoon with the lads from Busmen. Snow and hail this evening.

Fine sunny days alternated with days of rain and snow. The fine days began at 3 or 4 o'clock in the morning and were spent tracking up and down the spurs and into the nalas in search of bears, but although a number of bear tracks were seen across the snow, most of the animals appeared to have left the area. One morning a bear was seen crossing a snow slope at about 300 yards distance. A steep precipice prevented a nearer approach, and the shot quickly taken was a good one, as the bear was killed instantly. The only other animals shot by Burton on this trip were a number of marmots, which he had promised to obtain for the B.N.H.S. museum.

DIARY

28th. Started at 8 a.m., with four coolies. Found that the shepherd's hut which we hoped to occupy had partly collapsed and was too wet to be habitable, so made our way further down to some overhanging rocks and camped there. Rain and snow came on towards evening and it was very cold. I intended to have cocoa after dinner, but discovered at first sip that I had put in curry powder instead of cocoa! However, although it was sweetened with swiss milk, it wasn't so bad and WARMED me thoroughly.

29th. Up at 4 a.m. A fine day and went up the nala for about two miles. There were tracks of the day before of a wolf, also recent tracks of a bear. 'Mahusti' – snow pigeons, and cuckoo everywhere as usual. No use staying at Sain nala, so made our way unsurely back to Sukney.

31st. Up at 3 a.m. and off at 4 up the Sukney nala. Saw nothing and no tracks, so back to camp, packed up and moved off to Busmen. On the march I met the chokidar and eventually satisfied myself that cook had been charging me Rs.1/6 and 1/4 for fowls which the chokidar had supplied at 12 annas. Of course cook won't admit it. I shall prove the matter later on at Gumbu village. Gave the Sukney lamburdar 2/- and 'our host' 3/-, and the village shikari 10/-.

2nd June. Up at 2 a.m. and off at 3 o'clock up the nala. Did the bad bits by moonlight, climbed the hill and got to the place where we hoped to find bear by 6 a.m. Waited all day and in the evening discovered that a man with a herd of fifteen goats had also travelled up by moonlight, going this way to Pahlgam in order to evade customs duty on his grazing goats, and had evidently scared away the bear as we found his tracks going up the nala towards Sukney. Back to camp at 8.30 pretty tired.

3rd. Up the nala with three coolies and food for three days to bivouac up the valley. Tracks of a bear going over the snow and crossing over into Kashmir. Many snakes about the hills.

6th. Reached Gumbu nala camping place at 1 o'clock; a hill camp under deodar trees near a roaring torrent. Many iris now blooming. Sent a man to Inshin for potatoes, 7½ seers for a rupee. Very warm in the sun at midday, even at 10700ft. as we were today. This camp is 9317ft.

10th. Paid up the small amounts due: fowls at 10as. each, eggs 5as. a dozen, milk 2as. a seer – all about half what cook has been charging. Started 7.30 and went via Busmen as far as Kuzuz and camped at 2.30 p.m., the march was about thirteen miles. Tiny was very tired. Rain and thunderstorms came on soon after our arrival. A snow leopard is said to have killed several goats near here a few days ago. No grazing is allowed in Gumbu, but here there are several thousand sheep and many goats.

12th June. Up at 3 a.m. and to top of the nala at the foot of Sarital Pass. The shikari saw eleven small ibex through the telescope. I missed a marmot with the rifle, and shot one in the evening. 'Molly' had a good dinner of marmot stew and rice. The kit came from Mattigam, rice and stores.

This valley appeared to be a temporary halting place for bear, which were only passing through, so Burton decided to move over the Sarital Pass and into the Zojnai valley. After the stores had been replenished and sorted, they left camp on 13th June and crossed the Pass (14,200ft.) with as light a load as possible.

There were no further signs of bear and ibex or snow leopard, and Burton arranged for coolies for the return journey to the Wadhwan valley. On 18th June they crossed the Framsar Pass to Inshin where the stores were again sorted and reloaded. When crossing the Dargan Pass they were caught in heavy thunderstorms with rain and hail, but on 22nd they reached the shelter of the Shangas valley and camped in the shade of a chenar tree to dry out their kit. The next day they left for Islamabad where they hired a houseboat which would take them down the river to Srinagar.

The diary for this trip ends with a few notes, and a detailed record of all the marches and distances. Comprehensive lists were made of the supplies taken and the stores consumed; and a summary of expenses and wages of servants was recorded, as all costs had to be carefully noted.

DIARY ————————————————————————————————————

Camp in Wadhwan Valley at entrance to Busmen Nala: 6th May 1923.

Supplies taken and used

20 seers	potatos		2 seers	carrots	
7	"	onions	2	"	springe
10	"	rice	5	"	sugar
6	"	dried fruit	1	"	cooking salt
4	"	Dal	4½ lb.	fat	
40	"	flour			

Stores consumed

14 Jam	5½ Butter – eating (lbs)
17 Milk	2½ Tea (lbs)
2 Cocoa	1 Curry powder
5 Potted meat	1 Worcester sauce
2 Army rations	2 Cornflour
3 Oatmeal	1 Vermicelli
1 Macaroni	9 Bovril
7 Sardines	2½ Butter – cooking (lbs)
2 Soap – Sunlight	6 Soap – Lux
2 Paisley flour	1 Pepper
½ Table Salt (lb)	1 Matches (pkt)
24 Candles (pkt)	2 Raisins (lbs)

Wages of Servants etc.

	per mensum	
Shikari	30 + 8	for return
Khansamah	30 + 6	" "
Tiffin cooly	12 + 6	" "
Camp "	10 + 5	" "
Dak "	10 + 5	" "

Summary of expenses

Bazaar supplies taken from Srinagar	42	0	0	
Motor Lorry	41	8	0	
Marches	184	15	5	
Country Supplies	105	4	0	– includes wood
Tips to Lamburdars etc.	24	0	0	
Sundries	28	14	9	
Dak Bungalow	2	4	0	
'Molly'	9	3	3	
Dak cooly – for tongas into Srinagar	15	3	6	
Village Shikaries	23	12	0	
Boat – Islamabad to Srinagar	22	0	0	
Pay of Servants	244	0	0	
Bill of Ranijam Merchant (excluding articles which carry on to other trips)	100	0	0	
Bread etc. from Hotel	6	4	0	
Cost of Stores consumed, including candles	85	0	0	
Carriage of same, Bombay to Srinagar, say	13	0	0	
Rs	947	4	9	
Say Rs	950			(for the two months)

Food averages Rs.4(8) for the two of us, including firewood when paid for.
We did not do so many marches as is usual owing to being detained at Sukney

so long. Cost of two months shooting may be taken at not less than 500/-/- for two persons, and that with considerable care and economy.

I walked all the marches and did two hundred miles, and shikar climbing in addition, (all this with my left thigh having been broken in 1903 and my leg four inches short). We did not do so many marches as is usual owing to being detained at Sukney for so long. The cost of two months' shooting may be taken at not less than Rs.500 for two persons, and that with considerable care and economy.

The food these Wadhwan Valley people eat is of the coarsest description and it is extraordinary that they should be able to do hard work on it, as the shikari said '– it is such that a bear wouldn't eat it'. The grain of which the chupattis is made is very small and locally grown and mixed with sour milk, at least so it tastes – very nasty.

At Sungum I saw a pony on the side towards the hill and the precipice. It couldn't find a way across but eventually did so, and the snow bridge by which it got over the river fell in next day. I saw the tracks of this pony several times where it had negotiated most dangerous places, one slip at any of these and it must have fallen into the river and been swept away. It came down frozen snow slopes of quite sixty degrees and along such slopes parallel to the river – a lucky pony.

We got back to Srinagar on the evening of 24th June and stayed there making arrangements, repair of tents, purchase of supplies, until early on 3rd July, when we left in two boats for Gandarbul, getting there by 5 p.m. and camping under some fine chenar trees a mile above the bridge. Here we have to stay a week to wait for the cartridges which were left at Bareilly. No need for hurry and we can do some fishing here perhaps.

15th July. To camp on the left bank of river about ten miles from Sonamarg. Today's march was fifteen miles. My feet blistered, having got soft by three weeks idleness. There were thunderstorms along the hill tops in the evening. After three days we moved camp into the open as it was too damp and cold under the trees and there were many hairy caterpillars.

22nd July. Off on a jaunt by myself, leaving wife and Tiny at Sonamarg. Left camp at 10.30 having been delayed by one of the ponies being missing. It was found high up the Glacier Valley, probably ridden there by some gujar, I crossed the bridge over the Sind River and going by the path up the spur and through the woods got to the main nala at 2 p.m.

On this trip, Burton met F.J. Mitchell, a fish culture expert, who was re-stocking the lakes of Vishan Sar and Krishan Sar with trout. Gangabul Lake had been re-stocked in 1907 and Mitchell had caught the first fish there seven years later. Burton went fishing several times with Mitchell. All the small trout they caught in the Lake were sent with the fish watcher to re-stock other lakes. Very often these fish never reached their destination, being sold en route to chanpans and gujars in exchange for wool and ghee. The fishing was very easy. As many as fifteen trout were caught in half an hour, and sometimes two were caught at a cast – as Burton commented, 'Too easy for really good sport'.

The scenery in the mountains was beautiful. Himalayan wild flowers were growing everywhere throughout the pine forests. Unfortunately the weather was cold and cloudy with a fair bit of rain, but there were occasional sunny days to enjoy, and fresh trout for breakfast or dinner was an added luxury. Snow leopards were rumoured to live in the mountains, but Burton never saw one. Apart from a lot of marmots, the only wild animals encountered in the area were wolves. These frequently attacked the sheep and goats which spread in large numbers over the hillsides, where there were many shepherd encampments.

DIARY ⸻

Returned to Sonamarg on 15th. Marched to nala about six miles from Sonamarg elevation about 10,000ft. On passing Krishan Sar saw some fish rising and also saw two or three small ones, so now the Watcher has put some trout into the lake.

19th August. At Sonamarg. Tiny went off with Miss Royds for a month's camping up Liddar valley way. I moved camp to Sarbul nala to sit there until the stag shooting opens on 15th September. Rain on most days. On 3rd September disturbed three stags along under the cliffs towards Buttal, so there are stags about, and the only thing to fear is that bad weather will send them down the Valley before 15th.

15th September. Up at 1.30, off at 2.30, and a long way up the hill by 5 a.m. The shikari advised going west of the nala instead of east and this proved to be a fatal mistake. At 5 a.m. found a couple of thousand goats being driven along the hillside to cross over to the Kalshir Valley. It soon began to snow and for the remainder of the day was all snow and hail. My feet got terribly cold. Saw nothing and back to camp by candle light at 8.30 p.m.

17th. Up at 2 a.m. and up the east side of hill by 5.15. Shikari spotted a good stag through the telescope about one mile off, a medium stag and a small stag with him. We climbed to the place where the stags had been first seen and rested a bit, and then saw four stags on sky line of the ridge. They eventually came down our side and lay up at about 400 yards. By 4.30 p.m. one, the best of them it seemed, lay down at about 325 yards. I waited till he got up and then fired at him with 200 yards backsight. Quite a good shot. He pitched down hill and struck against a rock, but broke loose when we tried to rope him and went hustling down the hill for about four hundred yards. Too late to do anything but leave him up for the night. Ten points, 36in. – quite a big beast and exactly what I wanted for the Museum. Started for camp at 6 o'clock and got there four hours later after a horrid candle light journey over awful ground and along river bank; crossing really dangerous places on the way. Very tired after nineteen hours out of camp.

Next day, up at 6 a.m. and off at 7.30. Along the road for three miles and then across Sind river and up and up; two and a half hour's climb. A snow storm came on when we were well up the hill and it looked as if we would have to give up the attempt at skinning in such weather. Fortune for once was in our favour and the storm ended by 12 o'clock. We did the job by 3.45 taking all measurements and weighing the beast as well. WEIGHT – 550lbs.

19th. Went to turn out the sheep from the hillside as none of the shepherds had recovered their flocks as they had promised to do. This took from 7 a.m. to 3 p.m. and then one herd was still there. I met the Game Watcher and signed his book. The watcher says that the two Captains of 1st Pioneers in Tajans nala fired fifteen shots at three royal stags without result. Wish I could have had one fifteenth of their chance.

27th. Left Sarbul nala camp at 8 a.m. Gave lamburdar R.10, he was very obliging all our stay and I dragged him up hill several times in the middle of the night. Ten pack and one riding pony at 1/- and 1/4 a day respectively. On to Sonamarg and reached Chuttergool by 29th. Wife went on to Gandarbul.

For the next twelve days, Burton returned to the mountains in search of stag and red bear. Perhaps the breathtaking views and the adventure of being in the Himalayas compensated for the lack of animals seen. He records in his diary each day's events and his impressions.

DIARY

7th. Up at 5 a.m. and off at 6.30. Sky absolutely clear except for a cloud on Haramook, but clouds soon began to build up. A most magnificent panorama of whole of Wangat Valley and hills bounding it, also of the Range dividing Sind from Liddar Valley, and whole of the Vale of Kashmir. It is as fine a view, perhaps even more magnificent, than any I have seen in the Himalayas. On top of the Pass I saw a lovely bird, dark blue, smaller than a thrush; so beautiful that the tiffin cooly was led to remark that 'God had made it of wonderful beauty'. Pitched camp on edge of plateau intending to work down the slopes in the early morning. Soon after pitching camp, snow storm came on and is in full blast at time of writing.

9th. Snowing again and no sign of stopping, so at 3 p.m. sent four ponies, one pony man, and tiffin cooly to Chuttergool to stay the night, and sent coolies in morning to move camp down hill. Stopped snowing at 5 p.m., three inches of snow. At midnight I woke up and saw flashes of lightening and heavy clouds; whole sky overcast and a storm moving up along the Pir Panjal. It snowed heavily during the night, and at 8.30 we struck tents and cleared off down hill. The whole valley was in heavy mist and all snow thawing fast; trees dripping; very slippery underfoot. Went to a gujars' hut on the hill above Chuttergool.

We saw a light on the spur the previous evening after it stopped snowing and feared it might be a shooting camp. It was a camp of 'bukarouts' with thousands of goats and sheep. So no hope of stag anywhere up that way which had looked so promising. Jungle on this hill very thick in many places and possibly stag sheltering in that. Will take the gun on chance of something for the larder. Am lucky to be off the higher hills – shudder at the thought of my fate if I had gone to Vishan Sar on the 3rd October.

12th. Sat on the highest point at boundary of the Reserve, just under 12,000ft. and had the most wonderful view. Whole of Kashmir Valley, with Wular Lake spread out below: whole of Pir Panjal stretching away to beyond Islamabad: Kolahoi, Annanath, some of the Sind Valley: Haramook and then the whole Range of Snows, beginning at Kijnag near Baramoola and ending with the mighty mass of Nanga Parbat: all this by just turning the head.

Haramook 16,872ft.; Gangabul 11,714ft.; Pass above Gangabul (the way I came) 13,200ft.; Sat Saran Pass (the pass of the seven lakes) 12,072ft.; the place I climbed to see Nanga Parbat 13,000ft.

Returned to camp at gujars' hut and packed and off to Toontwar by 2 o/c. Struck camp and got to Gandarbul Tele Office next morning. Wired Hugo asking him to try and get me a permit for Duchijam State Rakh; and he replied that all permits now rest with Rajah Hari Singh and not with the Maharajah. Went and saw Wigram on 16th and he gave me a special permit for Dara Nala, which is one reserved for Residents in Srinagar. Was busy 13th to 19th packing kit for Bareilly and on 19th moved into House Boat 'Nightingale'.

The six months in the Himalayas ended with a short shoot of seven days when Burton obtained a stag of 36in. 8 points and this was sent to the B.N.H.S. Museum. Some serow and snow bear were also seen. Coming down the slippery hillside two days later, Burton fell heavily on his left thigh near his old injury, and this caused an enormous bruise along the whole of the leg. In great pain he crawled back to camp. Next day they packed up and with the aid of two sticks he struggled the seven miles to Shalimar Bagh where he was able to get a car to take him to Rawalpindi.

However, he didn't want to have to cancel the arrangements for the Kot Fatteh Khan and Salt Range, and although the leg was still painful he set out on 3rd November by train to Gagan.

DIARY _____

4th November. Off at dawn with Fazel Din and Bubadur, both of whom were with me last time I was here in December 1920. On getting to the hills saw some urial, all small or medium heads, eventually had a quick shot at 150 yards at an ancient looking ram and slew him instantly. He fell fifty feet and was too dead to hallal. Just as well as he does for the male urial for the Bombay Museum. Horns 28in.

Must be about a thousand urial in this Chak, but no use shooting more animals than are wanted. Most awful going on these hills, rocks like knives. My leg is black and blue nearly down to the ankle, result of the fall on 26th. Next day I stayed in camp to skin and on 9th we go to Mianwali and on 13th to Khushabu for Salt Range.

On 4th December, heavy mist from the previous days rain, but it cleared by 12 o/c. Shot a very BLACK buck, for the Bombay Museum, 20in. only, but mature and suitable for a mounted specimen. Saw immense herd of antelope, about ten thousand animals.

6th December. To Delhi on the way to Bareilly. Here I was laid up for five days with sciatica on my right hip. I left on 14th to stay with Phyllis and Dick at Lucknow before starting our next trip to the Pilibhit jungles.

In November 1923, Burton reached official retirement age, and in a burst of joyful exuberance composed a long poem in celebration. In fact his record with the Magistrate's Department was excellent, and his reputation for fair and just decisions is on record. Some of the verses from his poem are quoted below.

DIARY _____

On 5th November I should have entered my Birthday Poem. Here it is.

'Today I am a Happy Boy, all future days are full of Joy;
For I am fifty five and now, my pension earned by sweat of brow,
I'm free of those official cares, which bared my head and brought grey hairs
    Jungle Jaunts, my future Joy,
    Today I am a Happy Boy.

No longer do I sit on Bench, and fill my nostrils with the stench
Of criminals and otherwise, and hear their endless string of lies.
It may be stripes with many a wail, or years or weeks in Sircar's Jail,
It may be either or may be both, depends on whether R.B. is wroth.

Oh! All the miscellaneous work, no jot of which did R.B. shirk.
The very thought. It makes me quake, that cause of many a bad headache.
And oh! the smell of those Bazaars, which shortened life by many years.
    Jungle Jaunts, my future Joy,
    Today I am a Happy Boy.

Tiger, panther, bears of three varieties, I oft shall see.
The third, the red, I fear has fled and perhaps I only dream of he.

Of seventeen now sight remain, Snow Leopard, Cheeta, these are twain,
Neither of them I may see, the latter is a rarity.
Hog deer, Mouse deer, another two. The Tsaing of Burma is also new
To me, as well as Burma's deer, brow-antlered, and the next I fear
I shall not get (we've never met) the Markhor of Kashmir, I bet.
The last of all is Burma's Takin, which nature had such fun in making.
 Jungle Jaunts, my future Joy,
 Today I am a Happy Boy.

Besides the rifle and the gun, in mountain glades 'neath India's sun,
There's sport with rod and line to get, in seas and rivers which as yet
I have not seen, and these I hope to visit full of vim — — — —
For five and thirty years I've served. Yet as you see am fully nerved
For five and thirty years shikar, relieved of toil in Sircar's chair.
 Golden days and silver nights,
 Sunlit glades and water sprites,
 Jungle Jaunts, my future Joy,
 Today I am a Happy Boy.'

R.W.B. Poet.

On the road to Adelboden - to Lausdonne.
17.11.22.

I

CHAPTERS
10/11

1
The mountains and lakes of
Kashmir, view from L.
Ganugabad, October 1923

2
Urial shot at Zarghun, Quetta,
1925 (with Mahabat and Wazir
Khan)

3
The women of Pahlgam

All sketches are by R.W.
Burton's daughter Phyllis

TOM PUSS OF SONARIPUR.

9' 7"   24. 2. 1924

4

5

6

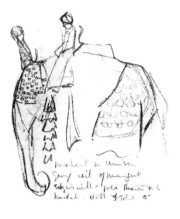

CHAPTERS
10/11

Chapter 11

THE TIGER OF SONARIPUR AND THE KUMAON HILLS

JOURNAL

All along the edge of the Himalayas, from Saharanpur and the Jumna River to the north west, to Gorakhpur and the Gandak River to the south east, is a belt of forest varying in width from twenty to fifty miles, which is the home of many species of wild animals. In the course of time the number of game animals may decrease but, owing to the protection afforded by the Imperial Forest Department, the denseness of the jungles, the heavy rainfall and consequently deadly malarious climate during five months of the year, this tract of country will harbour the larger game animals long after they have almost disappeared from many of the other forests of India. The rhinoceros and wild buffalo are gone, none of these now remaining in this tract. A hundred years ago the forest belt was many miles wider than it is now. Early in the nineteenth century, tigers were shot before breakfast a few miles from Bareilly. There are still wild elephants in the forests of the foothills, some of them become dangerous at times and are proclaimed as rogues by the Government.

The Reserved Forests are divided into shooting blocks open to sportsmen for the latter half of each month, on payment of a license fee of ten rupees. Elephants, unless proclaimed as rogues may not be shot; other game animals are allowed according to season and the number entered on the shooting permit. Unless the sportsman is able to obtain the loan of one or more elephants he will as a rule be unlikely to shoot a tiger, as the restriction against shooting after dark greatly limits his opportunities. The Terai forests to the west of the Pilibhit–Tanakpur Branch Line are drier than those to the east. The Sarda River has now been harnessed for purposes of irrigation and practically the whole river will soon flow into a canal three hundred feet wide to be conveyed to distant cultivated lands: a colossal work carried out in the past few years by the Irrigation Department at a cost of six or seven crores of rupees. It was above and close to the head-works of the canal that the mahseer fishing used to be of the very best, and it is likely that the construction of the canal will have done much to spoil the fishing. It was not far from the banks of the Sarda river that wild elephants were close to our camp in 1924.

DIARY

26th January. Forgot to note that a herd of wild elephants was all around our camp on night of 24th, and caused much excitement. Mahouts of our two elephants in much trepidation as to their animals. Forest guard borrowed my shot gun and some cartridges and made much noise, but this was not sufficiently heartening and he roused me out a second time and I let him loose off my .500 rifle. I went with him a couple of hundred yards up the road and got quite close to where the elephants were. They stopped feeding for a couple of minutes only, and did not appear disturbed by the puny firework display; the noise and my presence had, however, a comforting effect on the nerves of our attendants who allowed me to sleep peacefully for the rest of the night. Very bright full moon, but dense shade in the jungle. Last night a tiger came along from the north, not far from camp.

31st January. Moved from Mahdo Tanda to Puranpur seven miles, all through cultivated country where the 1884 map shows all jungle. Puranpur D.B. is an excellent one, close to Railway Station. Puranpur a filthy place; horrible smell from the hide drying business. Moved on 9th February to camp at Sarda River. Out from 6.30 a.m. to 4.30 p.m., walking all the time with only twenty minutes for breakfast; Army Rations, and slice of dry bread. Walked all over the Kadir in hopes of hog deer with aid of three dogs of the chamars of Dakka who were with me. Saw nothing and walked back through the Zemindari Forest.

JOURNAL —|——————————————————————————————————

It is a warm afternoon in mid February, we alight from our train with all our baggage and make our way along the forest track to the Rest House. We find there the elephant we have been fortunate to obtain on loan from a local landowner. The next morning we proceed on the elephant through the long grass and reeds on the borders of an extensive lake in search of swamp deer (gond). We put up a number of animals most of which rush away invisible in the long grass. One stag carries aloft on his many-tined antlers a small haystack of dry grass, a not infrequent sight as the dry grass is brittle and gets broken off by the rushing animal.

The lake is a beautiful sight in the rays of the rising sun. Narrow and serpentine in shape, the wide expanse of reeds along its nearer edge is relieved from monotony by some scattered thorn bushes and a knoll covered by large evergreen trees. The water is covered with wild fowl; cattle egrets and several species of snowy white wading birds are along the further shore; a fishing eagle screams loudly from a dead bough at the edge of the forest which borders the whole mile long length of the lake, and away in the forest we hear the grunting of a panther.

The Range Officer had told us that in June as many as a thousand swamp deer could be seen in this extensive plain; and we ourselves see not less than three hundred during this our first morning. We come across a number of hinds and it is a lovely sight to see them lined up in the water against the background of waving reeds and grass with noses in the air and big ears cocked staring at our elephant moving majestically towards them.

It is very interesting to sit quietly in the evening near a jungle pool and observe the ways of the forest; the jungle crow, the tree pie 'seven brown sisters chattering in the thorn', and others all ready at any unusual sight to give the alarm. There is a sound away to the left of some animal on the move, the sound advances, ceases, and comes nearer by slow degrees. I think it may be a kakur and am pleased when the russet form of a stag steps daintily from the bushes. Next come some peafowl, and three jungle fowl which are pecking among the leaves a few yards from the foot of the tree in which I am seated. A noisier approach announces the advent of a sounder of pig, followed by two chital hinds. Within the cover a peacock rises with a clatter and a 'kok! kok! kok!' at which the animals and birds in the open make a hurried exit from the scene. A sambur stag appears with four hinds and a fawn. One of the hinds goes deep into the water to eat the weeds which she obtains by plunging her head underneath to the roots of her ears.

It is fast getting dark and an attendant is sent to call up the elephant. His departure, quiet as it is, is detected by the hind in the centre of the pool. A ringing tonk gives the alarm and the sambur dash into the forest. The chital take no notice, not even raising their heads from the grass. The peafowl had already left, and one of us tries how near it may be possible to get to the chital. They take no notice of the figure slowly advancing towards them along the edge of the tall grass; it is only on hearing the voice of a man on the approaching elephant that they take alarm and vanish ghostlike in the shadows of the jungle. It is a common observation that animals are easy of approach in the twilight hours. This is true of all animals, not only the deer tribe, but the carnivora also. Probably it is that they seldom see human beings abroad at that time and that the twilight is as difficult to their eyes as to ours.

Our last morning sees us out before day-break being conveyed to the forest by the faithful Champa. We dismount from the elephant and proceed quietly along the edge of the forest. A large skein of geese comes up from the south with noisy honkings and, wheeling over the lake, proceeds onwards over the Himalayas to the breeding grounds in Tibet, or perhaps to the shores of the Arctic Sea. It has become noticeably warmer the past few days, there are fewer duck to be seen, and the migratory shore and water birds are evidently returning to their summer haunts.

DIARY _____

13th February. Marched to Mailani Junction, getting there midday. Put all the heavy kit and tents into a Railway Wagon – cost R.10, to Sonaripur: a cheap good arrangement. Slept in train and got to Sonaripur 10.30 a.m. Marriott D.F.O. in train with us; also the Engineer of the Railway. Floods which did so much damage at Lucknow in September came from here. Engineer told me Sarda River was ten miles wide at the bridge: all the rain local, not from the hills. Many cattle drowned, also wild animals, and some people. Much damage to small game and birds.

16th. Evening, went to Kahraha jheel: took the Court of Ward's elephant to assist in putting up duck. Got parted from the elephant. Very tall grass and deep water. Didn't bother to get in touch with it again and on return found the elephant was frightened near the jheel by a bear and bolted, and the shikari and the boy driving the elephant both had to dash off. Elephant went into the jungle. Mahout's fault in being lazy and sending the elephant out with only a 'helper' up. This he did well knowing the elephant to be nervous and very unsafe. Went next morning to see if I could find the bear, but failed to do so. Doubtless he was as much alarmed as the elephant, and having put her to flight fled in the opposite direction. The elephant went about 300 yds before getting to the lake and then went through about 200yds of water, deep all the way. The boy riding her must have lost his head altogether. Telephoned to Deputy Commissioner and told him of escape of the elephant. There is now a system of telephones throughout this North Kheri Forest Division. An excellent arrangement.

24th February 1924. Truly a Red Letter Day. Out on elephant at 7 a.m. to go up 85ft. fire line to north and search the jungle to left of it for bears. At 9.30 got out of the forest into the open country where grass all burnt. In this open space, which is the Sonaripur clearing and is about five miles long and a mile to two miles wide, is the Railway Station; and a mile to the east of it, the Forest Rest House and Rangers Quarters. When crossing the open space I saw two pig going from this patch of jungle and remarked to the Mahout and to Chandan (the Khairagarla shikari who was on the elephant with me) that there might be a panther in jungle patch as it seemed curious that the pig should be going across the burnt hot maidan at this time of day.

We went to the jungle patch and began to quietly pass through it backwards and forwards. All of a sudden I saw a tiger about twenty five yards away, about to enter a patch of very tall and thick grass which had mostly escaped burning. Fire had been through the whole of this Forest patch when the grass maidan was burnt some weeks back. By the time I got rifle up all I could see of the tiger was the back part of him. He stopped for a moment and I fired quickly seeing that my bullet, .500 solid soft lead, would probably rake forward and possibly kill him right away. On the shot he gave a couple of grunts and disappeared.

We circled back to find the place where the shot was fired and in doing so discovered a dead sambur stag at edge of thick patch of grass into which the tiger had disappeared. Marking the line the tiger would have taken in his rush, we got round the grass and soon located him. His growlings changed into the usual coughing grunts as he charged us from underneath some thick evergreen creepers and trees. The elephant turned and bolted with T.P. at her heels and I clinging on with left hand to a rope, fired two ineffectual shots with right hand. Rifle too heavy for me to hold properly with one hand and elephant being like a boat in a choppy sea, small wonder that I couldn't score a hit. The tiger did not catch the elephant and turned off into some tall partly burnt grass. As he went we could see he was lame in one hind leg, also that he was a very massive tiger with fine ruff and broad chest; and that he was extremely angry: so ended the first round.

The mahout pulled up the elephant within fifty yards and after a bit we started to draw T.P. again. We pushed down several small trees to clear the view; each tree as it crashed eliciting a growl. The old mahout, Ghulab, kept his head and manoeuvred splendidly throughout. Getting within what T.P. evidently considered the 'ring' limit; out he came a second time and same performance was repeated. Again the elephant bolted; again tiger pursued; again my puny right arm fired two ineffectual shots. This time T.P. seemed to have retired further into the grass as we couldn't exactly mark out where he was. A shot fired into the grass had no result. The elephant was making efforts to advance to the attack, a proceeding which might indeed have had very disastrous results as T.P. would have got to close grips and might have pulled the elephant down on her knees, and either Chandan or I (or both of us) might have been shaken off: however, the mahout was equal to the occasion and managed to restrain her. I told the mahout that the only way was to get me up a tree and for the elephant to draw the tiger so that I could get a shot.

We advanced from another direction, first pushing down a tree or two; and soon found ourselves within T.P.'s fighting limits, as out he came and again the same proceedings, except that this time the mahout pulled up too quick, or else tiger had more pace, as he got home with one paw on the elephant's near hind leg. I thought this had happened as I was unable to get off my usual second ineffectual shot because tiger was out of sight under the elephant's rump. I fired, both hands holding the rifle for the first time, as the tiger halted for a second before subsiding under an evergreen tree, and thought I had hit him. We now had the tiger in a better position as there was a small tree close to a big one into which, if tiger would allow me to get, I could stand ready for him being once more drawn by the now much more excited elephant.

There was only a pad on the elephant and no rests for the feet, and those who have ridden on a pad elephant can realise that it is not easy to shoot off a pad at any time. I was unable, owing to an injury of long standing, to sit astride as is usually done, so it was a hopeless affair to attempt to kill the rampaging tiger off Kandan Piari. The violent exertions of the elephant had caused the ropes securing the pad to get considerably loosened and the pad was slipping over to the right. Slowly the elephant was taken up to the desired tree, and naturally thinking it was to be pushed down, she was with difficulty restrained from demolishing it. There were several pushes and resulting cracks on the part of the tree. All this time the tiger kept up a continuous rumble. Nine shots had been fired, the first only being a hit. Six ineffectual shots having been loosed off during the attacks, and two into the grass to rouse him out: three cartridges now left. Having roped myself into the tree with the small rope I always carry, I felt we had hopes of scoring in the next round. All the time I was getting into the tree, which took time as I had to kneel on the pad listening to growls which might any moment culminate in an attack and be ready to sit and seize rifle, the tiger was keeping up an incessant growl and the elephant was wanting to again advance on him.

Now the final round was about to commence. The elephant once more demonstrated and after some little delay out came the tiger. I expected him from my left across my front, but he did a short cut as elephant bore to my right and my position was very awkward for firing. My two shots missed. First, I can't say why; second because a branch of tree arrested my arm when I was pulling trigger. The shots, however, seemed to have the effect of stopping the charge. Now the tiger got himself down almost below me; not thirty feet away. My opening rifle and putting in my twelfth and last cartridge attracted his attention. He looked up and peered at me round trunk of a small tree, which prevented me aiming at his head, – just as well perhaps, head shots often go wrong. By leaning much to my right and getting butt of rifle against biceps of my left arm, I was able to sight on to his back to left of spine, knowing that the solid bullet would pass through vital parts. To the shot the tiger subsided; he had been supporting himself on his forepaws, and in a second his head fell back and his gallant fight was over. 11.30 a.m. – one hour and fifty minutes.

No less gallant, and beyond all praise, was the conduct of the mahout, who kept his head and managed his elephant admirably; also he never suggested a retreat, although he saw I was quite unable to shoot the tiger while on the elephant. And the old she elephant – Kandan Piari, what of her. Had she had her way she would have been on top of the tiger. She had been twice before mauled by a tiger too. Chandan behaved well also; though his office was merely to sit tight. He kept his head all the time, when T.P. was breathing blood and fury under the evergreen bush, while I was getting into the tree, and after I had got into it.

It was lucky tiger did not come at us while I was getting into the tree as the rifle had to be handed to me. Tree very awkward to get into, a lot of small branches. Suppose he had come at us and sat almost under my tree, as he eventually did, and the elephant away with my rifle. I did think of this, my being left without rifle, but took the risk as with rifle slung on my back I would have made a lot of noise and perhaps betrayed my position and also could not have taken a shot had the tiger charged. All's well that ends well. The fight is over. Now for the autopsy and measurements.

Laid on his back, nose pressed to the ground and knives stuck into ground at nose, root of tail, tip of tail, gave his measurements in a straight line.

Length: nose to root of tail – straight line 6ft. 4in.
     "   tail   2ft. 9in. – 9ft. 1in.
     "   nose to root of tail over curves 6ft. 10in.
     "   tail   2ft. 9in. – 9ft. 7in.
Height at shoulder – 40in.

The first shot, fired when only hind quarters and a bit of the flank visible could not, short of killing the beast outright, have been better placed. If it had had greater penetration it would have gone on into the stomach and so to the other side, well forward, and this is what I hoped it would do: a .470 H.V. soft nose bullet would probably have done it. So even .500, 5drs, 480 grain solid soft lead has its limitations against the massive muscles of big tigers.

The fact of this off hind leg being completely crippled prevented the tiger getting home on the elephant; but even so his pace was very fast indeed. The last charge of all was the most determined and the longest. He had worked himself up to highest pitch of rage and fury. The shot which killed him entered well up left side behind shoulder and a bit far back and raked forward, through the lungs, and mushroomed against the skin on opposite side behind elbow. Anyhow the first shot crippled, the last one killed, and all the other ten were anywhere. Small wonder too.

I wanted the carcass of the sambur left alone as quite possibly a panther might be found near it; but some Thadus went and skinned it and cut it up and brought the stinking remains for us to see. The beast must have been killed quite five days ago and as the tiger's stomach contained pieces of undigested sambur skin, he had evidently killed elsewhere and just returned to have a look at his larder.

25th. Asked old Mahout if he had slept well. He said he had slept but little. I own I was so excited that I didn't get off to sleep until near twelve o'clock. Chandan says he couldn't sleep at all. Busy most of the day seeing to tiger skin; also the gond skin, which was still very wet. The following day, out on a new elephant, sent to replace the runaway. She was captured on 22nd or 23rd, having made her way to the village where she is usually kept. A bit lame in one hind foot from a knock against a tree stump, ankus lost, also red cloth on the pad, otherwise no harm done.

With ponies in the Kumaon Hills.
There were hectic days spent at Bareilly sorting the kit. Some of it was to go to auction, some to pack away in store, some to be ready for their stay at Pachmarhi in June, and the rest to take with them to the Kumaon Hills. They were to be accompanied on this expedition by Lapersonne, who had been sent by the BNHS to collect birds from that area. He had gone on ahead on 10th June to Kytuna to purchase pack ponies in order to give them greater freedom of movement, as local transport might be difficult.

DIARY
14th. Slept in railway carriage overnight and off to Tanakpur by 7 a.m. train. Found Lapersonne camped in D.B. compound. He had purchased six ponies, average price Rs.48. I was at Tanakpur for ten days anchored to the D.B. compound and unable to get to the river to fish having to look after ponies all day long. Couldn't even get coolies to tend them. After some days heard D.C. had arrived and found it was the Commander (Wyndham). Asked his assistance and he sent for the Government cooly agent, an individual I had been unable to get hold of before, and told him to supply me within two days with five ponies. By evening of 24th we had thirteen, but no men who had ever packed ponies or looked after them. However, a start had to be made so we prepared for an early rise having done up as many loads as possible.

25th. Got to Sukhe Dury at dusk. Rough tracks, first five miles level, then three miles up hill fairly steep in places, then half a mile down hill the camping place, a shanty run by Mr. Abbott, the founder of Abbott's Mount near Lohagat. He and his wife here, and I was much refreshed by copious mugs of tea. Their son Bruce shot the man-eating tigress in this area a short time back. It was very hard work getting the ponies along. A feat to have accomplished it with no sore backs or girth galls. Nearing the top of the hill I got dreadful cramp in both thighs, and this got worse and worse. We had to stay at Sukhe Dury as I couldn't possibly go on. Thirty six hours of purgatory here.

27th. Up at 4 a.m. and went on by myself walking slowly the four miles downhill to Ladya nala and after a rest four miles up hill to Diuri. Ponies arrived at 5 o'clock. Lapersonne bringing them along very well. He has turned out to be a great help with the ponies, and has good authority over the men. We have three very nice lads with us.

Arrived Diuri on 27th, and started for Champawat next morning. Progress was very slow and we couldn't risk going on over unknown road through dark oak forest, as we might damage kit and lose ponies also, so camped literally on the path. I had to hurry on through the forest two miles to get hold of cook and sweeper who had the three leading ponies, these had the bedding. Got them back just at dark, and we were enabled to get out beds and straighten things out a bit before it got quite dark. No lanterns with us, these had gone on to Champawat by cooly. Dined off Army rations and bread and butter. Fine clear night up to 2 a.m., then clouded over and a little rain at 4.30. Thunderstorm circled all round us and we were indeed fortunate to escape a real bad time of it. Rather a wakeful night as ponies kept on breaking loose and rousing us by walking over a plank bridge. Everything comes to an end and we got up to find two ponies missing; soon recovered one, the other was caught and brought back by one of the lads and met us on our way down. Wife walked as her riding pony had to be loaded in place of the runaway 'Roan'.

29th. We got to Champawat D.B. in a slight rainstorm at 11 a.m. Lovely valley, snowy ranges of Nepal to the east. Marched from Champawat to Lohaghat D.B. six miles. Easy road, down – up – down – up, passing over a small suspension bridge on the way. Lohaghat a pretty place. We now have a Tahsil chaprassi attached to our camp which should make things easier.

1st. April 1924. May as well give a list of our pack ponies all named, and their pack saddles numbered with writing ink laid on with a brush made of chewed end of a twig.

1.	38	He cost that and is worth all of it. A SLOW pony.	
2.	Hatrack	He cost 40 and looks like his name. Too thin to be likely to be of much use. A bad buy.	
3.	Boneshaker	He cost 36 Packed up wonderfully.	
4.	Cougher	" " 40 Coughed over his first feed of grain.	
5.	47	" " 47 V. good pony. Mane and tail dyed blue.	
6.	Roan	" " 50 His colour. A light pony; good beast.	
7.	Bell 40	" " 40 With his bell; hence his name: good beast.	
8.	Cream	" " 75 Named by his colour; excellent beast.	
9.	55	" " 55 Not turning out as well as hoped, weak.	
10.	Toss Up	" " 40 Tossed his owner 40 or 50; owner won.	
11.	Runaway	" " 45 A small pony; got loose one night.	
12.	Blaze	" " 40 A blaze down his face; good pony.	
13.	Fetlocks	" " 45 White fetlocks both hind legs; too thin.	

So of the thirteen, about four are poor beasts, rest fair or good. It remains to be seen what loss on sale will amount to. I am calculating on recovering average of 25/- each.

Up and down the valleys they journeyed with the ponies. Steep cliffs rose from the river valleys and the paths were treacherous and narrow. At one place one of the ponies stumbled and the load slipped and went hurtling down into the river. The box contained all the fishing tackle, it was retrieved somewhat damaged but with most of the contents intact.

DIARY _____

7th April. Pitched camp under the big pipal tree opposite the Rameswar temple which is a new one, built a few years ago as old one washed away by river in flood. Next day went up stream one mile and fished down. Saw a good fish in a deep channel, water too clear, fish shy off spoon directly they see it. Unless we get rain to colour the river, fishing will be a wash out. Ponies very thin; can't get any fodder that they will eat.

On 23rd went to see a place called Mayawati: four miles west, where said to be good grass for ponies and fine jungle. Took two hours to get there. Found several houses; one a Post Office, one a large house occupied by half a dozen Bengali Swamis, members of the Vive Kananda Adwait Ashram founded by Swami Vive Kananda, which is a religious society and has branches all over India. Saw them and asked if any objection to my camping on their estate. They were very pleasant, gave me tea and afterwards, breakfast. Tried to push me further on and suggested a place two miles away towards Champawat. Went to see it – hopeless, no grass, bad spot. Returned and fixed up to come here (Mayawati), and camp up the hill. Excellent grazing, oak jungle all round. Returned to Lohaghat and packed kit.

25th. Started at 7.30 a.m. with remaining kit on eight ponies. Thunderstorms came on. Pitched camp, with thorns all round, and ponies should be safe at night. I could move to any suitable place were it not for necessity of getting good grazing for the ponies. In this way they hamper movements; on the other hand, very difficult to move at all when more than two or three coolies required.

27th. Went across the valley to west to open uncultivated fields, ravines on the way. Met a Zemindian with a gun. 'the Knockabout' hammer ejector by the Midland Gun Co. He told me he killed a tiger with it last year, came on it by chance, slanting shot a little below him and killed it instantly. He shot a hare yesterday and has shot kalij all round his village. Game must disappear before many years. There are many guns now, two or three in almost every village of any size, and shooting goes on regardless of season or sex, all the year round.

12th May. Weather much warmer today. Moved camp to Debi Dura. Found that a pony had been killed by a tiger close to the camp, which is under large deodar trees close to the temple. The kill in khud two hundred yards away. Pony had been killed at top of ravine not far from road, dragged a long way down to stream, across it, and up hill where it was eaten and head and forelegs put into a thicket of green bushes and thorns. Two hind legs picked clean and left in open. Went with shikari to ridge two miles south next day; shot a kakur for much needed meat. No fowls or eggs procurable from here.

15th. Did a long round through various nalas; very thick cover. Found fresh tracks of tiger, same beast probably which killed the pony. This tiger was seen yesterday by some villagers. Shikari says it is the same which killed and ate his aunt, and killed his brother's wife this year, February 24th and March 10th. We came across the pieces of clothing of the unfortunate aunt, stripped off her as she was dragged through the jungle, and it was in same nala we found fresh tracks today. Lacchan Singh showed me the place where the woman was seized. Several other women near her, cutting oak leaves for cattle fodder. She was stalked from below and it was only known she was taken by one of the other women having her attention attracted by a cloud of dust as the tiger jumped down the khud. All the women ran screaming after the tiger, but it didn't drop the woman and ate the whole of her except piece of skull and part of pelvis. The sister-in-law was taken close to Debi Dura, also while cutting leaves. She was up a tree and out of fright, fell down when the tiger came under her tree, calling out 'the tiger has eaten me!'. The tiger wounded her terribly about the face with his paws, but did not carry her off as he was put to flight by the screams of the women.

Many rumours coming in as to tiger happenings in the neighbourhood. I heard three shots in rapid succession when on the ridge on 14th. The rumour arrived that five tigers had killed two cows and two buffaloes and that a sportsman fired fourteen shots and killed one tiger and two cubs. News also in, and said to be authentic, that a man was killed by a tigress some eight miles away and the tigress has been shot and carried by the villagers to Lohagat.

17th. Small buff killed in khud near tent, dragged about two hundred yards down the nala and a good deal of cover had to be cleared to expose it. I tied machan chair in the tree at foot of which tiger had placed the kill, and sat up for the night. I was safe as to tiger, a panther might have tried to get at me. I clearly recollect that I had no torch, as torch batteries had got wet when box fell into river and none to replace them yet received. Had torch been all right I must have killed this tiger, which was without doubt the man-eater. I very clearly recollect his footsteps close to me on hillside, and in the morning I found he had returned the way he came, as I saw his footmarks going down the path. Sat up again all of next night. Tiger did not come at all. Clear night fortunately and not raining as it was on 16th.

Burton sat up a third night for this tiger and on the 19th the man-eater returned to the kill. The moon had not yet risen and in the darkness it was impossible to see the tiger, but it could be heard tearing off pieces of meat from the carcass. As the moon showed over the top of the hill to give some light, a second tiger appeared on the scene with a tremendous roar. The man-eater slipped away and there, every stripe visible in the light of the rising moon, stood the newcomer. Burton took the shot and the tiger rushed off towards the nala. After a few minutes the roars subsided and in the morning they found the tiger dead in the nala. The skinning and pegging out took until dark when a heavy storm and rain came on to last all night and through the next day. As the man-eater appeared to have left the area Burton decided to move on and arrived back at Bareilly on 12th June.

DIARY ——

Note. A note as to how the former measurement of the twelve foot tigers were no doubt taken in earlier days.

While in the Kumaon Hills at a place called Debi Dhura I heard shots in a ravine far down the hill; this was in May 1924. Three tigers were shot in a beat by an Eurasian and his shikari; writing to the Deputy Commissioner at Almora, he gave the lengths of the tigers as – 13ft. 9in., 12ft. 7in., 11ft. 10in.! A human foot was said to have been found in the stomach of one of them.

At that time I also shot a tiger some miles from Debi Dhura. I remarked to the village shikari that the tiger was not a large one. He replied that it would be found when skinned to be a very big tiger. After the skinning he showed me what a big tiger it was. This he did by he and his helper pulling the just removed skin until it looked like the skin of a python. That way this between-pegs tiger, body 6ft. 0in. and tail 2ft. 10in., total 8ft. 10in. measured about 12ft. 6in. That is the origin of the twelve foot tigers of earlier days.

Lacchan Singh, shikari, told me of a man living near Debi Dhura who has wonderful powers! When he meets a tiger he throws some dust or earth towards it, and the tiger will then follow him anywhere! He can make a tiger come out anywhere in a beat that he likes by circling the piece of jungle, leaving a gap, and the tiger won't come out of the circle anywhere but through that gap! Also this magician can put a spell on any particular field of grain so that a marauding bear will not touch that field! Needless to say I wasn't able to test the gent's powers.

Another thing he told me of is that an extensive hillside to the south, which he pointed out to me, is never shot over by any native, and presumably sahibs can't shoot over it either. At any rate it wouldn't be any use trying as the whole countryside would be in opposition. The reason is that this particular piece of country is under protection of the Deity, and anyone shooting there always meets with no success: either gun bursts, or he slips and falls, or is mauled by a tiger. I asked Bishan Singh about it and he said the same. That piece of jungle must be full of game. A pity more of such sanctuaries cannot be established in many parts of the country.

TRANSPORT – No use trying to get about these hills of Eastern Kumaon except by owning one's transport. Then one can go when and where one wants to. Dependent on the country there would be endless delays and annoyances. I believe I am the FIRST to have ever tried buying transport ponies! Remains to be seen how much I am out of pocket over it. Am sure I couldn't have gone even along main roads except by giving a week's notice of each move. Except for the path near Tanakpur at foot of hill to Sukhe Dury, all the P.W.D. (District Board's) roads were quite good. Pack ponies could go, not too heavily loaded, almost anywhere within reason.

(*Note*. Cost of transport worked out at Rs.7/- a day: $90 \times 7 = 630/-$).

FLIES – Awful at Rameswar, Chira, Paharpani (extra awful!), and doubtless the same at all the other places now weather much more warm.

COST – of Kumaon trip.

Total cost three months = Rs.1482/-: = Rs.494/- p.m.

THE
JUNGLES
OF
THE
CENTRAL
PROVINCES
AND
BALUCHISTAN
1924
TO
1927

Chapter 12

FOREST SHOOTING BLOCKS IN THE SATPURA HILLS

From the mountains and foothills of the Himalayas, Burton moved to Bareilly and then on to the jungles of the Central Provinces. Three months were to be spent at the hill station of Pachmarhi, and nine months in the jungle where Burton had obtained a permit for six different shooting blocks. It took two weeks to sort and pack their kit, and Burton and his wife and daughter were glad to move on 30th June from the extreme heat of Bareilly to the comparative cool of Pachmarhi. For the next three months they suffered the unceasing rain and blustery gales of the monsoon, but at the beginning of October they were ready to set out for the jungle.

DIARY

While at Pachmarhi a buffalo was killed in an open space near one of the main roads beyond Rustic Bridge. The slayer was a large panther as I saw from the teeth and claw marks and tracks by the roadside. Eating was done from the hindquarters, tail intact. Such rubbish is written in many books purporting to be authoritative as to panthers invariably commencing to feed at the forequarters. They commence at hind quarters very frequently, also at stomach. I must in future take careful notes of any kill, as also to disperse the legend that a tigress kill can be known by her biting off the tail!

6th October 1924. Rain during most of September: culminating in very heavy rain whole of past week. This is the same storm which has created such havoc all over Upper India, Delhi to Naini Tal and Mussoorie. On 8th October we started at 11 a.m. for Tarnia. All our kit, our three selves, 'Molly', 'Simba', and four servants, all in a motor lorry – Rs.65 for the journey.

9th October. Pitched camp at Tarnia. Said to be a panther constantly about this Bungalow and our water man came across it in the khud just below, at about twelve o'clock today. A shikari turned up, gold bangles and ivory handled umbrella! Glad to learn he was ill, so he isn't fit for work. Another much less pretentious man, also a Khond, came and I impounded his musket and told him to come and stay and bring two men with him. Very difficult now to get men as they are all busy at the essential work of ploughing for the cabi crop.

Tonga arrived on afternoon of 11th. 'Dew' and 'Mildew' as the bullocks have been named by Mrs. Hamilton, require to put on a lot of flesh. 'Dew' a good beast. 'Mildew' has light bone and will never be of fine appearance. Tonga cost Rs.150 and bullocks Rs.155, a high price for such a pair. No news of tiger anywhere near but the panther said to have twice visited the village. I think the Khonds about here shoot a great deal; many guns, and they are all shikaris. We had unceasing rain from evening of 10th to morning of 13th, during which nothing could be done. All supplies are difficult and dear, small chickens a rupee each, eggs twelve annas a dozen.

24th. Left Tarnia at 11 a.m. and got to Dela Kheri D.B. the next afternoon and stayed the night, which was a bad one for sleep owing to a couple of hundred goats arriving just after dark. The owners drive them along and sell them en route: a big goat costs Rs.10. A tiger killed the buffalo on night of 25th, dragged it down and heaved it over a slab of rock about thirty feet, against a clump of wild plantains. The kill in a very dark place and not possible to tie lantern box. Not very hopeful for a return to kill. Tiny could not climb her tree, a difficult one, so we went back to camp. Just as well as T.P. did not return and night was very cold. NOW I am told that this tiger has been shikarried before and never returns to kill!

They decided to move on and sent their kit by train from Piparazia to Bagra Station and set up camp on the banks of the Tawa river. Every day Burton was out tracking through the jungle. He shot a few pigeon for the pot and one day a blackbuck, also a sambur whose horns measured 36in. This was sent off to the BNHS museum.

Fever was prevalent in this jungle, and after many fruitless nights spent in the machan hoping for panther or tiger, he suffered, with resignation, several bouts of fever. His wife and daughter were also affected, but Burton, regarded illness as an inconvenience, and expected his family to be as tough as he was. In the jungle, self sufficiency was important. As well as meat and fish for food, it was necessary to have some basic knowledge of cooking. The following recipe is from his diary.

DIARY _____

Bread: How to make Yeast cakes: 3lbs. flour = 4 loaves bread.
Use the cake maker: Put in 1 tbsp. sugar, 1½ large tsp. salt; then take 1 tbsp. of yeast and make a paste of it in LUKEWARM water in a cup: then fill up the cup with water: and add to the sugar and salt already in the cake maker. Stir and gradually add flour and more water, not exceeding 1 seer (2 milk jugs full). Stir for ten minutes. Put cake maker, covered with wet jharan, with contents, into bread box. In cold weather put a hot water bottle also. Put a blanket into the box and wrap the cake maker and h.w.b. in it. Then put another blanket, and cover box with mackintosh sheet, and a heavy weight on top. Leave till morning. In morning stir again for ten minutes; by spoonfuls put the contents into the bread tins. Put bread tins in sun on a box, covered by blanket (a white jharan over the tins). In hot weather don't put into sun.

Bagra block. 13th.   Took photo of view up Denwa river. Today began to feel feverish and fever all night.
    14th.   To Itarsi to put Tiny into Mail for Jhansi. Mail late, and we had to leave her on the platform to get in as best she could. She looked very weak and pulled down and wants much feeding up and tonics.

On 19th there was a kill by a tigress, and Burton decided to sit up for her in the machan. When there was no moonlight, he used a complicated lantern box to give some light in the dark and dense jungles. This was unreliable and often caused a great deal of trouble.

DIARY _____

Lantern in the new box was smoking, owing to want of air. Cut a hole in the top and now lantern burns all right, but light comes out at top and must devise a way to prevent this. Sat up all night, just enough light to shoot with, but tiger did not turn up. Lantern box shutter works splendidly and lantern now gives excellent light.

19th. Put up machan chair and all serene by 3.45 p.m. The lamp in box to my right about forty feet away. At 4.30 noticed volumes of smoke from the lamp box, pulled string and gave more air to no avail. Soon the box took fire, fierce blaze, and by 5 o'clock, as near as may be, the box lamp fell and continued to blaze on the ground. I heard monkeys giving the alarm a hundred yards or less behind me, and feared the worst. The tigress never turned up and I think she came near, saw the flames and smoke and then went back on her way being seen by the langurs. Her natural approach was through thick cover on the other side of the hill where the ruins are and where she would not have been seen by the langurs.

25th. Out at dawn and down to Denwa River. Near the river I put up a sambur. I go very quietly now in the canvas boots with jute soles. A mongoose, five yards away, did not hear me coming. Saw two lots of sambur crossing the river, five hinds with two tiny ones so small that it is a wonder they got across. Then two hinds with one tiny one. Noticed the baby kept close to and just down stream of its mother.

30th. Took twenty four men and three boys and had four beats of which the last one of no account. In first beat heard nothing except a grunt of a pig Second beat a sambur broke somewhere near me, couldn't see it, third beat the same. Shot a jungle fowl on the way home; so ended a rotten day. Cost of beaters Rs.8/9 – at 6as. for men and 2as. for boys. Man Singh Patel with me and he also saw nothing. As almost always these beats are waste of time and money. Worth trying on this, the last day of my shooting pass.

4th December. Last night was very cold and had little sleep and felt sure an attack of fever was coming on, and so it did. Back to Itarsi on 8th and on to Jhansi for Tiny's wedding to Surgeon Commander A.G. Malcolm R.N. Wife went to Delhi and on to Quetta. I took train back to Itarsi and Bagra, and on 29th left by the night train for Harda. Left black tin box with Deputy Ranger to keep for me. Contents H.G.B. camp clothes and some books of mine.

Harda. 1st January 1925. I had no desire when I went to sleep last night to 'See the New Year in', but was woken up at twelve o'clock by the discordant blasts and whistles of all the railway engines and factory sirens in the place. The kit from Bagra arrived at last and made arrangements to be off tomorrow. Five carts at 6/- each = 30/- from Harda to Indpura; twenty five miles.

2nd January. Off at 8.30 a.m. Caught up the carts close to the town at the river crossing. Went leisurely on in the tonga, had breakfast by the roadside. Passed through Gahal, a large village, at 4 p.m. No news of the carts and realise they must have gone by some other cart track. No use pushing on, so stopped for the night under a tree, and slept in the tonga, most fortunately having a red cotton quilt with me and found it quite enough. Ganput, the tonga man was all right with two waterproof sheets. Dined off bovril, two eggs and bread and butter. There was a tank close to Gahal village and a fair number of duck on it. Surroundings of the tank towards the village in a horribly insanitary state; the smell passing along the road simply beastly. Two men I met on the road very polite and helpful, gave me fifty pullas of grass for the bullocks. Up and off at dawn and got to Magardha 8 a.m., found carts there having fetched up at 8 p.m. yesterday.

Indpura block. Down with fever on 3rd, which lasted four days. Settled on tree for machan and will sleep there three or four nights. Sat up on 8th. No tiger or panther came. A bear woke me up at 3 a.m. by making loud demonstrations and scratching up of earth and chewing of my tree trunk. I tried to see, thought at first it was a tiger!, but soon recognised the visitor's voice. He was in dense shadow behind the trunk, as moon was on the opposite side. Very soon he made off and I saw him scuttle away. The same bear, probably, was among the bir trees in the early morning; the men heard him breaking branches.

9th. A sounder of pig came along soon after sunset; I could hear their crunchings of things they were eating long before they came in sight. Heard villagers having a 'honk' by moonlight and one shot fired; during the night I heard three guns altogether. I expect a good deal of shooting goes on. Shikari tells me of a pool of water some miles away which is the only water for miles around during the hot weather, and where all the animals jostle one another for drinking. I expect all the village shikaris take good toll there on moonlight nights and during the day also.

10th. Nothing at all last night and no jungle sounds except painted partridge calling after sundown. Will give the machan a final chance tonight and then go stalking and see all the jungles around until 15th. Villagers said they would beat the jungles around free of charge for sake of any meat, so fixed up to go there tomorrow. Back to camp, seeing two four-horn on the way, Evening had beats near river for peafowl, shot one jungle cock, three peafowl, one four-horn (48lbs). Total cartridges today – eight for seven birds. Camp people much pleased.

Thick jungle to the east, too thick to do any stalking, the grass chest high. Saw two half-grown sambur playing in maidan, chasing one another and the mother looking on and keeping watch from just inside the cover. Soon after saw two stags, heads about the same size. Could easily have shot either of them, but the heads too small, only about 28in. and thin.

Sent Ganput with bullocks to Magardha to try and buy a bullock cart for thirty to forty rupees. Sorted out camp kit in order to leave a good deal of surplus things here. I could leave more, two tents, beds, chairs, but place said to be infested with rats and to leave things liable to damage in that way would be a poor economy.

15th. Ganput returned yesterday evening from Magardha with a bullock cart Rs.29/8 and dear at that price as it has a wooden axle and wheels none too good. However it seems strong and will have to do. I shall make a bit by using it to carry kit on short marches and so save the hire of one cart.

18th. Moved camp to Bothar: two carts, two trips – Rs.4 plus my own cart which took all the tents. All the jungle between the two branches of the Gozra river are burnt clean, and there is bamboo cutting all over the place. No use staying here. (*Note*: On many jungle trips it would be a GOOD plan to buy a cart and pair of bullocks and so have some transport always at the camp.)

Jarkahu block. 21st January. Marched to Borpani, nine miles, crossing over the Satpura Range. Tomorrow is market day at Kaida, so bullock cart is going in to get supplies for the camp people. 'Mildew' is VERY thin, result of the cold probably, so I am housing the bullocks in the village at night. (*Note*: This Pachmarhi bullock never fit from the day I bought him; suffered from lian fever and eventually died of it, just wasted away.)

24th. Out at dawn. A mile from camp found tracks of a medium sized tiger and tracks of a large panther. The villagers have dug a deep square pit, 5ft. × 5ft. × 10ft. deep, in the hopes that some beast may fall into it. The shikari says that none have been so foolish up to date.

25th. Stayed in camp to mend camp bed. Evening, went up hill to the north of camp to look in nalas for tracks of tiger.

JOURNAL ——

We arrived at our Forest Rest House on 1st February and that night the whole country was stricken by a cold wave which passed over the whole of India and caused great damage to the crops and the foliage of the forest. In the valley of the Tapti River the cold was intense; the thermometer hung up in the verandah showed the temperature at 6 a.m. to be 30°. Not very cold to some, but really cold to us dwellers in this warmer climate. Following on that cold wave the forests of the low lying country were, and still are, a pitiful sight. All was brown where all should, at that time of the year, have been in every beautiful shade of green.

It is always interesting to be out in the early morning at the time when, as the native of the country expresses it, 'you can see the hair on your hand against the sky'. That is the time to see animals, and birds too. The animals who have been feeding, or on the prowl, are making their way to secluded places where they can lie up for the day and have undisturbed rest.

The sandy bed of the river shows plainly the tracks of all who have been abroad during the hours of darkness. There were the tracks of a hyaena, easily distinguishable from those of panther by the uneven shape of the main pad of the foot, of a porcupine which had come to drink, of several wild cats, of prowling jackals, and of otters. In one place a long smear in the sand showed where a crocodile had been for a waddling stroll. There were a few tracks of sambur, all hinds and small stags as was plain to the eye, and rounding a bend of the river we saw ahead of us two hundred yards away a small stag chital with several hinds. They were crossing the river to gain the security of the Government Forest, after having spent the night among the crops of a village on the further bank. Peafowl and jungle fowl had been to drink, white egrets were seen along the reedy borders of the pools, a pair of ruddy sheldrakes (Brahminy ducks) rose with loud calls of 'chakwee, chakwa', and circling in the sky was a Brahminy kite, a fine handsome bird of bright russet plumage with a conspicuous white head. This bird is revered also by Hindus as being sacred to Vishnu.

DIARY ——

4th February. A man arrived at camp to say there had been two kills. After breakfast I started out to see the place of tie up near camp, and found the fool who had visited the kill in the morning had merely put one leafy branch over it, and tied piece of cloth on a bush! Of course the crows had at once collected and vultures followed them, and carcass picked clean.

The second tiger kill had also been left uncovered, but fortunately the crows and vultures hadn't found it. Burton waited in the machan that evening and the tiger appeared just before eight o'clock. It stood at the head of the kill in the moonlight, but with the moon in front Burton couldn't see the foresight easily, and when he fired, the tiger dashed back into the jungle without making a sound to show whether it was hit. There were other animals which visited the kill during the night.

DIARY ——

A wild dog came during the night; they are very handsome animals, lovely russet coats and black tips to their bushy tails. I turned the light on him and he took no notice at all. I made a lot of noise getting the blanket round my shoulders and generally trying to get comfortable! and he took no notice whatever. At early dawn he came again and so did the crows; great fun to see him chase them off. A jackal came up and was no sooner spotted than he was quickly hunted off, and very nearly caught too as he raced down the nala. I called up the men from the field quarter of a mile off where they had slept for the night. At the sound of my call the red dog was much alarmed. I sounded four times and at each blast he jumped with astonishment. Eventually, not making it out at all, he sat down a little way off, and as nothing seemed to happen, returned to the kill and went on feeding till he heard the men coming up, then off he went.

The following day we followed the track by the blood for a good way and shikari was in quite a funk and said we ought to stop and wait for cattle. I could see the ground was fairly open and that no wounded tiger would have stopped before reaching the bamboo forest, so decided to follow on till it seemed foolish to continue. I was right, as on getting to the edge of a deep nala, where the blood tracks led, the tiger was soon spotted dead in the nala. He was near as may be two hundred yards from where fired at. Shot a bad one and a lucky one, too far back, but fortunately had travelled forward a little. Back to camp by 8 o'clock and cart brought tiger to camp by 9.30. Measured and skinned and weighed.

Over curves:	body 6ft.;	tail 3ft.	: total 9ft.
Between pegs:	" 5ft. 10in.;	" 3ft.	: " 8ft. 10in.
Weight	380 lbs.		

A typical hill tiger, girth very small, feet large for his size, forelegs and hind legs much developed as to muscle. When skinning I found a porcupine quill embedded under his chin. He was heavy for his measurements, I judged him at about 300lbs.

Shikari and the village Muccadam who has been with him as co-shikari grumbled, at least it was the latter who did, at 5/- reward for this tiger. I explained that the Government paid 15/- and they would get all of that for each tiger. Ten annas a day pay quite enough for such ignorant men and not much good at shikar either, and the Muccadam grumbled at that and said he always got a rupee a day! I didn't realise really what I was doing when I got to Junapani and should have turned down the Muccadam and kept only the other man, much better than he is, and a cooly; but the Muccadam sort of came into service without my much noticing. Forgot to note that this Korku village ate the whole of the carcass of the tiger leaving very little for the vultures. They must be pretty low in the social scale.

6th. Went to Ratamati, a large village with much open country around through which the road passes. Many hundreds of doves and peafowl. Had breakfast near the village well. At Ratamati I saw a travelling blacksmith at work, he comes from Minar; a wild looking sort of people. Their cart was a weird affair, a very ancient pattern I am sure, built on the wheel frame like half of a punt, and all studded over with brass nails.

12th February.   It never rains but it pours! Three kills last night: one on the main road by a panther; one of a red goat near the waterman's field also by a panther; one in stony nala east of camp by tiger. Sat up on 13th but tiger did not return to kill. Now they tell me all sorts of tales of this tiger; that he is very old and wary, ranges as far as Kaida and Bolidar, not yet known to return to a kill the second night and so on. It is always so, they never repeat these things until too late. I must watch events and may perhaps sleep in machan four nights. He was away seven nights after the 3rd so the nights to stay up would be 17th, 18th, 19th.

13th.   Tied the chair in a teak tree and sat up over the road kill. A hyaena came and had a feed. He was very scared and evidently feared Tom Puss turning up. He didn't eat much. The hyaena must have been a horrible beast; I smelt him every time he came near my tree, a filthy smell, foul beyond description. Bombay Natural History Society want a hyaena skin and skeleton from me for setting up. There seem to be many hyaenas in these forests; I am always finding their tracks.

A hyaena and a panther were shot from the machan during the next few days and on the 15th February Burton sat up over the tiger kill. The tiger came that night and prowled around the kill for nearly three hours without coming close. Then just as the moon rose and gave some light the tiger approached the kill, walked straight past without stopping and vanished into the jungle.

DIARY
_____

15th. I realise that it is useless attempting to shoot this tiger without a moon, and with the torch it is worse than useless. I could SEE him in the dark, just see his shape, but I would not be able to see which way he was facing, or how the bullet would travel after hitting him, so foolish to fire and very likely merely wound. Decided to leave here and go on to Kaida as only eight more days in this block.

16th. It has been very cold at night the past few days; now the weather is changing and for the first time there is a strong warm wind from the west. A clear precursor of the hot weather and unpleasant clouds of dust, wherever there can be dust. On the way down the nala saw a human skull and asked shikari how it came there. 'It is my son's skull' he said 'he was buried at the upper end there,' pointing. 'The rains washed the soil away and scattered his bones!' He seemed quite indifferent to the skull lying exposed and evidently does not intend to bury it again.

Got to Kaida 4 p.m. on 20th February, taking in some stores at Borpani and leaving the rest of spare kit there to be taken on to Pati on 1st April.

23rd. Out at dawn to north east. Shot a female four-horn, then three blue bull. Horrid slaughter, but forest people particularly ask for them to be shot and the village is pleased with the meat. All the people of Kaida village are Korkus, same as those of Junapani. The shikari said that they would not touch the meat of the nilgae if the Chamars skinned the animals. I asked him if he was a Khond and he said 'Yes'. In further conversation I discovered him to be Korku and all his village. Evidently they desire to rise in the social scale.

27th. Beat the hill south east of Kaida; three beats, all blank. One beat at the foot of hill, in which eight chital does appeared and one peacock, and that was all! Now wish I had stayed on at Junapani; I might have got that tiger. Had I known the place was beatable I would certainly have beat it out. I understood it was not! I feel sure that the Forest Ranger is anti-European and working against me, I wouldn't trust him half an inch. Have written to him for four carts to take me to Bori Rest House and wonder if I shall get them.

Chapter 13

TIGERS AND PANTHERS IN THE C.P. JUNGLES

Machaborcori Block. 1st March. Off early to Bori, had breakfast at river near Machabori village. At Bori found the S.D.O. Mr.Chadda. He came today from Dekhna and is evidently running round tying up all over the place and frightening or wounding animals as he is quite inexperienced and uses a twelve-bore gun with 'lethal'. Told me how he has missed several chances at tiger and panther, and I fancy told me much less than the facts! Stood up in machan once when a panther came to kill and so panther saw him and cleared, tiger also saw him. Did not know I was coming or I am sure he would have stayed here a week.

Shikari here an old man, seems reliable, brought news of a village buff having been killed yesterday evening at sundown while out grazing. He followed up the drag and found the remains under a rock in nala. He clapped his hands to ensure departure of tiger before he got to the kill! I went off with him, and found the tiger had returned after shikari had left and had removed paunch and taken off the remainder, head and forelegs and part of ribs. Tracked this up for a long way through bamboo jungle, and eventually found the remains at foot of a bamboo clump. Excellent teak tree, and I was quite well concealed. I had to climb tree and tie chair myself as shikari said he couldn't do it. Sital said he had never climbed a tree and so he couldn't, and the village youth evidently knew nothing as to lashing a chair. So up I went and did it, quicker and better than they would have done it, so all was well and for the best. Had great hopes of tiger coming to feed, but he did not turn up. Probably he had seen us or heard us when we found the kill and so decided, no fool, to stay away. Heard a few animals moving about during the night, but never the well known heavy stealthy footfall.

3rd. No kill: no use I think sitting up for this tiger. He is evidently very cute and shikari says he was missed last month out of a machan. Shikari says there are no bison in this block – perhaps that is why one is put on my permit! Or perhaps shikari doesn't know much about jungle beyond limits of his own village.

This tiger was shot at and missed a month ago by the lad who had this block. His machan is a clump of bamboos sixty yards away and though moon was good, much too far to be of any use. He had a splendid gular tree ten yards away! Shikari says that after firing the one shot at this tiger over kill last month, the sportsman fired five more shots at hyaenas killing one. Also that the lad got out of his machan and ran about looking for the tiger after he had fired at it! I wonder how much of this is true.

4th. Two four-horn bucks passed the bungalow at 9 a.m. Let them go as larder full. Could have killed with .375 from verandah of bungalow. Roads very unpleasant now: quite four inches of dust and carts go along smothered in its clouds. All country to east disturbed by bamboo cutting. Went towards river to look for jungle fowl. Nice path along the bank shaded by overhanging bamboos and large trees. Much water in the river and it is said to never dry up.

7th. Cart went to Harda to fetch rifle and potatoes. With it went the two Chamars to return to Itarsi: as it transpired yesterday evening, quite by accident, that neither of them will tie up bodas for kills, though they will untie. This Hindu caste business! But it was on clear understanding that they WOULD tie up and so save me from being blocked by Khonds refusing to do the work that I engaged them and entered that clearly in their written agreements. I never for a moment supposed they (Chamars) would refuse. They said nothing when Wilson read out the agreement to them! Perhaps, as they say, they did not understand and thought they only had to accompany jungle men who would do the actual tying. All for the best, except I don't get petty repairs to kit done, and I now save quite 17/8 a month by their going. Not so many tigers to skin that I can't cope with it myself with aid of villagers, as on many other trips.

9th March 1925. Thirty five years today that I left Southampton for India for first time and twenty one years today that I landed at Southampton with broken leg.

10th. News of kill and I wasn't in machan last night as I ought to have been! Tied chair in a bamboo clump and sat up next evening but tiger did not return and is evidently another of the many tigers of these parts which never return to a tie up kill. So I am well punished for not having slept in machan night before last! Will do so tonight and tomorrow night. Hyaena turned up soon after dark and was generally very jumpy, he finished off most of the bones, still some left for tonight. The whole business is keeping still. If, at critical time, tummy doesn't gurgle, all is well! But it so often does rumble, perhaps the sound of it doesn't travel as far as one imagines; but at night any sound travels far. The wooden bell clapper round the buffs neck can be heard a mile away. Machan creaky, as all these tied up affairs are. My big machan bed would make too much show in the bamboo clump, and now trees are mostly leafless it is not often I will be able to use it. Will have to use the chair which is little visible and easily tied, only drawback is one can't sleep much.

12th. I was in machan, same as last night, having had the floor of it re-tied and a thick layer of grass put down. At about ten to seven, just before moon came, I heard tiger moving about and soon buff began to snort at him; so he must have been pretty close. Then there was a great row of the bell and I thought buff was about to be killed, but nothing happened and then I heard T.P. walking away towards forest again. Later he again came and this time after scaring the buff I heard him gallop off, four or five big bounds, in the practically open bit of jungle to south west. He must have been just amusing himself in the moonlight!

Next day I was in machan by 4.30. The men had not been gone ten minutes when tiger's presence was announced by monkeys. He came fairly close behind, and I heard a low growl and a second one a little louder, and that was the end! When I heard the growl I at once concluded, which was probably correct, that he had expected to find grazing cattle. He had probably heard us at the machan and thought we were cattle men, then he came to the sound of the bell and was annoyed to find a tied up buff, much to be suspected and not to be killed in a light-hearted fashion! Nothing more all night.

Burton had just bought a new gun, .400 from Law and Adler, and on the first beat using this gun he shot a panther. There was some difficulty in obtaining beaters on account of the Holi Festival and on 18th, most of the village, including the shikari, were not in a fit state to appear. However, on the strength of an increased offer of 8as. a number of men turned up, twenty seven in all. The beaters, as usual, avoided all the thick places of jungle and moved five or six in a bunch, but a small stag was found and shot and the men were pleased to have the meat.

DIARY _____

24th March. Bori. I have several times told shikari that there would be a kill at the river bed place about 24th and sure enough, kill of the boda took place last night. It is in all probability the cunning tiger, as the tracks of last night are straight from the valley where he proved too cute for me direct to the river bed place. Shikari, reporting the kill, said men could be got today all right; and I saw a lot of men about yesterday evening as there is crop collection work going on. Now, he reports that beaters refuse to turn out, all pleading urgent business elsewhere! They are afraid to beat, that is the plain fact and the beat affords no danger to them. An island in the river with clear river bed on three sides of it and a natural nala on the hill side, a steep hill. An easy beat, couldn't be easier; Abdul gone with shikari to try and persuade the men to turn out.

I am afraid I maligned these people as they turned out after all, and the first report of shikari was wrong; fact was the Muccadam wasn't moving and he got a move on when Abdul went to him. Twenty six men turned up at midday, and we set off to beat the island. The shikari did not look on main road for tracks to see if tiger had left the river bed, I did this and found his tracks leading up nala into forest. Shikari said no harm in beating the island first and I agreed, but fear this was a fatal mistake, as the tiger was not on the island. The beaters made a good deal of noise and though shikari said the tying up place for the tiger was too far for this to matter, I fear it did matter as tiger was not in the second beat either. Must sit for the tiger or tigress whichever may turn up, each evening, and hope for the best. Blue bull saddle very good for dinner last night.

(*Note.* A long time after, a year about, Abdul divulged to me that the tiger WAS in the second beat and beaters let it out – funky).

Ganput told me today that Abdul very 'chitak' which is no news to me! Says he is using some of my food stuffs, and no doubt he is, potatoes and onions and some flour, and atta and rice too: but it can't be very much as I issue a few days supply at a time and know how it should last. I suppose that Ganput discovered at Magardha that I have a receipt from man who sold him the cart: and that it is 26/8 and not 29/8 as Ganput charged me! He is probably hedging against the evil day when I burst that news to him!

25th. Up at 4 a.m. and off by dawn. A small stag and three hinds came along, all trotting in a bunch, straight towards me where I was sitting at the foot of a tree. The leading hind didn't see me, but stood watching old man shikari. What a pity my camera not with me today. The first day I have left it for a long time.

28th March. Sat up till dusk again. A mongoose among the rocks close by saw me but couldn't make me out, and growled at me for a long time. Saw little bush quail following after one another like muskrats. Many bright flowering trees now: dhak, and erithrena of several kinds. Jamun trees all very bright green with their new leaves, also some shrubs, otherwise jungles bare and noisy. In evening shot some doves for larder, ten for fourteen cartridges, and one jungle fowl for the pot.

30th March. Packed kit ready for tomorrow. At 10 o'clock many vultures seen descending on the hill near the Bungalow. A big sambur hind killed by panther.

Arranged for men to stay and keep vultures off and sent for machan chair to be tied in suitable tree. All settled by 4 o/c but vultures still about so kept the men and 'honked' the vultures, which eventually got tired of waiting and being disturbed and sailed away. At 5.15 let the men go. Old man shikari, who isn't much of a shikari, said the kill must be by a tiger as so much eaten. Only stomach and some ribs eaten, no hind or fore quarters, and kill obviously by a panther by the teeth and claw marks. A big panther, and so he proved to be.

Two or three crows came to the kill. I was very well hidden and they did not see me. My chair very cramped, scarcely elbow room: these shikaris all think everyone can sit like they do, squatted like a frog. I managed to tie back the screening branches pretty well but had to shoot from left shoulder and couldn't make a rest for the rifle without causing a rustle when raising the barrel.

Shortly before dusk the crows gave the 'caw' announcing arrival of the panther, and I saw him stealing up on my right. He stopped and listened intently, quite three minutes, then came on a bit and stood again, then on a bit, quite close now and sat on his haunches, head and part of shoulders hidden by a tree. He approached kill and I had him sideways so raised rifle barrels. The rustle was very slight but attracted instant attention and he turned his head quickly, direction accurate but looked past my tree. He seemed to be looking straight at me, but wasn't. He soon turned his head away and then I took the shot. I had put on the radium sight, and not used to this aimed a bit low and hit where aimed, but it was too low to kill on the spot. To the shot the panther went (as they always do) same way he had come at a tremendous pace, steep down hill and I heard a great thud a hundred yards below and the last gasp. Bugled up the men, nearly dark; foolishly decided not to take the men down to look for the beast. Many bamboos, rough hillside, so went back to camp to look for Tom Puss in the morning.

Alas! Alas! Went at 6.30 a.m. and found no panther where I had heard him crash but signs of much flattening of leaves and fifty yards down a nala lay half the panther. The hind half, from ten inches or so behind the shoulders, eaten by hyaenas: and such a fine beast, 'half a tiger' (Adha Sher) as these people call this big type of panther. In splendid coat too, fine rich colouring; old beast. In skinning him, fore-part all quite undamaged, found about fifty wounds, fairly recent, of porcupine quills: and several quills still embedded under the skin, face, feet, side. He had a bad time of it after killing that porcupine – if he did kill it! The Korkus took fore and hind quarters of the sambur to the village to eat. Useless regrets. I was morally certain he was dead, but he might not have been. As the men came up I thought I heard a bamboo crack down below, that was really the deciding factor. This beast would have done splendidly for the promised specimen to Bombay Museum. Alas! Alas! One can't risk letting any beast lie out in these jungles which are overstocked with hyaenas.

Having skinned the (half!) panther, set off with sixteen beaters and my two men, and beat the hill, full of hope, but no result. A pig and a kakur turned up, several langurs came along, two didn't spot me which speaks well for my staying still. Went on three quarters of a mile and beat a long stretch of very dense cover; only peafowl and jungle fowl in it. Old man shikari never told me of this place before. A.1. for tiger to lie up in, cover and water and can be beaten. I think they all funk beating out tiger. At any rate for anyone they don't know – that is, don't know if he will kill or wound. I have shot four animals before them and missed nothing so now, the last day, they have confidence!

End of Machaborcori block and Hashangabad District. Start tomorrow for Pati in East Tapti block, Betul District.

East Tapti block. At Taori. Glad to find here a thatched wattle and daub Inspection Hut. No shady trees for a tent anywhere about, so I am lucky. A gawalla very solicitous to be of

3

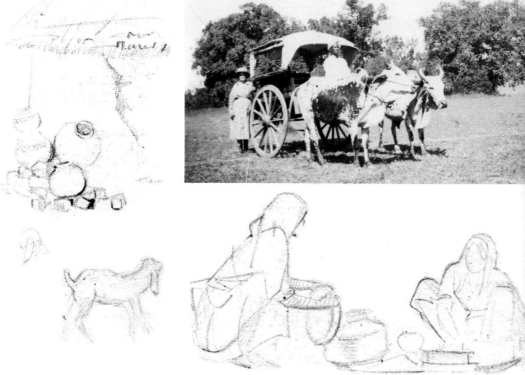

I

CHAPTERS
12/13

help as he has suffered losses recently by tiger killing his cattle. Very cold at night here and hot in day; at 1500ft.'. Not many tracks of animals, and tigers must be living on cattle. My twelve-bore gun none too safe now and shall have to scrap this gun and buy a new one. Plan to stay here ten days. On to Nanda on 16th, stay there till 20th and then go to Khandu Block.

The machan was tied in a terminalia tree, and arrangements made to sit up over the kill. A tigress came on the second night, and to a shot in fairly good light from the moon the tigress was hit and sprang away up the nala. A dying cat yowl a little later indicated that the shot was fatal and she was found next morning dead on the further bank.

DIARY _____

10th. Did a round towards Chuma village, up the hill and back to Nanda road and so back to camp, very hot. Muccadam of Taori with me failed to find a jungle pool of water which he knew of! These people seldom leave the main roads, and know little of the jungle animals and their haunts and ways. The people of this village have an independent and democratic spirit as instance the coolies objecting to Muccadam receiving more than they do for the same work. This morning shot a four-horn close to camp, so larder full for first time since 4th March.

13th. I feel sure I would be wasting time by staying here any longer. Kit of DSP on tour came today, no carts available for tomorrow, so emptied two of his and sent on to Nanda at night with my kit, plus my own cart, leaving a tent behind to come on later.

15th. Nanda has much open country round about. No tracks at river bed and whole place overrun by cattle. A new village established within forest a few years, and not shown on map. Vultures nesting on trees near the river and shikari says they are always here. Very hot.

19th. All settled down in machan at 4.30. I heard some animal prowling about after dark: may have been tiger but didn't sound heavy enough for him. Anyhow nothing visited the kill. Machan chair tied in good tree. Am not likely to be spotted and may, with electric light, get him: One can't shoot quickly as that means great possibility of wounding and not killing and that is the devil; especially in such thick jungle all entangled with creepers. So I must take a sure and careful shot or none at all. Found later that tiger had passed close by me, along the road, and must have seen the buff; but he didn't touch it. Evidently a very wily tiger and must now have a beat for him. Not a large beat and fifty men ample, but they ask for seventy. I can't afford many of these beats; 4as. a man I hear; which is better than 6as. of Hyderabad district.

20th. Evening. It was as I feared, beat blank. Tiger must have gone off somewhere to lie up near water. Sixty four beaters and two forest guards cost Rs.47/- for the beat. The kill had been taken about sixty yards down the nala. I didn't tie up again, as must leave tomorrow or the Malghat shikar will be spoilt. I will be truly glad to get away from this Nanda bungalow; it is like living in a lime kiln, the dust of lime penetrates everything, most unpleasant.

22nd. Up at 3 a.m. and off at 4.0. Got to Tapti at 7.15. Saw streams of women from Gozra village crossing river to go and gather mohwa berries. All the people of this country busy at that just now and since early on this month. Only pools of water in river, a small trickle from one pool to another. Bed of river very rocky, jungles on hill sides very thin, trees small, very little soil. Pushed on to Jamu getting there at 12 o'clock. Very hot, but a good breeze. In evening went with shikaries across river.

Whole country bare of undergrowth and burnt and roamed over by hundreds of cattle and buffaloes. Last night's tracks of a tiger going up the Betul river. Saw a few kakur, and so back to camp, tired, after a long day and walking about fifteen to sixteen miles at least.

23rd. Up at 4.30 and off at 5 a.m. across river. Saw three sambur hinds and one fawn, then one hind with fawn. This one left the edge of forest and galloped across maidan and quite by chance we saw her baby fawn at edge of cover from which she had come. It really looked, and perhaps was, as if she purposely did this in order to distract our attention! very brave of her. At same place as yesterday found the returning tracks of the tiger, this quite unexpected. I expect this is end of his beat and he is not likely to be this way again for ten days. Anyway, have decided best to push on to Rahu bungalow.

North Khandu Block. 24th. Up at 3 a.m.: and carts loaded by 4.15. I started out in bullock cart, one hired bullock and 'Dew'. Road very bumpy and rocky and got to Riparia, seven miles, by 8 o'clock. Very uninteresting march, open rocky plateaux or else sparse bare jungle. Carts didn't turn up till 11.30 and had had a lot of trouble. 'Mildew' lay down at the start in the mud at the camp water place and refused to move. Then bullock had to be changed at a village on the way, a cart completely upset. Let the carts halt at Riparia for two hours and then started off at 1.30 and got to Rahu F.R.H. at 5 p.m., blazing hot this last five miles, poor buffs and 'Mildew' suffered, but fortunately water at two places on the way.

Country round Rahu does not look very promising. No shikari here and I shall have to do all the hard work of finding tracks by myself. A good bungalow, thick thatched roof, large rooms and wide verandah; it stands on high ground well away from the village. R.O. came to see me, tells me fowls are 1/-, chickens 8as., eggs 6pi., carts 13/- a mile. He sends to Bainsdehi for post on Wednesday and Saturday and can get me oranges from Ellichpur and cotton seed for the bullocks. Wood felling going on about here.

With considerable honesty, Burton records all his misses as well as his successes. On 1st May he sat up for and missed a tigress on the kill. These misses were nearly always night shots when visibility was poor. In the daytime he shot kakur and peafowl and doves for the pot. The following day he found a pony in an open field which had been killed by a tiger only a few yards from the main road, and arranged to sit up here, having fixed the machan in a nearby gular tree.

DIARY ————————————————————————————————————

3rd May. Another bad failure! This time tiger came at about 1.30 a.m., his impending arrival announced by alarm given by a blue bull on the edge of forest. In a few minutes he was at the kill. I heard him beginning to break up the carcass. The moon had gone down and it was dark and I could see nothing except just the black mass of the kill. After a minute I put on the light and saw tiger was lying down at hind quarters almost end on to me. I merely saw a long yellow shape same colour as the yellow grass. If I had not known it was a tiger the electric light would not have disclosed the fact. I fired and to the shot the tiger went off with a roar, I heard him on the hard open ground for about forty yards and then no more. The night was stormy and it had rained several times. I was glad when dawn arrived. In the morning no blood, no tiger, and no tracks. He probably went on down the valley which was pretty open and has now gone for miles. The real difficulty is insufficient light and difficulty of defining backsight. All these misses at night due to bad torch bulbs.

4th. Thunderstorms and rain at night. Moved on to Rajadeo. Bungalow locked, but I easily opened it by pulling up door bolt, inserting my walking stick through broken window pane to do so. A small one roomed thatched house, wattle and daub, mud floors, a small bath room. Bath, as in most cases, useless so just as well I carry one about with me.

8th.   Spotlight torch came by cooly today from Chichole, and expensive torch, ordered last December from Bagra, they sent the wrong pattern and it had to be returned twice. It has now come at an opportune moment as my own bag of tricks requires repairs and the batteries won't last much longer.

Another miss! Panther on the kill at 3 a.m. Put on the torch and panther took no notice. No answer to the shot and panther gone and not a sound. No blood to be found, and feared a complete miss. A bad business indeed. So bad for one's prestige with the local shikaris. I missed nothing up to 7th April and now in one month have missed three panthers and two tigers, nearly as many as I have missed in the past thirty years!

23rd May.   Moved camp to Biba, thirteen miles via Jarida. Tracks of a tiger down the road. The jungles have become quite green lately. Many trees which were leafless on 5th May are now in full leaf: bamboos beginning to put on leaves also and some undergrowth coming up. Nights much colder now. Ranger wrote to me to say a girl had been seized by a panther in village of Boda and dragged fifty yards and rescued by the people. She was seized by the head when out behind her hut in the early evening.

26th. Last night's tracks of bear again on path near the water to east of camp and saw a very tall smooth trunked tree up which bears had evidently been many times to try and get at the bees of which there were three colonies on the higher branches; wonderful climb, even for a bear. Kill by tigress and cub; very little left of boda but quite enough to return to. They did not return to kill or pass along the road or come anywhere near. A high wind all night from the west evidently monsoon blowing up. A thunderstorm up in the higher hills to south. I fear the journey back to Betul 9 to 14 June may be an unpleasant one. Will sit up again tonight and quite possibly the tigress and cub will turn up. Machan chair quite well concealed. A bit creaky when tree shakes with the wind, but it doesn't much matter in high wind.

29th. Being third night in machan chair I wanted sleep badly and dozed off; waking every half hour or so; until 4 a.m. When men came soon after daylight, I left them to untie chair and went back to camp. On way back shot a kakur with .470. A female this was; but wanted for larder and no more can be shot as I have killed the four allowed on my licence. Peafowl and jungle fowl very plentiful in all these jungles also kakur; few sambur, four-horn or nilgae.

A cattle herdsman came to the camp to tell Colonel Burton that he had heard a tiger growling in the bushes by the banks of the river and took him to see the place. It was very hot, daytime, and it seemed likely that the tiger had concealed his kill and retreated to a more shady place to lie up. There was a green bush at the foot of the bank and as Burton approached, at about 40 yards, the tiger rushed from this bush up the bank and disappeared. The kill was found about 20ft. further on, in the open. Presumably the tiger had not dragged it under cover as this would have left him no shade to lie in free from the swarms of flies.

There was no suitable tree for a machan, so a number of thin trunks were tied together with a thick rope, the trunks about 5ft. from the ground, and some poles lashed to make a platform. The general confusion of all this no doubt alarmed the tigress as she did not reappear. It rained heavily during the night, and as it was his third night of sitting up in a machan, Burton dozed off and on. By morning nothing had been to the kill and the machan was dismantled and he returned to camp. As the trees and bamboos put out more leaf, the jungles would soon become too thick for shikar, also the regular monsoon rains were due.

On 31st May a heavy thunderstorm had cleared by early evening and Burton decided to sit up that night in the machan. As he approached the kill, he saw a grey shape tugging at the carcass and realised it was a panther. His gun was wrapped around with electric wires needed for the distant light, and it took some time to untangle. In his hurry to shoot before the panther slipped away, he fired too quickly. The panther jumped up the steep bank and walked quietly away into the long grass, and although Burton sat up for him, he didn't return. There was no sound through the silent night, except the dripping of raindrops off the leaves. At dawn he heard a rattling of stones and curious whining and grunting noises, and thought at first that it was a bear with its cub, but then he saw a wild dog, and soon there was a whole row of them tugging at the carcass.

DIARY ───

7th June.   Started 7 a.m. and got to Boda via Biba and Lakhiwara at 3 p.m. Passed the kill on the way, eaten by vultures, BUT the carcass had been moved and it looked very much as if tigers had returned to the almost putrid remains on the third night. Found at Boda that the village Patel had wounded a panther in the village, over a goat, night before last. Probably the same beast which attacked the small girl in May. Panther was seen next day but Patel didn't fire as he has only a single barrel! Not very venturesome people in these parts. In Chakrata hills they killed a panther with a hatchet. Saw the child, a lot of scars on her head and cheek, all by bites they say. No cover anywhere near the village. Panther attacked her in quite open ground. I put up for the night in a clean and comfortable grass hut kept set aside for use of Forest Subordinates on tour.

Nothing to do here so may as well close down diary of this very unsuccessful shoot with a few lists.

Expenses – for period 24th December 1924 to return to Itarsi on 15 June 1925. Say Rs.2350/- = 430 p.m. near as maybe. Deducting avoidable expenses, can safely say 400 p.m. as cost of shikar.

DIARY ───

8th June 1925. Nothing to do here, so may as well close down diary of this very unsuccessful shoot with a few lists.

Stores consumed

Whisky – 1/4 bottle		Jam	30 tins
Anchovy	0	Lux	9
Apple rings	4 lb.	Lime juice	2 bot.
Atta	40 lb.	Macaroni	4 pkt.
Army rations	3 tin	Milk	39 tins
Baked beans*	4 "	Marmalade	1 "
Bovril	9 bot.	Pepper	½ bot.
Butter	38 × ½lb.	Potted meat	7 tins
Biscuits	1 tin	Paisly flour*	5 "

Bandaloo (tinned curry)	4 tins	
Bloaters & herrings*	13 "	
Chutney	2 bot.	
Custard powder*	0 tins	
Cocoa	2 "	
Curry powder	1½ tins	
Cornflour	1 bot.	
Cocoatine for cooking	25 lb.	
– mostly consumed by servants		
Cheese kraft*	1 tin	
Cheese cheddar	6 "	
Dal	5 lb.	
Flour	–	
– no need to take when by myself		
Fruit dried	9 lb.	
Glaxo*	2 tins	
Haricot beans 3 "		

Potatoes	128 lb.⎤	much eaten
Onions	27 lb.⎦	by servants
Q. Oats	6 tins	
Rice	28 lb.	
Soap, cakes	22	
Salt, table	1/4 bot.	
" cooking	4 lb.	
Sardines*	12 tins	
Sauce, Worcester	4 bot.	
Sausages*	5 tins	
Sugar	10 lb.	
Tea	3 lb.	
Treacle	1 tin	
Vinegar	1 bot.	
Kerosine oil	3 tins	

*can v. well do without these but want a few sausages, sardines, and fish as a standby.

Expenses etc. for period 24th Dec. 1924 to return to Itarsi on 15 June 1925. including any expenses for Oct. Nov. which should be carried on etc. – say 5½ months.

				Recoveries and Credits
Bullocks: purchase	155	0	0	85 – bullock sold
" upkeep (after Bagra)	39	7	0	2.12 grain sold
" man pay (to 30 June)	108	0	0	35/8 earned by saving hire
" tonga purchase	150	0	0	sold on 9.2.26. for 50/-
" " sundries	35	14	0	5/- in hand
Servants pay: Abdul – 15 June	165	0	0	
" " Ghasar – " "	165	0	0	
Shikaris and shikar coolies;				
camp coolies	383	0	0	
Cart purchase	29	8	0	12/-
" hire	176	0	0	20/- earned by cart
Buffaloes and goats (bodas)	176	3	0	18.0.0
Beats	56	15	0	
Portages & telegrams	73	9	0	5.12.0
Stationary	9	0	0	3.4.0 in hand
Servants clothes	23	8	0	23/8
" blankets & jerseys	37	0	0	37/-
Photo films & printing etc.	15	0	0	
Tools	79	8	0	65.14 value in hand
Ammo. & .470 rifle licence	166	11	0	100.0.0.
Electric torch: batteries				
wire, radium sights	65	9	0	42.0.0.
Permit fees	86	10	0	36.0.0. refunded
Maps	13	10	0	nil, but maps in hand
Medicines & methyl. spirit	58	6	0	50. value in hand

Boots & shoes	52	10	0	25. " " "
Bazaar supplies	105	4	0	9/- 2 tins k. oil
Europe stores – in hand	147	0	0)	
" " new	192	11	0)	164/- value in hand
" " freight 5 12 0)				
Tea	9	13	0	5.0.0. in hand
Sundries	14	0	0	6.4.0.
Machan bed & new one	23	12	0	23.12.0
Camp furniture	10	0	0	10.0.0. bath in hand
Alum & saltpetre	24	2	0	10.0.0.
Whisky	17	0	0	14.0.0. 2 bottles
Own clothes	36	8	0	31.0.0.
Rail Fares & luggage etc.	118	9	0	
Rs.	3184	14	6	857.14

Say Rs.2350/- = 430 pn. near as maybe.
Deducting avoidable expenses, can safely say 400 pn. as cost of shikar.

Salt and Alum Pickle Water – 1 gal; Salt – 1 quart; Alum (powdered) 1 pint
Boil and cool.

9th. To Bainsdehi and Rahu, about twenty miles. High monsoon wind, and was glad to have it blowing me along and not facing me. Open cultivated plateau, 2474ft. People here very polite. Put up in a clean and tidy D.B.

9th June. Left Bainsdehi at 4.30 a.m. and got to Jhallon D.B. at 9.30. p.m., then went on to Tapti River, walked all the way, total twenty four miles, last six in pouring rain, a very heavy storm. Had to share the rest house at Tapti with a wedding party of eleven women and children and five or six men! Chapatti and cheese and tea for dinner.

10th. Up at 3 a.m. and off at 4.0. Walked twelve miles to Betul D.B. Next day, all kit packed, sealed and sent off by road van to Wilson for store (41 articles). Betul a very unflourishing place apparently; no rope to be got! Bazaar almost empty. Weight of luggage booked – tents, store boxes etc., twenty maunds seven seers. Cost Rs.5/7 to Itarsi.

15th. Betul to Itarsi. Travelled with Archdeacon Martin of Kamptu. He told me details of narrow escape of George D.F.O. Chanda, from man eating tigress. It seized him by back of neck and teeth actually went into the vertebrae of the neck. The khond with him, carrying his gun, did not know how to work safety catch so was unable to shoot the beast. He drove if off however, by hitting it with the gun and made it let go as it was dragging George away. George says that when he was in the tigress' grip he said to himself, 'this is hard luck and I am quite young'. He recovered consciousness and then helped by the khond managed to make the two miles to camp; followed all the way by the tigress which the khond had to frighten as much as he could. The Commissioner C.P. gave the man a silver bangle for his arm engraved with name and reason of the award, also a bullock cart and pair of bullocks and a piece of land. The King has awarded the Albert Medal to him, and well he deserves all this: a brave man.

The Archdeacon also told me a very extraordinary story. The first British Resident at Court of the Bhonstas of Nagpur in 1791 was one named Captain Ramsay. He died of cholera it is said, (but in view of the preservation probably a big dose of arsenic!), and was buried at Kanplis. Some few years ago the grave was in danger of being washed away by the river changing its course, so it was decided to exhume the remains and rebury in cemetery. When the coffin was exposed it was found to have completely crumbled away, but the body was perfectly preserved, and as if only just interred. Hands clasped across chest and face complete. Of course, all went to dust as soon as exposed to the air, but it is most extraordinary that such perfect preservation was maintained in a tropical climate.

17th. Left by Punjab Mail for Quetta and arrived 5 p.m. 19th June. Distance Itarsi to Delhi, 489m.; Delhi to Lahore, 336m.; Lahore to Quetta, 799m. Total 1624 miles.

Chapter 14

TRAVELS IN BALUCHISTAN

DIARY _____
June–July at Quetta. At McMahon Museum met J.C. Bond, Curator, and learnt something of his trade in skins. Some years ago, during Lord Curzon's time, he started trading in egret skins from Mussoorie. The business was put an end to – fortunately for the preservation of these splendid birds, by the passing of the Wild Birds Protection Act. He sent 3000 skins home and got an average price of 14Rs. each for them, having paid 6 Rs. each. Last season he sent home 3000 foxes of one kind and 2400 of another kind. The first fetching 15/- to 20/- and the other variety 30/-; he pays about 5 to 6 rupees for them. He showed me a reddish coloured fox which is not uncommon, but which has not yet been described by Blandford at the British Museum. He told me of a place called Koh-i-Sultan, thirty miles north of the Quetta/Dusdap Railway Line, where, he says, plenty of persian ibex can be got.

JOURNAL _____
Quetta. 1925. It was towards the end of September that the summer heat abated and I set out to visit the Zarghun Range. After two hard days east towards Loi Sar and the Wali Tangi when only a few female markhor were sighted, it was decided to go away for a few days with merely blankets and food, as to scale precipices and do the climbing necessary to get anywhere would be difficult for men with bulky loads. It was very cold at night on the high plateau, while the sun during the day was pleasant. Soon after leaving camp a martin and two yellow wild cats were seen. Down a steep gorge and up a terrific hill we went, there was no sign of markhor, and down up, down up, we went four times repeated to bivouac in the evening after a 'down' near a trickle of water. I shared the same food as the men – unleavened bread of whole meal baked on the red embers of a wood fire and washed down with icy water from the hillside, aided in my case with a tin of sardines.

On 24th September it was up and up to the summit of a high hill overlooking the valley below Loi Sar in which we sighted four urial rams. Having found no markhor we descended two thousand feet to try for a ram. In some places the descent was none too easy for a stiff knee and a short leg, but we eventually arrived within four hundred yards. Wazir Khan and Mahabat kept peeping and peering, and before I could catch them up, the old ram marked down as the one to be shot got up with a warning hiss. In an instant all four would have been speeding out of sight among the scrub covered ravines, but I made a very quick left shoulder shot and my beast was hit and the last away. A good shot that was, near 300yds with the 100yd sight, so Wazir Khan gave an approving look and Mahabat said that if he had my rifle he would never be without meat. However, I was quite sure these two men owned a rifle and that during the four years of the war, they had taken full toll of the good head of game which formerly existed.

Within a few hundred yards the ram was found, and it was surprising he had got so far. He was about nine years old with 27in. horns. Soon a hailstorm with thunder came on and it got very cold, so we made our way as rapidly as possible to a deep tortuous valley far below to bivouac for the night. Kebab of mutton toasted over the embers with a stick were very good, also some more of the unleavened bread. In the tongue-loosening excitement of making lawful the meat of the ram secured by that really fine shot, Wazir Khan said that 'Pathans could not shoot so well and quick as that,' and that 'Mahabat who had shot five hundred animals couldn't have done it.' If he had shot five hundred or even a third of that number, he must have killed off most of the markhor and urial of these hills! All next day we wandered through the hills back to the tent, sustained by mutton in one pocket and salty unleavened bread in the other.

I have now covered a great deal of country where no one has shot for three years – so says Wazir Khan – and where scarcely anyone ever goes as the country is so difficult, and seen only three markhor. Either the animals are in some other place or are practically extinct. Wazir Khan possesses a small-bore H.V. magazine rifle and he and Mahabat both use it. Mahabat can go to practically any place a markhor can go and no animal seen by him is likely to escape. He carried the carcass of the ram and the two coolies their loads of bedding, along the most awful places. Several times the coolies were beaten and Mahabat had to carry their loads for them. Every boulder to the smallest stone is rough, like a file, to the touch and so the foothold is very good, but one has to be careful of loose boulders of which there are many. Many of the juniper trees are very old, some of them must be several hundred years old.

After two days at camp we again set out prepared to bivouac, and working along precipices around Loi Sar found ourselves watching a wide ravine down which ran a fair stream of crystal water. Two markhor were seen to ascend and lie up in a sort of cave. This place was evidently known to the men, and I had probably been led around all these days to fill the purse of Wazir Khan with whom it had been arranged I was to pay two rupees daily for himself, one and a half to Mahabat and twelve annas for each donkey, about nine rupees a day: but on that account there was no rancour in my mind, for what would any of us accomplish in the way of shikar in eastern lands without the skilled and willing aid of the local shikari. On the first of these two days there had been thin ice on the few shallow pools of water on the upland slopes and a keen wind, so it was a relief to lie in the sun with the field glasses and watch the markhor make their effortless way up the precipitous hill.

DIARY _____

25th. A difficult climb up, the men went bare foot, I wore the rupee bazaar shoes. Sat down and made ready the .375. Mahabat went up and disturbed the animals, and the old white one came out. Hit him twice; and then he stood and I shot him through the heart. He fell 500 feet, first drop 300 and then 200, right horn broken off, skull smashed, bad fracture of off fore leg at shoulder, and I had to sew up 11in. of skin. Ribs broken, backbone pulverised at rump, skin a bit cut in places, but all pretty well invisible when sewn up, which I did next day at camp. Got there, about five miles, at dusk. The markhor a fairly old beast, men say twelve years, and that he has often been sought after. At the camp an old man turned up who had been a shikari and said HE had 'sat' for him several times without success!

Measurements – Horns 23in.

Much dangerous and difficult climbing done the whole time I was out, and pretty good at fifty seven years of age for me to be able to do it so easily. I was never in difficulties and always confident, of course I was much slower than the men were. The native chaplis worn by Mahabat were excellent and were infinitely better than my rope soles, which wore out entirely. Ticks very annoying and very numerous all over the hill. Chapattis cooked with cocoflour were excellent and good for three days, always palatable; that and a few eggs was all I had. The men cooked the flesh of the urial on the embers of the fire, that was all right, but carried the bones and lumps of meat covered with ashes in their pockets all day and gnawed them like dogs – (and with aid of penknife I did the same!).

The people are very hardy, as indeed they must be to stand the rigours of the winter months. The principal garment is a coat made of 'pushtar', the inner hair of sheep and goats and is woven into a felt like consistency, making it impervious to wind and so very warm. The sleeves are not much used and hang loose being also used as pockets. The men are all full of prayer, Wazir Khan especially so, putting on the saintly expression suitable to such occasions which is effected by turning down the eyelids and the corners of the mouth in a half smile. They are not very particular as to hallal. There was no life at all in the markhor and no blood flowed.

This short shoot was an expensive one owing to the very high pay given to shikaris, due of course to being so close to Quetta.
Expenses. Say 200/- for thirteen days = Rs.15.6. a day.

This short shoot was an expensive one owing to the very high pay given to shikaris, due of course to being so close to Quetta.

2 Tongas to Urak – 10 miles	10	0	0			
2 " from " -10 "	10	0	0			
Shikari Wazir Khan – 13 days @ 2/-	26	0	0			
" " " tip	9	0	0			
" Mahabat Khan – 11 days @ 2/-	22	0	0			
" " " tip	3	0	0			
5 donkeys @ /12/- for 13 days	48	12	0			
3 men @ 1/- for 13 days	39	0	0			
1 man @ 1/- for 6 days	6	0	0			
1 " to Quetta to get tongas	1	0	0	=174	12	0
Alum and salt for skins	2	0	0	= 2	0	0
Food supplies	19	1	0	= 19	1	0
	Rs.195	13	0			

Say 200/- for 13 days = Rs.15.6. a day.

19th October. Along the Spezand to Dusdap Railway Line for Persian Ibex and

Gazelle. I left Quetta this morning by the 9.46 a.m. train, my servant Sattar Shah with me. My kit comprised bedding, valise, two kiltas of stores, suitcase, tiffin basket, sack of potatoes, onions, and alum and salt for curing skins. No bed, chair, table, such things not necessary at this time of year on these short trips. Very nearly missed the train, which is bi-weekly only, as of the two tongas arranged for only one turned up. I got to the station nearly ten minutes later, and climbed into the train as it was moving off.

The train began late and continued to lose time all the way. The Railway Staff pay was being disbursed at every station and at wayside gangmen's huts also, so we dawdled along all through the night. The first part of the journey was very dusty, more especially as there were mostly downward grades and train went pretty fast. Desert country all the way, barren sandy wastes or low rocky hills. The Railway Stations are all built as defensible posts: some were of brick, some of stone and some of mud only. Walls high, twenty five feet or so, loopholed and provided with flanking fire by means of galleries supported on iron rails jutting out of the wall. These galleries had loopholed sheet iron walls. There were large iron or iron plated doors, and if doors kept shut the people inside would be pretty safe. Got to Mirjawa at 7 p.m. having passed Nok Kundi at 10.30 a.m.

20th. At Mirjawa is the Persian border and there were Persian soldiers on the platform. Khan Said Ali Khan, the Frontier Assistant (Political), met me here to take charge of me. A fine built young man of twenty five or so. Got to Kacha Road at 10.30 p.m., but there is no Railway Staff. My kit was put into what had been the telegraph office, and I slept outside on camp bed provided by K. Said Ali Khan (in future F.A.). A sentry paced up and down all night but I slept well.

21st. It was pretty cold towards morning. After tea and chupattis, started at 9.20 a.m. on camel. I dreaded this ride and with reason. Awful pain from stretching of legs and two miles from camp after going about thirteen miles I had to give in, so dismounted, lifted off, and walked the rest of the way. Saw eight seesee in an open plain, no other sign of life except a few larks and shrikes and linnets. Got to Kacha Thana at 10 o'clock, and found many buildings and a fort. This was formerly the headquarters of General Dyer (1916). On a rock is carved in big letters – 106 – this being the 106th Hazzars Pioneers. The Levy guard of some thirty men was turned out to meet us.

22nd. Obviously no use trying for ibex from this inhabited place, so am off this morning to a place ten miles away. This place well shot over by all the local people and every man, every goat herd, in this country carries a rifle. Very cloudy since yesterday; when I ask if it is likely to rain I am told, as usual in these Muhammadan countries, that 'God knows and it will rain if he wishes it'! I am told Baluchis always shoot males because they are the bigger animals and give more meat, not because the killing of females would reduce the stock: F.A. tells me this. Riding camel to camp today I sat sideways and so did not have to clench my teeth all the way.

Went in direction east by south of Kirtaka and searched a number of valleys. Saw nothing and no tracks and as we were bound to see tracks after the rain I am pretty sure there are VERY few ibex left in these hills. The three men with me, Duff Isa Khan, Gabey Khan, Kundil Khan, all of them shikaris, tell me there are now no big ibex hereabouts. All agree that on the Koh-i-Tuftan hills there are plenty of ibex: but F.A. told me it wouldn't be possible to go there – political people would object owing to the recent disturbance between Persians and Baluchis. If I can get nothing here I must try and go there and if that can't be managed then to Ras Koh, which is south of the line, somewhere near Dalbandin.

24th. Left at 7 o/c, which is now day-break, to go on camel to a hill some five miles away. After about half an hour, Gabey spotted a white buck about 1000yds off on the further slope. Horns seemed about 30in., four females with him. Watched them over a rise and into a valley between high black rocks. A long and very steep climb down, along a river bed, and then a long climb up to top of the ravine. The animals were a long way down, so made a quick descent to get round the hill as they were seen crossing over far below. Eventually about 1 o/c, arrived at a small ridge to find the buck standing on a col at about 350yds. Took a lying down shot and saw dust fly just short of him. Gabey said I went over him and that the dust was caused by his forefeet as he turned to flee; I don't think so, anyway he wasn't hit, as Gabey went off to see and followed his tracks for some way. On way home at head of the big valley we found his tracks going fast so he was unhurt.

Immediately after the shot the females came below us, all going fast. Isa Khan began to loose off contents of his magazine and wounded three or four with solid .303 bullets, a sad business. I waited my chance and shot the biggest female at two hundred yards, when the animals came in sight again. Isa Khan, we found, had hit her in the stomach; clean entry and exit wounds, and she would have gone miles and died days later. He certainly wounded two which got away. These people always lose their heads in sight of game with weapons in their hands. I had told him I wanted ONE female for the Museum. He said he fired because he thought I might not get a chance! These people very good about hallal and Isa Khan made a VERY small cut which won't show at all when sewn up. I will stay in tomorrow and see to skin and go out for ibex day after, Monday 26th and return to Kacha Thana on Tuesday. No use staying out here longer than that.

25th. I wrote to F.A. and said I seriously thought of Koh-i-Tuftan. He writes that apart from it being politically undesirable, owing to Persians not yet having settled their troubles with the Baluchis, the foot of the mountain is 6000ft. and forty miles from Mirjawa, and at this season shikar on the mountain would be very difficult. I can realise that. A lot of rains and thunderstorms about now and it would be exceedingly cold: so I must go no doubt to Ras Koh, from Padang Road.

On 23rd I saw a fine sheet of water in the plain over the Afghan border. It looked very blue and not far off. Overflow from the Helmand River says Isa Khan, and he is right according to the map: any number of wild fowl and water birds he says. It is a long way from the foot of these hills, he says forty miles, many lovely views today owing to the clear air. I have made a very good job of the skin of the poor innocent she ibex. Threatening of rain and some small showers all day, thunder all around. Gabey Khan told me how he got shot six months ago, and showed me the entry and exit of the bullet, a .303 solid, fortunately for him. It entered about the anterior superior iliac spine and came out centre of buttock, too low for spleen and intestines and seems to have only passed through bone and flesh. He still walks lame and complains of muscular pains in leg. Seems a Baluch didn't challenge him and just fired straight away! He is a very good ibex shikari, spots animals a long way off and good at stalk and patient. Probably very deadly when himself on shikar with a small bore rifle. There are many like him about the country and game must be diminishing very fast.

Saw many fine tamarisk trees in the deep nalas and some very tall grass, like elephant grass of the Terai. All this country wants is plenty of water and everything would grow luxuriantly. Isa Khan says Koh-i-Tuftan is an active volcano in as much as it smokes all the year round; says lots of sulphur and alum up at the top and that the mountain is always very cold. He says no end of ibex there as Persians don't shikar much and no Baluch people very near the hill. A month on the mountain would be very pleasant indeed, but time to go would be August or September; too cold after that. Sattar Shah was stung by a scorpion a couple of nights ago. I scraped the place

1

2

3

CHAPTER
14

1
View across Kacha Thana,
Baluchistan, 1925

2
Riding and pack camels,
Baluchistan

3
A yourt (Baluchi camp) in
Baluchistan desert, 1925

4
Photograph showing Burton's
position (·) from which he
shot a Markhor at (x). Quetta,
29 September 1925

5
Baluchi skikaris of the Ras
Khor

5

with penknife and he said that eased the pain a bit. He didn't make much fuss about it and was all right six hours later.

28th. Duffadur Isa Khan pleased with results of two strong pills I gave him a couple of days ago; also with the Genaspirin which took away his headache. Have now had to give phenacetin to Naik of the Guard who has fever. Probably Kacha Thana a feverish place as there are mosquitoes there and they have become malaria carrying; no doubt owing to the war as has been the case in so many other places. Clouds again yesterday and some rain in the night. I have a cold now, been coming on for several days. One gets very hot climbing hills and then has to sit at the top and survey the valleys for game, so it is likely that one will not escape colds and chills. Took 5 Genaspirin and 10 quinine and will stay in tomorrow.

30th. Still heavy mist at daylight and struck camp. Soon the effort of sun to dispel the mists proved futile and one couldn't see fifty yards so we made for the road and waited for the camels. The road is the old trade route Nushki to Rabat and telephone line runs along it from Kacha Thana to Sainduk. Left Kirtaka at 11 and got to Kacha Thana at 2 p.m. Rain and mist all the way. F.A. and Isa Khan told me of the fate which overtook twenty two Afridi deserters from a Punjab Regiment during the war. They deserted at Sainduk taking camels and water with them thinking they would have no difficulty in crossing the desert into Afghan territory. They wandered about and lost their way and nineteen died of thirst. Three tied themselves on to camels and these camels took them through the desert and they escaped. The fate of the party was known by some of the other camels returning to Sainduk and Levy men tracked the party up and found them all and removed all the rifles and equipment.

I asked F.A. what tip I should give Isa Khan and the other two men and he was very positive that nothing should be given. I wish I hadn't asked him and just given 10 + 5 + 5; as that would have been more satisfactory and cheaper as I shall have to send presents from Quetta which will probably cost more.

31st. Got to Kacha Road at 11.30, and waited for the train. Stopped it and got in and reached Dalbandin at 12 midnight. Dalbandin has about 1200 inhabitants. Height 2980ft., the country is all desert like, sand and sandhills, patches of melons here and there. Very little wildlife, a hawk, a couple of ravens, and tracks of rats in the sand. Much warmer than at Kacha of course, temperature runs to 118°.

5th November. R.W.B. fifty seven today. Left Dalbandin by 2 a.m. train and arrived at Yadgar Station at 3.40 a.m., no station staff just like Kacha Road. There was a heavy thunderstorm all over the country and train due to leave Dalbandin at 0.8 was over an hour late. Arnold, the Railway S.D.O., told me that quite possibly the line would be washed away in places as it gets very easily damaged. At Yadgar was met by the Levy Duffadur from Padang Road with two of his men, also the local Lamburdar. They had two riding camels and two pack camels for me. As the two tents lent by the Tahsildar had heavy poles the two loading camels were a bit too few, but about ten miles from the station we came to an encampment and got another camel for the rest of the way. Got to sleep at Yadgar inside the fortified Station, having been provided with a large charpoy by the people there.

Up at 6 a.m. and packed and off at 7.45. Took a photo of the black felt 'yourt' where we got the camel. These desert nomads live in a most primative style and are mostly very poor, camels and goats their only property. Got to a place in the hills, in bed of a hard rocky stream, at about 10 o/c and waited for the camels which arrived five hours later: distance about fifteen miles. All the way from the station the Duffadur was telling me of the generous amount in rupees disbursed by various sportsmen, and I soon realised that he was as expert as Wazir Khan of Zarghun in the business of extracting as much money as possible from the Sahib. He said the camping place would be a long way up the nala and camels couldn't go and donkeys would be necessary, and said the camels would wait at this place until we returned. This was obviously rupees for him, keeping camels idle at a rupee a day for an indefinite time, so I insisted on discharging them. Paid 12as. for the camels picked up on the way and left the other two unpaid with orders to come to same place on 12th.

The shrubs on these hills almost as universally thorny as those on Zarghun which is saying a good deal. At Kacha the shrubs were all aromatic, and thorny ones in the minority. When jumping off a rock I almost landed on a sun-basking cobra, a tap on the tail as it glided off caused a raising of the hood. The people of Ras Koh villages are very primitive: their dwellings the merest shelters. The women are not in any way 'purdah' and wear long red dressing gowns as an outer garment, and pyjama trousers underneath. They must eke out a very hard life of it and I am not surprised at their having killed off most of the ibex for their cooking pots.

7th. Off at day-break and up hills towards the highest part of Ras Khor. Saw nothing. The rain of 4th evening had washed the hillsides clean of all old tracks so new tracks should have been easily visible. Very few ibex left on these hills, twenty or even fifteen years ago there were many animals. No use staying here and I settled to strike camp and arranged for the camels to come to the nala tomorrow. There were further attempts on the part of the Duffadur to make me pay cash. Truly a cunning rascal. I paid 5as. a trip for each donkey, only a distance of three miles, and the Duffadur wanted me to pay 12as. each way! Took photo of three of the donkeys and their loads and the men.

On way back to camp I passed a water hole where a goat man and his women folk were. He was a very handsome, light coloured, biblical looking man. Light eyes, upper lip shaven in the middle like all orthodox Muhammadans, so that their prayers shall go straight to heaven unsoiled by the moustache.

On the 9th the camels appeared at camp. These were the camels which the Duffadur had sworn could not be found again if discharged. There were constant attempts on the part of the Duffadur to relieve Burton of cash, which he – since he travelled to a tight budget – was skilled at resisting. Five rupees was requested to buy a goat for a sacrifice to the local saint at one village, with which Burton complied, but he gave the money direct to the Lamburdar since he considered the Duffadur could not be trusted. In the daytime the desert sand was heated by the burning sun, but at night it was so cold that thin ice formed on the water. On 11th, Burton left Kacha Thana and made his way to the station at Padang Road. After tips to all the men the trip worked out rather expensive at Rs.60 for seven days.

JOURNAL ————————————————————————————————

With a fifteen mile camel ride over the desert, the trip came to an end, and also my first and last Baluchistan shikar. In all that ibex country I had found no ibex worth shooting, and indeed it was plain that but a few more years would see the total extinction of most of the few remaining animals. The time is now not far distant when all unpreserved game animals, more especially those in the border lands of the Indian Empire will be as extinct as the Dodo, and unless the Indian Ministers of the New Constitution speedily take the matter in hand, the same will be the fate of a number of species within the Empire itself.

DIARY

12–18 November. Got to Quetta at 3.30 p.m. Sent present of a warm jersey to each of the three men at Kacha plus fifty fever pills for the Duffadur. Sent F.A. two books, one on India 1723/24 and one 'The Wealth of Nations', as he leans strongly to Swaraj.

Chapter 15

A SUDDEN END TO JUNGLE SHIKAR

DIARY
We left Quetta on 11th December and arrived at Lahore the following evening. We stayed with Wardrops for the night. Mrs. Wardrop, her sister Miss Norton, and Capt. Mason, (their brother is the Maj. Norton who climbed Everest). Left Lahore on 13th and reached Itarsi 2.20 a.m. on 15th; put up at D.B. and had a very strenuous three days packing and sorting kit, on to Harda on 18th. We started out next day 7 a.m., five carts for kit, one cart for wife; good cart road all the way. At Kayagam, we saw a good duck tank, but as the Patel has a gun they don't have much peace. A great many coots on the open water, possibly a good many duck in the reeds. The road left the village and went on through small jungle to cross the Anjan River a mile further on. Made our way to river bank near an old brick kiln and stayed for the night without pitching tents.

20th December. Off early to go to village on right bank of Anjan river and camp there as it is central for Joga and Bainswara jungles. A lot of peafowl near camp. A mugger in the river opposite the tents. On the other side is Government forests. Camp very comfortable and sufficient shade for this time of year. Crossed the river in a crazy dug-out. Went on to Sontalai and posted letters etc. Was well received here and given a good meal of chupattis by the muktana (a baniah) of owner of the village. Saw sambur and four-horn on the way home. A mugger in the river opposite the tents. Fine old red sandstone fort on an island in the Narbada. Ferry boat plying also small dug-outs. Water deep, and fairly swift current. A splendid banyan tree for shade and decided to move camp here.

24th. Pitched camp at Joga. Lovely place, couldn't want a better site. In afternoon shot a doe antelope (blackbuck) close to camp; badly wanted, to make the camp happy and also for Xmas dinner. A lot of peafowl and grey partridge about, so we won't be short of food for the larder. Soon after return to camp, a man from the nearby village brought news of a cow having been seized at dawn and the tiger or panther frightened off by him rushing out with a lighted branch. Found cow's nose much torn and assailant a panther without doubt. A tiger would have killed the cow instantly.

25th. Christmas Day. Went with shikari and two coolies to find a place to tie up. Saw two day old tracks of tigress along the river bank, and found an excellent jamun tree to tie up in. A dhimar marriage takes place in the village tomorrow, hence much tomtomming and row going on. A lot of timber coming across the Narbada all day. Country opposite belongs to Indore. Shikari tells me there is a tiger in the Indore forest which stops carts and kills the bullocks.

A kill by tiger on 28th was reported by the shikari who failed to cover the carcass, much to Burton's exasperation. A thick cover of branches was essential to prevent the crows from exposing the carcass to the ever watchful and persistent vultures. He writes in his diary – 'sent them back at once to cover thickly with branches and stones on top to prevent crows uncovering and so calling up the vultures. Hopeless ass, Sital, he knew such foolishness lost me a tiger in February last.' The tiger came to the kill. Burton fired and missed and sent the tiger leaping away towards the river. He was having trouble with his new .470 gun, and also with the batteries for his electric light apparatus. The new acetylene lamp which he had ordered from Bombay was useless as it threw a column of light up into the tree and made a terrible glare reflected from the leaves and branches. He notes: 'Never used this lamp, great waste of Rs.45 and more. My own apparatus, if I can get sufficiently strong battery, is as good as any I have seen and far less trouble.'

Several days were spent at this camp. The people were not exactly helpful and charges were high. Coolies 8as. a day and carts 2/- a day which came to a total of 30/- for the transport alone. Every day tiger tracks were seen in the jungle, and on 11th January a tigress killed a boda down by the river. Having arranged a machan in a suitable tree, Burton sat up the next day. Later in the evening he heard a crunching noise and looking up saw the tigress had already settled down to eat. The river was noisy, and he hadn't heard her approach. Sighting from his left eye, as his right eye was giving him trouble, he fired at the centre of her shoulder and she fell and died instantly. A boat was used to take the tigress back to camp, and Burton did the skinning himself as the men didn't appear to know how. He judged the tigress to be about twenty years old, 'an ancient beast', and her teeth were blunt and broken.

There were no further kills or signs of tiger and Burton decided to move camp on 19th back across the Anjan river to Jhangira. He stopped here for several days, searching the jungle for tracks, a few pigeon and peafowl and also a blackbuck were shot for the pot, and on 26th January moved on to Bainswara. There was much tree felling in the jungle, and no point in staying, so he moved on to Joga.

DIARY _____

The two ferry boats at Joga belong to Indore State and the ferrying fees are farmed out to a Contractor, a Punjabi, as the villagers don't care to deposit the 200/- security asked for. The fees are small: a loaded cart 2as. and if with bullocks 3as., each person one pie. The contract is sold now for 400/- and the man is said to make a profit of 250/- or so.

Forgot to note that again langurs mistake Simba for a panther. The little hanumans never make such a mistake or deceive one by uttering the 'double knock' note except at tiger or panther. Old shikari man recognises this to be so, as have other jungle men I have asked about it. Skies now clearing, moon not much use after next two days. The tiger the other day, when he killed the boda, spotted it from out towards the river and swam across a lagoon of water to stalk and kill.

DIARY _____

1926. 10th January. Went up river beyond Saliakheri to Mural village. Much open country and a fair amount of small game there. Just walking along saw peafowl, partridge, quail, sandgrouse, green pigeon: much thorny jungle, ber trees now ripening.

11th. Kill by tigress at Bariaghat. Of course the FIRST day I have not gone to see that tie up! Probably would have got her on the kill as I stalk it under the sandy bank at fifteen yards. Very good tree for machan, but has to be thickly screened from the side towards the hill as it is rather close to ground there. Much noise from river so I can't be heard. Might be detected by smell, but not likely as tigers have very little sense of smell. Would have liked to be higher up, but can't be managed and other available trees very bare of leaves.

12th. Went to machan at 12.30, and settled down at 2.30. River very noisy and I heard no bone crunching or tugging at kill. At a little after 4, thought I heard some noise at kill so looked through peephole and found tigress settling down to eat! She must have been there five minutes or more. Let her get up to tug at kill but first had a look at her, left eye along sights. Then when she got on forelegs to pull and gave a good chance, fired at centre of shoulder. She fell over to the shot and died almost instantly, just a few gasps and a twitching of tail. Sounded horn, but it wasn't heard, so settled down for the night. At 5.30 heard 'wuff' to my front and later, a few minutes later, a growl somewhere behind me. Think it must have been a tiger but found no tracks, may have been a panther; anyway it didn't turn up again.

Men came at 7 o/c, shot not heard at camp. Best to take tigress down to camp by boat. Had to do all the skinning myself. Sital no use and also had to have his food. Didn't finish everything until sundown. Skin nicely stretched and should turn out well; very well marked and quite long fur but just beginning to put off winter coat. An ancient beast, may be twenty years, teeth yellow and blunt, left lower canine tooth broken; eyes very filmy and looked as if getting blind.

Measurements	Curves: body	5ft.7in.	tail 2ft.8in.	total	8ft.3in.
	pegs: "	5ft.4in.	" 2ft.8in.	"	8ft.

Weight – 240 lbs.

Decided to move to Jhangira on 19th and from there to Bainswara on 26th. Saw Chumilal shikari, man with warty nose and he is, I should think, more of a shikari than any I have yet seen this trip; has a gaspipe gun. He was quite frank and said no use staying at Bainswara as no tiger near there for two months past owing to hundreds of men cutting wood on islands in the river, which used always to hold tiger. Now this felling of timber will go on for two years more. Decided to move on to Joga and got there 6 p.m., sixteen miles for carts, fourteen for me as I went along river bank and tied up a boda at old place near jamun tree. Bhagwan met me at Joga and told me tiger was back here two days after we left! Will sleep in machan at Bariaghat in hopes of tiger coming along. Took photo of camp.

There were no more kills by tiger or panther and on 7th February Burton left Joga with five carts to go the sixteen miles to Kayagam, remarking that it was a good cart road except for the first six miles as far as Ooah! which were very stony. The next day they moved on seven miles to Harda and there caught the Calcutta Mail to Itarsi. Extra luggage and tickets cost altogether Rs.33 and Burton, who had limited funds, remarks rather anxiously 'All this moving runs away with a lot of money.' From Itarsi, his wife left by train for the Hill Station of Pachmarhi, while Burton returned to Betul for more shikar in the Central Provinces jungle.

DIARY _____

11th February. Arrived Betul 4.57. Found tahsil chaprassi and two bullock carts ready waiting. Packed carts up for an early start next day and slept in the station waiting room.

12th. Up at 5 a.m. and off at dawn. Walked to Tapti River, eleven miles and waited for carts which didn't turn up until 3 p.m. Axle broke twice, same cart each time and cart had to be loaded and unloaded and so delayed two hours. Had breakfast under big banyan tree on the left bank, and walked on to Jhallon D.B., ten miles, twenty one in all, getting there an hour before dark. Got chokidar to cook me dhal and rice, cost one rupee six pies for two meals! and felt well fed. Carts came in at 8 o/c, had a cup of cocoa and so to sleep, which I really needed after four bad nights: noise of Railway Station kept me awake after the silence of jungle life.

There is now a motor bus service Betul to Bhainsdehi and back. Each passenger Rs.2 and 15 seers luggage free and 2/- a maund for luggage. So I will go by bus on return and send carts ahead. Forgot to pay the D.B. charges when leaving, so sent cash by M.O. to the chokidar. I had entered up the book and put 'paid' against 1/8, and gave 8as. tip to chokidar and forgot to pay him the 1/8, and he, poor ass, said nothing. He must have thought a lot after I left!

14th. At D.B. Bhainsdehi. 2500ft. and nice and cool. Walked to Jarida, fourteen miles, country very pleasing, open spaces, forest, park-like land, waving crops in the hollows. Stayed one day, then on to Rajadeo.

17th. Walked to Rajadeo by the short cut, saw nothing and no tracks. Carts turned up shortly after I arrived. In afternoon went down river and tied up machan chair in tree a few yards from where I tied it last year. Hope for a kill before 1st March so as to give me benefit of moon which is full on 28th February. Put out another boda along the Raipur Road nala. Only these two places now available as wood cutters to west and bamboo cutters all over the hills east of river and in Chopi Kua valley.

19th. On the way back to camp heard a stick crack and getting near heard a loud puffing and snorting and thought may be a pig or a bear. There was a three foot bank to left of road and a fifteen foot steep drop on the other side. I picked up a stone and got on to the bank and found myself looking into the upturned face of a bull bison! He was about twenty feet from me. I looked in astonishment and as the snorts didn't diminish threw the stone at him. It missed his nose, a bad shot. He didn't budge and as I didn't want the complication of having to shoot him in self defence I got back into the road and went on towards the tie up. On way back, at same place, but further in the jungle, more loud snorts: but we didn't chance his coming any nearer and went quickly on. He was jet black, a young bull, five or six years by his horns, which seemed about 30 in. in length and fairly massive. A great hulk of a brute he was.

20th. Evening. Went up hills to north and did a fairly long round, leaves too noisy, and hopeless to try and find sambur in such noisy jungle. Tracks of panther along the road to camp. In a few days now jungles will be quiet for five days as all work stops during the Holi. Find that the villagers will not now take two and four anna silver coin – only rupees and nickel; so must send my two and four anna silver to Treasury to be changed.

1st March. No kill: up at dawn and went to Chopi Kua Valley by the main road way and then over the hills. Shot a peafowl for the larder. Tracks of a small bear on the main road. Yesterday at midday a number of people turned up from Kamida village. Eleven women and about fifteen men and boys. They arrived singing and banging drums and had sprigs of green leaves stuck in their puggries. The object of the visit was to extract 'baksheesh' for the Holi Festival: blackmail it is, as one has to pay up and look pleasant. The woman danced in quite a well trained manner and some of them carried peacocks feathers in their hands. A photo of the group may prove successful, I hope so. Five rupees as 'baksheesh' was not enthusiastically received and it was represented that that was for the men and now the women want something! So another two rupees was given, seven in all.

6th. I heard the staccato cries of kakur up the hill indicating the presence of the panther. Later, I heard his quiet footfall on the leaves of the road and then a sambur close by called at him. He replied with two or three grunts and came to the kill very soon after. Pitch dark: after a few minutes I turned on the light. He didn't take any notice and went on eating. Took the shot right shoulder and left eye, as I found I couldn't see well with right eye which is very bad in bad light. He was instantly slain. Out of machan by 9 o/c having called the men up from camp on my bugle, then skinned him as specimen for the Museum. A fine male panther: oldish beast; teeth a bit yellow and some of the small teeth in upper jaw worn down level with gums.

Measurements	body	tail	total
pegs:	4ft.3in.	2ft.9in.	7ft.
curves:	4ft.6in.	2ft.9in.	7ft.3in.

Weight – 120 lbs.

Mounted on pedestal in Prince of Wales Museum, Bombay. Took leg bones, but by mistake they were boiled. However, put in place they should give the necessary guide as to limbs.

About dusk a tremendous row of tomtomming down below and I almost gave up as hopeless: then the row ceased. It was the people of Kuluribi having heard of success of Kamida in extracting seven rupees from me on account of Holi, making a similar effort on their own account. They were wanting to come to me at machan but Abdul stopped them telling them to come again in the morning. This they did but they didn't get any rupees!

7th. Moved camp to Biba. A thunderstorm and fair amount of rain. Selected tree for machan, one which I couldn't use last year as it was infested by red ants, now it is free of them. Shot a green pigeon with .22 for larder. There is now some colour in the forests: erythrina in flower, also the few dhak trees that there are, and several other flowering trees and shrubs. Must be well hidden for this cunning tigress. On way out shot a kakur at sixty yards, male, weight 64lbs, one horn broken. I see Col. A.E.Ward says not much difference in colour of sexes, but I have always noticed the male to be much darker, same with four-horn. On way back saw three four-horn feeding in the open. Nice to see animals again. Rajadeo too noisy, here there are several roads and paths to walk quietly on.

12th. A flying squirrel in my tree this evening and early morning, and making same cry as the animal I saw at Rajadeo on 23/24, so that also was Pteromys Oral – the Large Brown Flying Squirrel, and not civet cat as I thought it must be. About 4 a.m. turned on light and saw head and shoulders of a tigress! She had the boda's neck in her jaws and was standing like a statue waiting for poor boda's struggles to cease. The opportunity was splendid. Tigress in act of killing and not minding the light. Foresight light now very dim, just a speck, foolishly never thought of the bulb carrier having got pushed out of place, and jumped to conclusion that the battery was giving out. Oh! that I had just felt towards the muzzle and put it right. That neglect cost me the tigress. At the report the tigress dashed away, back the way she must have come and across the nala. Dawn up soon after, and when the men came, found a splintered rock which gave the alignment of bullet low, under her chest, JUST under it looked like.

15th. I was settled in machan by 4.30 and not in much hope of tigress return. After three hours I heard the well known footstep on the leaves of the road just under me! He waited about three minutes and then went to the kill. I began to make ready and then removed khaki handkerchief over the loophole and waited. He had been crunching bones and let the gas escape out of the stomach, which it did with a loud hiss and must have given him a very bad smell under his nose. The boda very putrid and swarming with flies and horrible to see and smell. Filthy beasts these felines and a marvel that anyone ever wounded by them fails to die of blood poisoning. He then seized the boda and seemed likely to pull it wrong way from my point of view, which was to get a sideways shot. So I turned on the light and aimed to hit him behind top of left shoulder blade. To the shot he grunted and putting on the light I saw him all legs in air and completely knocked out: before I could get a second shot in he was up and out of the circle of light. I heard him stumbling among leaves not far in front of me and knew he was hit, and then all was quiet.

Half an hour after the shot, a hyaena turned up and had a great feed. Pulled out the stomach and removed it and returned for the tasty! morsel and had some bones and came again several times in the night. At 2 a.m. I heard bullock bells in the distance and a cartman singing and feared he would come along and disturb the tiger, possibly to damage of man and bullocks!, but fortunately he turned off somewhere. About 4 a.m. I heard what sounded like a dying 'cat call' and rejoiced as it meant no charge by enraged T.P. In the morning I searched all around within fifty yards and did not find him or any blood marks. There would be no tracks owing to leaves. Then made a cast up the nala opposite and a hundred yards up it found tiger lying dead.

I had looked all over the open space without seeing him and suddenly he 'jumped into view' and I realised once more how easy it is to look for these beasts and not SEE them. Lucky he wasn't able to attack. He would possibly have got me. A fine big tiger, feet small for his size. A regular hill game killer.

I went to camp with one man to send bullock cart and left the other three men to dismantle machan chair. Was tired after four nights out of camp and had a long day's skinning in front of me. Did all the skinning myself and finished skinning and pegging out at nearly 6 p.m. Tiger in splendid condition; some fat, not very much; fine ruff to his head and good coat.

Measurements

Length: curves: body 6ft.6in. tail 3ft. total 9ft.6in.
   "   pegs: " 6ft.1in. " 3ft. " 9ft.1in.

Gave rewards to men; Tota the best cooly, 3/-, and five others including water cooly and boda boy 2/- each = 13/-. Abdul looked expectant but I don't see why one should tip one's well paid servant, working in camp, every time one shoots a tiger or panther.

17th. In evening went to Khari village. The village of the usual style; a long straight street with houses, mostly detached from one another, on either side, the gawalas house at west end of village. Patel had his bed swung on chains on his verandah and it looked very comfy!

18th. Out soon after dawn and went east along the upper road to Chobita where tiger killed. Selected a fine tree for machan bed and will tie up there for rest of time here. Back along the river and so to camp. On getting back find kill to west and most likely by the tigress which I missed so badly on night of 12th. Perhaps I am to have another chance. *Fortune does not often forgive such failures to seize the opportunity given in the first instance.

19th March. 'There's many a slip' is a very true saying: and also 'It might have been worse': and how truly I wrote yesterday as at *!

My machan was a very solid one in a very solid tree, and bamboos ready all round on which to fix fresh screening branches. I had three men with me, two cutting branches, and the third, Tota, at the foot of the tree sending the branches up to me by the rope I let down to him. I always like to work myself and not sit looking at men doing the work contrary to my ideas. I had placed most of the branches in position when the bamboo on which I was placing a branch suddenly gave way. I crashed through the screen and the resistance of the branches kept my head and shoulders up a bit. This was fortunate as had I reached the ground head first, the smash would have been far worse. I reached the ground sideways, at full length, landing on my right side. The fall was about eighteen feet and the nala was covered with granite boulders. Almost the whole weight of the fall was sustained by my right thigh, but my right wrist came in for some of it. My injuries were at once apparent to me, as my right foot was lying across my left leg at a right angle, and my wrist very obviously dislocated. I at once got two coolies to pull on to my leg to get the bone into proper position, and tried hard to reduce the dislocation of my wrist by putting one man to pull at my shoulder, I also helping him by pulling my arm, while the two other men, Dadu and Tota, held on to my hand. Our united efforts made no impression and I had to give up the attempt. I was pretty sure there was a fracture at the wrist also.

I then sent one man to the village to get help, and began to arrange to splint myself. I had the machan dismantled and saw to collecting together of all my odds and ends and unloaded rifle. I had a bough cut with a fork at end of it to use as a Liston splint for my thigh, padding it with a blanket. Using the puggries of the coolies and one of my putties the splint was bound on to me securely. Dadu's puggrie was round my chest and the aroma of it – perspiration and general 'aroma de Dadu' – was somewhat overpowering. After the splint had been fixed I got a thick bamboo and had it split in two. This, padded with a pillow case and bandaged to my arm and hand, with the other puttie made an excellent splint. When lying on the machan bed I lashed my hand to the carrying pole and so kept up extension on the wrist until I got to hospital at Nagpur. This kept the wrist in quite good shape and I had almost no pain with it. I then had my left leg tied to the other leg in two places and set to work to show the people how to make a dooly out of my machan bed. As soon as it was ready I was lifted on to it and my left leg released. We then set off to camp, about a mile and a quarter, maybe less, leaving Mrs. Tom Puss the free dinner I had given to her, and doubtless she had a good meal.

We got to the forest hut about half an hour before dark, and I had my guns and rifles properly oiled and put away. Carts had to be procured and carriers arranged for and all my kit had to be packed and the men to have their food. All this took time; a violent storm, mostly wind and dust, came up and delayed things for a bit. At day-break we got to the Bhainsdehi Dispensary. The coolies had never done any carrying of this kind before, but they brought me through quite quickly without a single jar or jolt, and were happy at receiving Rs.1/8 each. The passenger motor lorry plying between Bhainsdehi and Betul was sent for and after folding back the seats on either side, my machan bed could be run in without any alteration or movement. The Tahsildar provided tea and biscuits and another Indian Official wrote some necessary letters at my dictation.

My two carts with my kit arrived at 7.30 a.m. I took my suitcase and tiffin basket with me and the lorry took me to the Civil Hospital Betul, thirty five miles, by 10.30 a.m. There Col. Watts, the Civil Surgeon strongly advised me not to go to St. George's Hospital Bombay, as I was intending to do, but to save delay and movement by going on in the lorry one hundred and six miles to Nagpur, where there is X-ray apparatus, skilful surgeon, trained nurses, and all the necessary appliances. He gave me an Assistant Surgeon, Dr. Shandal, to accompany me. We started at 12 noon and got to the Mayo Hospital at Nagpur at 7.30. The road was bad and bumpy in many places so we could not go very fast. The Assistant Surgeon gave me a morphia injection, not because of pain exactly, but to make me feel the jolts less and so enable the car to go a bit faster. My improvised splint was left for the night as it was quite comfortable, but my arm splint was changed.

I went a second night without sleep and next morning to the X-ray room and was there chloroformed, photographed, and splinted. On coming to I found to my great disgust that I had been fitted with a long Liston splint. I could feel it was of no use and it very soon gave me great discomfort. It seemed they had not got a Hodgins sling large enough for my thigh and one had to be made. I had to wait until the 22nd for this and was then again chloroformed and put into the Hodgins sling. This proved unsatisfactory on an ordinary bed, so on the 24th I was chloroformed (at my request!) and moved to a fracture bed. The Matron had to struggle hard with the Doctors to get this done and they were havering over it from 9 a.m. to 3 p.m! The Doctors didn't know much about the fitting of the sling and the very competent Matron did most of the work. Lucky indeed for me as I feel sure the excellent result obtained could never have been had if the Doctors had been left to their own devices.

The fracture is in same position as that of left leg in 1903. It was not possible for me to be taken to the X-ray room again and enquiries all over India failed to find any portable X-ray apparatus! All that could be done was to keep quiet and remain as cool as possible under the electric fans and hope for the best. The X-ray of hand showed a fracture at the head, involving the joint. It was put up in a special splint and seemed all right. Once on the fracture bed and properly fixed in the Hodgins sling I felt more hopeful. The Doctors seemed to do nothing but talk and each seemed to lean on the other and Col. Tarr seemed to leave everything to them, and again I say I owe my good join up to the Matron (Mrs. N.H.G. Puttick). I had an enormous bruise all along my leg and side. That of 1924, when I fell in Kashmir, and broke my left thigh was a big one, but nothing like this.

Chloroform was very well administered and I never had it better given. For the first six weeks I slept very badly, seldom more than an hour at a time. The knee was very stiff and took a long time to bend. The massage and bending was done by the Matron. Two goes of chloroform hastened matters, but it was not until 7th July that knee became almost normal as to bend, but I shall have to keep it on the move for some time yet. Hand splint was removed on 10th April and massage commenced. By 7th July wrist was stronger, but fingers still very stiff and obstinate. Movement is complicated by gouty rheumatism. Thigh bone is quite straight and feels strong, but I am running no risk of bending it and go about on crutches. I have much pain in back muscles, but that will get better in time.

We left Hospital on 4th July 1926 and are now staying with Mr. and Mrs. F.W.A. Prideaux. I was 106 days in the Hospital. Several people were very kind in coming to see me. Hospital charges were low. Rent of room 2/- a day; electric light and fan 2/- a day; and 2/- rent for wife occupying a bed. We made our own arrangements for food. On the 14th June, F.H.G.R. Gentle I.F.S. sylviculturist, came in with a wound in face caused by blow back of bolt of a .280 Ross Rifle. His injury much the same, though not so extensive as that of my face from the bear in 1913. I shall be interested to know final result. COL. TARR EXPECTS HIS ANTRUM TO HEAL UP! I doubt if it will close as there was a hole into it as big as end of one's thumb; so Khisty who operated told me. His eye ball damaged but that will probably clear up.

Soon after leaving the Hospital, Burton learned that the Matron had been taken seriously ill. He and his wife visited her before leaving for England, and gave her as a present two gold mounted tiger bone brooches, also some money to spend on a holiday for herself and her daughter. They heard later that she was never able to take advantage of the holiday and had died soon after they left Bombay.

DIARY

We left Bombay in P & O *Rajputana* on 17th July; (Note: *Rajputana* was torpedoed in Atlantic 1941) and disembarked at Tilbury on Thursday, 5th August, being met at Docks by Graham Malcolm, Tiny's husband, now stationed at Chatham, and then on to St. Pancras, and out to Gillingham on 9th. The two things which up to the present have struck me most are the dustless motor roads and motor bus services all over the country, and the disgusting state of the streets and countryside covered with loose paper etc., the refuse of the people eating their meals during holiday outings. The whole country is spoilt by this untidy habit: let us hope a future generation will have better manners.

Much of their time in England was spent visiting relations and friends and seeing as much of the country as possible. One of their close friends, Mrs. Fellowes, whom they hadn't seen since the days at Satara and Mahabupura, took them on a motor tour through Kent, Sussex and Surrey. A beautiful and impressive contrast to the Indian scenery they were accustomed to. On 16th August they went to stay with their daughter Phyllis at Thetford.

Their friends and relations were scattered widely in different parts of the country, from Jersey in the Channel Islands to Cumberland, from Cheltenham to Norfolk. In September he visited Oxford to stay with Frank Marshall and his wife Louise, (the widow of his brother Aubrey), and met also her daughter Ellen who was born in 1905 after Aubrey's death.

In October 1926, he returned to London and into the King Edward VII Hospital for Officers to have his wrist manipulated under gas and massage, and then moved to Gillingham for several months. In March 1927 they went to Cheltenham to see his brother R.G. Burton and his family and also his sister Clara and other members of the family before going to Jersey to stay with his eldest brother Charlie. In February and March he was back in England at Gillingham but in April returned to Jersey in rented accommodation to spend more time with his brother Charlie, whose health was rapidly failing.

DIARY

Left Jersey on 3rd August, sorry to leave old Charlie, but it had to be. Went same day to Marnhull, Dorset to stay with Gage and his wife. We went for a day's fishing to River Nadder, very cold windy day, so none of us did anything. Made a gun sling for Gage to use and hope it may obviate his having to buy a lighter gun than his favourite old twelve-bore. Left Gage's on 18th, a very pleasant stay indeed.

They made a short visit to North Wales to visit another old friend Col.V.K. Birch and his wife and were able to do a little fishing in spite of the rain; and then returned to Cheltenham to stay with his eldest sister Clara and see something of the countryside.

DIARY ——

On 2nd September went to see Phyllis and children off to India, and on 5th went North to stay at Temple Sowerby with my brother E.B.B. and his wife. While there went to Carlisle and saw the old Cathedral and the Museum in which are some heads of Indian game animals presented by Edmund. Went and stayed with sister Jo at Burwain Hall, Kings Meaburn, and met her three daughters, all very charming girls and hard working. Took them all, Jo and the three girls, for a drive to Haweswater 25 miles, and to Mardale at the head of Haweswater Lake.

The Haweswater Lake is to be enlarged to furnish water to Manchester and we saw the water level marks high up on hillsides showing how many houses and farms will be submerged. The Mardale Church is to be re-erected at another site. The Dun Bull Inn will be fourteen feet under water! Back to Gillingham on 12.9.27 and busy getting things together for India. Rods and tackle from Ogden of Cheltenham £30, gun by Webley & Scott £17, some tools, etc, and some motor car accessories. I also bought a typewriter and must make it pay for itself by writing articles.

BACK
TO
INDIA
1927
TO
1929

Chapter 16

BY CAR — BOMBAY TO PACHMARHI

DIARY
3rd January 1928. Camp at Joga on the Narbada river. I now begin to write up this Diary in the same manner as up to 18th March 1926, when I fell from the machan and broke my leg and arm.

We left Tilbury on 14th October, 1927. Voyage same as most. Met Champion I.F.S., author of a new book – and first of its kind about India – *With a Camera in Tiger Land*. I have since written a Review of it which will appear in the Journal of the Bombay Natural History Society. A very good book, and I conclude that, to do any good at animal photography such as achieved by Champion – and he has only just broken ground, – one would have to do no shooting whatever, or very little. First of all go through a thorough photographic training and in fact FIRST become an expert photographer. I, at sixty years of age, have too many other things I want to do and see, to care to give the time and spend the money necessary. The output is expensive, but I have little doubt that an increasing number of sportsmen will take to animal photography.

We landed at Bombay on 4th November and stayed at the Grand Hotel, expensive, Rs.32 a day for the two of us. We were very busy at Bombay, unpacking and packing kit to go on to Itarsi, and seeing to purchase of Ford car. We left Bombay on 9th November taking a Ford car driver at 5/- a day! until I learn to drive.

JOURNAL
The country we pass through can well be described as 'the side uplands of the Deccan' and forms part of the Great Trap region, a distinctive feature of which is the occurrence of immense quantities of loose basalt stones of all sizes which look as if they had been showered on the land. The fields are covered with these stones and the raising of crops is hard work. Hard country breeds hard men, and the Mahratta Regiments were found during the Great War to be second to none in stubborn fighting qualities. In days gone by the most dreadful famines have all but depopulated this Deccan land; plagues of rats ruined the standing crops on many occasions, and the hordes of marauding Pindari horsemen devastated and oppressed the country for many miserable years.

Except in the vicinity of the scattered villages and the few water courses, few trees are to be seen, The countryside however, is looking its best now. The dust has been washed off the foliage of the trees, and the winter crops are thriving under the influence of the recent rain.

The road has little traffic on it. At Toka the pontoon was on the further side of the river and took some time to complete its cargo of passengers, bullock carts and grain and make it's way back, by means of the current and a wire hawser worked by a pulley running on a steel cable stretched from bank to bank. The Godavery here, is some four hundred yards in width, and where a week ago a motor car was able to cross by means of its own power and the aid of a team of bullocks, there is now six feet of water. The source of this, to Hindus, very sacred river is at Trimbuk on the eastern slopes of the Sahyadri hills of the Western Ghats. Close above Toka the river is augmented by the combined waters of the Pravada and the Mula. The army of General Wellesley crossed at this place on 21st August 1803, and as the river was at that time both deep and rapid the crossing took six days.

The broad masonry zigzag approach to the water's edge presents a busy scene and reminds us of the occasion over thirty five years ago when we performed this journey in a tonga. We recollect that, some little distance before arriving at the river, we saw the left wheel of our vehicle trundling along before us until we came to the ground with a crash, but without damage to ourselves or our conveyance. It took us then seventeen hours to travel from Toka to Aurangabad and fear that if the nalas are unkind we may not proceed much faster on this occasion.

At the first nala after crossing the river we stick in the sand, the water almost up to carburettor level, and have to be pushed through by some eighteen village men and boys. Beyond a slight difficulty in crossing another unbridged stream no further trouble is experienced, and the comfortable Inspection Bungalow at Aurangabad is reached without mishap; the distance covered was sixty eight miles. It is interesting to see again the old Cantonment which has not now the orderly aspect of its former days. We receive much ready assistance from the Executive Officer, and are surprised to find him carrying out both judicial and executive functions; an arrangement concerning which there was, a few short years ago, much outcry on the part of the extremist element of certain Cantonments, and which had been condemned by the Government in considered terms. However 'necessity has no law' and we know that the arrangement is liked by the people of the bazaars who are those whom it most intimately affects.

On their journey, Burton and his wife took the opportunity to stop and visit the Fort at Daulatabad and the Ellora Caves. The Fort is constructed with massive walls and battlements and dates from the thirteenth century. The mosque was originally a Jain Temple and also at one time a place of worship of the goddess Kali. The evidence of it's Hindu origin can also be seen, illustrating the dynasties of Hindus and Muhammadans which successively reigned.

JOURNAL ————————————————————————————————

Passing through a fifth gateway we come to the central portion of the fortress. The way to the upper battlements is by a stairway excavated within the solid rock. A lantern is necessary, but after the manner of the East, we find that the light brought with such forethought from the guard room has no oil in it and the bearer of the useless article has no matches! We produce matches and a resin torch is unearthed from a dark recess to guide us by its fitful and scented light to emerge eventually from the tunnel and reach a platform overlooking the way we have just come. Continuing to ascend by alternate steps and pathways, we reach the extreme summit of the Fort. It is very peaceful on the top of the hill. The distant hum from the scattered hamlets arises faintly to our ears, the cattle bells and cries of goatherds are heard among the overgrown ruins of the city of former days. We have to go on to the Ellora caves, so reluctantly make our way downhill, taking another path for a part of the way to see the perennial water supply in the absence of which the fortress would have little strength.

Few places in India have been more magnificent or more celebrated in former days than Aurangabad, and few have suffered more in every sense of the word from the hand of time, and the changes of fortune. All is now dust and desolation, but the grand mausoleum of Rubia-ud-Daurani is an exception. It is in an excellent state and much attention is paid to its proper preservation. It is similar in design to the celebrated Taj Mahal at Agra, and from the top of one of the four minarets, we obtain an extensive view of the city of Aurangabad. We also visited the Pan Chukki, or water mill, which afforded the pleasing shade of trees and sound of running water.

There was a cold feeling in the air when we left the cantonment of Aurangabad to go to Fardapur where there is a Guest House maintained by the Government of His Exalted Highness The Nizam of Hyderabad for the convenience of visitors who have obtained permission to occupy it. Entering the city, we pass through several gates to emerge through the Delhi gate on to the Ajanta Road. Two rivers the Girja and the Purna are crossed, the deep sand of the former necessitating the willing help of a number of cartmen to push the car through. The crossing of the Purna gives no trouble and thereafter the road is good.

Throughout this journey, Col. Burton was intrigued to be following in the footsteps of General Wellesley's army which fought in the Maratha Wars of 1803. His interest in history – and army history in particular – took him to Ajanta and the battle-ground of Assaye, where against an army seven times as numerous, Wellesley gained his first great victory of the campaigns.

JOURNAL _____

The new ghat road now under construction is blocked to traffic, so we have to find our way down the steep age-long bullock cart track, the path by which the Maratha hordes came thronging to sustain utter defeat at the battle of Assaye. The descent is a difficult feat for the car, and is not made any easier by the half dozen bullock carts laden with brushwood which we meet and have to pass on the way. Had we 'looked before leaping' it is doubtful if the descent would have been attempted. We reach the foot of the ghat without mishap, in spite of many boulders and deep ruts, and emerge undamaged at the main road to arrive soon at the Guest House, a distance of sixty three miles.

Next morning we proceed to the celebrated caves at Ajanta. The scene is very beautiful, the caves being in the perpendicular scarp which sweeps round in a semicircle and closes the upper end of the ravine. The clear and rapid stream of the Waghora river sparkles over the rocks, and wherever a hold can be found is the green carpet of creepers and a canopy of trees. There is not a motorable road to Burhanpur and the car has therefore to be railed the distance of thirty four miles. We are told that within a year or two there will be a good road connecting Burhanpur to Jelgaon.

It does not take long to realise the truth of the saying regarding this place –
'Char chiz ast tofaye Burhan,
Gard, garma, gad-o-goristan.'
'Burhanpur is noted for four things: dust, heat, beggars, and graveyards.'

At this season of the year (November) the heat was absent, but the other ingredients noticeably present. It is also noted for muslins, and for the silk cloth embroidered with gold and silver lace. The railway station is two miles from the town, and we make our way through an endless string of cotton laden carts and the choking dust raised by them, to enter the town by a gateway through the crenellated wall of the

1

2

CHAPTER
16

1
A panorama of the Ajanta
Caves

2
A Banjari family, the women
showing the impressive head-
dress which caught R.W.
Burton's attention

3
Richard Burton with his Ford
car in which he travelled
extensively across India

4
A boy in charge of a bullock
cart, near Akot, 1927

Sketch by Phyllis Burton

fortifications. The streets are narrow and crowded with carts and people. We emerge from the city to find ourselves on the banks of the Tapti River. The water at the crossing did not appear so deep as we were told, as we see a venturesome cyclist pedalling most of the way through. Mounting the steep exit from the bed of the river we pass by Zainabad, now in total ruin, built about the year 1399. During the Maratha war, Scindia camped here with his sixty thousand horse and so desolated the country that it did not recover for many years.

Burhanpur is on the right bank of the Tapti and was, in former days, the capital of the Faruki dynasty of Khandesh established in 1388. During the years 1630–32, while Shah Jehan, was encamped at Burhanpur, an appalling famine desolated the Deccan and Guzerat. Records of the time state that the numbers of the dying caused obstructions on the roads, and every man whose dire sufferings did not terminate in death wandered off to the towns and villages of other countries. At Burhanpur also it was that Mumtaz Mahal, the dearly beloved wife of the Emperor Shah Jehan and mother of his fourteen children, died in June 1631. Her remains were afterwards transferred to Agra to repose eventually beneath the world renowned Taj Mahal erected in her memory by her sorrowing husband.

In this part of the Tapti valley the land is being fast taken up and reclaimed from the clutches of the forest growth. There is a motor road from Burhanpur to Berar, and we see the village people sitting by the roadside 'waiting for the bus'! The country is now safe and easy where formerly none could move abroad without fear.

We see many Banjaras along the road. Formerly they were the principal carriers of grain from one part of the country to another, but with the advent of the railway their occupation is almost gone and they are taking to other pursuits. They are a picturesque people. The dress of the women is strange; they have a stick about a foot long placed upright on the top of the head, the hair being wound round it and the scarlet headcloth drawn over it. Married women wear bracelets of lac, ivory, or coconut, both on the upper arm and on the wrist. Clothes have borders of cowries, and cowrie necklaces are worn. The men have a necklace of coral beads, and carry slung round the neck a tin toothpick. At weddings the bride and bridegroom walk round a pack saddle with bags of grain, thus symbolising their former nomadic life.

Nearing our destination for the next few days we pass through a village, the whole of the human and animal population of which is on the road. It is the weekly bazaar day and people from the surrounding smaller villages and hamlets are here to buy the supplies they require. The sellers are from amongst themselves, and there are also dealers who earn their livelihood travelling from one village bazaar to another. We are now on the edge of one of the great forest tracts of India. Soon we see the massive outline of Asirgarh Fort, and the glow of the setting sun lights up the red sandstone battlements silhouetted against the sky.

At dawn we awake to the noise of numerous peafowl sounding their trumpet-like alarm call and know that some feline is on the move. Sure enough, we find the fresh tracks of a tigress in the dust of the road a short distance away. She had passed along the bed of the ravine not fifty yards from the house; but on the present occasion we are here to shoot with a camera and not with a rifle. The car takes us three miles up the road which winds along the northern slopes of the hill. Before us are the massive minarets, seen yesterday from afar, of the mosque, a smaller replica of the Jamma Musjid at Burhanpur; below us is jungle clad and hilly country which stretches as far as the eye can reach in every direction. The fort is on an outlying spur of the Satpura Range. Below the foot of the walls is a bluff precipice eighty to one hundred and fifty feet in perpendicular depth.

The district of Nimar was devastated from end to end during the first twenty years of the nineteenth century. In 1802 Holkar reduced the then opulent town of Khandwa to ashes and the country was overrun by Scindia's hordes. After the peace with the British

Government which ensued at the termination of the Second Maratha War, the Pindaris took up residence in the forest country between the Satpura and Vindhya hills under the leadership of the robber chieftain Chitu. The originally peaceful inhabitants formed plundering bands of their own. Every village was put into a state of defence by means of a masonry or earthwork wall, and the cultivators crowded into these fortified places. The whole country was ruined, neither life nor property was safe.

It was this lawless state of affairs which led to the outbreaks at Poona and Nagpur, and resulted in the Third Maratha War. Chitu, after many wanderings, joined the fugitive Appa Saheb of Nagpur. Appa Saheb escaped in disguise and fled to Rajputana, but the doomed Chitu, a monster in human form, hunted and tracked through the jungle, was devoured by a man-eating tiger. Although Nimar was now freed from the nightmare of oppression, there were other turbulent robbers harrying the country for the next sixty years. Sheikh Dulla Pindari continued to plunder the country until he was killed in 1828. The Bhils of the Asir hills also gave trouble; and from 1878 to 1889 the notorious dacoit Tantia Bhil murdered throughout the length and breadth of the land until he was eventually caught, tried and hanged at Jubbulpore.

There is little that remains now of the Fort of Asirgarh, and passing through the main gate we descend the hill. The following morning we return to Burhanpur and then move on towards Akot, a distance of close on a hundred miles. The first forty miles are mostly level, along the valley of the Tapti River, but we soon come to continuous forest and reach the Gawilgarh hills which run parallel to the Satpura Range. The term Satpura Hills, the Sat-Putra or seven sons of the Vindhyan Mountains, is now customarily applied to the whole range from the sources of the Narbada River at Amarkantak on the borders of the Rewa State, nearly to the Western Coast, a distance of some six hundred miles. The highest point is Dhupgarh near Pachmarhi and there are many parts over 3,500ft. in elevation. Only in the last fifty years has travelling been made safe and easy throughout these wild hills by the construction of metalled roads up the steep passes. From the summit of the Pass we have a wide view of the rich plains of Berar. Ten miles further on we arrive at Akot Rest House and go in search of the Tahsildar to make arrangements to visit the site of the battlefields of Argaum the next day.

We jolt over the eight miles of rough cart track to Argaum in a larha, as the small cart drawn by trotting bullocks is called, and pass through waving fields of millet and of cotton. The air is cool, and there is water in the nala; as it must have been on that day one hundred and twenty four years ago when the Maratha Power was finally crushed and the country freed from a vicious rule. Beneath a tree, a grave enclosed by iron rails but otherwise uncared for is all that remains at the site of the Battle of Argaum.

From Argaum they moved on to the Hill Fort of Narnala. The Fort covers an area of about three hundred and ninety two acres, and the full circuit of the walls is twenty four miles. The first gateway is ornamented over the arch by two carved stone tigers, and the main gate – the Mahakali Gate – is flanked on either side by galleries and stone lattice work and was built in 1487. Burton comments –

DIARY ————————————————————————————————

Everywhere it is evident that the pipal and banyan trees are fast disrupting the masonry of buildings and battlements, and that in the course of years all the laborious work of men of former days, no doubt believed at the time to be everlasting, will be but shapeless heaps of stone and rubble. At the Dhobi Talao we see grooves in the granite stone under the pipal tree, indicating that water was bullock drawn for many years, and we also notice recent tracks of sambur which come to drink here in the hot weather, when water in the surrounding hills is scarce.

We leave Akot at eight o'clock next morning, at which hour the streets are not congested by cotton carts and pedestrians, and take the road for Ellichpur. Cotton provides the greater part of the traffic and leaves its traces in patches of white caught up by the roadside trees. Here and there we see snowy heaps of freshly picked cotton awaiting transport to the nearest market town. The Rest House at Chikalda overlooks a deep ravine. We hear the moan of a tiger in the valley below and the distant bark of a kakur. At dawn we awake to the familiar jungle sounds, the boom of the lungoor, the call of the peafowl, and chattering of tree pies. In the freshness of the morning when the first rays of the sun are lighting up the mountain tops and the stars have just faded out of the sky, we stand and enjoy the scene with which we were so enraptured at the close of the previous day.

The road winds through the attractive Civil Station of Chikalda over the open downs to the North gate of the Fort of Gawilgarh. The reflections of the crenellated walls are sharp cut in the green stagnant water of the tank. We approach the fort by the path to the north, and it was this way that General Wellesley led his troops in 1803, when he stormed and captured the stronghold which the enemy had believed to be impregnable. Immediately upon the fall of Gawilgarh the fort of Narnala capitulated. On the 17th December a Treaty of Peace was signed with the Raja of Berar, and on the 30th with Scindia. Here we come to the end of the campaigns of Wellington in India and he was only thirty four years of age at the taking of Gawilgarh.

The Musjid is a handsome stone building in the Pathan style, the front of the mosque is formed of seven arches, and the covered portion had originally twenty one domes, however the western wall has fallen away and now only fourteen domes remain. Leaving the fort, the path takes us back through the high over-arched and pillared shade of a banyan tree, and next morning we are ready to leave for Betul, a distance of ninety miles. The road is an excellent one and we soon reach the causeway over the Tapti River. The Tapti, rising near Multai, drains much rocky country and in the rainy season soon becomes an impassable roaring flood, while in the dry months of the year it dwindles to a succession of pools connected by a trickle of water. After crossing the river it is eight miles only into Betul; and from there another fifty five miles to Itarsi.

Itarsi is an unlovely spot. The valley of the Narbada river is not well served with motorable roads, and as far as Itarsi there are numerous unbridged and difficult streams to cross. Our destination is Piparia the railway station for the Hill Station of Pachmarhi. We cross the sandy bed of the Tawa River by an earthwork causeway, and have thirty miles of second class roads to cross. The cart bullocks are more frightened than those on the more frequented roads and a string of carts scatters like a covey of partridges at the approach of the motor. We are aware of the sweet-smelling and lovely golden puffball blossoms of the scented acacia trees where the road passes near them, and see hanging from their thorny branches the swinging nests of the weaver birds.

Arrangements were made at Pachmarhi for rooms near the Club for the six months from 5th June 1928 to 5th December. The right axle of the car was found to have rusted, a result no doubt of getting wet in the Tapti river, and the repair cost 5/-. This accomplished, they drove on to Nagpur to stay a few days with friends.

Chapter 17

PANTHERS AT RAJADHO AND A FOREST SHRINE

After the long drive from Bombay to Pachmarhi, Burton made plans to return to his favourite haunts along the Narbada River and the jungles of the Central Provinces. Although he now had a car to make travelling easier, the camp kit and luggage still had to be transported by train and bullock cart, and as many of the roads were just rough cart tracks the journey was often erratic and uncomfortable.

DIARY ——

21st December 1927. To Itarsi one hundred and sixty two miles in one day. Stopped at D.B. Multai for an hour and took photo of Multai tank. Arrived at Itarsi 6 o'clock, having left Nagpur at 9 a.m. On 23rd, railed car and kit and selves to Harda and stayed at D.B. Next day, sent carts off to Joga via Oowa. The first ten or twelve miles were not difficult, but after that it was pretty bad, and there were many boulders when we got into the forest past Oowa. When removing stones to clear road side for motor, under first stone a snake (non poisonous), under second a scorpion, and under third a centipede! At that rate what a population of horrid things must the forest contain.

1928. 2nd January. At last weather has cleared. Cloudy and rain threatening and unusually warm ever since 10th December, now temperature is down to 46° at 7 a.m. (it was 58°!)

Joga: the Narbada River. On 11th January saw tracks of tigress along the river bank where she went to drink; this was in the early morning as the drops of water which fell from her were still on the sand. She was sneaking along close to reeds, taking all the cover she could, as I could see in one place she went belly to ground UNDER some reeds not eighteen inches high! Coming round a bush she came right on the boda which was in the open on the sand. She stuck claws in and turned and went off into the jungle, and did not return. Decided to change machan from Bariaghat to Saliakheri about a mile further up stream. Many tracks of the tigress there and she lies up either in the hill or on island in river. Saw carcass, very high, of a defunct mugger stranded on a shoal.

Burton often saw the tracks of a tigress along the river. One evening she killed two pigs on the far side of the river, but when Burton went over the following morning, the Korkus had already removed the carcasses. The clear tracks of a tiger were also seen along the nala but by 23rd they both appeared to have left the area and it was unlikely they would return for at least a week. At the end of the month Burton was due to strike camp and move on to Harda.

DIARY ——

26th. No kill: tigress came along from direction of Bariaghat, saw boda, stopped, went up the bank had a look, then went on and along the path towards Joga and turned off into jungle! Evidently a very cunning beast and fears a tethered boda – probably for good reason. The wire rope which was stolen found replaced. I am not sure who took it! but rather suspect Joga people, my own boda men! Villagers cunning and grasping and quite different from last time we were here.

On 2nd February motored via Hindia to Harda, twenty seven miles. At Harda a tremendous rain storm came on and we feared all the kit would get wet, but Abdul was sensible and housed it all, paying Rs.3/- as hire for the night. This delayed the carts as it rained heavily all the 3rd so carts did not turn up until afternoon of 4th. Rushed them off to Station and managed to book the whole lot, 23 maunds, by parcels to Betul: an expensive move. Harda to North Khandu block, near Rs.200 one way and another.

5th. Went by 8.a.m. train to Itarsi, motor in wagon with us, and on to Betul next morning, a good run, fifty five miles. Got some things in the bazaar, saw Tahsildar and arranged for carts to Bhainsdehi at Rs.7 each. Saw D.C., Brown I.C.S. at his Court House and met with a very curious reception, when I asked him to sign a Life Certificate for me, he asked me how he was to know I was Col. Burton – stinker! We got to Bhainsdehi at 1 o'clock on 9th. Saw Tahsildar and arranged carts and sweeper, no bodas to be got. Sent off carts on 12th and went in motor to Jarida, down to Rajadeo and on to Biba. The man eating panther rather a myth, only one person killed and that in the rains.

13th. February. Pitched camp at Biba. Tied up machan chair at Chobita crossroads, same place where I shot a tiger on 15th March 1926, just before breaking my leg. Much traffic of bamboo carrying carts along the road unfortunately. Out early on 20th, all up valley of Tingra river. No animals, no tracks; put up one small sambur on hill near camp. Temperature at 6 a.m. 55°; at one o'clock, in sun 106°, in shade 84°; so getting warmer now and will do so daily. Kachnar trees in blossom looking very nice and jungles lovely in the early morning. On 23rd crawled home from machan to a seven days illness. Temperature 104 degrees: malaria skotched by quinine; Abdul also had high fever.

3rd to 6th March. Heard peafowl this morning early, for the first time. Mohwa fruit beginning to ripen, and jungle now turning brown very fast. No kill, and bitterly cold at night. Will put out bodas from tonight as I am fit again now, and Abdul's fever gone. A dust haze all over the country: there must have been a big dust storm in the plains and it has blown up the Tapti Valley. Moved camp to Rajadeo.

12th. Kill by panther one mile down river. Sat up, and at 6.20 heard male panther rampaged all over the place with two females. He came to kill once, and I was getting ready to take a shot when he moved off into jungle, a lovely dark coloured panther. He was incessantly roaring and growling and chasing the females. At the last of daylight, almost beyond shooting light, I felt tree shake and heard an animal running up and in a second I saw – only just enough light TO see – bullet head of panther on bough not five feet from my head. The electric cord for backsight battery was very short, and with difficulty I pulled muzzle of .470 round far enough. The shot caught her full in chest and blew her off the bough to fall dead below machan.

At the shot the male panther continued to rampage and didn't go away; went on chasing after the other female. It got dark and soon I heard the brute scratching and growling below me and felt tree move once, so fired a shot to send him off. Then sounded bugle for men to come. In twenty minutes a female panther, by the size, came to kill and I had a steady shot by the electric light: it must have been a miss. She dashed off into the bamboo jungle and I heard no more of her, but before she could possibly have got to my right I heard the male panther again chasing about in the jungle, as I thought with a THIRD female. Anyhow that was the end of night of 12th. Men came up and we went back to camp.

Female panther: 41in. + 28in. = 5ft. 9in: weight 60lbs.

13th. We found that a lot more of the kill had been eaten, so I sat up again and at ten minutes to six the male panther, without any demonstrations, turned up from the direction of the river. He was much on the alert and instantly spotted the slight lift of corner of khaki handkerchief over loophole. He and I stared at one another for full three minutes but he couldn't make me out and turned, apparently satisfied, and lay down facing the kill. I waited till his head turned away and then poked out rifle and took careful shot: left eye, right shoulder. Male panther – 7ft.1in. weight 110lbs. A wound in his off fore foot, probably by a bamboo splinter, was filled with maggots. Panther had an extensive fresh bruise over the ribs on right side and possibly got this when he was killing the boda.

The name is not Rajadeo as I thought, but Rajadho 'the Great Pool' after the deep pool in bend of the river east of the now dismantled hut. Semal trees just coming out in blossom, and langoors feeding on them. The lantana is bad now, strangling the jungle in all low lying places and thick hillsides too, where the soil is favourable. It seems clear that the panther on 12th did not come up my tree by accident, but on purpose. She first went up the tree at foot of which was the kill, climbed that and got as high as to be able to see into my machan, see my head at any rate which she did by accident no doubt; THEN she came along and came up tree very fast and straight for the small bough on which she sat and from which she could have got me, had I been a langoor for instance; and me too if she had wanted to! Forgot to note that owing to demands of baniahs, four annas nickel is not now current in these parts. Government having withdrawn two annas silver from circulation, the baniah taxed four as silver; that having become scarce because villagers wouldn't use it, they have now taxed it as nickel!

Nine nights tying up here and no kill is unusual, as also is this very wet weather, almost like the monsoon. Went three miles up Kamida Road and then over hills to Chopi Kua and then down nala and back over hills. It is two years today that I broke my leg at Biba; leg QUITE strong now and same as before break except knee does not bend as much.

22nd. Found kill by tiger on Raipur road, men said they had seen the tiger and it wouldn't let them near, and it had broken the wire rope. Went at once and found this to be so, the most decrepit of my four remaining wire ropes (new wire is on its way from Calcutta). Followed up the drag and found the kill about two hundred yards away on edge of thick lantana. Towards dusk tiger sounded a couple of 'whoofs' to scare away anybody and announce his presence. Then I heard him using his nose, loud sniffs, and he came round to my left and close below me. It was towards the last glimmer of daylight, only a FEW minutes within which to shoot without aid of electric light. I heard him advancing to the kill, but before I could see him, he went off with an alarmed 'wuff' and rushed through the jungle. We had slightly moved position of kill, it might have been that. He didn't return, and I heard no jungle alarm noises during the night. He was a BIG tiger, and his tracks were all along the road when we returned to camp. He MAY be the same wily tiger which has defeated me so often; anyhow is more than ordinarily suspicious and has probably been fired at before over a kill.

25th. I have tied up, at Biba and here, twenty six nights and there have been only two kills by a tiger, also two by a panther, which works out to the usual average of one kill a week.

Nothing has visited the defunct and now highly odorous boda. The crows have found it and I cleared the brambles a bit to expose it. The tiger evidently cleared out of the place that night. Another lesson learnt as to how careful one must be.

Lost opportunities seldom recur, so I leave Rajadho tigerless. On morning of 2nd April loaded up carts and motored to Chunkheri and stayed at F.B.; saw a bear in the moonlight. Next morning took photo of fine banyan tree in front of the bungalow and then motored to Makla, steep ghat and many hairpin bends. Makla F.B. is well situated at 3016 feet and has a good group of mango trees close to it. Water from two wells some 600yds or so from the house. It would be nice to shikar all over this plateau and down the ravines.

My right eye has been inflamed for four days and I won't get to Semadoh now until 12th and can't expect to get settled until 15th. Ford car giving trouble, battery weak and may have to go to Akola 100 miles to get it recharged. A heavy duststorm down below and all hazy this morning and much cooler. Fazal Ahmed stung by a scorpion last night and making a great fuss over it. Pain must be nearly all gone by now, twelve hours after, and yet he can do no work! A chicken-hearted fellow. Am arranging to go to Semadoh and Kolkaz on 12th.

temp. at Rajadho 70° in evening, 56° morning, 94° noon. At Makla, 80° in evening, 75° morning 92° noon.

12th. On to Kolkaz, bungalow on Sipna river same as at Makla, stone floors, thatched roof. Jungle very extensive. Semadoh means semal tree pool in Korku and Sipna means teak tree.

16th April. Went early to the Bhopra nala. Saw a lot of sambur, hinds and small stags. Later saw a bigger stag and shot it, poor thin horns and shouldn't have killed it, but there are many such and meat wanted for the men. Next day, went a short round through the forest. Came across a sounder of pig and let them get quite close; amusing to watch them. One was above us and got our wind: at his warning grunt all the pigs of the sounder instantly 'froze' and listened. I moved the rifle, and off they all went. Tracks of tigress along the right bank of river.

21st. No kill: but tigress saw the boda, prospected all round and lay on bank – clear shape of body, tail and paws in sand – and watched the boda at ten yards distance! She retraced her steps and went off into jungle to south of the path. Only thing to do is to sit up over the same boda tonight, on the likely chance of her coming along to have another look, and being tempted to kill. A very quiet vigil it will have to be! The slightest possible sound will put her off. This tigress seems as cunning as the one at Joga.

22nd. There was much sound of sambur and pig all night. The tigress did not turn up. Some animal, may have been a bear, was behind my tree a good deal during the night. Forgot to note that yesterday found at the pool half an eel; remains of meal of an otter. Korku gleefully annexed it for his cooking pot! Also should have noted that the old Korku of Korku Dhana who went to Betul from Rajadho to fetch motor parts, had never seen railway and was highly delighted at going. He came back to Makla full of his sight seeing. A tough old man.

The tiger and panther that roamed through these forests appeared to be very wary, and the noise of cartmen along the road to the bridge no doubt kept them well back in the thick jungle. Two bodas were killed by a tiger, but it didn't return to either, and Burton decided on 1st May to pack up and leave for Amrasti to have the car foot brakes checked and the battery recharged.

DIARY ————————————————————————————————

10th May. To Bhainsdehi; thirty two miles. Car gave no trouble, except for one puncture by babul thorn. The fourteen miles Jarida to Bhainsdehi was worse than before owing to track having been cut up by bullock carts. At Bhainsdehi; no help from Tahsildar to recover the Rs.7/- kept by the sweeper Basaratu who took Rs.10/- in advance and deserted after four days. Wrote to D.C. Betul about it, and will see whether he will assist or not. Could get no reliable information from anyone as to the road to Kanela via Kotal Kund. Would have gone up it in car, but wife too nervous and wouldn't be left to wait while I went on! So decided to go by cart and leave car at the Kotal Kund Rest House. Got to F.B. at 3.30 p.m., a very good one on top of a jungle covered hill, but it was locked up and the Forest Officer about to arrive with his family, so we camped in the verandah. All things considered, decided wife should return to Bhainsdehi, going to Kotal Kund by cart and thence by motor; her own decision.

15th. Learnt that D.F.O. Kasar Singh, who had given me only fifteen days permit as he wished himself to shoot for fifteen days, had not been near the place and apparently never intended to! Whichever way it was he should have let me have the whole month when he knew he was not going. I went myself to Kanela and got hold of Forest Guard, and arranged for three carts; also had kept the two carts which we brought up from Kotal Kund; so all arrangements satisfactory. Met Miss Jones of the American Mission, and went to see her at her house on the hill. Fine view; but a lonely life. The Mission works among the Korkus and the Bhils. Was offered loan of tent and took it as it MIGHT rain and cause a lot of discomfort in the forest.

16th. Got to Bhandia Kund at 11 o/c, both the carts upset on the road. No damage to kit and a miracle, at the first upset, that the cartman was not seriously hurt. Road very bad in places: a mere footpath becoming used as a cart track. It will be difficult to return by that road and will probably have to get all kit carried half a mile up the hill, from where there is a good cart road to Kanela. Said to be a tiger round here which has killed a pony and several head of cattle lately. Hills sparsely covered with forest, very stony, a good many green trees. Ate a lot of ripe 'goolu' fruit, as I was hungry, ate skin and all!

17th – 26th. Saw one four-horn, very few tracks of sambur, no tracks of panther or tiger. Jungles contain scarcely any animals at all; very little undergrowth. A bad block altogether and I cannot understand why Cox told me it is good for tiger. A tiger roams about occasionally, no doubt and that is all. Forest Guard tried to take away my only two coolies this morning. Quite by accident found he was doing it and got them back. Am told by old shikari that they suffer much here from oppression of the forest underlings; and that is why Antarmal has been deserted. These people, Bhandia Kund, also intend to abandon the village. Have decided to strike camp on Saturday 26th, and return to Bhainsdehi: no hope of tiger from here. Shot a peahen this morning for larder, no fowls procurable. Have heard cuckoo every day up in these hills since 14th May. On 20th a large panther turned up at the kill. When torch was turned on it took no notice whatever; then raised its head to look towards the ravine and I shot it high up on shoulder, and was instantly killed. Weight 100lbs. Length, 6ft.11in.

26th. Got to Kanela at 9.30: managed to get three carts. Started off 6.30 p.m. and walked for two hours: had dinner, sardines and chupattis, by roadside. Walked 8.30 to midnight and camped below the ghat, at 12.30, near some water. Cartman and servant thought it wonderful and daring that I should walk at night all alone with only a stick, through jungle etc! Had no camp bed with me, slept on blanket on sheet rock!

27th. Up at 4.30 a.m.: got to Kotalkund 7.15, made tea and waited for motor which came at 8.10, and so back comfortably to Bhainsdehi. Recovered Rs.7/3 from the deserting sweeper. Failed to recover 3/- advances to cartmen, and which I had forgotten when paying them up. Tahsildar didn't show up again, without doubt the extraordinary reception of me by D.C. (C.Brown) at Betul was notified to Bhainsdehi, and hence change of attitude of Tahsildar. Hope to meet Brown some day and tell him of it.

4th June. Off to Itarsi, kit by two motor lorries 15/- each, nineteen maunds of kit, and arrived there in the evening, 100 miles from Bhainsdehi. At Itarsi for two days sorting kit, and left for Pachmarhi on 7th to stay at Hill Hotel for six months.

JOURNAL _____

It was early morning when we arrived at Khandwa Junction and from there to Piparia we saw the blue outline of the Satpura Hills on our right. The railway line crossed many streams, some of them of considerable size. Soon after the ascent of the hills commenced we saw on our left the gloomy gorge of the Denwa River into the depths of which we were unable to see. The road winds upwards through thick forest, and on our left was a tremendous ravine with precipitous sides. It was down this ravine, some years ago, that an officer lost his way and remained for five days.

Hogshaw of Pachmarhi told me the extraordinary story of Major Rodrigues of the I.S.M.D., a man who had been much on active service and had two rows of medals. He had been to Gallipoli and other war areas during the Great War. It seems that Rodrigues and his family went down the Piparia Road for an afternoon's jaunt, somewhere near Bormar. Walking up the road, I suppose to get to their motor car, Rodrigues saw a path leading downwards. He went down this, saying he wanted to see where it led to; the others walked on. He did not return. They went to look for him and called but it became dark and they went back to Pachmarhi.

Next day a search was made without result. Hogshaw's father, a great friend of Rodrigues got three hundred coolies and searched the whole jungle. For four days there was no trace. On the fifth day Hogshaw Senior said there was nothing for it but to follow the deep ravine downwards to a hamlet, unoccupied much of the year. There, up a tree, they found the missing man. He was in a bad way mentally and physically. He had not had anything to eat or drink. He had been afraid to come down the tree. The first night he had slept up a tree, then he went down and down and down to where he was found. He saw a tiger; he was afraid of the lungoors; he stayed up the tree day and night. He met calls of nature up the tree, and would doubtless have died if he had not been found. He recovered under medical care and died not long ago. The whole thing is almost incredible, but it's true. He must have known that the way back to the road was up hill, and to Pachmarhi also; yet he went down hill. And his pluck was nil, a very chicken hearted man indeed, unless he was mentally afflicted in some way and that does not seem to be said of him. I know the ravine, a deep gorge, but not in any way difficult to get out of; and he had no reason to get into it! Why didn't he follow the path back to the road? Why not make his way up hill instead of down?

On 6th July I went to top of Dhupgarh (4454ft.) with two lads from Bombay who are staying at the Hill Hotel: Ritchie of Lloyds Bank and Durran of a firm of Chartered Accountants. There is a break, a very unusually early one, in the monsoon. We had a clear view in every direction. 'Water's Meet' is about a mile and a half by a steep path from the Long Chukker. Here four streams meet and form the upper waters of the Denwa River. At the back of the Club is 'Club Hill'. It is about 300 feet in height and can be ascended without difficulty from the eastern end, and yet very few visitors to Pachmarhi go to the top of this hill. From here they could see the whole plateau and surrounding hills laid out before them. The view from Malcolm Point is one of the finest on the whole plateau.

The hill of Mahadeo and the adjacent hill of Chouragarh are conspicuous from Pachmarhi. On 7th July went to the Mahadeo Cave with Durran and Ritchie, walking two and a half miles by the bridle path to Nadia. It was by this path that all access to Pachmarhi was had in the days before the construction of the Itarsi–Jubbulpur Railway. Passing the entrance to the cave, we set out to make our way to the top of the hill by a footpath shown to us by the poojari. The path is little used and soon disappeared, so we just followed the line of least resistance to the east of the hill, and so scaled the precipitous southern face of the mountain. The foothold was good and the exercise all that could be desired. We were amply rewarded for our exertions by the really magnificent view of all the country to the south of the Pachmarhi plateau. The Denwa River, its main sources under the slopes of Dhupgarh, cuts its way deep down through tremendous gorges along the western base of Mahadeo, the slope of which is almost sheer to the invisible river. Looking east we saw the Chouragarh Hill, and the well-worn path plainly visible up the knife edge spur, up which twice every year many thousands of pilgrims toil to the summit of this mountain. Where in former times human victims hurled themselves over the precipice in sacrifice to the bloodthirsty Kali, the consort of Siva the Destroyer, now they go on to the Mahadeo cave to leave their gifts to the Deity.

9th July. Went with Durran and Ritchie to Rori Ghat and Alimod villages, very hot. At Alimod preparations were going forward in anticipation of the heavy rain which would soon arrive. Thatching of the bamboo wattle and daub houses is an urgent matter at this season of the year. A layer of fronds of the date palm is covered with the green leaves of the camels foot creeper, laid after the manner of tiles, and over this is spread a thick layer of coarse jungle grass. Such a roof is proof against the heaviest rain.

Had a hard day, not enough exercise, but it is difficult to go walking with no object in view and in beastly wet weather. Golf is almost a necessity in civilised life in the Cantonments. Went twice to the Denwa river to fish, I also visited the coal mines at Parasia. Another day I went to the top of Chouragarh Hill.

Am tired of Pachmarhi and don't want to go to the place again.

(*Note.* Did, in 1931, and disliked the Central Provinces people even more than before! so never again.)

The forest shrine of Nagadwiri is known to few Europeans, the number who have visited it is probably less than half a dozen. The Hindu festival of Nag Panchami is held on the 5th of Sawan, corresponding approximately to the 20th August, and it was on this day that with two friends I took the path with the pilgrims to Nagadwiri.

During the night there was a heavy thunderstorm, accompanied by a deluge of rain, and at daylight the rumblings and growlings of the elements had only just subsided.

The cooly who was to have accompanied us did not appear – a sign of the independent spirit of these days, so it was after eight o'clock before a man was found who would brave the elements and the long and difficult path to the place of worship. After three miles over the Plateau of Pachmarhi in a thick mist and drizzling rain, we dropped down the hill by a rough boulder-strewn path to reach the hamlet of Rori Ghat, a matter of another three miles.

Pilgrims had been passing through Pachmarhi for several days, and we soon found traces of them on the path. When night had overtaken them they just slept on layers of green grass gathered from the forest, and half-burnt embers of several fires indicated their attempts to keep warm. It was not difficult, we being already wet through, to realise the miserable night they had passed. At the foot of the hill, where the path crossed a turbulent mountain torrent bordered by a grove of ancient mango trees, stood a solitary policeman. His duty was to allow no pilgrims to return up the hill to Pachmarhi as there was danger of cholera being brought into the station.

Nearing Rori Ghat we sat down for half an hour to a damp and frugal meal. The village was full of pilgrims who had crowded into the huts for food and shelter. There is one street only, ankle deep in mud and mire, and the wattle and daub huts, thatched with leaves and grass in the style of the past several thousand years, appeared miserable habitations at such a season. Passing through the village we began to meet a stream of returning pilgrims; men were carrying children, women had babies in their arms, and all were soaked to the skin. A special feature of this pilgrimage is that it is made by women in want of a child, and it behoves all who have attained their desire to make a return pilgrimage taking the child to the shrine with them. This is not a fashionable pilgrimage to which people of rank proceed; the majority of the pilgrims are of the agricultural and labouring classes.

About a mile from the village a stream was crossed, on the banks of which had been a considerable encampment. The pilgrimage of 1926 was in worse weather than the present one, as we learn that ropes were stretched across and the people assisted through the rushing torrent by two policemen, who were strong swimmers and specially selected for the duty. Now we began to overtake a mile-long procession of pilgrims and heard occasional calls of 'Mahadeo, Mahadeo', uttered by both those proceeding and those returning. The strain of the journey was beginning to tell on some of the older and more feeble folk, for this is an arduous tramp along a rough and boulder-strewn path with many steep ascents and descents. A charming old lady we met was making slow and toilsome progress. The spirit which gave her the fortitude to undertake this arduous journey is an indication of the zeal with which the people of this land perform their religious pilgrimages. The rain came down more heavily, small rivulets had to be waded, the path itself was a stream. Three miles short of our destination the path became level and for about two miles there was a broad savannah, covered with high grass and beds of reeds, bordered by heavy forests.

Towards the end of our journey the way led over two spurs of the higher hills. Through the mist and rain could be seen precipitous scarps of red sandstone gashed with jungle-clad ravines and laced with waterfalls many hundreds of feet in height. The calls of 'Mahadeo, Mahadeo' became more frequent. At one place an opportunist had established a subsidiary shrine to attract offerings from the pilgrims. It was of recent origin and had nothing to do with the main place of worship. There was a young banyan tree, a vermilion daubed stone, and a scattering of coconut shells and faded flowers. Round the tree the pilgrims paced seven times circling it with cotton thread unwound from a spool.

Now we were making the final approach, and shouts of 'Mahadeo' echoed among the ravines at the foot of the precipice. In the centre of the path was another lingum at which all the pilgrims made obeisance with offerings of grain. Further on were two snake charmers with each a cobra, whose fangs had been extracted; lifeless they were, chilled by the mist, and the men also looked miserable. The pilgrims were not paying much attention to them and 'business is bad' they said, when receiving a small sum for the taking of a photograph. A deep and gloomy ravine was crossed and the last steep ascent to the place of worship accomplished. Under the cliff was a crowd of pilgrims and a dense throng of them against the strong barrier erected at the mouth of the cleft in the hill, at the far end of which could be seen the fire of the officiating priests. Only a few people were admitted at a time, for the passage is very narrow. Outside the entrance is a tree of considerable size around which the ceremony of seven times circling with thread was performed. The passage into the hill is about a hundred feet in length and the space at the end admits of only a small platform for the priest and the worshipper. There is a stone image of Siva and of the serpent Nag.

It was a great pity that the weather conditions were so bad. The scenery must be grand, but all was shrouded in mist and rain. Only a short stay was possible as it would be well to attain the Pachmarhi plateau before dark. As the afternoon closed in the rain became more incessant; rivulets we had crossed with a long stride were now wide and ankle deep; two streams were over the knees, and that near Rori Ghat a rushing thigh-high torrent. The returning pilgrims, their fervour abated, formed a miserable procession. It was pitiful to see the slender women and tiny children wet to the bone and without any material comforts. Our own attendant came down with a bump, unhurt however; bare feet have sometimes their disadvantages, and our heavy hobnailed boots were a welcome protection against cuts and bruises on such a path.

It was quarter past five by the time we passed through the village and the plateau was gained at seven o'clock, in time to avoid the scramble in the dark up the hill, but the black of a moonless night closed down with exceeding suddenness. We missed the direct path and put an additional toilsome mile behind us before arriving at the Hotel at just after eight o'clock. Nearly twelve hours on the move with only half an hour's halt; a hard day. However, we were glad to have done this pilgrimage and to have been once more in close touch with the millions of India who know nothing and care less (still less would they care if they knew more) of the Self Government aspirations of the small quota of urban population, which is nowadays so noisily clamorous. Are they really working for the greatest good of the greatest number?

Chapter 18

FROM THE BANKS OF THE NARBADA, THROUGH RAJASTHAN TO DELHI

DIARY ————————————————————————————————

Left Pachmarhi 27th September 1928, stayed Itarsi that night and left at 6.50 p.m. next evening. Trains to the smaller stations are apt to halt at inconvenient hours, and we turn out at midnight to sleep on the platform until dawn. A cup of tea, a few bananas, and the two waiting bullock carts packed with our kit we are off soon after the sun is above the horizon, to accomplish the eighteen miles to a Forest Rest House before night fall.

JOURNAL ————————————————————————————————

The Narbada has the reputation of being a difficult river because the mahseer in it have a marked partiality for gram, and aschew fly spoon and natural bait. However, the mahseer will take natural bait at some places, and Dhariaghat, where the river roars in foaming falls and cascades over a wide barrier of basaltic rocks is the best. This place is seldom fished because it is not on a motorable road and is some little distance from the railway. From the small wayside station of Bir (pronounced Beer) on the main line east of Khandwa Junction it is twenty four miles by bullock cart to the river.

It is cloudy, rain threatens, and the air is close and sultry. After the first three miles, the road is very bad. In places the track is deep in tenacious mud; here and there outcrops of rock throw the carts about with violent jerks and bumps. Once one of the carts overturns, but without damage to contents as our things have been carefully packed. A two hours' halt at midday is necessary for man and beast, a change of bullocks three miles short of our destination causes delay, and it is not until eight o'clock, thirteen hours from the start, that we arrive at the Rest House. We have been fortunate to escape the rain. Now that we are under shelter and secure, the downpour commences, and it rains on and off all the next day.

On 1st October we walk six miles through the forest to see Narbada Mai and select a camping ground. The road to the river runs between two blocks of teak forest. Where there are deep ravines thick with bamboo and undergrowth. Several painted sandgrouse are flushed on the path, and a sambur stag with horns in velvet clatters up the stony hillside. As we near the river the roar of the Falls can be heard. Below the Falls the river is confined in a gorge some ninety yards in width, and boils deep and sullen for half a mile to open out and again contract, and so make its way for twenty miles to Mandhata.

By the side of the path approaching the sacred river is a temple dedicated to Mahadeo, from within which issues the unceasing chant of the solitary priest. All through the day and night, with only short intervals for rest and food, he drones away; and so passes the monotonous days of his earthly existence, hoping for the Nirvana he wishes eventually to attain. He is one of the really earnest devotees and has been here three years, alone in the tiger-haunted forest, with no human dwelling within miles of him.

3rd October. Weather conditions seem to improve, so we proceed into camp, pitching tents in the shade of some small teak trees. Sorted out fishing tackle.

6th. Did not start fishing as early as I intended; water very dirty but is clearing a little and this evening river is quite a foot lower. I struck a murrel, fishing with gram, and he bit through the gut. Saw a man on opposite side of the river where the rapids sweep in rushing eddies along the rocks, catch three big murrel in the morning and one in the afternoon. He uses a long bamboo, about twenty feet of line and a dead fish on a single hook. When he hooks a fish he drags it out by the skull! 4lbs, 6lbs, doesn't matter; nothing to break so out he comes without any niceties of playing! 'Sometimes' says our dhimar 'they catch as much as three maunds of fish in a morning.' It is mahseer we want and not these coarse fish, but the water is too thick for spinning. Weather very unsettled, hot and steamy, thunder about and will certainly be a storm before long. River has risen, which is a pity as it was just getting into good order. Saw several large packs of white winged teal.

12th. About three thousand people collected for the Dashera Festival on both banks of the river. Shikari says an order has come from Dhar State that there is to be no fishing. I suppose it is for this festival only. There were joy rides in boats and whole scene is festive and picturesque. A feature of the boat business was the chasing of coconuts which floated down the stream. There was a special poojah performed by a few of the men, by evening of 13th nearly all the people had left.

An old man of Takari killed a panther one night a couple of months ago with his hatchet. It got in among the calves. He went in, another man carrying a light, and found the panther fastened onto the throat of a calf. Using both hands he severed the panther's spine near the loins with his light axe, gave it several more cuts and ended by slicing half its head off!

21st. No kill: fished further side of the river using the ordinary general utility rod, greenheart butt cane top, A.& N.S., got one tengra 2lbs, also a small yellow fat bellied fish which barks, grunts rather, when it is out of the water, put it back. At 5 o/c was taken by a heavy fish which made off like an express train; difficult to get along rocks, so put on good strain. Rod gave a loud crack and I could see the cane of last few inches below first ferrule had split. Followed as fast as I could, 100 yards line out. Found the line under a rock further down, got it free, and up flew the line another 20 yards. Then got on terms with the fish and after more time, keeping him out of the flood in a small bay had a sight of him. Well hooked fortunately. Dhimar very good with landing net: Mahseer – 20lbs. A fine handsome fish; deep blue back. When dhimar picked up his rod from where he had hurriedly put it down when he heard my yell, he found a water snake had pinched his minnow and got well mixed up with the line. Slew him with a piece of drift wood, a mottled green snake 2ft. 6in. long.

A blister fly got me badly on lip and tongue. Felt it bite me and brushing it quickly away was at once sharply blistered; quite unpleasant for twenty minutes or so. Beautiful sunset, crimson sky, water a lovely colour as we poled across the river; may rain soon. Minnows seemed to be moving a lot and wonder if they sense another flood.

I saw a wonderful display of leaping fish of all sizes making constant efforts to ascend the falls. We sit and watch them; none succeed that we can see, yet some must do so. Our greatest admiration is gained by the tiny heroes which leap from the foaming torrent against the slippery sides of the rocks, cling there panting with down-pressed pectoral and ventral fins, wriggle up a little, take a rest, wriggle again, and so by difficult inches climb the five feet of rock, mostly perpendicular and sometimes overhanging, until they meet the water trickling over at an edge. A final effort is made and the gallant minnow rushes into the flood, to be instantly borne away down the fall he has been vainly endeavouring to ascend. It is only the very wee minnows which attempt the ascent in this manner; the others are ceaselessly leaping, leaping, without apparent success.

We catch a few mahseer before the water again becomes too coloured, then our fishing produces only small tengra. These scaleless fish do not afford much sport, but are good eating and have no small bones. Early in the month there were flights of duck and teal moving up and down the river. Daily while fishing, we see three varieties of kingfisher, blue rock pigeons, red-wattled lapwings, fish hawks, kites and the ubiquitous crow. One day we saw an immense mugger cruising down the river like a Thames steamer.

During this fishing trip frequent heavy showers caused the river to flood which made fishing impossible. It took ten or fifteen days for the water to clear after a storm, and in the intervals when the water was fishable, Burton caught a few small mahseer of 3 to 5lbs. He was unable to leave until the last day of October as there was a full moon Festival at Mandhata and there were no carts available until after that.

DIARY

The dhimar caught a perrun 14lbs., also a small mahseer. Stopped fishing late and dhimar discovered he couldn't get the boat up stream in the dark; nor indeed in daylight without help. To have been swept down either of the main falls, as would have happened if the boat got into the heavy force of the stream, meant certain disaster, so we decided to sleep on the rocks for the night. The sky was clear and a cleft in the rocks was found which would shelter us from the night wind which would be somewhat chilly. Luckily I had a box of matches in tackle box so we had a fire midnight onwards, any amount of drift wood available, and the dhimar had his evil-smelling tobacco to comfort him. The full moon shed a silver radiance over the placid reaches of the river and over the wild turmoil of the roaring waters of the falls and cascades.

Soon after day-break the moon set behind a giant mango tree on the Dhar side of the river, the stars faded out of the pale blue sky, and the sun rose over the forest trees. The dhimar now set about making arrangements to get the boat away. A long rope was called for and he waded and swam to the bank to fetch it and bring a man back with him. They arrived at a rock at the head of the rapid and the man left there with the rope while the dhimar returned to the boat, which we poled to a place on the near side. The dhimar, like an otter in the water, fetched the end of the rope and fastened it to the boat. It was nervous work to see him swept in an instant some twenty yards down stream before he obtained a footing. The boat was taken up stream as far as could be managed, and taking the force of the water, was whirled down and pulled with success to the eddy below the rock: once there all danger was over and we safely gained the bank. As we did so the swollen bulk of a dead bullock came floating down the stream to be carried over one of the centre cataracts. We were glad to have had a long drink of river water before THAT came along.

29th. Again went to middle of river and found the fish still busy leaping. Got plenty of live bait and fished under the archway. Got a 10lb. mahseer almost at once. He tried to escape by the further channel and had to be dragged back by main force as, if he had turned the corner, he must have eventually cut the line. Caught another small one, and a perrun; then had to leave early in order to get away before dark. Would do very well if I could stay on a week or two more, but arrangements made for the Rajputana tour and I must be off.

Six miles takes us back to the Forest Rest House where there is a sandstone fort about one hundred and fifty years old. The remaining eighteen miles to the railway station we do in a trotting bullock cart during the cool hours of a moonlight night to take the train at an early hour in the morning of the last day of October. Narbada Mai – when will I see you again?

JOURNAL _____

For the purpose of travel over all sorts of roads and tracks there is, to a slender purse, a limited choice as to a touring car. The Ford car we had purchased at Bombay took us from there to the Central Provinces, where we spent several months in the forests of the Satpura Hills. The monsoon months were spent at Pachmarhi, and then came the recent fishing trip to the Narbada. But one cannot always be on shikar, and when the instinct to 'see things' which is the urge to travel, becomes insistent it is time to be once more 'on the road'.

The valley of the Narbada is not, as yet, traversed by motorable roads, so we had to rail our Ford car to Khandwa. We set out from here early in November with the intention of motoring by devious ways to Delhi. The road from Khandwa was in good motorable condition, but we were much hampered by thousands of cattle which were being driven to distant jungle pastures to graze there until the next monsoon. Buffaloes remained stolidly in the road until quietly pushed by the bumpers, and irresponsible calves ran about after frightened mothers. It was also the celebration of the Diwali Festival and many people were assembling for the Fair at Mandhata.

There are some crops of millet and cotton, but the land is mostly stony and unproductive. At Mortaka village we reach the fine iron girder bridge over the Narbada. At the bridge head we paid a toll of two rupees and followed bullock carts at crawling pace over the one-way track which is beneath the railway line. About the centre of the bridge we stopped to look downstream at the place where, twenty two years previously, my canvas fishing boat sank under me necessitating a long swim to safety. After crossing the bridge – it must be about a mile long – we proceed through wooded and cultivated country to reach the foot of the ghat which surmounts the western end of the Vindhyan Hills.

Having replenished stores and petrol at Mhow, we proceed to Mandu by an excellent road. It was pleasant to stop halfway and have breakfast under a shady tree. Mandu was at one time the capital of Malwa, and from 1304 until 1564 when it came into the hands of the Emperor Akbar, was constantly the scene of siege and battle. The Emperor Jahangir, liked to visit here and it was early in the seventeenth century that the beautiful Nur Jahan, the celebrated Persian wife of Jahangir, shot four tigers while at Mandu. All is now ruin and desolation, where formerly there was great splendour; the Hindu Raj was displaced by the Muhammadan, of which no trace now remains. The aboriginal Bhils still cultivate the plateau as they have done through all the strife and turmoil of the ages, and sambur, tiger and other beasts of the forest wander through the ruins.

1

2

3

4

golden lions
and his whol
riding chair
golden scales
shoulder blac
magnificent
trappings. Af
horses; then

The morni
time to settle
tongas. Half
limestone bri
crossed it on
annual flood.
seven gateway
battlements
Padmini, and

It has been
fortunate tha
and never se

The train
After breakf
Chambal riv
cultivated co
Bungalow at
while slowly
laden luggage
end ring of o
by the blacks

The road t
extensive she
very pictures
is said that th
am sure there

The road f
was nearly da
we were fort
thirty miles
surrounded b
ground. Abov
again is the F

The thirty
the previous e
from here to
from Deoli w
engaged in re
monsoon floc
remained, bu
running from

CHAPTER
18

1
The Chambal river pontoon
bridge en route to Gwalior

2
Saryasi, a Narbada devotee,
1928

3
Chitor, the Tower of Fame

4
Udaipur, the Jaghiwas Water
Palace

5
20lb Mahseer caught by
Richard Burton in the
Narbada river

6
A packed service bus,
photographed after passing
Deoli

licensed for eighteen passengers and full up inside, had quite half that number hanging on outside! Seeing me stop to take a photo there was a hasty unloading, and energetic action on the part of the driver, who took me for some police or other Official. We passed quickly through Nasirabad to arrive at Ajmer as the sunset glow was fading from the surrounding hills; the day's run was one hundred and nine miles.

Ajmer is situated on a plateau which is probably the highest point in the plains of Hindustan, and the range of hills between it and Nasirabad marks the watershed of the continent of India. The fort of Taragarh, built of huge stone blocks, encloses eighty acres of the top of a hill to the north west of the city. The Anar Sagar lake is the source of the Luni river and the beautiful marble pavilions on the embankment were built by the Emperor Shah Jehan.

The road from Ajmer to Jaipur is in first class order. We pass one of the large Kos Minars, or milestones, placed every two miles in the time of the Emperor Akbar, to mark the distance. In the days of slow travel by bullock cart and palanquin it must have been a solace to weary eyes when one of the minars was seen in the distance. We, however, cover the seventy nine miles to Jaipur by lunchtime, and have time to see around the city in the evening.

Jaipur is a great and pleasing contrast to Ajmer, where the drive through the narrow streets was a horrid experience. Narrow streets congested with every imaginable variety of vehicle, including municipal carts, smells, flies, loose cattle, sheep and goats, mangy dogs, the halt, maimed, and blind in dozens pestering for alms, itinerant musicians, insulting urchins, sweetmeat sellers, their wares almost hidden by the swarms of flies, the incessant cries of the tonga driver to clear the way; the noise, the hubbub, the dirt, the squalor. We talk of legislation to abate street noises in England; I think that such turmoil as continues without cessation for all the daylight hours in a city like Ajmer would speedily drive one to an asylum.

Here, in Jaipur, it is a pleasure to drive about the wide, well kept streets, where there is room for all and very little noise. In all India there is no city planned with the spaciousness of Jaipur. The modern city was built in 1728, and is encircled by a masonry crenellated wall twenty feet high; there are seven gateways. Weavers, dyers, carpet makers, ivory carvers, and others can be seen at work producing the fascinating things which visitors so much wish to acquire.

From Jaipur we motored on to Alwar. The road from Rajgarh deserves special mention. It passes over the Aravali Hills and through the big Game Preserves of the Alwar State. There is not in the whole of India a mountain road constructed on such generous lines, or maintained in such perfect condition. The drive of fifty two miles was a great joy. We saw a number of animals; sambur, nilgai, chinkara, pig, and all of them as tame as if they were in a park. At Alwar there was much going on in preparation of the festivities on the occasion of the twenty fifth anniversary of the rule of the Maharajah.

The first twenty five miles of the road on to Delhi was within the Alwar State and its condition indicated that perhaps His Highness has no game preserves in that direction. After passing through Ferozepur Jirka and into British Territory the road improved and was good all the way to Delhi, with the exception of half a mile or so through the town of Gurgaon where the road was dangerous owing to deep pot holes. So here we are at last at Delhi, the speedometer showing the run from Alwar to be one hundred and three miles, and the distance travelled by the car since leaving Khandwa, exactly one thousand two hundred miles. There has been nothing to say as to motoring troubles, not a single puncture, or tyre trouble of any sort; but I do not employ a native driver, and as an owner driver I am more careful.

Chapter 19

MORE TIGERS, AND A JOURNEY SOUTH — 1730 MILES BY CAR

After a short stay at Delhi, preparations were made to return to Itarsi and the C.P. jungles; this time they took a more direct route, generally on good roads, and some of the way by train.

JOURNAL _____

It was on a bright and crisp morning in January that we took the road past the Purana Kila to head for Muttra and the South. The distance was ninety miles and an easy run. The picturesque frontage of the city of Muttra along the banks of the Jumna with its many bathing ghats and small pavilions was admired from the river, and a visit was paid to the ruins of the ancient town of Mahaban. A second class road running through cultivated country took us to Bharatpur. The provisional road map of India indicated a first class road from Bharatpur to Fattehpur Sikri, so it was followed for three miles, to peter out into no road at all! The skeleton arches of long neglected bridges were found here and there, and the barely visible sandy track of fourteen miles took four hours to cover.

Fattehpur Sikri and Agra are on the beaten track and seen by all tourists, so a description of these famous places is not necessary. Travelling from Agra, the Chambal river was crossed by a pontoon bridge, and as on former occasions at other points of its course, we were struck with the beautiful turquoise blue colour of the water. The fortress of Gwalior has witnessed many historic happenings, and is at last in times of peace, in which it is not likely to be again disturbed by the sieges and assaults which it has endured through the ages. After Gwalior we travelled along excellent roads passing through much jungle country, and came to Bhopal late in the afternoon of the second day. From here the train took us to Itarsi, and we stayed for the next two months in the jungle of the Satpura Hills.

Camp by the Tapti river, Rangobehi.
February began with heavy rain and thunderstorms which continued until the end of the month. There were no tiger or panther kills, and few animals were seen when tracking through the jungle. Some green pigeons and duck were shot for the pot. On 17th Burton decided to move to the F.B. at Chaurakund. Two days later the tigress killed and Burton sat up for her. She did not return, although tracks were found of both tiger and tigress up and down the road and along the river bed.

DIARY _____

22nd. Forest Guard brings news of another tiger, big male, having finished off the tigress' kill! I think he may return tonight so will sit over boda. Full moon and well worth it. George D.F.O. came to see us yesterday on his way to his camp; he estimates there are one hundred tiger in the Mulghat Forest Division.

23rd February. Sat up over live boda and slew the tigress (it was she and not a big male as F.G. said). As well to relate history in detail.

Was in machan chair and all settled by 4.30 p.m. At 9 p.m. tigress started her roarings and whole forest aroused by the noise – sambur, and monkeys. She roared around for some time and appeared to have gone off to the west and I was despondent. Boda was tethered under small leafless tree by side of cart road. At 10.10 p.m. I heard the tigress' steps among the leaves and saw her form stalking in a very purposeful way – towards the boda. The boda moved and she instantly rushed at him, and seemed to straddle across him, pulling his neck – which she had taken into her jaws from above – backwards towards her. He uttered a few small shaking bellows and was then silent. She stayed still, quite still and I heard the neck bones break.

In about three minutes from the attack she had him dead and let her jaws open and the boda's head fell to the ground. Immediately she seized him by neck to drag the carcass away and, finding she couldn't (because of the wire rope), dropped the neck and seized the hind quarters and gave some tremendous tugs. Then she lay down head on to line of boda's body and tore him open and gulped down the meat! I could get no shot, so I waited for about ten minutes or so, in hopes of a chance, when she suddenly got up and went straight off back into forest, making no end of a noise, careless of how she crashed about and making all sorts of cries, belchings and grunts. Then I heard her roaring and grunting and making zoo noises all over the place for about half an hour. Then no more and I feared, needlessly, that she might not return.

For five hours there was no sign of her. Then at 3.10 she noiselessly and unannounced came and sat at same place as before, and recommenced her meal. I knew I must now take a shot or get no shot, as she would go off the same way and give no chance. I could see with field glasses how she lay, but there was a good deal of confusing shadow. She began to feed down one of the hindlegs, both of which lay out towards the open, and I saw that I could get a shot at her head if she kept on at this, so put on the torch. Instantly she looked up at machan, I took careful aim and she fell over without a sound and lay with legs and tail twitching. Her breath left her in one big sigh and she was dead.

Next morning, when men turned up I went to camp and fetched the car. A fine tigress with an unusually long ruff, so much so that I thought on first seeing her stalking boda that it was a tiger. Her coat unusually long and thick. Bullet went a bit higher than I thought, but her head was raised, looking up at me and went just over top of her skull between the ears and an inch or so to right of spine. A very fatal shot.

Measurements
Length: straight – between pegs   8ft. 2in.
      "   curves   8ft. 5in.
Weight – 250lbs.

Skin and skeleton sent to Bo.N.H.S. to be mounted in Museum with the tiger and this LOVELY skin stolen. Well covered, no hollows or 'points', a massive powerful beast. It was very noticeable how invisible she was in half shadow, half moonlight.

Next morning gave the kill over to the vultures. Too tiring to sit another night and will wait for a kill.

2nd March. Out stalking, saw two lots of sambur. Kill at west; big tiger: broke the root which I thought was strong! Took kill about three hundred yards. Tracked it up and found it in grass. Put up machan chair and ready by 4 o/c. Tiger turned up at 7 o/c. He took no notice of the distant light over his head, or of the torch when turned on to him; and I killed him with one shot in the head. Bugled up some villagers who went and told people at camp and when they came I got down and went home. In morning found a tigress had gone along the road and eaten bone of hind leg left by the big tiger!

Measurements

Curves – body	6ft.9in.;	tail	2ft.10in.	= 9ft.7in.
Pegs – "	6ft.3in.;	"	2ft.10in.	= 9ft.1in.

Fine tiger – 450lbs. Faded colouring. Skin prepared for Bo.N.H.S. for Prince of Wales Museum as a mounted specimen.

Shikar at N. Chaurakund block is finished. In most years there is no water near Chaurakund after the middle of March. The rain of February filled up the streams, and it was because of this that the game was scattered.

5–6th. Packing up and sending off kit to Dhakna. Forgot to mention very nice Khond F.G., Manigoo of Rangaheb. Gave him tip of Rs.20 for excellent service the month he was with me. Drove in car to Harisal to fetch petrol, road very bad because under construction to make it pucca.

At Dhakera, his next camp, there were sambur, nilgae and four-horn in the jungles, as well as tracks of tiger and panther, but although there were kills by both these, and Burton sat up in the machan at night, neither returned to the kill. The daytime was spent stalking, and a sambur stag was shot as food for the camp Burton notes in his diary, and not as a trophy. He was out early most mornings and describes this jungle trip in one of his articles for the journal.

JOURNAL _____

All the forests of this part of the country are of teak and bamboo. The hills to the south of our present camp extend by successive ridges and valleys to the main backbone of the Gawilgarh Hills. Many of the trees, as in the Tapti Valley, are withered by the recent severe frost. As a rule there is not much colour in the forests of tropical countries, but at this season there are autumn tints of every description. One tree, a species of erythrina, has brilliant red flowers; and there is the tree known as 'the Flame of the Forest' on account of the brilliant colour of its velvet-like orange red petals.

The hot season is now approaching. The temperature in the verandah rises to 100° in the middle of the day, but the nights are cool and in the early morning it is as low as 56°. On arrival here we were greeted with the news that there are seven tigers in the vicinity. I was also informed that the news of the countryside is that I have recently shot eight tigers. I fear the story of the seven is as inaccurate as that of the eight, for in walks abroad there is no sign of even one of the reputed seven. A bad sign of this camp is the silence at night. There are no alarm calls of sambur and other animals, and no tracks of tiger – old or new.

News came that a panther had killed a calf near a village five miles away. I went at once and tracked up the kill, which was very neatly 'butchered' and placed in a clump of bamboos. There was a suitable tree close by and my machan chair was soon in position. Shortly before dark a lovely mongoose came and had a feed. Such a lithe, graceful animal with grey points to the hair of his sleek body and a fine black tip to his long tail. He reminded me of several of his species which have been such interesting pets from time to time: no snakes, cockroaches, or spiders, and such like, in one's house when there is a tame mongoose on the premises.

The darkness of the tropic night is not as you imagine it. One soon becomes accustomed to the light afforded by the stars; except when in deep shadow one can see quite well. There are certain colours which are not readily visible in twilight and darkness, stare as hard as you wish you will not be able to make out with any distinction the form of the larger carnivora, even at a few yards distance. It is the ground colour of tawny yellow which is their concealment.

There is a pool in the river not far from this bungalow. It is shaded by large trees and has much life around it, daily we see the otters at play and catching fish. On any bare rock in the stream are cormorants, and there are four varieties of kingfisher. One of these is like the bird one sees in England, the other is a black and white bird twice the size of the other. His habit is to hover over the water about thirty feet up and then plunge deep into the stream to catch the minnows crosswise in his beak. He has been described very well as 'the pied fish tiger o'er the pool'. The other two are alike in colouring, but differ in size, the larger being about twice as big again. They both have bright red bills, and their general appearance is blue and white, but mostly blue. The larger one is the more rare.

On the 29th March the tiger killed and dragged the buffalo a quarter of a mile to conceal it under a mass of creepers. There was a suitable tree for the machan chair, but it was necessary to cut away much of the creepers in order to be able to see. The nights are very still and one can hear the slightest sound at that distance. The tiger was extremely cautious, stopping and listening and slowly coming nearer. He took half an hour to approach. Having come close enough to see the kill, he was able to see then that it was not as fully concealed as he had left it. For a tiger of his experience that was sufficient warning. He had no doubt had a very convincing lesson on some previous occasion and had no intention of taking risks. Of the watcher in the tree he had, I am sure, no knowledge. I heard his retreating footsteps and that was the last of him for that night.

The only way to get this tiger would be to sit up every night until he came along again. By the sixth night I was getting tired of the game, but determined to sit him out. On the eighth night patience was rewarded. I heard his moaning call by the river and coming nearer. There was no sound on the part of any forest animals to announce that the tiger was on the prowl. At ten minutes to eight there was a rush over the leaf strewn pebbles and in an instant I was sitting up with the rifle out of the loophole. One very quickly decides where exactly to place the bullet and the foresight gleamed brilliantly on the centre of the shoulder blades as the trigger was pressed. To the shot the tiger fell on his side, his tail beat the ground for a few seconds, and then he was still. The buffalo's hind legs kicked out again, so the tiger breathed his last before his victim ceased to live. The bite in the back of the neck killed the buffalo, the tiger had not had time to break it's neck. The claws of his left paw were still hooked round buffalo's nose! They fell together, so that when the tiger fell on his left side with his hind legs drawn up in the act of killing, boda fell on to his left side also and all three of the tiger's feet were under the buffalo. His length was nine feet between pegs, about the normal size for these jungles. The villagers were very pleased to be rid of this beast which had taken toll of their cattle for years.

Many people do not sit up at night, but to me there is a great charm about it. One learns to recognise the alarm calls of all the animals of the jungle, and the cries of the night birds also. It was on one of the eight nights' vigil that I learnt to know the sound made by the porcupine, but whether he always makes this noise I do not know. There was a loud expulsion and taking in of breath, and I could not imagine what it could be.

The tracks in the morning showed beyond any doubt who had been puffing and blowing all around my tree.

One day I was seated in a tree by a jungle pool when a picketted goat called up a panther from a neighbouring ravine. The panther came trotting through the trees, halting for a second or so now and again, as if he could hardly realise his good fortune at obtaining such an easy meal. Up to the goat he trotted to be met by a lowered head. A feint of a lifted paw by the panther was countered by a butt from the fearless goat – the fearlessness of ignorance. Another feint by the panther, and in an instant he would have made the fatal attack; but his intention and his life were ended by a bullet in the chest. Down he sat, exactly in his tracks, and as lifelike as possible to the astonished goat, which just sniffed at him and went on unconcernedly with his meal of thorn leaves. A panther without experience this, and though full grown, his weight of 100 lbs for his length of 6ft.11in., showed that he had not yet attained his full proportions.

I often get up in the dark and go off into the forest to see the animals. Often the sambur feed along quite unaware that anyone is near. The hinds with fawns keep separate from the stags. One day several sambur came to within a few feet of me as I sat at the foot of a tree. Alas, I had forgotten to bring my camera. When one gets on in years there is more desire to see than to destroy and, during the lives of the coming generation, public opinion will more and more condemn the killing of wild animals. The time is approaching when, if the hand of man is not stayed, there will be few animals left. 'What about your own slaying?' you might say. My answer is that my softness of heart does not extend to the greater carnivora – not yet at any rate!

DIARY ───

A very big forest fire for past week away to south west in Dhulghat, whole sky blazing red like sunrise. Still, four days later, a light sky all night in that direction. I went yesterday evening to look for a handkerchief left in forest some time ago at a place where I sat down to mend boots, and found it! Saw seventeen sambur, and three pig. There might be a tiger about but they evidently have other haunts which they prefer.

11th April. Finished packing. Sold meat safe for 15/- and the big bath tub for 7/- to the Forest Department. Got rid of several kiltas and packing cases to reduce baggage.

12th. The lorry turned up at 7 a.m. packed it and sent it off and followed in the car. Went on to Ellichpur and stayed there the night. Lorry went on at 5 p.m., the men saying it was cooler and they would get to Itarsi D.B. at midnight. I started off at 6 a.m. and got to Itarsi, one hundred and seventeen miles at 12.30. No lorry! It turned up at 2 o/c or later, having had a lot of tyre trouble. Paid the stipulated 100/-. The recognised rate is 8as. a mile – Rs.85/-, but I agreed to an extra 15/- on account of the lorry having to go empty to Dachna.

17th. Saw wife off in evening to Bombay for Coonoor. I started 6 a.m. the next day in car for Nagpur. Have gone 5800 miles with only TWO punctures, and today had two punctures and one tube giving way. Took car to garage to have the universal joint seen to, which had been heating up ever since skid of last September. No doubt the chassis was never straightened properly.

JOURNAL ───

At Mull there was news of a man-eating panther which had been killing people for the past six years, and has killed more than two hundred people. NEVER known to take a human being standing or walking, always lying down or sitting. A native Forest

1

2

CHAPTER
19

1
A camel cart photographed on
the Burton's journey south
through India. They travelled
1730 miles by car

2
Dhakna, Korka women in Holi
festival attire

3
Dhakna, the Forest Rest
House, 1928

4
The tigress shot at
Chaurakund, 1928

5
The boat, rods and dhimar
used while fishing on the
Narbada river, 1928

Officer sat up in a pit with a companion over the body of a woman. Panther came, a few feet away; the other man flashed the torch and panther made off. Later it came back and sniffed around the pit, and they cowered and were afraid to move! So the killing goes on.

This brute was shot in October 1929 and the killing of it is a thrilling story related to me by the young sportsman concerned (Goodchild). Seated on his machan, a flimsy unscreened structure only eight or nine feet above the ground in silent vigil over a tethered goat, he heard the choked cry of the goat as it was seized and turned on the torch attached to the rifle in his hand. Instantly the panther launched to the attack; the machan collapsed with the weight of the beast, and as it fell the rifle was discharged. Clinging with one hand to a branch, the growlings and rushings of the brute were answered by several shots from a revolver. In a few minutes there was silence. After an anxious four hours dawn appeared, and the slayer of over two hundred and thirty human beings was found dead a few yards away. It was fortunate for the watcher in the machan that the murderer's eyes fell first upon the goat, for otherwise one more might have been added to the long list of victims.

The Civil Station of Chanda has changed little since last seen over thirty years ago. The railway and the motor car have arrived, but the broad shady streets and the peace and quiet of a typical out-station of the Civil Administration remains as it always has been. There is a timber depot at Allapilli, so all along the road the carts were a real terror. One can't take any chances in passing them as it is never safe to try and guess which way the buffaloes and bullocks will shy. Along the east side of the clearing at Allapilli is the Government Forest Reserve, which is also a sanctuary for all animals, except the greater carnivora. Here are buffalo, bison, sambur, chital, four-horn antelope, nilgae, muntjac, pig, wild cats and civets. The bird life is also abundant. I passed Rest Houses every ten to twelve miles along the road from Chanda.

Allapilli is in the Ahiri Zemindari, a large tract the length and breadth being each about eighty miles. It will be instructive in these days of organised belittlement of the achievement and benefits to the people of the British Rule, to say something about it. From the Official Gazetteer of 1909 it is learnt that within six years of the assumption by the Court of Wards, on account of mismanagement, of the estate, that 'it has been fully cleared of all it's debts and has now a clear field before it. It is safe to say that the estate has made almost as much progress in the last six years as in the whole of the previous six hundred years of it's existence.'

DIARY _____

1st May. At Allapilli found D.S.P. and his wife in District Bungalow. I am told much shooting goes on, so all the game will soon disappear. The tigers will remain and kill the cattle and the people, as these sportsmen do not shoot tigers! Went on to F.R.H. and found District Forest Officer there, and he gave me a room. Next morning went out on his elephant. Saw a few sambur and the early morning tracks, at a pool of water, of the tiger which had stirred up the sambur and chital which I heard calling at 4 a.m. In evening went with D.F.O. in his car along cart tracks through Sanctuary. He evidently does much of this night touring after tiger and panther and says he has fired at sixteen panthers and shot three of them! A lazy and unsporting business, and he rouses up all the jungles at night wherever he may be. I hope other D.F.O.'s don't do the same! He is too grossly fat and physically unfit for any other form of shikar. I stopped at Allapilli to do some fishing, with little result.

3rd. Set off for Sironcha, 57 miles. Very nice D.B. Former Residence of the D.C. here, double story, fine views over the Prenhita river.

5th. Went nineteen miles east to F.R.H. Kopela. Road has, in former days, been a good one; now much neglected. Very bumpy and rough and heavy sand in many places, and very hard on a car. It is easy to see how slowly the bullock carts have to travel and how easy for tiger to bag a man off his cart; for that is what they frequently do. The man-killing appears to almost cease in hot weather months: the reason given being that the tigers then only move at night, and so come across no men; who are not about at night. Quite likely it is the proper explanation. Some of the killings are by tigress with small cubs and in one case by two half grown tigers: so the trade is carried on from one family to another. There have been man-eaters in Chanda District for many years and probably always will be.

From Allapilli to Sironcha is fifty seven miles and except for the first few miles being cut up by the converging carts, is good all the way. A cart track to the east was followed to the village of Palli on the right bank of the Indravati river. The going was reasonably good and the average pace twelve m.p.h. The Ahiri Zemindar had caused a track of bamboo matting to be laid across the sandy bed of the Bandia, just beyond the village of Damarincha, near my shooting camp of over thirty years ago. It was here in 1898 that I got fever, and had to go back before my leave was up.

During the past twelve months a number of people have been killed by tigers. Three were killed in December and eight in January. Only one tiger had been killed during the past year and there were said to be quite a number within thirty miles of the town. It is not for want of other food that human beings are killed, for while motoring through the forests a number of sambur and chital were seen. In some cases the men were taken out of the bullock carts they were driving, or else from behind the cart if they happened to be walking. In one case the victim was taken from the centre of a string of thirty carts. Always are the victims taken from behind, seized by the back of the neck, and it seems that in the case of both tiger and panther the animal never attacks a man from the front.

Two men were killed on the road near here 23rd March this year. First kill 9 a.m. – man dragged off; next kill 5 p.m. It was found that the tiger in taking off the first man somehow let go hold of neck when negotiating a nala. The corpse fell in sitting position with its back against the bank and arms spread out – graphically illustrated by the Sub. Inspector! – and in that position it was found. It was seen that the tiger had paced around in front but had been afraid to touch the body as whichever way he was the staring eyes of the victim looked at him, and he couldn't get behind it to again take hold of the neck. However this may be, the fact remains that the body was not touched and the tiger was there all day, for at 5 p.m. another cart came along and the tiger killed and completely ate the cart man.

The Sub. Inspector says the people won't let the Police sit up over corpse; and I expect the Police don't want to! but probably a relative would let a sahib sit up. If I don't go to Burma, I might come to these parts December, January, February; plenty of fishing also. At Sironcha are the buildings of the American Baptist Mission, established here in 1892, and the scattered houses of the settlement. The country is flat and palm trees a feature of the scenery. From the sap of these trees is brewed a potent liquor.

6th May. Leaving Sironcha at dawn to cross Prenhita and so to Kazipet via Channur and Mancherial: but fear the crossing of Godavery will be difficult. Neither the Prenhita nor the Godavery rivers are yet bridged for road traffic.

7th. At 5 a.m. I was at the river bank as told by Tahsildar. The men were only just beginning to make the raft! Four dug-outs, one of which was leaking badly, were lashed together with two poles and some rope, and over these was placed a layer of bamboo matting. By pushing and pulling this way and that, the crazy craft was eventually adjusted to the satisfaction of the 'foreman of works', a dhimar of few words, who evidently knew his job and had measured the wheel track with a bamboo lath. A couple of planks were placed in position and the car run on by hand as it seemed unsafe to do so under power. It was fortunate that this was done as one of the improvised trestles slipped and the back axle had to be prized up with a pole. At last the car was perched up on this primitive arrangement, and in ten minutes, the baler busy all the time, we were against the further shore and safely across the wide, deep water. We were then pushed through quarter of a mile of deep sand. All the kit had to be taken out and sent across the river first, and car had to be reloaded.

A few words of Telegu enabled the correct one out of many confusing cart tracks to be followed. But what a road. Twelve miles of truly awful cart tracks. Bumps, deep ruts, rocks, pot holes, a wonder the springs did not break. There was a great deal of deep sand. Some part of the way was through jungle and many stumps of trees had to be avoided. Nearing Channur, got stuck in 120 yards sandy river bed. Bad approach or I could have taken it at a run and perhaps got through. Had to send for some men, and got pushed through. At Channur saw Tahsildar to whom I had sent a letter two days before. He knew nothing of the road beyond Godavery, but had sent on two chaprassis to make arrangements.

Went twenty four miles along fair road, and found chaprassis with fifty eight villagers waiting by road. Started to be pulled and got along by using engine, mostly on lowest gear. Many times coolies dropped the two ropes and pulled off puggries and loin cloths to put their feet on to; car red hot and could scarcely be touched! Four channels of water were crossed, and then we crossed the deepest channel. Water up to carburettor and I feared the worst. However all was well: I had tied up mouth of engine oil pipe with cloth to prevent water getting into it. Poor coolies – they had a horrid time of it. It would have been more sensible for Tahsildar to have arranged for four pairs of bullocks and ropes.

When the coolies had rested they were ready to drag the car through remaining fifty yards of sand and up steep bank. Paid 12/- for coolies, 2/- to the Chaprassis, and 1/- to the Kansidar of village. I don't know how much the coolies were allowed to have! I ought to have had the forethought to keep out small change, but expected bullocks and not coolies. No tyre trouble so far.

Took one man as guide who turned out to be totally ignorant of the roads and country south of the river! Found myself in a big village and then saw a huge thorn sticking in a front tyre! Pulled it out and put on spare wheel. Got another man as guide who took me to Railway line and told me to follow the line. Did so, and got badly hung up twice in cart ruts: once had to jack up wheels and fill up below tyres with earth and back car to get engine sump off the ridge. Eventually after crossing many bad plains, got through to Paddapullu Station. A miracle! Was relieved to quit the awful cart tracks, all stones and sand and thorny bushes, and reach a pucca road; a mile short of the Railway Station. Next morning three tyres were flat owing to small thorns having worked through and caused minute punctures. The deep sand had worn the walls of the tyres down to the canvas in some places, and it might have been cheaper in the long run to have railed the car from Chanda; but that would have been very dull and unadventurous.

JOURNAL ———————————————————————————————————————
In the Hyderabad State are many good roads, and that from Karimnagar, through Kazipet

to Secunderabad, is as good as any. Nearing Secunderabad it was very interesting to see well-known haunts of former times. A wonderful city is Hyderabad. In the thronged streets are to be seen men of all the countries of India and the East; but the days of even forty years ago, when the place was almost mediaeval in appearance and atmosphere, are gone for ever. The city now has fine, broad, dustless streets and the traffic control is admirable.

Motorists to the Nilgiris from Secunderabad generally drive to Mahbubnagar, rail from there to Kurnool, and take the road via Bangalore and Mysore to Ootacamund; but the yet unsatisfied spirit of adventure asked for the longer route and parts of India as yet unvisited. Over the Hussain Sagar bund, across a wide bridge which spans the Musi river and the road to distant Bezwada was gained. The route was through a hot, arid, and mostly shadeless country. Many mile sped by before the desired shade for lunch could be found. There was nowhere a tree large enough to shelter a goat, so the car was run off the road to a large tamarind tree. Good shade, but plenty of cattle ticks. In the bed of the unbridged sandy stream which is the boundary between Hyderabad and British India, the car stuck fast, and had to be hauled out by bullocks; and the wide bed of the Munyeru river twenty miles further on necessitated the help of villagers.

I went by train to Kistna Canal Station. When the wagon arrived there was no car in it! I had to wait for another train with the correct wagon. Went on to Guntur and took in petrol, but after leaving here I took the wrong road and did sixty three miles of cross country roads – some good, some mere cart tracks. I was nearly stuck in one nala, and again had to be pushed through the sand of a river bed. On arrival at Ongole in the evening I found a very nicely situated Inspection Bungalow. A heavy storm came on and I only just got the car into the garage in time. I was lucky this storm wasn't a few hours earlier, or I would have been hopelessly stranded on the other side of that river. The violent storm during the night had laid the dust and cooled the air for the next day's run of one hundred and sixty miles to Cuddapah, through country as arid and shadeless as can be imagined. However, nearing Cuddapah there are hills covered in thorny jungle and the causeway over the Pennair river was a welcome surprise. On leaving Cuddapah the roads were lined with trees, mainly the kanji (Indian beech) and the tamarind, and I drove happily along, freed from all thoughts of unbridged, sandy rivers.

Winding through forests and jungly hills, the Mysore plateau and Bangalore were soon gained; then the level road to Seringapatam and on to the City of Mysore, and it's wonderful electric illuminations. Passing onwards along the shaded highway leading to the Nilgiri Hills the dense forests of the foot-hills closed in on either side. The road turned upward and the air became cool and invigorating. The morning of the 18th May was almost cold when the car throbbed up the steep winding ghat after Gudalur. Then the open country was reached – the far famed Ooty downs. We followed the endless undulations of the slopes, in the hollows of which are dense patches of evergreen forest 'sholas', so sharply defined by years of grazing that they give the appearance of English parks. Thirty miles from Gudalur the road passes along the shore of the Ootacamund lake, it's four hills towering above it. In this beautiful scenery and climate it was difficult to recall the troubles and discomforts of the journey; and from here it was just a few miles to Coonoor where I would now be living. Total mileage from Itarsi to Coonoor – one thousand seven hundred and thirty miles.

A
TRIP
TO
BURMA
AND
SOME
FISHING
1929
TO
1930

Chapter 20

TRACKING IN THE BURMESE JUNGLES

There was a brief period at the beginning of this century when Northern Burma was open to western travellers. During and after the second world war the country was closed to the outside world, and there has been little contact since then, especially with the more remote areas of Northern Burma through which Burton and his wife travelled in 1930.

They sailed from Madras on 14th December and arrived on 16th at Rangoon. It was the first time Burton had visited Burma since he was posted to Mandalay as a young soldier in 1891. He noticed quite a considerable number of changes. New buildings, tarmac streets, and large numbers of cars and tramways. His intention was to fish in the upper reaches of the Mali Hka and the Confluence of the Irrawaddy, and to see as much of the country and its wildlife as possible.

For several years now, Burton had shot animals only for sending to the Bombay Natural History Society Museum, and did not retain these for personal trophies. On this occasion he had been asked by the Society to obtain a saing, if possible, for the Museum. Even this controlled shooting began to be not to his liking, and apart from shooting game animals and birds for food, and the greater carnivora when they became a threat to the lives and livelihood of the people, he had developed a lack of sympathy with the shooting of wildlife for sport. Perhaps it was on this trip to Burma that his interest in conservation began to override his love of hunting. In future, he found much of his enjoyment of sport in fishing and the discovery of new places to visit.

DIARY _____

Left at 6 p.m. for Taungdwingye: Pyinmana Junction 3.50 a.m. Saw the pagoda at Pegu lit up by many electric lights, looked like a christmas cake. Left Pyinmana 6 a.m. and crossed the Pegu Yomahs, very thick forest. Saw men in conical pattern leaf hats. At Taungdwingye, at the Bazaar, there were many articles made of bamboo for sale – rolls of bamboo matting and bamboo baskets. The bullock carts are more ornamented than the Indian ones, and all squeak loudly to keep off 'Nats' (evil spirits). Many men and women were smoking big home made cheroots. Taungdwingye is rapidly increasing in size now that the Railway is here and being extended further.

21st January. To Kodu, seven miles, by bullock cart. A small forest village, F.R.H. is on highest piece of ground near the village, and one can see over the near jungle to some extent. Much bamboo and very thick undergrowth where there is water near the nala beds.

24th. Out to the north east. Impossible to track for any distance in this dry jungle. In one nala there were tracks of bison, elephant, sambur, saing, kakur and tiger. Evidently a great resort for all animals in the rains. The men caught a number of small fish, pulled them out of deep pools among the rocks using crickets found under boulders as bait.

25th December. A day of rest after three days hunting, not very cold at night now and 80° in Verandah at the hottest time of day. The elder tracker wears his hair long and tied up in a 'bun' at the top of his head. He has delicate ears and small feet, altogether a womanish type, with narrow shoulders. The other tracker is a big fellow, with broad shoulders, head cropped, an oriental Malay type of drooping moustache. Both chew betel nut at every opportunity. If we halt in jungle while tracking for only a few minutes, out comes the betul box, a red lacquer affair with two inner compartments and about five inches in diameter. One could track a Burman through the jungle more surely than one could track a saing in this dry season, by the copious red saliva ejected every twenty paces. They walk very silently and are good trackers, even in this hard condition of the ground. In early rains no animal would evade them.

31st. Both trackers went west of the hill north west of Kodu. It seemed pretty hopeless as there has lately been marking of trees for felling but, as we were waiting in a nala for the tiffin cooly who had lost track of us, the elder shikari went a few yards up the nala and put up a bull saing. Following on we found him in open forest. Saw his whole body and his conspicuous white stockings, his colour a rusty brown. I couldn't see his horns. He stopped and I saw part of his flank between two trees and had plenty of time to put a bullet into that but refrained, since if wounded – as he would have been unless by lucky chance the bullet had got him in the kidneys or spine – I would never have got him, as the ground very hard for tracking. So off he went, and now I am rather wishing I had taken the chance!

We went to a pool of water and stayed there till afternoon and at 4 o/c two cows and a young bull came along. Fine big beasts, lovely chestnut coats, a little white each side of the muzzle, beautiful large eyes and big ears with a lot of white hair about the inside and edges of them, white buttocks and stockings from above the knee downwards. Must be very heavy; about 1600lbs – not less.

Forgot to note that when clearing a place to sit yesterday evening, a snake was found curled up in the dead bark of a log which the tracker and I were stripping. It threw many coils and wriggles and was off pretty quick; I couldn't see what kind it was. Glad I began to clear the loose bark away before sitting on the log! Heard peafowl for the first time a couple of evenings ago; the call is different to that of the Indian peafowl. I often put up jungle fowl when stalking about.

1st January 1930. A rest in camp. Cloudy this morning; a lovely sunrise over the low hills to the east. Temperature has been 80° or less in the day, and as low as 50° at 6 a.m.

JOURNAL ──

The saing of Burma is also found in parts of Siam, Sumatra, Java and Borneo. Their eyesight is remarkably keen. It is interesting to watch a herd settle down for the day and to observe how a young cow, for it is always on these that the duty devolves, post herself as a sentinel, taking up the best possible position of approach. To see the animal deliberately leave the herd and take up this isolated position is an instance of how freely animals can communicate ideas.

One learns much about the saing when tracking; how for instance, the snort of alarm which has something of defiance in it, on the approach of the intruder being detected, does not necessarily mean that the bull has departed. It is only experience that can teach such things as that. Such knowledge of tracking that one may possess will be improved for in that science one is always learning. To watch the expert tracker affords endless interest. The manner of his noiseless progress as he works through dry jungle where every leaf can go off underfoot like a cracker, the constant use of the ever ready razor-edged dah with which an obstructing bamboo is noiselessly sliced off, or a leaf overturned to disclose the hoof print beneath it.

On one memorable day the gymnasium footed progress through the dry teak leaves was given a first class commendation by coming upon a cow lying down just twenty feet away, her rest was disturbed by the loud and unnecessary warning whisper of the tracker whereupon the cow was up and off after a startled look at the apparition which had come unnoticed through the silent forest.

DIARY _____

3rd January. At midnight I was woken up by the bungalow shaking, an earth tremor, quite a good one! The younger tracker when he met me in the morning pointed to the sun at noon and then touched the ground and indicated by quivering his hand that he also had felt the tremor. They are used to these 'shakes' in Burma. We worked up the slopes and side of the big hill (Myinmanidaung +1324ft.), and got right to top of it. Then along the crest and down a long spur and we came to a very deep ravine, perpendicular sandstone cliffs, all crumbling away, and nala with much water in it. On the way up the hill we found a dead tortoise, very high! The elder tracker (Maung Thet She) was up a side nala and the younger tracker (Chaung Yo) and I waited to see if he could smell it. He picked up his bundle and dah, within six feet of it, and passed it without notice. We had a good laugh at his want of nose! The tortoise had evidently fallen down the steep hillside and smashed his carapace: we found this on turning him over, a wide gaping crack.

At a turn in the ravine Thet She stopped and pointed with his dah, there was a big snake, about twelve feet long, in act of mouthing a large frog – a giant of a frog – as if he was about to swallow it. It was jet black, and its mouth – into the widely extended jaws of which I looked with my binoculars – was terracotta. There was a slight whitish marking on its neck which I took to be the flattened hood. I signed to the men to keep still as I wanted to see the further operations. One of them must have moved for it suddenly took alarm, up went its head, it's eyes glistened as it saw us and it turned to go up the bank into the forest. It scaled the perpendicular bank with wonderful ease and lithe grace, its black scales shimmering in the sun, and gave a great impression of speed and power. Its head went into the hollow of a tree and emerged on the further side. Then it slid along the top of the bank and disappeared from view. It was about twelve inches in girth at the thickest part. I could have killed it with a bullet from my rifle as it was mouthing the frog, but was too interested to think of it. It had no markings of any kind on the body, but it was undoubtedly a King Cobra and could have been no other snake. The men explain it as killing men in a few minutes and they lose cattle by it too. Such a brute, if it made for one, would take some knocking out! A dah would be a sure protection in the skilful hands of a Burman, but I doubt my walking stick being quite sufficient.

Post in this evening so I stay in camp tomorrow to write various letters. D.F.O. has sent me a Rs.5 licence, under which I can shoot all unprotected animals and birds subject to prescribed close seasons.

JOURNAL _____

From the appearance of the inhabitants of this forest village it was evident that they suffered much from malaria, so I was not surprised one day to find myself down with fever, and a temperature of 103°. It was a short attack of five days only, and in the intervals there was time to admire the view from the verandah. Below was a field of millet, bright green, but beginning to ripen. Beyond the field a wide belt of feathery bamboo, and stretching away to the hills is the forest of all shades of green and brown. The hills have an undulating outline and reach an elevation of over 2000ft. They are wholly covered in forest, the ravines being defined by the colour of the foliage. I gazed at the dark places and wondered what beasts were harbouring in them.

This is a jungle hamlet, just a forest village of a dozen houses, built on posts as is the fashion of the country. Beneath the houses are the cattle and dogs, the ducks and fowls, the carts and the farming implements; and in the evenings, around the smoking wood fires, are the slanty-eyed little children, solemnly warming themselves in the chilly air, for the temperature falls rapidly after sundown at this time of the year, being as low as 50° before sunrise and as high as 85° in the middle of the day.

After the bout of fever, another day or two was spent roaming the forests from earliest dawn to late in the evening in vain search of the bull saing, and then I realised that hoping for a lucky chance would be of no avail and further efforts must await the onset of the rainy season. Back to the first village we went, passing through patches of charred jungle, for the forest fires had commenced and in all directions could be seen a pall of smoke. The bungalow had suffered slight damage from the earthquake which had roused us at midnight the week before, the doors and windows would not close and the posts were about four inches out of plumb. At night from the verandah, long lines of light could be seen, with here and there huge beacons of leaping flames where the hungry fire had found dense patches of grass and dry bamboo. All this was strange to see, after being so long used to the strict fire protection force in India. It seems that the policy of fire protection was abandoned in Burma some years ago, much to the relief of the jungle people no doubt, and it was with evident delight that the men with me used to expend the best part of a box of matches during the day in the forest.

DIARY ——————————————————————————————————

11th January. Packed kit; paid the trackers, thirteen days tracking of which Rs.12/- to Thet Lat, Rs.10/- to the younger man, as they were away one and three days respectively. Boy carrying tiffin etc. (THEIRS as well as mine!) 12/- a day = Rs.9/12 = 31/12. Moved camp to Mycurintha. A tamarind tree shades the left end of the verandah from the western sun. In front are two siris trees, and beyond the river bed one can see between some trees the pinnacles of the local Monastery.

13th. Up at 4 a.m. and off at 5.0 in bullock cart. Too dark to see anything more than twenty yards away. It was after 9 o/c when I saw a thamin stag, he must have been lying down and we had just chanced on him; thick cover, grass, bushes, ravines, green shrubs, and trees. So all I saw of my first thamin stag was a fifth of a second 'snap shot' view of a very dark animal about the size of a chital with a semicircular appearance of horn. This village has a thickset hedge and gates to keep out cattle thieves. The Headman sent a present of plantains, papayas and Indian corn, this afternoon. Lovely golden appearance of the air in the jungle in the afternoons and grand sunrises in the mornings. Moon now nearly at the full. 'Silver nights and Golden days'!

17th. Out too early and had to sit half an hour waiting for dawn. We sat round a fire, the men very merry – headman, tracker, and three coolies. One had long hair, one clean shaven head and one cropped hair. Evidently now all do as they like about their hair, also as to tattooing of legs, for of the five men, two were not tattooed – the two youths. Tomorrow is the last day of shikar this trip. Last night tremendous jungle fires were seen to north and north east. I see the Southern Cross every day when I set out in the early morning. Full moon rose last night like a ball of fire.

18th. Out after the thamin stag by dawn. Searched everywhere until 10.30 and saw no sign of him. Back to camp by 11.30: and so ends the hunt. No saing: no thamin: and if there are no thamin up Myitkyina way I get none at all. For two days or more I have had a thickening and inflammation of the ear and could think of no reason for it. Today, H. looked at ear through magnifying glass and found a small tick! Had him out and swelling beginning to go down.

20th. To Myolalin and Taungdwingye. There I packed the spare kit for Kalaon and set off next day, 21st, by midday train and got to Kokkoda at 3.45. A buffalo cart waiting and put all kit into that, and so to the F.R.H. by sun down; a short four and a half miles I think. Here is the edge of the wet zone and jungle much more green and undergrowth thick. This bungalow is the same as others with the welcome addition of a 16ft. × 16ft. unroofed extension of the front verandah. Nice to sit out and see the stars. Heavy dew here at night. Thick forest right up to the house, within 40 feet of it. To the north, 100yds away is the wide sandy bed of a river with a trickle of water meandering down it, on the other bank is the village, with a most formidable bamboo stockade round it to keep out robbers – men of neighbouring villages I suppose!

Much more life in this forest as more food supply for both birds and beasts. The fact that the jungle is thick and there is plenty of water in all the nalas, preserves the game here to some extent. At 8.30 a.m. heard a gunshot to the west inside the Indavery reserved forest plot. No doubt the lads with me know who the firer is likely to have been.

24th. The last day. Off before dawn, did a round in the forest to north and west, nil. Yesterday evening a male panther was grunting about half a mile away. I also heard alarm call of thamin for the first time, it is a call something like four-horn with a higher note, couldn't mistake it for chital or four-horn. A bevy of laughing thrushes was around the back of the kitchen this morning, all hens with exception of one cock which had a splendid white crest. With them were two beautiful drongos (racket tailed) but far more brilliant in colour than the Indian bird. Today I met a long string of bamboo laden carts nearly all drawn by buffaloes. There are many roads leading from here; one of them is bridged, wooden bridges and wide, fit for motor traffic but the deep sand and the occasionally broken down bridges would make one a bit uncertain in a car. Bullock cart probably faster in the end!

25th. Afternoon, went off to Meegyoungye to go on Ferry boat. Motor Rs.15/-, thirty three miles, fairly good road, took selves, servant, and all my kit. Had tea in the anchored barge and went on the down mail steamer when it came in. Then on to the Ferry boat 'Kalawe' when it arrived at 8 o/c. Dinner and bed: lovely sunset – wonderful.

JOURNAL ———————————————————————————————

It was late in the afternoon when the many spires of the pagodas on the Sagaing hills were sighted. Earlier in the day we had seen in mid stream the iron frame work for the borings which are being made preparatory to the foundations of the piers for the railway bridge over the Irrawaddy, which will be constructed within the next three years. We tied up for a short time close to the embankment and the three piers which

1

2

3

1
Burmese girl working a
primitive loom at Nkrungtu

2
Fish seller at Kyoukuyoung

3
Structure built over a grave to
ward off 'evil spirits'

4
Chinese muleteer and pack
mule used by Burton on his
travels through the damp,
impenetrable jungles of Burma

5
Elephant carrying her fodder
to camp

6
The village 'herdsman', a child
and buffalo

have been built on the right bank of the river, and saw on the further side the long sweeping curve of the earthwork to which the bridge will make a connection.

We arrived at Mandalay on 29th January. Soon after the steamer leaves the shore for the upstream voyage, the eye is attracted to the massive brickwork of the Mendohn Pagoda, lit up by the rays of the early morning sun, and the many domes of other pagodas along the lower slopes of the hill. The wide expanse of water was studded with native craft, the square terracotta sails of those labouring upstream flapping in the breeze. Not long after this we grounded on a sandbank; a kedge anchor had to be got out and in one way and another there was a delay of over two hours. At Kyaukmyaung a number of people were awaiting the arrival of our vessel which was the weekly bazaar steamer. Some of them had goods for sale, such as long tubes of cooked rice, fresh fish, plantains and other fruit, but the majority were seeking their weekly supplies.

The Third Defile was entered and we made steady progress in deep water for about forty five miles, the river being about three hundred yards in width. The jungle of bamboo and small timber trees grew down to the water's edge and here and there were small fishing villages, or just a solitary hut, and the large square drop net ingeniously raised and lowered by the easy leverage of a long bamboo framework, with which large quantities of fish are captured. Sailing up the river were many large craft, for this is the season during which the wind blows steadily from the south west, and the river journey to the trading centre of Bhamo – the commencement of the trade route into China is made with a fair amount of speed. The return voyage will be when the river is in flood after the beginning of the monsoon. We were five or six hours late in getting to Thabeitkyin. At sundown the northern end of the Defile was reached at Male, and there the steamer tied up for the night.

Next day there was a very sudden change in the temperature on account of a biting wind straight from the far off snowy mountains to the north. The river now rapidly widened and once more the call of the lascars, heaving the lead and plying the bamboo sounding poles was heard throughout the day. It was under a sunless and overcast sky with occasional rain squalls that we steamed the next day, the most important stopping place being Tigying, a large straggling village at the foot of a small hill on the summit of which is a white and gold pagoda and a monastery. The costumes of the people comprised every colour of the rainbow. Some of the women wore large Shan hats of bamboo work, circular in shape with a cone in the centre, others had coloured silk handkerchiefs placed in graceful folds on their heads, while not a few were satisfied with the dressing of their raven locks in the Burmese style with white or pink flowers. One girl had a long drooping cock's feather as an adornment, and her small infant was in a fold of her shawl at her back.

Yet another day of slow progress against the stream took us by sundown to an anchorage within three hours of Kathe. On the left were hills covered with dense forest, while to the east the country is level and high elephant grass grows up to the water's edge. It was quite a change to find ourselves on the morning of the fifth day anchoring alongside the barge at Kathe, and see the railway trucks in the siding of the small station which is close to the landing stage. The golden domes of two pagodas glittered brightly, for now the storm was over and once again we were warm in the rays of the sun. Our intention is to go by rail to Myitkyina, hire a country boat and drop down stream through the First Defile so seldom seen by travellers, and so return to Kathe by the daily ferry boat.

Chapter 21

THROUGH THE JUNGLES OF THE UPPER IRRAWADDY

JOURNAL

Thirty miles upstream from Myitkyina, which is the northern terminus of the railway in Burma, two large rivers, the Mali and the Nmai join together; and from that place – known as the Confluence – the combined river is named the Irrawaddy. The Nmai, when clear, is crystal clear and is colder than the Mali. In it's upper reaches it is not so accessible as the western river, but it contains many fish. The waters of the many spring-fed streams which flow into it are warm and it is in these and at their confluence with the main river that good fishing is to be had. However, the fishing season is short and the distances considerable, so it is the more accessible Mali river which attracts the fisherman.

Tents are not advisable owing to the myriad creeping and crawling insects which abound. If there is no Rest House, the Kachins of the nearest village will put up a weatherproof hut in a very short space of time. Only two years ago the journey to Fort Hertz took twenty one days, but this is now shortened by four marches as there is a motorable road as far as Tiang Hka, fifty six miles from Myitkyina. After Tiang Hka, mules are necessary. The mules and muleteers are Chinese and have to be hired for the whole trip. With the exception of rice, which is procurable in the neighbourhood of Fort Hertz and of which a month's supply will suffice, all supplies have to be carried from Myitkyina. Fowls and eggs are occasionally obtainable.

DIARY

20th February. I went to see D.C. and lorry was loaded up at Circuit House. I saw the off front wheel was very wobbly and the driver said it was 'like that' and wouldn't come off. We left Myitkyina at 11.15 a.m., and twenty miles out the axle broke off short at hub of the wobbly wheel which shot off ahead at a great pace and disappeared into the thick forest. The lorry ran 80 feet on the hub before pulling up. I waited in the forest, under a bamboo clump until 5.30, when a lorry loaded with P.W.D. cement came along, destined for Tiang Hka where a suspension bridge is under construction, and my kit was put into the lorry. It got dark after we had gone about five miles so I saw nothing of what must have been fine scenery. The road has hundreds of hairpin bends and it is a marvel how the man drove the heavy lorry in utter darkness without mishap; his lights not too good either. However, we fetched up at Tiang Hka at 9.15, having only stopped a few minutes at Nzop Zup, where is P.O. and T.O. and a small Military Post.

My two Kachin servants are Mathu, who has been in service of P.W.D. S.D.O.'s, and cooks, he also he owns a D.B. gun which I told him to leave at his house, consoling him with prospect of using my gun to collect jungle fowl. The other man Magam, was in Kachin Regiment and also talks Hindustani. An ugly little fellow, but very likeable and more of a worker, likes doing things, than Mathu. By degrees I have discovered he has various accomplishments. Army signaller (reads and writes), shoots with rifle and gun (pot shots), handy with tools, can use a fisherman's casting net, make bamboo grass shoes, and can – he says – consume a full bottle of rice spirit at a sitting and get pleasantly drunk. This he prefers, I gather, at bed time after a tiring day!

In the morning I woke to see a thick mist. The river is 150 yards away down a steep bank, and rapids a few hundred yards below. Opposite is The Triangle, of which so much has been heard of late years, on account of the releasing of slaves by Sir Harcourt Butler. In that tract, as on this side also, are many hills and all is thick forest. The whole of this country is one network of deep ravines, and over the whole is a smother of tangled jungle. There are many sambur and kakur and some tiger and panthers. No doubt there are clouded leopard, but to come across them, or any animal, in such forest is merely a matter of luck. Jungle fowl are numerous and other birds also, such as the Peacock Pheasant.

22nd February. I went up river to find the Third Rapid mentioned by MacDonald, but no sign of it. Visited a small village on way back. The villagers asked to see my rod – 14ft. greenheart, so I put it together for them, also showed my watch and knife and leather rod rest, and they were quite pleased with the 'pavee'! The path back was through the forest for about two miles. Horrid going, up and down ravine banks and roots and debris all the way. Just a foot wide path through impenetrable forest. This took us on to the main road. Great energy of P.W.D. to get it ready for the Governor of Burma to motor up to Sumprabum in March or April.

23rd. A thick fog. Went at 9.30 with Magam to a village a mile inland. One long house, apparently one family. The man was away, gone to some other village, his wife was making rice spirit. The rice is fermented in hollow bamboos about 4ft. long. This she pours into a big shallow wooden vessel, mixes in hot water, and ladles it into another bamboo. From this it is afterwards strained into bottles – 4as. a bottle. Another woman was attending to silkworm eggs, which would soon be hatching out. I took a leaf on which the worms feed and will find out the name of the tree. Around the hut were goats, pigs, fowls. The fowls are not killed except as sacrifice to the Nats. They said no tigers or panthers trouble them and I expect carnivores only work along nalas and river beds. They could scarcely progress through the undergrowth and would seldom get a meal that way.

The mules have turned up so we will be off tomorrow. There was a wonderful glow of the setting sun on the bare rounded slopes of a high hill in The Triangle. The hill is of a red soil and was thus a bright golden red colour. I went down river in the evening, and could see rocks and swirling water far downstream. This looks like the third Rapid of Tiang Hka which Macdonald described as ABOVE that place, for further up stream there is no rapid for miles. I got no offer from any fish and the water seems to me lifeless, just as it so often is when the water is too cold.

The pack mules had come unladen from Myitkyina and expressed their displeasure at taking to the open road in the morning by much kicking and arching of backs; but only one succeeded in getting rid of his load, which rolled down the hill until stopped by a bush. The Chinese system of packing articles on a rigid frame, which is dropped onto the wooden saddle is quite perfect for travel in mountainous country as the load cannot work loose, and all that is necessary is to lift it again onto the saddle. So the mule was quickly reloaded and gave no further trouble.

The mule saddles and gear are Chinese and different to any seen in India. A wooden saddle, lined with soft leather and a numdah; on the saddle two battens perpendicularly on each flap. These are to take the legs of the crutch of wood on which the load is tied – a great weight either side – before it is lifted, load complete, onto the saddle. There is no girth, all is by balance. The load is tied on by a complicated arrangement of leather thongs. The animals have rope net muzzles to prevent grazing.

The muleteers are Chinese. They wear a wide hat of the usual shield shape made of very finely plaited bamboo and this has two ribbons attached to it which can be tied under the chin if wanted. This wide hat gives excellent shade and when the sun is at the back, it is just slipped behind and protects the spine. The men wear a short blue jacket and baggy blue trousers, and have woven grass sandals on their feet, and usually a pipe with a small bowl in their mouth. Cheery, hard working fellows and nice to deal with.

24th. When we got into camp after nine miles the muleteer at once unloaded the mules and looked at their backs and aired the saddles. Then the mules are turned loose to wander off and graze until nightfall. Shortly before dark, they return to camp in response to the shrill cries of the muleteers and receive a feed of unhusked rice and are picketed for the night; each animal being supplied with fodder brought in from the forest. In the morning their nosebags are filled with a good measure of dhal, and the animals munch steadily while the loads are prepared. Each saddle is made for a particular animal.

This D.B. is Supka Ga: it is a bamboo hut with two rooms. Cool and airy, built on piles, a roughly built and cheap affair. Elevation is 1200ft., which is 600ft. above the river at Tiang Hka. Already there is a change in the vegetation, fewer ferns and bamboos and wild plantains, and it is cooler. In places the road is deep in mud, and would be almost impassable in wet weather.

JOURNAL _____

It is when going into the interior beyond Tiang, which is where the road leaves the Mali river not to rejoin it until near Fort Hertz, 150 miles to the north, that one realises what evergreen tropical forest is like. The road passes through solid walls of green jungle, the more tangled and impassable by reason of the network of dead bamboos.

Some portions of this road were made in 1927 by men of the 2nd Battalion of the 1st Madras Pioneers, as can be seen at mile 63 by the lettering cut by them into the perpendicular clay cliff. To make any advance possible, the men hewed and hacked through a scene of great beauty. Everywhere magnificent giant creepers, some delicate as wreaths of English clematis with gossamer woven flowers; others so weird looking as to be almost repellent with their snake-like stems, thick as one's arm, all clinging like iron bands for strength, and for all their delicacy equally impassable.

After leaving the Mali river, the road rises by easy gradients. Along the road are a few open grassy spots where can be seen tiny blue and white flowers resembling forget-me-nots. One does not see many animals. The home of the takin, that weird beast half goat and half buffalo in appearance, is far to the north. Occasionally a hoolock monkey will be sighted as he hurls his black form spread-eagled through the air from one tall tree to another, and the black giant squirrel and two smaller species of brown squirrel, may be seen. Of birds, one sees two varieties of Imperial pigeon, pin-tailed green pigeon, and several doves of the same species as met with in India. Great hornbills flap across the valleys, and from the thick undergrowth comes the call of skulking pheasants, but that is all the acquaintance one can make with them. There are tigers and panthers, the latter mostly of the black variety, but during all my wanderings I never once saw the track of these felines or came across a kill.

Beyond the first two marches, the post is carried by pack bullocks or buffaloes, so the mail travels slowly to these distant outposts. Even in what may be considered as the dry season, the moisture oozing out of the hillsides turns many of the re-entering angles of the road into a quagmire; and when the torrential rains of the monsoon arrive, the road is well nigh impassable in many places. The path conducts the traveller over ridges, along hillsides, and across streams, in some of which can be seen sizeable fish in the deep pools. About every ten miles along the road are Staging Bungalows, mostly sited on rising ground or the summit of a ridge, well cleared of trees and commanding entrancing views. At Kadrang Yang is such a one, most welcome after a march of eleven miles. To the east the tall white branchless tree trunks and the brown grass of the steep hillside, recently cleared for cultivation after the wasteful manner of these people, are lit by the soft rays of the setting sun: away to the south are the high ranges of the peaks in The Triangle, glowing in the last fiery shafts of departing day.

The deep sombre valley below the house is all in shadow, silent, dark, impenetrable. Diagonally across the view runs the single wire of the telegraph line connecting the back of beyond with civilisation. From the outhouses comes the low hum of voices and the occasional whinnying of a mule. Away in the forest a woodpecker drums on the bole of a dead tree and there is the crashing of branches as the monkeys settle down for the night.

DIARY _____

25th February. A thunderstorm and heavy rain last night. This morning a thick mist. The mules were packed and off by 8 a.m. A few miles on we caught up two bullock carts carrying the up-mail bags. Six letters were for me. Further on met two pack bullocks with the down-mail. They take over the contents of the carts and return up the road. The road very deep in mud and slippery after last night's rain. Nice and fine and warm today, and the road became wider with a grassy surface. I said that Magam could shoot with a gun – pot shots. He now tells me he can shoot birds on the wing and that at Magango he got a tip of 10 Rs. from an officer because he shot sixty four snipe with sixty four cartridges! He goes with Mathu this evening to beat out a hill and shoot jungle fowl on the wing. I am too lazy to go and see him do it.

26th. Eight miles to Kawapang D.B. Two mules strayed so we didn't get off until 8.30. After about two miles the road crossed over the Daru Hka by an iron suspension bridge. All along the road dense forest. Many dead bamboos, and it is on account of the bamboos having died that these jungle Kachins are having a time of scarcity now. Heard a pheasant calling, very like koklass' call. Magam disappeared into the thick forest, a hopeless quest. He came back without the pheasant but with a big thorn in his toe, which he very skilfully cut out with the razor-edged hunting knife he carries.

Kawapang D.B. is on a bare knoll and commands a fine view. The bed of the Daru Hka can be seen below to the west, and away to the east is the bare top of the Pumlum Bum Military Police Post (also P.O. and T.O.). It is about sixteen miles off as the crow flies, and overlooks the valley of the Mali river. Away beyond that I see streaks of snow on a hill, and far beyond through a gap, is a line of snowy mountains, evidently eternal snow, and probably over 16,000ft. in height: it is in China. On the road I met a number of pack mules returning to Myitkyina. I took a photo of the leader, a much bedecked mule with a circular piece of looking glass on its forehead. With the mule was a Chinese mule driver and his white chow dog.

27th. At Kawapang this morning all the valleys were filled with mist, which soon dispersed when the sun came up. The hoolock monkeys were in great voice. When one is close to them the sound is like that of a pack of puppies all howling at the same time. A weird shrill call, difficult to describe, their alarm note is very gruff and deep-toned. The people keep many fowls, but do not kill them for food in the ordinary way, only when the 'Nats' (the evil spirits), require to be satisfied. But as life always has it's little worries, no doubt they fare off 'murghli' pretty often!

28th. Ten miles to D.B. Maithong Ga. There is a decided change in the jungle now, much less palm and plantain, more fern, flowers and butterflies. It was hot when walking fast along the road, but the temperature here is just right and a cool breeze is blowing. On the way I met a string of pack bullocks, the leading ones with bells swinging in arches over the saddles. Very musical. Magam shot a jungle fowl on the march today, also a squirrel with a very long tail.

JOURNAL _____

Every part of the journey is of interest. Being the only highway through the country, people of many tribes are met with. The country south of Kamti Long is that of the N'Hkums and the Kaku Kachins, two of the many sub-divisions of the Chingpaw, which is the racial name of this people of Tartar origin. Between the Mali and the Nmai rivers, the tract of country known as The Triangle is inhabited mostly by Maru Kachins, a people amongst whom slavery is a natural custom, and who eat dogs, fattening the 'friend of man' for the pot! Nice friendly dogs too, of the chow type. The Marus of the Triangle claim to trace back to forty generations of ancestors, so the immigration of the Chingpaw over the snowy mountains which separate the head of the basin of the Irrawaddy from Tibet must have occurred a very long time ago. Lisus, Nungs, and many other tribes of Chingpaws are there; and in the Kamti Long plains is a colony of Shans, long separated from their fellows hundreds of miles to the south.

As a result of centuries of freedom the Kachins are a very independent people. Not long ago some of the tribes deposed their overlords – Duwas, as the headmen of a group of villages are termed – saying they did not require them and could manage their own affairs.

The villages are always situated on a ridge or other well-drained site and many of them are approached by a long avenue. On each side of the road are placed a number of short, carved prayer posts, and beyond these a number of bamboo structures sacred to the spirits (Nats). The houses are constructed on the communal plan, and many of them are as much as two hundred feet in length. The floors are about four feet from ground level, the space below being fenced in for the pigs and fowls. The pigs keep the village sites clean. The fowls are very handsome birds, some of the cocks display tails with feathers two feet long.

House building is a communal affair, and 'house warming' the occasion for the consumption of much curry and rice, and rice-spirit. House cleaning is unknown, and when the accumulated filth of years renders the construction of another dwelling desirable, the old one is burnt down. The universal habit of spitting is a nuisance, but the people are likeable and easy to deal with. They have no written language and so have wonderful memories. Every child knows the name of every living and growing thing in the forest, and what is edible amongst the wealth of vegetation which keeps the people from starvation when a calamity overtakes the rice crop which is their staple food.

DIARY _____

1st March. D.B. Hpauhtum Ga (2000ft.) eleven miles. Crossed Sinan Hka on the way; an iron suspension bridge is under construction. There is no bungalow now between this and Sumprabum, so the march tomorrow will be seventeen miles (it was eighteen!) A long day.

2nd March. The road was uphill all the way. Saw a P.W.D. elephant, whose job it is to haul logs to the sawing places; a good deal of work going on. Saw an old Kachin man and an old woman, both really old, – of course Magam was away on in front with the camera. The old woman's legs were tattooed in circles like football stockings. Magam said she had good socks, and he and Mathu were hugely pleased when I said they were better than mine as they wouldn't wear out!

At Sumprabum I met Hector S.F.O., P.W.D., Not favourably impressed; doesn't meet one's eye and I wouldn't trust him an inch! After seeing some maps and hearing what Hector could tell me, I decided to work down Hpungui Hka Valley round to where Sinan Hka runs into Mali Hka, and to take a month over it.

(*Note*: this was the turning point of the trip. I should have gone on to Fort Hertz and not gone aside as I did. Had I gone on, all would have been well and not the blank trip as to mahseer).

There are about one hundred Military Police at this Post, all Gurkhas, which is in Helio and Lamp communication with several other Posts, and also the two columns now operating in The Triangle. I don't know what these Expeditions are for and don't like to ask questions. Another Expedition is in the Hukong Valley. It seems that no game shooting licence is necessary up here and any and all can slay what they like. The flesh of a sambur was openly brought to the house for sale today. I saw a Kachin having his tiffin and tea: the teapot is a hollow bamboo into which tea and water is put and the joint put into the fire; other end of the joint (the bamboo is sliced in two, one third of the way between two joints) is the tea cup. It might be thought that the bamboo would be burnt before the water boils, but it doesn't. These people's whole existence is bound up with the use of bamboo and without it they cannot exist. Water is carried in hollow bamboos about 3ft. long or more, which are put into baskets on the back. No need for a bucket or water holding utensil in these parts. Bamboo supplies all one needs. My rod cases have been protected by strips of bamboo. The D.B. Supka Ga is all bamboo, not a nail in it. The piers of some of the bridges are made by boulders heaped into circular bamboo baskets.

6th March. To D.B. Phungin Hka, ten miles. The last few miles close to the river. I fished till dark, but caught nothing. I met a man of Putao this morning, he had a crossbow, and of course I was far ahead and the camera behind. The heavy 3.A Postcard Camera size is a mistake, as on account of its weight it is not always on me.

7th March. This morning the whole valley swathed in thick mist which was dispersed by the rays of the sun by 8.30. Magam shot a male hoolock monkey. Yesterday I saw a sooty coloured long-tailed monkey – the lungoor of these parts is different to the Indian one. The hoolock weighed 12lbs only, full grown male. A very soft skinned animal, delicately made hands and feet. A shame to have slain him, but my fault as I had told Magam I wanted one for the Museum. The skin and skeleton taken to go to the B.N.H.S.

8th March. A thunderstorm last night and heavy rain. Started late, 9.30: near the suspension bridge met the Putao Post, on bullocks. After going four miles it came on to rain, pretty heavily. The umbrellas were packed up! The men did very well with wild plantain leaves and the Chinamen were sufficiently protected by their big hats. At seven miles, having gone a good deal up hill, we came to a hut where the post relays change. Found that the cleared path from here to Jakun was not practicable for mules in this slippery state – very steep. I found a path going to the right and guessed it must go to Jakun, so sent Magam back to fetch the mules as path would be quite all right for them. I waited in the house of some Kachins. All the men were away, only three old women there with two children and three dogs. Pigs and fowls were under the house. Inside it was quite warm, a good fire, and everything black with smoke. One of the old women fetched me a bamboo stool to sit upon which was polite of her and good for me, as I fear that a floor seat would have entailed sitting in spittle! They spit promiscuously anywhere. Dried up my topee and shirt which had got wet through.

When the mules turned up we set out along the path, recently cleared for the Civil Officer when on tour. The grading very steep in places and very slippery. The mules were led by a well conditioned mare, who was wonderful in the way she slid down the inclines and rushed the upward slopes; but so were they all, game, plucky animals. It was about four miles to the ford, all through dense forest, the hoolocks making much noise. Near the river the path went through dense wild plantains and other murky growth. The ford was deeper than expected and about 80yds across. The mules were well up to the girths and the loads of the small animals dipped into the swirling water. One small mule nearly overbalanced; that would have been a calamity indeed. Seeing my bedding likely to get wet, I had it carried across. One of the Chinamen took the whole load on his shoulders, quite 130lbs with saddle, and went across safely through the slippery stones and boulders. The water was nearly up to my waist, and cold. The bank on the opposite side was very steep and the mules had to be led up one at a time. Lucky my rod cylinders were well protected by bamboo laths, as one of them slipped off and dived into jungle.

I had led the way all this time so as to spy out the bad places and was a good way up the opposite hillside when Magam caught me up to say the mules couldn't manage the hill. I expected this as the path was very steep indeed and slippery, so we went back a few hundred yards and camped where the path passed under a leafy tree and close to a small brook.

The muleteers stacked the packs and the saddles along the three foot path, covering them with birch bark mats, and then drove the animals up to the village for food and shelter. A space was cleared with dahs by the side of the path and beneath the dripping shelter of a tree, camp was prepared in the pouring rain. The bed was protected by a 6ft. x 6ft. waterproof sheet lengthened to the ground on one side by a thatch of wild plantain leaves, while the two Kachins made a similar shanty for themselves on the other side of the tree. I ate my cold dal and rice and chupattis, the men cooked their meal. The Chinamen's simple arrangements, after cooking their food, was to lay leafy branches on the path, over these a sort of rug and one of the birch bark mats. Two poles propped up the large white felt wrap, impervious to weather, which completely covered them. A small trench having been excavated with their entrenching tool (an adze – axe shape) to drain off the water, they were snug enough with a blanket apiece wrapped round them.

It rained all night, but all slept comfortably through it. All day the men had been picking off leeches, only one got hold of me. When saddling up in the morning I picked a fat leech from the eyelid of one of the ponies. The only birds seen on the march were a jungle hen and an emerald dove. The chinamen are real experts at starting a fire. All this dead bamboo makes first rate firewood as it burns wet or dry and only wants starting with dry chips. Food there was in plenty. Close to the now impassable ford dwelt a solitary Chinaman who eked out an almost hermit existence by supplying fish to the villagers.

10th March. It rained all night and very heavy rain this morning. What a country! It will be a difficult business getting up the hill out of this valley. Lucky there is a village,

Ngawma, of six houses not far off on the road up. Some loads will have to be carried as the path is getting cut to pieces by the rain. The Phungin river has risen a couple of feet, and is not now fordable; lucky we crossed it and are on the right side as it would have delayed one a week at least. I saw the Chinaman start his fire this morning, a few drops of Kerosene oil! So he isn't such an expert as I thought. These plantain leaves are splendid for keeping out the rain – an excellent roof.

At midday it stopped raining for a bit and I went to have a look at the river. Going back to camp I took the path from there and followed it half a mile along the river. Leeches in millions, I picked off quite fifty. No water worth fishing so I will move tomorrow, as the sun came out for a few minutes at 3 o/c and the storm is evidently over. Some coolies came from the village and took up six loads. The Headman came to see me and brought food as a present. When he was about to go Magam told me a present in return was expected, so I gave him a rupee.

11th. Got off at 8.30: lightly loaded as they were, it was difficult for the animals. One mule fell head over heels backwards, his load fell on the path and he hustled down a 20 foot khud into a stony ravine. Marvellous that he wasn't hurt. A path had to be cut to enable him to get back on this path again. A few yards further a pony fell and the load pitched down the hill, but couldn't go more than a few feet on account of the dense undergrowth. It was with some difficulty the two Chinamen and Mathu got it up on to the path again. At the village, it took an hour to get there, all loads had to be sorted out and retied. While this was being done I took two photos of women and children. The camera had got wet in spite of special American cloth cover. By 10.30 we started off, and soon came to the path from Sumprabum. A few miles further on we came to one of the camping places got ready for the Civil Officer on tour; five good huts, a stable for three horses. All very neatly built and quite weatherproof. I don't suppose they are paid for. Here is 'begar' in full swing! We went along the bank of the Phungin Hka to a camping place on the bank of the river where there is a small bamboo bungalow and a couple of servants huts.

12th. Magam told me of stinging nettles today. Showed me two kinds; one is like the English nettle – he says that sting only lasts a short time. The other has a large leaf and grows to considerable height. The sting of that comes on slowly, not instantly like the other, and lasts for days. If you tell others that you have been stung it will last longer than if you say nothing about it.

13th. Went to the ford to fish, three miles. There is a barrier of rubble and stones, a natural one, aslant across the whole river bed, like a weir, and through this are half a dozen runs into the deep water of a pool about half a mile long. A feature of the scenery is the swinging fronds of huge wild plantains and the clumps of bamboos bending like fishing rods over a stream. At 11 o'clock I landed a small mahseer, thick-set olive with reddish fins. I could command the whole of the water with 30 yards cast. I think the water is still too cold for many fish to be on the move.

14th. Moved camp to Gacheung. Only a short march now to the Mali River at Hpunyang Daru where I will probably camp for some days and hope for big fish. I saw a few butterflies, one or two big and gorgeous. The firing of guns which has been incessant for the past few days is now over, as the ceremonies following the death of a man of importance are ended. The villages are full of women and children and puppies; all the men are away in the train of the Civil Officer who is on tour just ahead of me. Passed another of his halting places where a small village had been erected for him and his followers and escort.

The village of Gacheung consists of one long (60yds long) Communal house. The big house faces north and south and has its sides exposed to the weather, eaves low to the ground on east and west. All around the front of the main end gable are bamboo structures to keep away Nats. In a post in the centre of a large entrance room are skulls and horns of eight buffaloes which have been sacrificed on various occasions, funerals and the like.

15th. At 11 o'clock went off to see the river. A steep path, like the side of a house in places. The Mali placid and deep, about 60 to 120yds across. A heavy run just below the Dam and a roaring rapid half a mile lower. Went up for an hour to as far as I could see; going very difficult, all big rocks and climbing in places. At one spot I had to cut two trees and make a platform to get across. The river runs in a deep gorge, high hills either side. Except for the dead bamboos lying all over the hillsides in tangled, broken, masses, the gorge is exactly like the First Defile, and a photo of one could be taken for the other. The water is very cold, snow water, and appearance like that of the Tons in Garhwal.

16th. Evening: went to river and found it a brown flood! Nearly four feet of water came down while I was there, also much drift wood. Post in; a licence sent to me for the whole of Burma for saing and thamin and hog deer for May, June, July. The problem is – where to go? Maps received; 92 E. Fort Hertz, 92 F. south of that, and a poor sort of map. Survey evidently not yet completed. Must move on to 'Nkruntu, about four miles, and hope for some fishing when the water clears.

JOURNAL ──

Leeches abound in these evergreen forests. After every shower of rain – and there is no month when it doesn't rain – the horrible things appear in thousands. The whole forest moves. On every leaf and blade of grass is a leech, crawling in humpbacked fashion along the ground are myriads of the loathsome pests. When the muleteer has to leave his path after a mule or a load that has slipped, he is lucky if he emerges with less than half a dozen fastened onto him. On what do the uncounted millions subsist? Where are they when it does not rain?

After my visit to Sumprabum, I returned to the main road to follow it for a couple of miles towards Putao, as the district around Fort Hertz is called, and then turned down the valley of the Phungin Hka to strike the Mali Hka opposite a village called Shukrungtu. Here the Mali flowed in a deep rocky gorge, fifteen hundred feet below, access to it being by a precipitous path – the only way to the ferry, which consisted of a large raft of giant bamboos and enabled people to cross over into The Triangle country at this point. After a few days we reached an elevated ridge overlooking the deep gorge of the Mali Hka and the village of Shigram Ga.

DIARY ──

22nd. Thunder and rain during the night. Of course the people all say 'never known weather like this!' Mathu and Magam have changed work; Mathu going out with me and Magam cooking and doing camp work. I get names of fish written down by Magam from mouth of local fishermen, Kachins, who get them with casting net. The people of these hills along the Mali are having a bad time of it now as the rice crop failed owing to plague of rats, three kinds of rats apparently. They dig up roots in the jungle and, as Magam says, can never starve like people in India do in times of famine. I found a woman at the river washing large roots which she had dug up after digging five feet down to the root of a tree. Like potatoes to eat says Magam, I must try some. He also has shown me a number of plants and shrubs all of which are used as food in one form or another. They get plenty of vegetable food, not much in the way of flesh except such pigs and bullocks and fowls as they kill to placate the 'Nats'!

Went at 12 o'clock to the river and found a good run between rocks at the head of a pool half a mile long and deep. On the rocks I found a big mahseer, Himalayan type, which had been killed by two otters of which there were tracks on the muddy foreshore. Fish was 48in. nose to end of tail, 43in. to fork, too much had been eaten off shoulders and belly to enable girth measurements to be taken. A fine feat on the part of the otters to have killed such a fish. It looked as if fish had shot out of the water and got stranded in his efforts to escape. Kachin cooly boy took all possible flesh, no doubt his household had a great feed.

24th. Again rain all night and thunder. Stopped about 10 o'clock and the sun came out, so I decided to be off and chance the weather and not waste a day. Path very slippery; near the place where the otters killed the forty pounder a mule fell backwards, his load went over and over down to the water's edge, and he rolled after it and pushed it well into the water. Of course it was something that mattered! The gun and rifle cases. Only well soaked, no damage done. The leeches were bad all the way. Saw a quantity of wild strawberries at one place. Got to Ningwa R.H. at 3 o/c, a short march and a lucky one. I feared the steep hill, but the mules wonderful, as usual. At 4.30, thunderstorm and rain!

I have wasted this valuable month, wandering about looking for places. Have seen something of the country, but came to catch fish! No doubt I ought to have made straight for Nonghkai, below Fort Hertz, and would have got there by 16th March, and could have fished down the best parts and then raced back to Tiang Hka. Perhaps another year! But I can't do it for four years quite, and will then be sixty six! Will see what sport I get in April–May and then think about it.

Chapter 22

THE CONFLUENCE AND PIDOUNG SANCTUARY

JOURNAL _____

As March drew to a close, the heat of the valleys increased also, and the number of biting and stinging insects, mosquitoes, horse-flies, sand-flies, gigantic spiders, beetles of brilliant colouring and amazing size, and a myriad of creeping and crawling things appeared. The wonderful growth of the forests was always a source of interest. Sometimes it was possible on rising ground to make one's way into the dense cover. The ground, where it could be seen, was a crumbling black mould, rich with the decayed vegetation of centuries, and gave out a damp, fetid, feverish smell. There was an upper storey of forest trees growing straight and tall, their branches wrapped in mosses, which often supported, midway down the trunk, a great clump of mould from which grew ferns and orchids; a kind of aerial garden. Every tree trunk is draped and sometimes completely hidden with creeping vines, canes and rattan hanging in great festoons from tree to tree, so that the entire forest is linked together. In all the ravines are ferns, gigantic in spread and marvellous in design, while delicate small ferns covered every stone with their moss-like growth.

DIARY _____

29th March. Moved camp intending to go to Laza, but was told mules can go via Magawng, so went that way. The path crossed this stream five or six times. It was after the last crossing the path became steep, and all the loads had to be taken off and carried up a steep bank quite impassable for loaded animals, on account of the cliff which would knock off the loads. Got to Magawng 1 o/c and had to camp, mules and men had had enough. Fortunately found a new house under construction and so quite clean and occupied it, no roof, but rigged up waterproof sheets overhead. Manankhang looks near, but probably a good six or seven miles: one deep ravine to cross. The sky is much overcast, so the headman of the village, fearing rain sent the young men and women of the village to thatch over the roof at edges of the waterproof sheets, and to extend the covering to the ridge and half way down the other slope. Path to Manankhang said to be overgrown with bamboos when it gets beyond the limits of this village.

30th. I went ahead with one man with axe and dah to get road cleared, but there was not very much to be done. The path was quite good, a bit steep on approach to stream. On an almost level bit, I slipped and fell and in falling put out right hand to save myself. This time a piece of jungle wood about ¼in. in diameter which had been sliced in two with dah when clearing the path some time before was unfortunately just where my hand hit the ground. The spike entered in the fleshy part of base of thumb, and punctured about one and a half inches. Lucky it wasn't a dry bamboo or it would have gone right through the hand; it was partly green and the force skinned off the bark. Very painful and made one feel a bit faint. Using earpiece of sun-glasses I probed for bark but found none; tied up with handkerchief and went on. Mules arrived at the stream just after I had crossed it.

I saw in one place path a bit narrow and overgrown so had grass cleared. I went on about a mile to open place on a hill and waited. After an hour or more as mules did not appear I realised there was difficulty and went back. Met six mules just coming away from the steep part and found two mules had fallen down khud at the very place I had noted and cleared for them to see. One mule, the new one with curly coat which replaced the dead one, fell three times! I am sure he can't see properly. The other mule fell twice. All this caused a delay of two hours. When I arrived and asked what was the matter, Magam loudly told me 'There is great trouble, a mule is down there dying, both its eyes are put out'. 'Which mule?' 'The new one from Sumprabum, there, it is dying', and he indicated great disturbance among the bamboos where I could see the mulemen and Mathu. In a couple of minutes up walked the dying mule, a bit bleary about the eyes, and no wonder, but only a bit stiff in his walk!

In five minutes he was again loaded up, having been led unloaded past the nearly fatal alteration. I was holding the other mule to prevent it wandering on and told Magam to take hold. In a most hysterical way he said he would not touch it, that it was all the Chinamen's fault, and he had told them this that and the other. I sent him on to get the other mules together; he was quite unfit to have anything to do with them. In times of stress and trouble a man's true nature is disclosed and I clearly see that Magam is a man I could never trust in any emergency. Mathu quite different, very calm and collected, as also the Chinamen. After the open space at top of hill, a quite excellent path up to the village, and I was glad to get to the Rest House (very much in disrepair) and lie down. Had waterproof sheets rigged up over bed in case of rain, also to keep off all the dirt etc. falling from the rotting roof.

Hand painful and soon got fever which remained for about forty eight hours. Thermometer not registering properly; I was not 110°! Glad when fever left on 1st April. Two girls from village were brought in by Mathu to see me; he said they had never seen a 'sahib' and wanted a view of one. With them they had the fifteen month daughter of the Duwa. I gave it a fistful of brown demerara sugar, much to its delight: nice merry girls, not beautiful. Mathu seems to attract all the girls at each village we stop at, as I hear laughing and giggling all day long. The Duwa came to see me. He corresponds to Siana of Chakrata Hills, and has about twenty villages under him. A man of about thirty, mongol features, black hair, brown goatee beard, the hair rather scanty and curling back under his chin, and straggly moustache of the same colour at corners of mouth; an unsmiling and self possessed man. Presented him with twenty five cartridges, No.6, at which he seemed greatly pleased, saying no Sahib before me had given him any! So of course his elder brother, who was Duwa before him turned up next day with his gun, and I had to give him some too – eight not twenty five!

2nd April. Hand improving and I can hold a pencil. Dressed, shaved, and went for a stroll in the village. A squalid life these people live, and the women a very hard one. Watched one of them at weaving, a very slow process. Saw a leopard cat which was killed in the night. It had slain five fowls before being killed by a thrust from a pointed bamboo. Took it and had it skinned by Magam. It is different in marking to the one of Koda; quite big rosettes, tending to streaks like a clouded leopard. Gave a rupee for it. Have decided to abandon idea of Mali Hka – Sinan Hka, as I won't be able to hold rod for a week or so, and to go tomorrow and camp on Sinan Hka at Khabayang. In this way I will be able to collect fish in Sinan Hka and so not waste time doing nothing. Dressed hand in evening, seems to be some foreign matter, may be a bit of bark, coming to opening of the wound. Every sign of speedy healing, and full use of hand by 13th, when get to Tiang Hka.

Got a few new fish, and set all in pursuit of fish (and an anna for each one brought). A lot of fly about this morning, exactly like mayfly. Magam shot two green pigeon – pintails, two pin feathers, beak blue-green, eyes brown, iris orange, legs vermilion: and now a partridge, male, bill black, legs greenish, eyes brown, iris dark chestnut, top of head brown, above eyes whitish, all under parts black and white, primaries uniform chestnut tending to dark brown at tips, wing coverts green-brown, each feather adorned with chestnut and black oval marking, and the tertiaries also tipped with white; rump greenish brown, under parts tail feathers and all wing feathers reddish brown: a handsome bird, seems to be a swamp partridge. Length 14in.

Wound in hand has been discharging great quantity of fluid. Pulled apart and with scissors caught hold of something and extracted nearly two inches of bark! Now the wound should soon heal up. Chinaman back with mules and rice, so will be off to Gumshen tomorrow.

6th April. Village headman came to camp and said it would be sure to rain today. Always two fine days and then rain! Thunderstorms and rain in evening and still raining next morning. Mules loaded and started at 8 o/c; Must try and make Bumpat R.H. tomorrow. Truly this is a disgusting climate: never stops raining. Fact is that there is so much moisture in the soil and the vegetation that no sooner has a couple of days sunshine begun to dry things up, than down it all comes again in rain.

The mule saddle – weight 11lbs.
" " loading frame – weight 12lbs.
Cost of saddle, 1/-: cost of Loading frame, 1/-: cost of all rest of gear, 5/-. Total: saddle plus gear to last for no end of a time, 7/-! And so efficient: scarcely a nail in the whole thing, dovetailed and morticed and sewn together with raw hide thongs.

10th. Kadrang Yang to Sup Kala, eleven miles. Three leeches got me on the hand yesterday. Stayed in camp to sort kit and rest. Very hot; 6 p.m. 90°; 7 p.m. 80°. Saw several butterflies and a curious green dragonfly. Part of the road very heavy with mud. Several mules got bogged and the wonderful Chinamen carried the loads through for them, although the yellow tenacious clay was up to their knees.

13th. Went down the road intending to fish rapids. No path to river, but found a track which led to rapids and good water. 14ft. Greenheart and big 6in. reel too much for hurt hand and rheumatichy wrist. Didn't cast well, lost two whole traces leads, spoons and all of another except top swivel and lead. Mathu has sent atta by bus, so I have something to eat! Simply couldn't carry on without atta.

14th. 6 a.m. 70°. Went down river along bank; some good runs and places where there must be big fish; no offers. Tried several kinds of spoons, large and small; lost two whole traces, leads, spoons, by getting hung up. A very bad river for tackle.

15th. Went down river to place where I stopped yesterday. Lost two spoons and traces and leads complete. Both these without any more lead than ½oz spiral. The swirls and eddies and backwaters of this rapid river take the spoon in all directions; everywhere rocks, and when one sees above water the rocks over which one was fishing, one marvels that any cast fails to result in a 'hang up'!

16th. Lovely water all the way here but hopeless without a boat. Dug-out of little use. Why have I not got another £1000 a year! Then I could do all sorts of things of this kind.

Note: Spoons I had made up according to pattern sent by Macdonald to me at Coonoor; NO USE. All people here use a spoon sold by Manton – the Myitkyina spoon. It is the one made by Manton to Macdonald's specification and totally different to what he sent he! They are dull copper and brightly tinned inside, and spin like a table spoon: not zigzag and slow like those he sent me. So I fish the Confluence after all my careful preparations, with ONE spoon lent to me by Woolaston P.W.D., a lad I met at Nzop Zup!

18th. Thumb much better and can use rod. Some women brought about twenty small fish, the beginning of new collection. Rain this afternoon and is cloudy so may rain tonight, which is very unpleasant as I have not a rain-proof roof.

22nd. Went down river in boat: a huge affair, 33ft. long, and quite useless for quiet fishing. The men can't hold the boat at all unless they tie up to bank. Got to Confluence at 2 p.m. and mules arrived 3 p.m.; very hot. Temperature in hut, 2 p.m. 86 degrees; 6 a.m. 68 degrees.

27th. Up at 5.0 and went by lorry to 'Nzop to get the post – mail bags were in the lorry. Hyde Clarke buys the 14ft. greenheart rod and gave me a cheque for 120/-. It cost 133/- including import duty and excluding freight, agency etc., which came to quite a lot; anyhow better than keeping it.

28th. River again risen during the night. Not much use hanging on like this and had better pack up and be off, and write the trip off as blank also blankety blank! Fever came on in the evening and all next day and 30th. River still high and coloured but looks like becoming fishable in a few days; however I own defeat and packed up tackle and rods and go tomorrow.

1st and 2nd May. Sorted out kit and arranged with Game Warden at Pidoung to go there 3rd morning for a few days. River in flood at Confluence until end of April. Total trip, fifteen days only fishing – three fish under 3lbs!

I collected eighty specimens of fish, all under 8in. long, and hear from B.N.H.S. that among the fifty two species included in the collection are quite a number of NEW species. Dr. Hora of Calcutta who is revising Day's Fishes for the Fauna of India Series for the Government of India, will report fully later. He regrets that so many of the new species are represented by only one specimen each. A pity I didn't make a point of collecting two or three of each kind. This was my first effort at collecting fish – 'experientu docat', and I will do better another time.

One new subspecies is named BARBUS CLAVATUS BURTONI! Such is fame! My tagging of labels wrong: should be through fleshy part of tail and not lips – but why didn't they warn me of this?! Suppose I ought to have known.

JOURNAL ——————————————————————————————————————

Pidoung Game Sanctuary. There are several Game Sanctuaries in the extensive forests of Burma, but for the purpose of observation of animals, only one of these is readily accessible. The area notified by the Government of Burma as the Pidoung Sanctuary comprises two hundred and sixty square miles of country. There are hills and valleys, thick evergreen forests, and more open jungle: north of the railway station are rolling downs bare of trees in the hollows of which are dense thickets, also long winding green valleys of lush grass.

The elephants, of which there are about one hundred and forty in the Sanctuary, stay mostly in the evergreen forest, so are not often seen. On all the game trails we saw numerous scratchings of tiger, also some fresh tracks. Many of the trees had the marks of claws upon them; on the trunk of one large tree was the unusual sight of both tiger and bear clawing, the latter ascending high up the trunk where could be seen hanging under a branch the wild bees nest which had attracted his sense of smell. Near the Manaw lick, several trees had in them platforms of branches broken off by black bears during the previous rainy season.

Saing are the wild cattle of Burma; the bulls are massive animals attaining a height of 17 h.h., yet these immense animals fall victim to the tiger. We saw in the Sanctuary the recently slain carcass of a grand old bull bison. He had been done to death by a large tiger which had hamstrung him by slashing his hind legs with his claws. Such useless destruction, as only a portion of his tail had been eaten. The tigers destroy much game. Already the stock of hog deer is largely diminished and this extensive area of forest could support many more animals than there are in it: but everything must have a beginning and the Sanctuary is just a few years established.

The Sanctuary contains many birds. The Chinese francolin is often heard, and the bird occasionally flushed as one wanders about in the early morning. The Burmese peafowl is seen and heard and there are several kinds of quail, among them that tiny member of the species, the button quail. The peacock pheasant lives amongst the evergreen, whistling teal, white-winged teal, and wood duck are on the quiet pools of many a stream winding through the dense forests. A green imperial pigeon is seen; she flew off her scanty platform of twigs which satisfies her as to a nest, and looking up we could see one of her eggs through the interstices of the flimsy structure. A very beautiful bird, the Burmese red-billed blue magpie, we also disturbed upon her nest by the side of the 'tiger walk'.

Everywhere in the jungles of Burma the nests of a species of ant is conspicuous in the trees. It is a curious round or oblong affair, looking like a black cellular papier-mache football; some of them are larger than that. They are built at the fork of branches or just around a stem, and in substance are very tough. In many of these ants nests is seen the round hole indicating that the Siam rufous woodpecker is, or was, nesting there.

One evening a snake of brilliant hues was seen on a path near the camp. The main colour was coral red, and when tapped on the back with a stick it made a white corkscrew of the underpart and end of its tail. No doubt this habit is a means of protection as it was repeated every time the reptile was touched. Pythons are met with in the evergreen, and the dreaded hamadryad is quite common. In the pools are large water lizards, some of them nearly six feet in length. One which was recently killed by the Game Warden had consumed no less than forty one frogs for his breakfast. From the rising ground above the station we have a wide view of comparatively level country, and beyond are hills covered with evergreen forest. Would that there were more such sanctuaries to protect the animals of the Forests of the East.

Among the game animals of Burma, the elephant and the wild cattle will long survive the ceaseless war which is being waged by mankind against the wild animals of the country, the reason in the case of cattle being that the people do not appear to have any liking for the flesh of these beasts. Other large animals, rhinoceros, tapir, buffalo, mythun, are so near extinction that they are protected throughout the year, and may not be shot. All that is possible is being done by the Game Warden of Burma, but it is a very uphill fight.

DIARY ———

3rd May. Pidoung. With D.F.O., Carroll, and Hodgkinson, doing cinema photography, went in afternoon to Game Warden's Camp. By the evening train came

1

2

3

4

CHAPTER
22

1
The confluence of the Mali
and Nmai rivers which form
the Irrawaddy river, a 'Mecca'
for fishermen

2
Shikari, Maung On, 1929

3
'Bears nest' in a tree, Pidoung
sanctuary

4
Ants nest in a tree, Pidoung
sanctuary

5
Mokidars hut, Inle lake

6
Leg rowers on Inle lake

of the Excise Department from Kathe, also taking photos, an amateur photographer with expert knowledge.

7th. Went out early and by 8 o/c got near the Manaw salt lick, not a salt lick really, just a pool of water in forest glade which is now dry and bare, but green and swampy in rains. Nearing the 'lick', a fine old bull Saing came towards us. Game Warden, Smith, has quick eyes and saw it. At eighty yards it saw movement of Edwards and his man getting camera ready; stared, but came on again, and twice stopped to stare, having not made out what he saw; then he suddenly got our wind and went off at a gallop.

8th. Started early and found herd of saing to west. Edwards took photo of sentinel cow, which snorted and went off to the herd. They were not alarmed and seemed to little heed the warning of their watchful sentinel. I went up under meagre cover of a small bush, the animals merely stared my way and continued grazing. Smith came up to me and we much enjoyed watching them; one big bull, some smaller bulls, several big cows and some younger ones, and some calves, twenty in all. The herd moved over a rise and then went off at a gallop, frightened by Edwards working at his cameras in the open.

On 11th went by train to Kathe. Onto Steamer 'Shwelan' on afternoon of 12th and at daylight set off down stream. At Tangamy found Smith on his launch and he told me all arrangements had been made there instead of Thabeitkyin. This was once a wonderful game country and shot out by a generation of sportsmen. Pollock and Thom did much slaughter in all these parts.

16th. Instead of a pony, a cart was produced! Off at 4.30 a.m. circled a long way through the jungle and back to camp. A tree in the forest is shedding all its beautiful cream colour trumpet shaped petals, very nice scent, something like jasmine. Kachnar trees in flower and also a number of shrubs with white flowers.

17th. Up at 4.30, but late in getting off. Rode the pony of Maung On. A willing little beast and as the Burmese saddle has no flaps and pony small and narrow, the riding didn't hurt my left leg. On the way passed through much thick bamboo jungle, with swampy places here and there and many tracks of elephant. Saw kakur and heard many jungle fowl. Left the pony and a Korean Forester, Po Thum, at a glade, and went on with tracker Maung On. He had told me to wear heavy nailed boots, but the ground was all loose gravel and stones, and he in his boots and I in mine made a great noise. After a couple of miles found a herd of saing. Sentinel cow was a bit suspicious, having no doubt heard us. When the animals grazed along a bit they got aslant of our wind and made off. Did a longish round and put up a cow which was an outlying animal for scattered herd. Then saw a good bull, took him at about 120 yards, a long shot, but can't let chances go, tremendous rain may begin at any time. To the shot he went off. Solid bullet, got him near neck and came out at left buttock, and yet with that he went off as if unhurt! Must in some way have missed all vital parts. He went up into some bamboo forest. Followed the tracks and came on him once, then two hundred yards on he stopped and I got in a bullet which broke his shoulder, then one through the neck killed him. A fine bull and just what is wanted for the Museum. 26½in. horns. White face, grey rather, and black on outside of forelegs.

Sent off Maung On to get men to skin etc. and while he was away took as many measurements as I could. Heavy shower of rain came on, so found shelter under bank of nearby nala. I thought the men would never come and began to suppose that tracker had forgotten the place! This thought caused by my having seen him pull out and study a compass; I expect he was just proud of his possession of compass and showing it to me. Beast too heavy to move so could take no front face photo. Curator of Museum must do with this photo and that of bull I took at Manaw lick which will do very well when enlarged. Poor old Saing; a shame to have killed him; lovely eyes and eyelashes. I can't imagine anyone wanting ever to shoot two, still less a dozen and more as some used to do, (Pollock and Thom!). Took further measurements and it was late when the skinning finished, and got to camp as it was getting dark. The tracker didn't want me to follow up after he found the blood. Said, by signs, that the bull galloped away and would go for miles. He had seen me pretty well cooked on the march from the river and thought poorly of my walking powers and no wonder. The heat, that day, was great and I get quite exhausted in this damp heat with a blazing sun. I insisted on following the tracks and we got him within half an hour or so.

At camp skinned the head by candle light and then thoroughly washed skin which had got stained with blood in many places, and put it into bath tub with strong solution salt and alum – brine. Tub would only take eight gallons. Used 20lbs salt and 16lbs alum.

Measurements: Horns – 26½in.

On way from Kyauk Ank on 14th, Maung On took a bees nest; I heard the humming and we found the bees in a clump of bamboos. He merely filled his mouth with tobacco smoke and going quietly to work, quite calmly, removed the honey covered with bees. He was not stung and it is apparently the way they get honey. I expect that if I had tried to do it I would have been badly stung.

21st. Wednesday. Saw one kakur and four or five thamin hinds and a big pig; also skeleton of cow saing killed by a tiger. Cart should be in today from Tagaung with alum and salt and then I will close down and be off. The skeleton of saing still smells horribly and I can't go until it is fit for travel. Very hot, no rain, a good thing to get over this twenty one miles of road before heavy rain comes when it gets almost impassable.

23rd. All packed and ready to start 4 a.m. tomorrow for Kyauk Ank, twelve miles and to Tagaung next day 25th on to Steamer, 26th Mandalay and Thagi, 27th arrive at Kalaw.

JOURNAL ———————————————————————————————

From Thagi Junction there is a choice of going by rail or by motor to the Hill Station of Kalaw. From Kalaw to Taunggyi there is forty seven miles of excellent road, then the broad emerald valley of Yawnghwe is reached and beyond it the hills on which is Taunggyi.

It is bazaar day in Taunggyi and the town is full of the Lake dwellers of this valley. The road to the waterway takes one past some fine pagodas on the way to the boat house. Here we find a roomy boat about thirty feet long by four feet wide, with a very shallow draught, and a cabin in the centre. The light craft glides quickly along, passing for the first half mile a number of houses standing on piles in the reed covered water. Beneath and around these are fat black pigs and ponies up to their middles in mud and water. On the platforms around the houses are dogs, hens, and children. Ducks and geese swim in and out among the reeds. Both the people and the livestock seem to be amphibious.

Soon a wide expanse of reeds is entered and the view restricted to the twenty foot width of the channel. Over the waving reeds are seen the green hills, with here and there the red soil of a field hewn from the forest. This wasteful method of cultivation is to be seen all over Burma, and rapidly causes the disappearance of timber trees and denudation of the soil; for directly the dense cover is cleared and burnt, all kinds of rank growth favoured by the dampness of the climate takes possession and allows no return to forest.

The boatmen use the oars in several ways. They always face the way the boat is moving, standing and working the blades with a backward sweep of both arms; also they have a very effective method which is peculiar to the people of this Valley. Standing on one leg, the top of the oar is grasped with one hand and the shaft is held along the outside of the thigh and the inside of the leg, the foot being bent inwards so that the big toe can curve round and keep the oar in position. By bending the body forward and sweeping the leg backward and then outwards, the oar is given a movement in the water as in ordinary rowing. After a couple of miles of tortuous progress among the reeds, the boat emerges into the clear waters of Inle lake which stretch far away to the south, and are about five miles in width. Boats on their way to the north of the lake pass by, swept along by flimsy makeshift sails rigged on bamboo poles. These lake dwellers are very expert fishermen. Fish spearing is practised by day and by night, the Inthas being particularly expert at this. Standing on one foot on the gunwale of the boat and using the oar with the other leg, they have one hand free for the fishing spear. At night resinous torches attract the fish to their doom. So the markets are kept well supplied with fish, most of them being of the murrel species, which can live for a long time out of its natural element.

With the wind astern, the return journey is quickly accomplished. The market is beginning to disperse, and boat loads of people pass on their way to their houses over the water. All are laden with purchases which have to last for the ensuing week. Our boatmen are well satisfied with a rupee each, and our day is ended with the forty mile drive back to Kalaw.

DIARY ——

11th June. Motored to Thagi, sixty miles, train to Mandalay and on to Ferry Boat and next day to Thabeitkyin. Next day by bus to Mogok to see the Ruby Mines, also sixty miles, and stayed at Circuit House.

JOURNAL ——

Nothing definite was really known concerning the mines until shortly after the Third Burmese War in 1886. Very few Europeans had made their way to Mogok by the path which wound it's difficult way from the banks of the Irrawaddy river for sixty miles through dense tropical forests; and apart from the natural difficulty of the route, the country was infested by robbers who levied systematic blackmail upon all who entered the tract. In these days the journey is easy and pleasant. On the left bank of the Irrawaddy and one hundred and fifteen miles from Mandalay is Thabeitkyin, from which there is an excellent motorable road to Mogok.

The road descends to the large village of Kyatpin where one sees the busy workings of people mining for precious stones by the pit method. The whole of the level space is honeycombed with pits sunk in the alluvial soil and the long poles of bamboo erected at the edge of each pit gives the impression of a forest of masts. The gravel is hauled out by means of balance poles fixed yardwise to the bamboo poles; a method similar to that used in many parts of India for raising water from wells. The gravel is washed in shallow baskets of finely woven bamboo and the rubies and precious stones are picked out by the expert eyes of the sorters. This primitive method is greatly improved upon by the Ruby Mines Company whose modern workings are now at Kathe, a mile nearer to Mogok than Kyatpyin.

After visiting the Ruby Mines, Burton and his wife returned to Mandalay, where they took the train for Rangoon. The steamer Edavana B.I.S.N.Co, left on 27th and arrived at Madras on 1st July, a day late on account of a strong head wind and rough sea. As regards fishing, the trip had been a disaster, but they had seen a great deal of the country, and Burton was glad to find the trip worked out less expensive than he had calculated.

Chapter 23

FISHING — TROPICAL RIVERS OF SOUTHERN INDIA

Colonel Burton and his wife were now settled in rented accommodation in Coonoor, their first fixed address for several years. He had discovered a place for fishing on the Bhavani river where few Europeans ever went, and every year for the next five years spent two or three weeks there in September fishing for mahseer. He also enjoyed some sea fishing off the West Coast of India.

JOURNAL

On 18th September 1929, I loaded up the lorry with my kit and set out for the Bhavani River. The road winds through tea gardens, the shrubs shaded by orderly lines of Australian silver oak trees, most of them pollarded to throw out side branches and afford more shade. On these trim hillsides now open to the view, there were, only twenty years ago, thick forests so dense that the sun's rays scarcely penetrated to the earth.

One of the many roads which traverse the hills and valleys took us to the Taimalai Coffee Estate Pulp House. Here we unloaded the car and put the kit (seventeen packages) on to the heads of a similar number of coolies. We started at 11.45 down the steep ghat road, paved with rough stones and consequently rather trying to walk upon, leading to the valley, 3000 feet below. This road was built many years ago and the construction of it was sound. The paved surface ended when less precipitous slopes were gained, and I observed half a dozen 'scratchings' of tiger, both old and recent, which shows that the road is used by these animals to gain the cooler forests of the uplands.

The sun's rays soon became more powerful and the heat oppressive, so I was glad to reach the banks of the Kundah River and sit in the shade of a giant terminalia to get cool and have breakfast. The Kundah was coloured from the frequent thunderstorms on the hills up the Emerald Valley, but was less than two and a half feet deep. The coolies waded across, holding on to one another in two's and three's, and I crossed in a coracle. The camping place was reached about 3 o/c. The only tree in the open, where it is better to be on account of the breeze and absence of mosquitoes, gave us little shade. The open space is a wide one covered with short grass and thorny bushes, and the Bhavani is a little over one hundred yards distant, its course marked by a fringe of large trees. The width is about seventy yards and there are rapids every few hundred yards. The men speak tamil only, but we get along well enough by use of signs.

Many rivers have their sources in the mountains and plateaus which form the Western Ghats, and most of them hold mahseer. The Bhavani is one of these, and probably the least fished on account of the bad reputation of the valley for malaria. I do not think the valley is malarious before the north east monsoon, which commences about the middle of October, if one goes high enough up the river; and I did not see or hear a single mosquito on the banks of the river during my recent three weeks stay at Sundapathi.

Along the banks of the river the trees grow to a great size, but away from the vicinity of the water, all the trees are of the thorny varieties and cactus is everywhere. The river is a rapid one between the pools, some of which are several hundreds of yards long. There is a large variety of bird life, and I counted over fifty species without difficulty. Conspicuous among them were the hornbills, the kingfishers, and the large racket-tailed drongo, while the flycatchers and the swallows were always busy over the placid stream.

Some twenty years ago, the Bhavani became almost denuded of fish owing to the unceasing and merciless methods of destruction employed by the inhabitants of the valley. Dams were built across the river and plaited bamboo baskets set at the prepared outlets, pools were poisoned, traps were placed at the natural ladders up the many falls, and by all the poaching methods at which natives are so adept the fish were destroyed, to such an extent that the people complained that their main food supply was no longer sufficient. Preservation has caused the river to be again fairly well stocked. Carp are numerous and so far as I could judge, fishing but four miles of water, mahseer are becoming plentiful. I was interested at one place where the fish could be seen in shallow water to observe how the mahseer of about two pounds hunted tiny minnows from their shelter under the stones, and pursued them as they bolted out on the other side. This is evidently one of the methods of obtaining the cannibal diet to which the species is so partial.

On 22nd September there was a heavy thunderstorm, the presage of several more days of tempestuous weather, marking, it is to be hoped, the end of the S.W. monsoon. Through the leafy screen of the trees before the tent, the turbid flood of the Bhavani River is seen rolling by.

DIARY ⸻

23rd September. River again in spate and very thick. Red ants everywhere, at least on almost every tree within two hundred yards of river. There is a long green creeper all over the open spaces, as good as rope, and no need to bring rope up this valley. White ants very bad; all boxes put on to tent pegs. Altogether an unpleasant country to shikar in.

25th. More tremendous rain last night, tent flooded but no damage as everything was on tent pegs 4in. off the ground. There must be a break before north east monsoon and big fish should be coming up on these floods. The white ants are all devouring: nothing that touches the ground escapes. I will have to be careful of tent flies, ropes at the pegs are sure to be eaten. The lime juice bottle lay on ground, on a piece of paper, since yesterday. Just now lifted it up and found a mound built up to the cork which they were busily devouring.

Evening. Went up to the junction with the Varagaar river, a small stream now in flood. The path up the valley is through scrub jungle and passes several hamlets. Near the Varagaar river is a grain shop: rice, ragi, jowari, soap, green coconuts (grown in the valley). Said to be several tiger about, and that they kill cattle fairly often. The village a wretched cluster of leaf and bamboo and grass huts. The people look very unhealthy. One child has smallpox apparently and none of the people or children vaccinated. The shopkeeper offered me coffee and milk, but I COULDN'T take it in such beastly surroundings. Promised some Oxide Zinc powder for a man with a bad foot. He spiked it and wound has spread over whole of upper part of his foot. He keeps a small shop, but has been unable to go and replenish his supplies. Came home through pouring rain and still, 7.30, raining hard. People say it won't stop till the Dhivali – 12th October!

27th. The head of the valley which is south west from here is hidden in mist and rain, but the river is now clearing at the edges. The boatman is making new bamboo framework for the coracle. It is 6ft. in diameter and 16in. deep and holds two comfortably, and can ferry three. These Irulas eat the fruit of the cactus, the ordinary 'chappal sen' or 'nag punnie'. Just pick it, carefully!, take a thorn and cut a ring round the middle of the fruit. It is very soft and can then be opened into two halves, contents not unpleasant, mostly small stone seeds. Saw track of a wild pig yesterday.

2nd October. This morning a number of yellow wagtail along the edge of the river. From here the river goes up and up, and there must be splendid pools and rapids. It is never fished. Old coracle man spoilt many good places by not being able, or not wanting, to stop the coracle. I am sure there are fish lying behind almost every rock as they used to do in Kistna, and do in every river in the world. The junction pool which I thought only as long as I could see is, so says coracle man, two miles long. It must hold some big fish. A good place just below the Siruvani junction pool is spoilt by big trees come down with former floods which make spinning impossible. Can't get the old man to bring me small 4in. fish as bait. All are 6in. or so; too big for the shallower runs.

6th October. Went up to rapids and fished down. Got a good fish at place where I have always hoped for one. One terrible moment! Line went slack and I was sure fish was off, but it had got behind some boulder and hung up the line. What a relief when I felt it still on! Heavy run; remembered to put off casting brake soon as possible so all went well. Net on small side and fish not properly in and the hook fouled it! A horrid moment again: Coracle man put finger and thumb into eyes and hauled it out that way. He always does that, and would be a bad opponent in a Paris 'Appache' row! Fish: 18lbs.

Old coracle man (he is not more than 40!) uses the two foot by three inch piece of bamboo which forms his seat and also a shoulder piece by which coracle is carried, as a 'priest' with which to knock poor fish on the head. I took photo of him holding the fish at place of capture. A gale of a wind blowing since nine o'clock, wild scurry of clouds, all from south west, but good sun too; lovely evening light on the river. Siruvani still muddy so no hope of fishing below Kundah junction this trip.

Forgot to note, – when spinning with SMALL fish, one of the very few I have been able to get, a kingfisher plunged at it and almost carried it off. It was spinning very naturally. Next time I come to this river I will bring a good supply of prepared baits. Whole country under rain and Bhavani in full flood this morning. So this trip comes to an end, with but seven days fishing: I look forward to next year.

JOURNAL _____

The flood was so violent that it was best to walk down to Sundapathy and avoid the half dozen rapids of that portion of the river. The coracle ferried coolies and baggage to the further bank, taking four men and about 250lbs. at each trip, I was astonished at its capacity. The first five miles down river entailed only two portages which the coracle man and I managed between us. Where the Kundah stream comes in on the left bank the river is broken up into many rapids, so two coolies were obtained from a village close by and walked two perspiring miles in the hot sun, which was turning the saturated valley into a Turkish bath.

It was only a short distance the coracle took us after re-embarking, and then a walk of about four miles, much of it high up above the river, which could be heard roaring down the deep chasm far below. The boatman told me that this rapid portion of the river holds very big fish, mahseer up to sixty pounds or more, and the time to fish for them is in December. I will hope to try for them in August to September, for from the appearance of that deep gorge I can imagine it must be very malarious. Along this part of the river there were silent witnesses of the violence of the elements, as the stream was blocked in places by giant trees blackened by lightening, uprooted and hurled into the flood. A thunderstorm in the depths of that gorge must be a terrifying affair.

Now that the difficult part of the journey was over it was delightful beyond expression to sit and enjoy the river in the soft light of the evening as the coracle glided, almost without aid, down the stream. On either side is the dense tropical jungle, huge evergreen trees entwined and festooned by giant creepers and flowery bamboos grow all along the water's edge. In one pool, the lengthening shadows of the trees were faithfully reflected in the water, and the long reach of the river bordered by the gloomy jungle. At the end of the pool towered the forest-clad mountain capped with fleecy clouds and laced by a mighty cataract tumbling headlong from above. I think the Bhavani is one of the most beautiful rivers I have ever seen.

There was heavy rain for the rest of this month, and Burton was glad to be back home and not still sitting in the tent by the river. The following year, when he went to the Bhavani to fish, he left at the beginning of September when he felt the weather should be better, and planned to explore further up the river.

DIARY _____

31st August 1930. Arrived Seerakadaon 9.30 p.m. Pitched camp half a mile further on near the river. Met a Muhammadan Contractor for forest produce, very polite, gave me coffee. The Contractor says a lot of tiger about and that they constantly kill cattle, also says there are elephant seven miles off; and that all this bit of country belongs to a Zemindar at Palghat.

JOURNAL _____

The scenery as the valley closes in is magnificent, and in the precipitous Attapadi Valley where the Bhavani has it's sources below the peak of Kolaribetta, it must be extremely wild and grand. Somewhere in that valley the river leaps down in a foaming torrent of four thousand feet, so there can be no mahseer above that, but to view those Falls would be worth all the trouble and difficulty a struggle up the valley would entail. In the pools and rapids accessible from camp, carnatic carp were numerous and in three days, using the small halcyon spinner, I took twenty four fish averaging 3lbs. My camp was where the river debouches from the narrow part of the valley and I planned to walk up stream by the paths through the jungle each morning and fish down to camp.

The weather was fine, not too warm, and there were no mosquitoes or biting and stinging insects. The long hours in the coracle were all too short. I soon knew every rock and swirl in the four miles of water. The spinners were small and light, thrown like a fly; the lure would sometimes be taken the instant it touched the water, and sometimes in still water under the shade of a tree and deep down. More often it would be taken in the swirl by the side of a rock, or in the quiet eddies along the edges of the steep banks, in fact where one's 'fisherman's eye' judged a fish should lie there was usually a fish.

At the tail end of the wide pool below the village the coracle was put into the water, the putting together of the rod and other preparations being intently watched by the observant throng. If a fish is about and on the feed, he will usually take the bait on the second cast, and so it proved. There was a murmur of varied exclamations from the crowd of onlookers as the rod bent and the reel screamed to the violent rush of a good fish, hooked some twenty yards down the rapid below the pool. Alas, after a run of about fifty yards when the fish showed at the surface in shallow water, the line came slack and the rod straightened. Nothing was broken, it was merely that the hook hold was slight. The waiting crowd groaned with disappointment.

The first three days at this camp had produced seven fish, the largest 12lbs then much rain in the hills brought the rivers down in heavy spate for three days. The next four days six mahseer (the best 24lbs) were taken and several others hooked and lost for one reason or another.

DIARY ───

2nd September. Lost one good fish by hook breaking. Bait taken close to boat and line went against top ring of rod. No further results. No doubt fish communicate ideas, and I expect that fish told all the others what an unpleasant mouthful he had come across. Fell while wading and soused to the neck. Clothes dried on me without harm in spite of a fairly strong wind. Three days with the smaller fish of these upper waters was sufficient, so I moved camp to the Varagaar junction six miles down stream.

4th. At Varagaar. River rather low now; one wants heavy water for spinning dead bait. Old boatman, sulky old beast, same as I said last year, unless everything exactly as he likes he growls like a bear, muttering to himself; always spoils the best bits of water. No doubt a coracle is the only craft for this river of many rapids and shallows, but a berthon boat is best boat to fish from. The Muhammadan Contractor passed through camp in the afternoon; he told me that in the Varagaar pool are fish as big as bullocks, and to bait for them one must use fish a foot long, for they won't look at small fish! I swam a 5in. fish for 400 yds down the pool using a float and certainly no 'bullocks' touched it!

9th. River in high flood this morning and head of the Valley still under cloud and mist. I find from Thomas' book, and by asking the boatman, that nearly all the smaller fish I got up river were Carnatic Carp (tamil – Shel Kundai). There were a few mahseer among them as I saw at the time. In the evening the lights and shadows on the green mountains were very lovely. The sky in the west looks as if this spell of bad weather is coming to an end; the boatman seems confident that there will be no more rain.

11th. Many heavy clouds up the Valley, Went up stream to just above the falls, and fished down. In first five minutes took a 5lb. fish; nothing in the splendid pool below the falls, but got a 10lb. fish further down in the almost still water. At top end of Halcyon Pool got into a good fish which took me 200 yards down stream, 22lbs: hen fish. Up river to same place next day, nil. Lost traces; one by getting hung up in rapid below the falls; the other in a mango branch over rapid near camp.

14th. Evening. Fished from the rocks and hooked a big one which went off at a great pace and took out nearly a hundred yards of line, down the still pool. I felt a jab and a second jab, and then the rush of the fish. The hook had not penetrated above the barb and dropped out of the fish's mouth after he was landed. It was heavy work getting him back up the pool and he bored heavily down and had to be shifted with rocks. Eventually tired him out and boatman netted him – 24lbs fine fish: 36 to fork; (39 to end of tail); 24 girth.

15th. Moved camp down to Soondapathy. Started fishing 8.15; again no small baits, most obstinate swine of a boatman, big baits not only make too much splash, but are bigger than the fish are accustomed to hunt and difficult to spin in placid water. Saw much lovely water today, all new to me as I was not able last year to fish any of this water between Koorapathy and Soondapathy owing to floods. Many portages of coracle necessary and water too fast in many places for coracle.

The river was beginning to rise on the last morning and a fish of 8lbs was taken in water so muddy that the bait could not be seen six inches under the surface. The last two miles down to camp were unfishable owing to the rapidly rising flood, clouds were banking up, so the trip was ended.

19th. I am sure the time to come is about middle of August, and what with the interruption by spates, best to arrange for six week's stay. Came down by coracle and walking to Mettupalyam. The coolies demanded 2/8 each, through a spokesman, who told them to 'fall in' to be paid. Before they started I spotted him as likely to give trouble. Refused to pay Rs.2/8 and eventually they were quite satisfied with 1/12 which I didn't grudge them for such a long march, but probably a native would have paid them 1/4 each only. Of course, the Head Watcher's idea was to get them paid 2/8 and for himself to snaffle 1/- or 12as. annas from each man! Swaraj in its normal working.

Burton and his wife were invited to spend Christmas 1929, with friends who ran a tea estate in the country near the Peryar Lake, Travancore, and this included the opportunity to go fishing on the Peryar river.

DIARY _____

17th December. Arrived Mount Estate; overlooking a deep heavily wooded valley on further side of which is a tremendous precipice. Hills mostly bare of forest except in hollows, ravines. Dam of Peryar Lake visible seven miles away. Nice and cool, but bad climate in rains; heavy mists and 150in. of rain: leeches abound in the forests. Went one afternoon, to Thekady by car, and took a boat out on the lake in the evening. Whole catchment area is a Reserved Forest and Game Sanctuary; except for Viceroys etc. Travancore State doesn't even allow planters to own a motor boat or a sailing boat on the lake; very anti-British native Officials. Heard sambur calling on further side of lake.

25th December. The party at dinner was fifteen; others came in after dinner. Fireworks, dancing, a merry party and the planters seem to pull very well together. To bed at 2 a.m. Up at 7.0 next morning and back to Thekaddy to arrange for dug-out and three men to take me to Thanakudi Forest Rest House, where the Peryar River runs into the lake.

DIARY _____

27th. Got to Thanakudi, 5.30 p.m. and a leech got me within two seconds of landing! Found the Rest House to be of three bare rooms, with back verandah and verandah three sides with two small rooms at ends. All round a 'V' trench to keep out elephants.

1st January 1931. Went up river by an inland path guided by a man of the hills. Fished down from where path met the river about three miles up stream. 1.30 p.m.

1

2

3

CHAPTER
23

1
The coracle at work ferrying
supplies over the Kundah river

2
Fully loaded with five men the
coracle crossing the Kundah
river

3
Coracle boy with a 5½lb
murrel caught by Burton

4
Men with catch of mahseer, 11
and 12lbs

5
Bhavani fishing scenery, this
was described by Burton as a
'good fishing pool'

killed a mahseer 8 lbs, on dead bait, and soon after had a run from another fish; all this would be good water when river high.

JOURNAL _____

All these mountains, except where the land has been opened up by European planters for the cultivation of coffee, tea, and cardamom, are clothed in forest in which wild elephant, bison, tiger, sambur and all the lesser jungle animals roam at will. The people of the hills are Mannans, but in a deep mysterious valley below the western slopes, the human race is represented by a tribe of extremely primitive people called Pandarums. True dwellers of the jungle they are, having bark of trees for their clothing, and rocks, caves and hollow trees for their houses. Very little is known of them and before long they must become extinct; for at the Census of 1911 it was recorded that they numbered fifty one. Perhaps there are more, perchance less, for it is likely that the Census Enumerators did not venture over far into those gloomy and forbidding solitudes.

The slow journey of eighteen miles over the winding waters of the lake to Thanakudi was done by wallan, but there are even more primitive craft than these in use by the hill men, who paddle across the wide expanse on rafts of bamboo awash with the rippling surface. Sometimes we were close to the shore, and occasionally could see the tracks of elephant and bison, for the whole catchment area of the lake is a sanctuary for big game. The sun blazed down and an occasional puff of wind made a flash of rippling darkness over the smooth water as a wider expanse of the lake was entered. In September, which is spring time in Travancore, the grassy uplands are covered with balsams and ground orchids, and most of the herbaceous plants are blossoming; and now (December) the country is varied by the autumn tints of the changing foliage.

JOURNAL _____

During the day there is not much to be seen; but up this secluded creek hemmed in by dense jungle there is more life. Monkeys and large black and maroon squirrels are busily feeding on the scarlet blossoms of an immense silk cotton tree; with them are numbers of black drongos. Grey hornbills flap from tree to tree in undulating flight. The strident noise of the cicadas is incessant and from the depths of the forest comes the booming call of the black lungoor.

The trunks of immense trees are invisible behind festooned draperies of creepers, and the great roots interlaced like writhing serpents are lapped by the glittering blackness of the almost stagnant water. The angry scream of a bull elephant a short hundred yards away made one glad not to have been able to penetrate more than a few feet into the undergrowth on exploration. Helpless indeed would one be in such cover with the trunk of an angered elephant in outstretched pursuit.

On 2nd January, the moon being nearly at full, it was good to wander in the dug-out. In the stillness of the air, every tree, every leaf, every creeper was apparently immovable. Nothing stirred but the paddles slowly dipping and the slight swirl on the water made by the oar of the steersman. The darkness deepened fast and the smooth veil of night was spread over the magic scene as we slipped along within the dark reflections of the trees. The hills became black shadows towering high in a clear sky and then the bright moon, soaring above the dark line of the forest changed the gloomy flow of the creek into a stream of silver.

We waited in the deep shadow of the overhanging bank. There was the occasional splash of a fish to break the stillness, the monotonous croaky call of the barbet was incessant, a giant horned owl uttered his loud and deep drawn out 'dur-goon dur-goon' which, when heard from some distance away in gloomy ravines, can almost be mistaken for the moan of a questing tiger. A large snake was seen making its way across the creek to the further side.

DIARY _____

Next day back to Thekady. A visit was made to the tunnel outlet to see the imprisoned waters emerge and hurl down the ravine in foaming rapids and falls, to find their way to the distant plains. To Ernakulam by bus as before, and into train going to Mettupalayam and had a much more comfortable journey than when coming.

SOUTHERN
INDIA
1930
TO
1935

Chapter 24

ELEPHANTS AND OTHER ANIMALS IN THE BILIGIRI HILLS AND THE C.P. JUNGLES

In January 1931 Colonel Burton and his wife went with Mr. and Mrs. McCarthy, to visit the Biligirirangan hills. At Sivasamudrum they saw the Cauvery Falls, and the bridge being built which would give a connection from Coimbatore to Bangalore. Burton noted that its estimated cost was Rs.415,000,000 and it was hoped to be completed in a year or two.

JOURNAL _____

In the Madras Presidency, the Biligirirangan Hills – 'the White Rock of the God Ranga', extend north and south for about fifty miles. At the southern end they are separated from the well known Nilgiri Hills by the deep valley of the Moyar River, also known as the Mysore Ditch, and a pestilential fever-stricken ditch it is. Forty years ago almost terra incognita to Europeans these hills were opened up by an enterprising coffee planter from Mysore, and at the present time privately owned motorable roads cross the hills. Along the length of them to east and west are good highways and a regular bus service. The country at the base of the hills is level and covered with brown thorny jungle. On the lower slopes is jungle of all sorts, bamboo and scattered trees, teak forest, and high grass; and mounting higher some of the slopes and all the hollows of the hills are carpeted with thick evergreen sholas. Paths made by wild animals are numerous, and without these progress would be exceedingly difficult.

There are many quiet valleys full of sunshine and deepest shade; streams of running water trickle down over polished rocks to be lost to sight in the deep ravines, where they tumble noisily over boulders, beneath the foliage of enormous trees. It was interesting to wander about the hills and valleys of these upland forests. In the course of an hour you may perhaps see half a hundred species of birds, and innumerable numbers of butterflies and creeping things.

The morning after our arrival at a Forest Bungalow, I went for a stroll with McCarthy through the thorny jungle beyond and came to a rush-bordered pool, at the edge of which were the night's tracks of elephant and also those of chital, pig and barking deer. A hundred yards further on, a turn in the narrow game path disclosed, at a distance of less than a dozen paces, the wrinkled hide and immense bulk of a bull elephant! He was motionless, listening, but the wind was in our favour, there was nothing to be done but curb our curiosity and retreat as quietly and quickly as possible. Although a .470 rifle is an adequate defence against an aggressive pachyderm, it is of no avail as an argument with the Forest Department!

Retreating, we made our way towards another pool, indicated by the large trees growing near it, to find ourselves a bare ten feet from another elephant, which was feeding on the further side of a dense thorn bush. Hurriedly we left this second danger spot (dangerous to the poor elephant if aggressively inclined), and made our way back to camp, where we learnt that there were two elephants in the vicinity about to be proscribed.

One of these had recently killed a man, who, passing near with some others had shooed him away and thrown a stone. The animal resented this and pursuing the fleeing party caught the stone-thrower – the others said that the beast knew his assailant and singled him out! The man was seized round the body with the trunk, dashed to the ground, and stamped on. Hard luck to slay an elephant for such an attack!

Within the few days of my stay I was able to give an accurate description of both these animals; but it is required that the description must be vouched for by an Official of the Forest Department, so there will be further delay. He of the cradle tusks and eight killings to his credit, I came upon one evening at the edge of a large water tank. As I neared the water a chital hind and fawn ran off, and several peafowl clattered away, and these alarmed an elephant at the water. The still surface was disturbed by ripples, followed by a loud squelch as a ponderous foot was pulled out of the mud. He was hidden from us by a big thorn tree, but almost at once the enormous yellow tusks appeared followed by the huge bulk of the body.

He came out of the river behind the cover and stood on the road; so long were the great curved tusks that they appeared too heavy to be carried and seemed to be resting on the ground. He didn't see us, thirty yards away, and we retreated, fearing the dog would bark. His tusks quite six feet out of his head, very yellow. We were told later that he is known to have killed eight people within the past few years.

The following morning I went alone to the pool hoping to obtain a photograph of this elephant. I was making for a large tree in which were some birds I wanted to look at; suddenly what I took to be a small brown monkey ran up a branch. The branch shook, and the 'monkey' became the curled tip of the trunk of a bull elephant whose whole outline suddenly sprang to the eye. I saw at once that this was the villain of the stone-throwing incident. It was six o'clock and the sun was well up. The bull advanced to the water and drank, but remained in the deep shade of the trees, so in none of my three exposures can he be clearly seen, although the distance was only twenty five yards. In spite of my standing in the open, he did not see me.

Daily, morning and evening, we tramped the jungles, but only saw a few chital. The presence of elephants made things very difficult, as the local villagers were afraid to leave their huts until well after sun-up, and hastened home long before dusk. The inhabitants of the hills are Soligars. They count themselves as caste people and will not eat the flesh of bison or touch the animals. Speaking a patois of old Canarese they live in primitive bamboo huts and are essentially jungle people, although the advance of civilisation and the opening up of the hills is beginning to change them. Their staple food is ragi, and wild yams which they dig up in the forest at considerable labour, leaving most unpleasant pits for unwary feet. Parroquets they regard as their children and will not eat them, but contrarywise, black monkeys they are very eager for, and I was many times asked to slay them; but one can't bring oneself to kill such animals, not for any reason.

The elephants were such a nuisance that we left this camp sooner than we might otherwise have done and did not wait for the return of the tiger, which had passed down the ravine and did not return.

The next camp was thirty miles towards the southern end of the range. I searched around very carefully and in ten days got to know pretty well all the jungle contained.

Bears there were, but we did not happen to meet them. One day news was brought to camp of a kill eleven miles away by a panther. By three o'clock I was off in my car prepared for a night out. The kill was in a deep thorny ravine, two miles from the road. By half past five I was settled down in the machan with the defunct bullock thirty feet from me. The stillness of the evening made every little sound distinct, the quiet rustlings of small animals and birds in the thickets and the staccato calls of jungle cocks. Then the night shut down and the stars came out with oriental brilliance, although it was very dark in the deep shadows of the ravine. At eight o'clock the familiar sound of quiet crunching came to my ear. There was no preliminary warning sound of any kind, as these formerly famed forests are now very empty of game animals. The panther was instantly killed.

DIARY _____

29th. One evening we went out for the pot, and shot one peafowl and six green pigeon flighting into some mango trees near the village. Shot nothing else all the time. Want of knowledge of the language – Canarese (Tamil would do), is a great handicap in every way. Many birds about, and saw a paradise flycatcher.

7th February. Left Bailur and went to Bellagi F.R.H., fifteen miles, which is on top of the Biligirirangan hills and three miles short of bungalow of Honametti Estate. owned by R.C. Morris.

10th. We moved camp to Hoolpatchayhalla, (which means 'Green grass ravine'). Camp is in a hollow at head of a shola; where there is a ring of shady trees and a spring of water close by. Morris had sent men on to clear the site and pitch his tents.

11th. Lined up all the men and sorted them out. Eight men plus Mulla plus Ira who is Morris' shikari. Better to have kept two more, but McCarthy doesn't want them. It is he who wants a bison and not I, so I didn't insist. Cold wind at night; a very sheltered camp all the same. Wild elephants have been known to visit it at night, so we keep fires going. Necessary to be up at five and out of camp at dawn if we wish to get bison.

12th. At 2.30 a note came from Morris to say that a donkey had been killed by a panther in the valley below the Estate and five miles from our camp. McCarthy wouldn't go. I was ready, bed and all machan kit, at 2.45; and after cup of tea set off and got to machan an hour later. A great deal had been eaten, both hindlegs and much of ribs. Much noise from cicadas and frogs. At 8 o/c heard distinct crunching of bones; torch showed panther lying down eating at ribs. He took no notice of the light. Bullet got him high in shoulder and out at opposite elbow – same as in case of female panther. He never moved.

Men came at 7 o/c. Decided to skin on spot and finished by 8 o/c with help of Banwa, quite a good skinner. Back to camp at 9.15, and pegged out skin. Panther was infested with ticks, which fastened on to me while skinning him, and so firmly did they attach themselves that they could only be removed by tearing them loose from their gory feast; the irritation of the bites remained for many days. Besides the ticks the animal had been much worried by spear grass, the needles of which had penetrated through his skin in many places. No tape, so didn't measure panther, and besides he was so stiff that proper measurements could not have been taken. Male panther: full grown: big teeth, all perfect; dark skin. Probably weighed 100 or 105lbs. The teeth of the female had been much damaged and blunted.

JOURNAL _____

The day before breaking up camp I set off at six in the morning to visit the Biligiri

Ranga Temple from which the hills take their name. It is about ten miles, through undulating forest all the way. At one place the night's tracks of an elephant crossed the path. I liked to think that perhaps this was old cradle-tusk, for he is a great wanderer, and twenty miles across hill and dale is nothing to him. Nearing Billigiri I came on a small lake, half clear water – half covered with lilies. The Range Officer accompanied me up to the Temple on the hill.

Seated a few yards from the temple wall one can dangle one's feet over a precipice a sheer five hundred feet in depth, and enjoy a wonderful view. Below and to the north is a tract of dry thorny jungle, threaded by the pilgrim route from the country round Mysore. Beyond the edge of the forest is open cultivated land, and a chain of tanks in the bright green setting of the rice crops; winding past them is the Honuhalla – or 'Golden Stream', which flows on to join the Cauvery River not far from Kollegal. To the north west, the blaze of electric lights which outline the Chamundi hill and illuminate the city of Mysore, can be seen for many miles. Eleven miles north of Mysore is Seringapatam (Sri-Ranga-Patnam, the City of the God Ranga) and from there can be traced the line of the great Cauvery river until it dives headlong into a deep gorge at the head of which is the Island and Temple of Sivasamudram.

Before admittance into the temple courtyard I was asked to remove my boots, after which the attendant priests showed the God Ranga to me by means of mirror reflected sunlight, but would not permit a photograph to be taken. However they very kindly arranged for me to photograph the image of the God and his attendant wives seated on a throne of gold in a setting of silver. This is the image which is taken in procession among the people on festival days. About 5000 people come to worship at the temple in month of May

DIARY ——
Came down hill and back to R.O.'s house and had breakfast in his verandah. He says there are many bears in these jungles and that they come close to his house after berries when they are ripe. Gave me cup of tea and couple of plantains, and I set off at two o'clock to get back to camp. This time did not go through the hamlet but by a more direct route. McCarthy much disappointed no doubt at getting nothing. I pressed him to go for both the panthers I shot but he wouldn't. We broke camp on 19th and went to Honametti – Morris' place, and stayed there the night.

20th. Motored to Ooty via Gudalur, one hundred and fifteen miles. 9 a.m. to 7 p.m. Had to follow slowly (and get all the dust) behind McCarthy all the way down the ghat. He goes VERY slowly.

In March 1931, Burton returned to the jungles of the Central Provinces it was to be his last Shikar to these jungles. The journey began with a drive of 100 miles to Mysore, which took all day as the car wasn't going well. He left next morning, but the car was still giving trouble, added to which, thirty miles out of Mysore the speedometer stopped working. On reaching Bangalore the car was checked at a Ford garage. It was the clutch which was faulty and this was repaired, but the speedo couldn't be mended, so he continued the rest of the way without one. He notes in his diary that he soon learned to accurately judge the pace at 20 m.p.h!

Bangalore to Anantapura was 132 miles. The road was reasonably good, but the heat in the car was stifling. At Kurnool, a further 121 miles he had the car railed to Mahbubnagar, it being conveyed in an open cattle truck at a total cost of Rs.25 His own fare and that of his man came to Rs.8/12. It took several days to drive

*to Nizambad passing through Secunderabad, and he again railed the car in an
open cattle truck from Nizambad to Hingoli. At that time there were no road
bridges over the Godavery river, nor the Penganga and Wardha rivers. From
Hingoli he drove through Basim, and Akola, and on to Ellichpur.*

*At Itarsi he met his wife, who had caught the Punjab Mail train from
Rawalpindi, where she had been staying with her daughter, and they arrived at
the Hill Hotel, Pachmarhi, at 4.30 on 14th March. The only loss on the trip was
a hurricane lantern stolen from the side luggage carrier when stopping for petrol
at Ellichpur.*

*After arriving at Pachmarhi, Burton sold the Ford car, as he wouldn't be
needing it again. He made arrangements for a four month shikar trip to the C.P.
jungles and booked a passage for England to leave Bombay on 12th March 1932.*

DIARY _____

1st April. Have been here a fortnight and have scarcely spoken to a soul! Called on
everyone, and of the nine ladies of Permanent Staff of the Musketry School only
two have as yet returned call. Pachmarhi is always like this: very peculiar and very
rude. Governor of C.P. (Sir Montagu Butler) came up today and soon there won't
be turning room in the Club. Hope never to come to Pachmarhi again.

It was a dull time at Pachmarhi all three months. No people congenial to me.
August, September, much rain, and again up to the very day we left, – 17th
October. An abnormal year: over thirty inches excess in Pachmarhi, and forty
inches excess at Itarsi.

DIARY _____

On 27th set out for Punasa. All together, six carts, five for kit of which one was for
two servants; H.G. in one, quite comfortable with two mattresses.

6th November. In camp at Borphal, Indaori Block. River Denwa very high
where we passed over it on way to Pipaya; another hour later and we might not
have got over. Took midday train for Itarsi and got there 3 o/c. Had a strenuous
week sorting and packing kit, mending store boxes, until 26th, when took 9 a.m.
train for Bir, where we put up in top storey of new Serai; quite clean, and sufficient
for the night. Have much kit, thirty four articles by goods transit, 22½ maunds:
and fifty articles with us, about 6 maunds: say a full ton of kit! Four months
supplies with us. Both servants new to us, and have to be taught much. Muhd.
Khan cooks and Karim Shah does tent work.

7th. Panther killed a small nilgae and put it up a tree to keep it safe. After the
gawala had moved on, it came back and removed it, as when the shikari went to the
place in the evening only one foot remained, caught up between two branches.

17th. Not a moments leisure since 8th, to write up diary until now. Only one
servant, others down with fever on 14th, and sent Karim Shah off back to
Pachmarhi; and today sent Sk. Rasool back to Punasa, a useless fellow, no guts; and
we can get along better and cheaper with two camp coolies for wood, water, and
kitchen help. Muhd. Khan doing well but lacks camp experience. I had to pack all
the camp kit and pitch and arrange this camp, see to loading of tents, in fact
everything down to all details.

On 10th, news of kill at gawala encampment said to be by small tiger. Got there by
3 o/c and found it was by a panther. A pretty white calf taken from the line of picketed
animals without disturbing anyone and dragged quite three hundred yards. Decided

to sit up for it and shikari put up machan in an ebony tree by tying three poles and stringing them – cot fashion – with a long rope. Panther came after dark, 7.0 o'clock, and I killed it with .470; instantly dead, no movement.

Male: 90lbs. Length 3ft. 11in. + 2ft. 7in. = 6ft. 6in. Skull – 8 $\frac{7}{16}$ × 5 $\frac{5}{16}$. Full grown and very muscular. Good coat.

On 15th, having packed several carts the night before, I expected to start by 7.30, but didn't get off till 10.30. All these people listless and lethargic from fever. Cart track to Nankiar Ghat four miles to north very bad and some nalas gave a lot of trouble. A yoke broke going up a stony ghat and fortunately I could get out my tools and was able to bore the necessary holes in a teak log cut to make a new one. In a deep wooded valley saw a panther, disturbed by all the row we made. Got to camp at 5 o/c: six miles in six and a half hours! Could only put up half a tent, for wife, and just unpack what was necessary for the night.

JOURNAL ——————————————————————————————

November 1931. Between the Tapti and Narbada rivers in the north west corner of the Central Provinces lies Nimar, a tract for the most part sparsely cultivated owing to the nature of the soil, but also not yet recovered from the devastating Mahratta wars of the early nineteenth century. In the hilly parts a deadly malaria prevails from the close of the monsoon to the end of the year, while in the low country towards the sacred river, there is some risk of fever until well on in November; so it was taking some chances to pitch camp near the jungle hamlet of Borphal early in that month.

The first evening in camp a panther passed close by, grunting to call up his mate, and extra care was taken to make sure that Little Ben, the perky cocker spaniel, was well chained in the tent: in the ten months of his life he had seen two panthers. He is a disappointment as to retrieving; I was never able to get any game birds to train him on.

JOURNAL ——————————————————————————————

To a lover of wild life and wild places there is a wonderful fascination in setting forth at a new camp. It was very cold, and a white shroud of mist lay over the village fields hiding all but the crowns of the distant trees; the heavy grass dropped under the weight of dew, and clothes below the waist were soon sopping wet. Before long the sun broke through, the mists rolled way, and the diamonds vanished from the grass. A chattering flight of parakeets swept in a green bow from the jungle to drop into the fields, and the call of the grey partridge was heard on every side. The local tiger had obviously been in a great rage, for he had scratched up the ground in a number of places and torn up and chewed two teak saplings. 'As mad as a man after eight annas of arrack', remarked my henchman.

The .22 rifle had to do great execution among the green pigeons, as no chickens could be procured, so Little Ben had plenty of lessons in retrieving. It appeared the dearth of fowls was due to propaganda on the part of the Hindus, for Korkus of the valley country are becoming much Hinduised. In response to enquiry they said 'Gandhijee is our God'. There were further instances of Hindu influence. A porcupine was shot for them, but because the Sahib had touched it, it was unfit to eat: and these same people in the hill country, fifty miles to the south, eat pretty well everything from owls to tigers and panthers which I have helped them skin.

DIARY

26th. Moved camp to gawala's encampment north of Borphal. Road very bad, and much delay by carts sticking in mud; one cart broke down three times. Took five hours, distance less than five miles. Went to put up big machan at the same place as before, and found that the big tiger had returned to the putrid kill, no doubt on night of 13th, and dragged it over a spur and into nala on other side; about 150 yards. If I could have stood another night over the putrid remains I might have got him! But it didn't seem likely he would come back. One never knows. What foul feeding beasts tigers can be; no wonder that a mauling by one is usually fatal.

Late one evening news came that one of the gawala's cows had been killed by a tiger one mile beyond where I am tying up to east. It is the mother of the pretty white calf, killed by the panther, which was the victim. Gawala says all eaten but the head and not worth going to sit up. May be work of two tigers. Slept four nights in big machan at place where boda was killed, in hopes of the tiger coming along. He didn't; so I don't get him.

5th. Sharpened tools, fitted handles to chisels, sorted and repacked stores. Struck camp as far as possible, to move to Punasa tomorrow.

7th/8th. At Dhariaghat, pitched camp, not much shade; very rocky. Found a Sadhur–Brahman camped in the cave: he consented to my taking his photo. A wonderful sunset: flaming sky, orange and red; and finally a glow like a furnace. Rain threatens.

On 12th, one fish, 6lbs, took me down river. Very cloudy. Sadhu enquiring why haven't yet taken his photo! Those wonderful sunsets and sunrises portended rain, and on 13th the sky was overcast all day and it rained in the evening. I went to the centre rocks and found a way to main channel. If only the fish were on the feed! No use stopping here for too long. I can fish 15th to 18th, pack on 19th and be off on 20th to Punasa.

Having failed for UNKNOWN REASONS to obtain a permit for the several adjacent and vacant shooting blocks, camp was moved through Punasa and we made our way through very uninviting country via Balri to Barkesar on the right bank of the Narbada. We crossed the Narbada in a big ferry boat, two annas a loaded cart; but we unloaded the carts as it was not safe to take them over in that way, hanging over the side of the barge! Anything at all loose would have fallen into the water and been totally lost. It took a long time to cross so we were only just able to camp down for the night.

24th. At Barkesar: overlooking Narbada and the Ferry. Camp quite well arranged and comfortable. Not allowed to shoot peafowl in this Jaghir so they are all over the place, and very tame. They don't object to shooting of anything else, but don't like the small deer shot. It is only under the influence of religion that game can be really protected in the East. Mukhtear has arrived back and sends word that he is coming to see me. Curse Cox: that on his account I should be at Christmas looking for a place to camp and shoot.

25th December. At Barkesar. Several tracks of tiger which killed a cow some ten days or less ago; saw a herd of sambur. Spent the afternoon soldering tins and lamps. Full moon tonight. 'Ben' is better at fetching doves, brings them at a gallop, but doesn't bring them to hand yet; hates the feathers in his mouth. Christmas week was devoted to exploration in search of a place at which to camp.

26th. Went to see Chandgarh. Started before day-break, very cold. As the cart driver said when lighting his chillum; 'I don't know where my fingers are'. Crossed

CHAPTER
24

1
Travancore, the Sabermalai
Temple, 24 November 1934

2
A sadhu at Dhariaghat,
December 1931

3
Barkesar ghat, a ferry used for
crossing the river

4
Swami of the god Ranga,
Biligirirangan temple

5
A view of the Narbada river
below the Makra camp

6
Korkus with a sambur at
Ratamalti, Suklu is holding the
horns

7
Shikaris with a panther Burton
shot at Chandgarh. The dog is
'Little Ben', Burton's cocker
spaniel who was,
unfortunately, not a good gun
dog

the Pari River, very little water, steep banks. Went up the path worn by generations of buffaloes taken by gawalas to graze in the forests near the Narbada at a place called Keralia. Half a mile short of the river found their encampment, which they left a month ago. On way back, saw half a dozen four-horn and a party of nilgae also put up two four-horn and a sambur at Keralia. Evidently the protection of small deer by the late Rao Saleb of Chandgarh has good results. Back to camp at Barkesar at 4.45. Small cart took us along very well. Paid Rs.1/8 and think man well satisfied, but one never knows: probably paid him double what he should have had!

27th. Packed camp. A visit while I was away yesterday from Jellalin of Gimar – nice old man, and brought a big basket of vegetables as a present. On 28th, moved to Chandgarh; camped on knoll as arranged. Very nice camp, shady, dry, no white ants, which were very bad at the river camp, so much so that nothing could be left on the ground even for an hour. Little Ben is looked at with much interest. They have never seen a dog like him before. Not often are cockers taken into the jungles. Have seen but few animals as yet, and must go further afield. At dawn saw a hyaena, he looked quite handsome, through the field glasses, with his black muzzle and prick ears. Little Ben didn't see him which was as well.

10th January 1932. Up at 3.30, off at 4.30 in bullock cart, to Tatwas. On getting to camp found that a calf had been killed in the village, by panther. When I arrived there, found the carcass picked almost clean by vultures. The idiots had not covered it up. It lay against hedge by side of a street in the village. A good tamarind tree close by. Quite soon after dusk I heard crunching of bones and with separate hand torch, made out the panther. Moved some twigs and the panther heard the movement, as he looked up. I had not intended to shoot that way for fear of injuring people in the hut beyond, but got rifle torch to bear and took careful shot from left shoulder. Not a move – panther instantly dead. Bullet s.n. cum split, took him low down in neck and smashed his innards to bits. Much excitement by villagers; back to camp in bullock cart by 8.45. Male panther: 125lbs. body 4ft.7in., tail 3ft. = 7ft.7in.: and the biggest and heaviest I have yet shot.

14th. To Balri, crossing the Narbada at Barkesar as before. The parao had been swept but a dusty and unpleasant camp. On next day to Khirkya, fourteen miles. Found D.F.O. H.S. Gadhi there. Evidently he considers Cox's order all wrong and not justified by the Rules. Cox has ruined my cold weather outing as he no doubt intended to do.

17th. We got to Marghari, thirteen miles, by 3.45. I went in a small cart as a dull job walking through level cultivated country. The cattle of the district all the way from Balri have a poor time of it. They are driven several miles to graze and back again for the herdsman to have a meal and then out again. So during daylight hours they get but two or three hours to graze and nothing at night. No wonder they are all bags of bones and in the hot weather die off in hundreds.

From Marghari to Ratamali was fifteen miles, and we arrived on the 20th, crossing the Nimar–Hoshangabad Boundary on the way. Tracks of a tiger all the way along the road from Bagwar to the nala close to Ratamali. Camped near the Garajul stream: good site. My ribs got covered with 'cow itch' – most unpleasant – not had it since 1898. Cow dung put on in a paste and pulled off when dry was the cure then. Tried it this time without much success. Then put on wood ashes, the Korku remedy, and had quick relief – quite wonderful in fact.

29th. News of kill and the men say it is by a big tiger. Kill is in open, no shadows, but no moon. I shall be able to see with field glasses how the tiger is lying before putting on torch. The chair is in tree at entrance of small nala and tigers must pass under it to go to kill. A faulty arrangement as I saw when I made it, but there seemed no other choice. At 7.30 heard footsteps among leaves in forest, and then quite close the deep grunt of T.P. which was instantly answered a hundred yards back. A tigress to dine with him no doubt. I was very still and crouched in chair with cheek resting on rifle stock. I heard every rustle of the stealthy approach: the deep throat sound, a sort of threatening rumble, and the sniff of nose being used. By slow degrees there was the push of heavy velvet feet down the steep bank and the rustle of the grass and leaves against the tawny flanks as the tiger almost brushed against my tree, and I pictured him in all his majesty standing on the rocks in the open. Then came similar sounds of the tigress following closer and just then a gentle breeze swept down the ravine to rustle the leaves and make the bamboos creak. Suddenly a peculiar noise, a sort of scarcely audible hiss from the tiger not thirty feet away, the advance of the tigress ceased and that was the last of them. Possibly a slant of air had carried the warning scent of the watcher in the tree. It would have been better to have chosen the tree on the farther side, and not risked detection in the near one. Had the tiger been alone he would have been less cautious; although HIS advance was much more bold than that of the tigress.

At 7 a.m., just before the men came, a stag sambur came along. Small head, but I felt I should give the men a feed. They don't often get meat and there are plenty of sambur. Took him at ninety yards as he was slowly walking across after having 'tonked' several times. Soft nose .470 got him at junction of neck and shoulder and travelled forward and stuck against skin half way along ribs on further side. The Korkus very pleased of course. Took a photo of the stag with five of my cooly men squatting behind him. Suklu, constituted the leader of them, is holding the horns.

Yesterday evening nearly had a fatal fall. I went up the ladder and into machan and had things arranged as I wanted. The ladder seemed safe then. In the afternoon I went up first, and the top rung of all came away in my left hand. I went backwards and tore a gash across my right hand. It was my left elbow and back going against one of the boles of the trunk which saved me. A narrow escape indeed! I could not have escaped serious injury and would probably have been killed: quite twenty feet. These bamboo lashings work quickly loose when dry.

JOURNAL _____

In the Western Satpura Hills of the Central Provinces early in February, at an elevation of some 1800 feet, the early mornings are really cold. Camp is pitched beneath shady trees on the banks of a rocky rivulet. The shale strewn slopes of the low hills are covered in high grass, while in many of the hollows is the ever spreading lantana with its orange blossoms and prickly stems. Jackals serenaded us at sundown and before dawn, the well known 'pheal' call being heard several times, occasioned by the approach of a prowling panther or hyaena, for the sight of either will elicit this hysterical cry. The staccato bark of the fox was also heard.

DIARY _____

4th February. All quiet in machan at 4.30. Soon the jungle crow and tree pie appear, and then comes the heavy swish of pinions and there is a general settling of vultures in a neighbouring tree. At 7 o/c there was a rush and the hyaena at the kill made a hasty departure with a terrified grunt. After a few minutes, hearing the crunching of bones, I put on torch, and saw tiger at kill. I decided for neck shot as shoulder shots at lying down animals not always good. To the shot she did not move and in a second rolled over as she was on a slight slope. Hyaenas came around but funked approach, as the tigress kept – to them – silent watch over her kill. I settled down, blanket over shoulders; and unloaded rifle so as not to keep at full cock for so many hours. At 3 a.m. there was a tremendous pull at kill. I thought it too hefty for a hyaena, but it might be. I put on light to see. A tiger! A tigress! I really thought it was the tigress and that I had shot the cub. I didn't dare to keep light on long, just had a look, saw the stripes and the big eyes looking up at me, blinking, not fully open.

I began to load as silently as possible: then I put out rifle, and put on torch. The tiger was standing almost at right angles. Circle of light lit up whole of shoulder. The tiger took no notice of the light and I aimed at the centre, avoiding the big bones and muscles of shoulder as I used soft nose cum split bullet, thinking it was the tigress. 'She' looked very big. No time to think too much! To the shot there was no vocal answer, but with a tremendous rush the stricken beast was in a fraction of time across the nala and crashing through the bamboos to my right. Then a few yards behind me, a deep sigh, expulsion of the breath from the lungs, and no more.

It was very cold and there was a strong wind blowing. At dawn I packed up odds and ends and removed screen on my right, and there he was, a big tiger lying on his left side. He had gone only thirty paces from where hit. The tigress looked bigger by daylight and I realised she was full grown, though not very large. Men very late in turning up, said it was so cold! Measured the tiger, the tigress was too stiff and bunched up. Measured her in camp, before skinning.

Tiger – curves: 9ft.11in.; body 6ft.11in., tail 3ft.; girth 52in.; forearm 20in.
        pegs: 9ft.3in.;   "   6ft.3in.   " 3ft.;
        Skull: 13$\frac{7}{16}$ × 9$\frac{9}{16}$. Weight: 420lbs.
Tigress – curves: 8ft.7in.; body 5ft.9in., tail 2ft.10in..
        Skull: 11$\frac{10}{16}$ × 7 $\frac{5}{16}$. Weight: 245lbs.
A heavy massive tiger; finely marked. Tigress well marked too.

It was the tigress which had killed and the tiger had come in during the night from the south, the men saw its tracks all along the path, and had passed under my tree and probably stood there a while staring at the unexpected appearance of a tigress lying quiet before her kill. Lucky I was not restless just then; but I was pretty high up and by habit extremely quiet in all movements, for one never knows but that a tiger may be close at hand. Started skinning tigress at 12.30: finished in three hours, and skin laid out without pegs. Finished the tiger by 6.15. Had some help from some of the men and the F.G. Mahmet Beg, and Muhd. Khan.

6th. No kill. Went to Junapani, and selected camping ground. Whole village away at Kaida Market. Shot a peafowl, missed a four-horn from the cart, – 'Ben' spoilt the shot, fighting to get out and shikar!

8th. Men came and said they had seen a blue bull. Had a beat, and came on a herd of nilgae, and shot one. Anyhow meat for the feast, and one is asked to shoot as many blue bull as possible on account of damage to crops of the Korku forest villagers. I have only 2lbs alum! Plenty of salt. Sent for alum a week ago asking the R.C. to send on to Harda for it if none at Magardha. Ass sent me 20lbs salt which I didn't ask for and said alum must be got from Harda and I must send a special man for it! Fool. Now I can't get it till 14th; man went yesterday morning, 10th; 14th is the earliest.

15th. Kill at Mirbu nala. When I got there found vultures busy at it! Fools hadn't properly covered the carcass. Kill by panther, may be two of them, and not by 'burra sher' as the men said. Put up machan chair and left a man to keep off the vultures. Hope he won't fill the chair with bugs. He is afraid to sit below, although it is a public road and plenty of traffic and in any case no chance of panthers coming to kill before I get there in the evening. Panther came at dusk. I let him feed and watched him; very 'skeared' he was, a bite or two and then head up and looking and listening. He fed at chest, evidently not liking the mess at the other end which the vultures had made. When I could scarcely see him any more on account of the fading light I put on torch. Shot him through centre of back behind shoulders and bullet came out at throat. Not a move, stone dead. Male: 4ft.6in. + 2ft.10in. = 7ft.4in.: Weight 136lbs. This is heaviest panther I have yet shot; but not such a big beast as the Chandgarh one. A very handsome animal: perfect teeth. Did his best to drag the kill, evidently not liking his dinner by the roadside.

25th. Very cloudy last night and much warmer, 52° at 6 a.m. Permit up at midnight. Packed camp: paid up coolies. Tip to F.G. Walud Beg, Rs.15/-. He wasn't satisfied, I heard; they never are. Also I am SURE he stole two of my cotton ropes for his pony! I started this trip with eighteen and ended with thirteen. Four stolen by F.G.s; one used by bodas. In future must dye them a distinctive colour.

It was twenty seven miles to Harda, sixteen in the bullock cart and I walked the rest. Had trouble on the 27th as cart wheel gave out and had to be replaced. Jarkahar is a big block and requires two months permit. We were very lucky on the last march in to Harda. Storm came on, threatening all afternoon, a few minutes after we got to D.B. So all kit dry and it, and the skins, might have been all wet, and ourselves and the poor coolies too. We got to Itarsi on 1st March and, after packing and sorting kit, left on 9th for Bombay. Sent 'Little Ben' to Jarkyn Forests, Nagpur.

JOURNAL —————————————————————————————————————

There was much to enjoy in these forests; the charm of the night-long vigils under the silent shining stars, listening to the many sounds and movements; the deep 'dur-goon, dur-goon' of the great horned owl, and the flute-like call of a smaller relative, and now and again echoing among the hills is heard the grand 'a-ough, a-ough' of a roaming tiger. Then there were the quiet evening prowls, the talks with the village folk, and the hearing from the weekly bazaar of the news of the country side from far and near.

'How I wish I could do all that, enjoy that life', many people say to me. Well, it isn't difficult. A ticket by the G.I.P. for a few hundred miles, the hire of a bullock cart, and the thing is done.

Colonel and Mrs. Burton left Bombay on 12th March and arrived at Tilbury on 1st April. After staying in England for nine months he sailed on 31st December for Colombo, Ceylon. His intention was to visit the Yala Sanctuary, staying two months in Ceylon, armed this time with a camera, and return to Coonoor on 5th March 1933.

Chapter 25

TRIP TO CEYLON, YALA SANCTUARY

Yala Sanctuary. February 1933. At Bombay about 350 passengers disembarked and we sent off our heavy baggage to go by goods train to Coonoor and so save all the bother and the heavy charges on the Ceylon Railway. We left Bombay about ten o'clock and could see the Western Ghats dimly visible about ten or fifteen miles away. The second day out was hot – the hottest day of all the voyage – as there was no wind and a glassy sea. We got to Colombo at 7 o'clock on Sunday 22nd January and anchored in the harbour. The *Empress of Britain* was close by with 300 tourists, including G.B. Shaw on board, and local papers full of it.

The passing of baggage through Customs gave no trouble but I had to leave my revolver with them to be kept 'in bond' until I leave Ceylon. In the afternoon the President of the Ceylon Game and Fauna Protection Society and his wife called for us and drove us out to the Mount Lavinia Hotel. The place was crowded with people of all grades of society and of every kind of colour as to complexion that it is possible to imagine. The East and West appear to meet much more freely here than in India. There was much consumption of small drinks, but after one potent drink R.B. took refuge in tonic water!

Next morning I bought a pair of canvas shoes in which to go through the jungles of the Game Sanctuary as I can't afford to spoil my expensive boots. It is arranged that I go on 6th February to stay with Mr. Tutein Nolthenius, one of the Society's Committee, and we meet Mr. Brown the Government Agent and his Assistant Mr. Leach. We stay in the Sanctuary for three days and get back to Tissa on the 15th. After that I make my way to Kandy. This visit to the only Sanctuary in Ceylon which is at all accessible should prove very interesting.

A very damp country is Ceylon, and I would not like to live in it. We are both a bit disappointed. I suppose it is that we have seen so much wild tropical scenery in other places, Burma, Kachin hills, Nilgiris, Travancore, and are a bit blásé in consequence. We had continuous rainy weather all the time we were at Kandy; and on 1st February left by train to see the famous ruins and temples at Anaradhapura.

On 5th February I was met at Haputale station by A.C. Tutein Nolthenius a tea planter and a keen naturalist. On the 9th Nolthenius and I started off for the coast, and in the evening we arrived at Tissamaharama Rest House. The Government Agent has to make a Report to the Government on the Sanctuary and we others are just accompanying him.

We transferred all our kit into the carts, and then we set out for Yala, twenty four miles distant on the banks of the river Menik Ganga, which is the western boundary of the Sanctuary. It soon became pretty hot and had it not been for the interest in new country and the life on the jheels it would have been very tiring. The water edge was thick in places with waders of many kinds – ibis, stilts, golden plover, pelicans. On the path we saw tracks of elephant, spotted deer, leopard. All the way we were within sound of the sea and in places there was but the sand dunes separating us from a view of the surf beating on the sandy shore. There were many wild flowers along the side of the road and in among the bushes; we also saw a hawk crested cuckoo which was jumping in the grass.

At 6 miles we stopped at Palupatana Rest House to have a drink and give the bullocks a rest. There were four bullocks yoked tandem fashion to each cart, the ropes to the horns of the leaders being passed through iron rings on the cart pole and on the yoke pole. The bullocks were small, as all the cart bullocks of Ceylon seemed, and were much scarred with branding. Not only were they branded in the usual way of the east, but the man with the hot iron appeared to have been tracing out designs on the hides of the unfortunate cattle and on most of them there was writing in a native language – Tamil or Singalese according to the ownership, the name of the owner being traced along the ribs. Our seven carts were all lightly loaded, some of them only carrying us as we sat from time to time, more to get out of the sun than for a rest; and it would be cruel to take heavily loaded carts through that sandy country.

After leaving the rest house at Palupatana we began to see game. At a sheet of water there were several herds of buffalo and a number of spotted deer. Counting the animals it seemed that there were in sight perhaps a hundred buffalo, as many deer, and a number of sambur. A flowering acacia was new to me. It had sweet scented blossoms of two colours, mauve and white. Among the many acacias were a few with the yellow puff ball blossoms and these were very like the acacia of India. A hoopoe, a green pigeon, an emerald dove, and a painted stork were seen. Some three miles short of Yala the party split up into three, the idea being to gather a beast to provide meat for the many hungry mouths. I went with the carts and saw a fine stag chital at a few yards distance, but I was not one of those carrying a rifle! The hunters arrived at camp without any success in spite of the quantity of game that was seen. The moon was at the full and we stood and watched the silent waters of the Menik Ganga sweeping down to the sea close by. The sound of the crested waves beating on the shore had been with us all day and lulled us to sleep in our tents. It was hot, but tents were desirable as protection against a heavy dew.

We were up early in the morning as the river had to be crossed. I don't know how the Ranger and the watchers had done their job of looking after the sanctuary with no means of crossing the river when it runs high, as it does for pretty well all the period June to January, as not even a dug-out is provided. They have a wire hawser to hang on to when wading across, but that was broken and had to be fished up out of the stream. So no doubt the watching is done from this side of the river!

A man went across and cut a strong liana, hitched it on to the wire, and the hawser was again complete. We all stripped and got across, the water up to hips only, and the carts were unloaded and everything taken over on the men's heads. Then the carts were driven in, and when the bullocks got out of their depth they swam, while the men wading behind pushed. The getting up the steep bank on the other side gave some trouble, but all were across in a couple of hours.

On leaving the belt of jungle near the river we got into a plain, partly open and partly studded with trees. There were scattered pools of reedy water, and everywhere the buffalo were grazing and wallowing. Stopping for a late breakfast there was the remains of an elephant by the side of the path. I used his skull as a seat and some previous party – the watchers probably – had used the leg bones instead of stones to prop up the cooking pots. At one of the sheets of water there were many golden plover and storks besides smaller waders.

It was late in the afternoon when we emerged from the forest, and there was a wonderful sight to greet us. The animals had begun to come out into the open. In every direction were buffalo and spotted deer. It was estimated that there were about 700 deer in sight and half as many more would have been along the fringe of the cover or out of sight round the bend of the plain. Of buffalo there would have been about 200, and besides these animals, there were pig and jackal.

There was no shaving done for the past two days. Good stories were exchanged and by 9 o'clock we all hit our pillows. I was the one to be early awake, and roused the others with the hearty call – 'The dawn is up, the day is here; for me the tea for you the beer.' The joke being that the tipple of the beer topers had been left by mistake at Yala. Next day we went with two trackers to a line of hills about four miles to the north. In the morning we saw thirty seven pigs in the open plain. All were feeding along, grubbing up roots and it was very amusing to see the little ones at play, chasing one another round and round and sparring on their hind legs with one another.

As we crossed the plain we saw a number of garganey teal in the lagoon and several old buff bulls. One of them had a broken horn and the watchers said that he and another big bull we could see shared the plain, neither permitting the other to trespass on his side of the stream. There was a reedy tank, which invited a stay, but we had not the time. Egrets nesting, herons, waterfowl, sambur stag, buffalo, crocodile, tracks of elephant, and lots of bird life.

Not having any shikar kit with me, I had to dull the whiteness of my topee, so what more effective and simple than to rub it well in a buffalo dropping? I was asked – 'Is that your hat or is it a cow pat?' It might well have been taken for either! The climb up the steep slope of the hill was a perspiry business. We followed an overgrown elephant track and then turned up the slope and wound round to the north of the hill to the top which is a bare rock. Height is 523ft. above sea level. A photo was taken to commemorate the climbing of Mandagala, to top of which no one had been since the Sanctuary was declared in 1894! From the hill we could see our tents at Pahala Potana, and the sea beyond, where also the lighthouse was visible. Away out to sea we saw a big steamer on its way to Colombo – probably the Australian Mail.

To the east, a river, the boundary of the sanctuary in that direction, could be made out. To the north was an unbroken sea of forest with some hills of varying height in the distance. To the west, far away, was the line of the Menik Ganga. Close under the hills we saw, looking from our rock, several small parties of buffalo in their wallows, a sambur stag, and some chital.

We could see plainly that what the Sanctuary requires is more open spaces, as grazing grounds; more water to allow the animals to spread over the forests; and plenty of broad paths from water hole or tank to water hole, so that the game watchers can really patrol the area. At present they never leave the open country near the sea; and can hardly be expected to as they would see nothing and would always be running into elephant and buffalo. Above all the animals want more water, for in the hot weather when practically all the water we saw is dried up, the unfortunate animals have to congregate on the rivers, which are then merely a succession of water holes, and have a very bad time of it I am sure.

All these forty years, during much of which time there was plenty of money, nothing has been done, and now the lean years are with the Government it is but little they can spend on keeping animals alive. Nolthenius is doing what he can to foster and advertise the idea of a National Park as that is the only way in which this wonderful game preserve can be made what it should be. We had a meeting at the end of the trip and G.A. asked us all for our ideas. These were mine. Repair that big tank and as many others as could be found; make wide inspection paths; clear open spaces in suitable places to increase the grazing; do not allow any thinning out of game, and do not kill off the leopards, but let nature work out the number of each species the country will hold.

There were several flowering shrubs and creepers. One bush with a conspicuous brimstone yellow flower is called Bethang Mala, but no one knew its botanical name. On the hills we saw the 'nilu' which gives such colouring to the Nilgiri Hills when it is in flower – strobilanthus as it is called; and there was one stalk of lantana. No doubt in course of time the whole of that clump of hills will be smothered with it.

On the morning of 14th February we had regretfully to strike camp and set off on our return. There were many buffalo and deer in sight, same as on our way in. One bull had the best head I had seen on this trip and I got a photo of him at about 60 yards. In the afternoon we crossed the Menik Ganga again at the same place as before. We got to camp just before dark having put up a surly looking bull on the way, of which the tracker was much afraid. He fears elephants and buffalo although he will track them for sportsmen.

This night was the coldest we had had, and there was a heavy dew. In the morning I went with G.A. to see Elephant Rock. The Rock is a very conspicuous landmark, and I wish I could have gone to the top of it, but time did not permit as we had a long way to go. Shortly after passing the rock we saw a female elephant with a calf but I couldn't try and take a photo as G.A. and the tracker seemed in a bit of a fluster about it. Reluctantly I gave up an excellent opportunity. Later we saw a big boar lying asleep in the path. G.A. is no shikari and instead of approaching quietly and then breaking a twig and so getting the boar to his feet, he fired at his hinder parts! Poor piggy. I am glad his shot went high and so did not inflict the non-fatal wound which would have resulted.

Nearing Butuwa Wewa where we had arranged to meet the others and three of the carts, we saw the splendid tank which should have been there, had the bund been properly mended. A rascally contractor had scamped the work and so the tank breached at the first opportunity. The others had shot nothing. Hughes missed a stag chital. It was quite dark when we got to the cart road where the motor cars were waiting for us. We reached Tissamaharama about 8 o'clock.

I met the President of the Ceylon Game and Fauna Protection Society in Colombo, and told him what I had seen, and left on the 20th midday for Kandy. The Mousakande tea estate group is at about 3500ft. and Phillips' bungalow gets all the force of the north east monsoon which sweeps up through a gap in the hills a mile or more away. Above him is a jungle covered hill and a perpendicular cliff. It has been most kind of the Phillips to have Hilda to stay with them all these twelve days I have been away. He is a keen zoologist and has written much about the mammals of the Island and discovered several new species.

We left next morning after I had been up the hill to get a view of the surrounding country – and been bitten by two leeches for my pains – and at Matale we got a hired car and returned to Kandy. On the 24th we set out with all our kit in a hired car to go to various places and eventually to Manaar and the steamer for India.

The country now became dry and thorny. Nearing Manaar we crossed an arm of the sea by a long causeway to find the Rest House full up, and the only thing to do to return along the road 14 miles to R.H. Murungan. We were up at 3 a.m. and took the train at 4.0 having paid up the hired car which had brought us from Kandy, 342 miles for Rs.171. The train got to Talaimanaar at day-break and we were soon on board. Customs people saw baggage during the crossing and were uninquisitive, but we had nothing to declare. I told them my revolver was in bond with Thos. Cook at Colombo who had not sent it along as asked and was endorsed on the customs form to this effect, and that it gave so much trouble that I did not want to see it again, and they could do what they liked with it. So far I have not heard anything further, but no doubt red tape is being spun!

We had a long wait at Daneshkodi, then we ran through sandy country and palm trees and lagoons and crossed rivers, and about 2 o'clock left the level country and began to see hills, the hills near Madura. We had a compartment to ourselves for the whole journey. We changed train at Podanur in the middle of the night, but it wasn't very disturbing as our onward carriage was waiting in a siding and the railway staff at Daneshkodi had wired on to have it ready for us. So we got to Mettupalayam at 5.45 and into the train for Coonoor at 6.30 and back to our cottage at 9.30, and so all our journeyings and excitements at an end – for the present!

The whole Ceylon trip from landing at Colombo on 22 January to arriving at Coonoor on 5th March, came to Rs.1771 or Rs.41 a day. As we can allow ourselves only Rs.650 per month or Rs.21/8 a day, such jaunts cannot be done too often; but one can only live one life, so what matter! And Coonoor is cheap to live in. There are so many places I want to visit, as my friend Cleeve tells me 'You must live to a hundred and fifty, nothing less will be of any use'!

Chapter 26

FISHING — INLAND RIVERS AND THE MALABAR COAST

DIARY
Attended a meeting at Government House, Ooty, on 7th June 1933, for purpose of forming a Wild Life Preservation Association for South India. The Governor of Madras, Sir George Stanley, presided. Doubt if much good will result. Sent in a long Note giving my views beforehand. At Coonoor all the time after 5th March, just 'kicking heels' until end August when I go to the Bhavani to fish.

24th August 1933. I am again at Sundapathi on the Bhavani River, under similar arrangements to 1929 and 1930. Very hot today, and coolies evidently felt it a good deal. I intended to camp tonight at Koorapathy, but men very done, and thunder growling all around and a few drops of rain, so stayed here in the grass hut. River full, but a lovely colour, great push of water; as well to go up to Seerakadam tomorrow, although lazy Avanashi, the boatman, says only small fish up there! It seems a tiger has been killing a few people some miles from Sundapathy. Met an Overseer of Electricity Department on his way by what he calls a 'short cut' to Avalanchi! He is to lay out Power line Pykara to Calicut.

29th. In morning went up river to where the small nala runs in. Lots of good water, but no fish. Back to Camp pool at 10.30, at tail end of it was taken by fish which scooted at once down the rapid and fortunately kept my side of bush in the middle of the pool. He did a great run and fought a fine battle. Seemed bigger than he turned out to be, 11 lb. At 5.30, when fishing, a big thunderstorm came on. Fortunately only light rain for my walk back through the village; buckets of rain just after I got back. All the Irulas peeping out of their doors at me, DOZENS of children, about five to each house. Houses in a double line like Korkus', and made of bamboo wattle and mud, with grass roofs; flimsy affairs and very small. They have lots of buffaloes and goats and cattle. Unfortunate buffs are corralled in the open, hock deep in mud and dung, and barely room to lie down. I stroke the little buff calves noses to alarm of their mothers.

All these days fishing, I used 9ft. trout rod. It is a bit of a strain on it in this heat, and with sometimes heavy bait, so now put it away and start using, for first time, the 10ft.6in. Hardy Greenheart spinning rod. A barge pole affair and best suited for heavy spinning, such as sea fishing and big rivers like the Cauvery. I have always regretted not getting a 16ft. Treherne grilse rod, Farlow's, same as the two I lost in rivers: one in Nerbudda at Mortakka 1906, and one in Jumna near Kalsi in 1914. Best pattern of all for all round work. The 7ft. Hardy Victor Greenheart spinning rod is with me, but not having had any practice with it, it would be difficult in the coracle, as old man twirls one round at all sorts of angles.

JOURNAL
The Bhavani issues from behind the Matteswara Hill and takes a direct north-east

course for Mettupalayam. Six miles down the Varagaar comes in on the left bank, a small stream which seldom affects the main river from a fishing point of view. Four miles below that, two rivers – the Siruvani and Gopanari – come in together on the right bank, the combined waters producing a muddy flood on very slight provocation, for they drain an area of tea plantations, which causes much denudation of the soil. Nine miles further down, the Kundah river, also from tea planting areas, brings frequent turbid waters, so it is not unusual for those ten miles below the Siruvani junction to be spoilt for many days.

There are elephants in the valley further down towards Mettupalayam and when the ragi crop, which these villagers have just sown is ripening, it will be raided no doubt, as it was last year. The sky became overcast and thunder growled among the hills: the conspicuous Matteswaramalai Hill (5855ft.) with its 400ft. tooth piercing the sky, and which dominates the whole valley, was lost to view, and the hills changed from purple to pitch black. The dark deepened into night as the storm came nearer heralded by loud thunder claps and long flashes of vivid lightening. These disclosed a turmoil of leaping waters, for the rapid mountain torrents had already brought the river down in spate. The big trees lining the banks of the river swayed before the wind and in a few minutes the camp was flooded deep with torrential rain. Storms along this river are very violent, as witnessed by many charred and riven giant trees along the banks and lying in the pools and rapids.

There are some very heavy mahseer in this river, but one does not get them by spinning, for they are too lazy to hunt for their food. The record is said to be 118lbs, and all the big fish one hears of in South India are taken on paste made of ragi or atta, after a thorough ground baiting; but one can do that anywhere, it is the searching of the river for fish with spoon or dead bait, which is the real sport. The fisherman must have both time and patience, as there are many spates during which no fish can be caught, and the angler has to assume the role of 'rusticans expectans'. On my first visit I sat seven days in the tent 'dum defluit omnes', for heaven's sluice gates were open all the time.

My coracle is rather a wonderful affair. It is six feet in diameter and fourteen inches deep, yet it will ferry in safety five men and several hundred pounds of luggage. One man can carry it for miles without difficulty. The covering of the coracle is of buffalo hide stretched over a basin-like basket of bamboo, the leather being kept soft by an application of mustard oil. There is only one seam, and kept in condition by the oil, a hide lasts a long time. The whole affair can be made for twenty rupees. I pay Rs.2/14 a day for the boat, two men, and a boy who cooks their food. The watchers, who have a boat of their own, tell me I pay too much!

After keeping the river in high flood for five days the storm ceased, and the water is now running down. The sun is drying up the earth almost as fast as it was saturated by the rain. Those exquisitely beautiful insects with soft plush-like bodies of vivid scarlet, about the size of a small cherry stone but flatter, are making their appearance. So thickly will they soon lie about that in places they redden the earth. Brilliant butterflies are beginning to appear and dragonflies and other insects are to be seen.

DIARY ————————————————————————————————

30th. Wednesday: The storm was a big one and has sent the river down in a flood a foot high, so this morning although much of it has run off, the Bhavani is a coffee coloured torrent. Sent Ramaswamy off with sixteen coolies to take camp to Koorapathy. Came down in coracle but had to do many rough scrambles on boulders and through jungle along the banks.

5th. Tuesday. Both rivers in flood. Bhavani subsiding; whole valley under cloud. Yesterday a high wind and cold, no sun. Put stones under bed legs, as white ants getting busy. Went up stream to same place as on 31st, and caught a 4lb. fish. No other offers; water just right and must be fish about. Fact is the spinning has to be EXACTLY right or the clever fellows shy off at the last moment. No doubt in a day's spinning the bait is seen and inspected by many fish and only at the moment when it happens to be just right is it taken. The bait can't spin too quickly, so as small a bait as will spin quickly must be used.

9th. River still high. I went up to above the falls but coracle could not be worked, so landed and got in again at 'Grandfather's Run' and in half a dozen casts was fortunate in hooking fish on a single treble. He took out 70yds line and was very strong and hard on the 10ft.6in. rod, which stood up well to the work. There were anxious moments when he bored to the bottom and seemed immovable and hung up. At last he came up stream into calm water, and was landed without trouble in shallow sandy bay; 24lbs. A fine handsome fish; very slightly hooked as barb had apparently not penetrated. One of the men removed the hook without aid of scissors. Took photo of fish held by two men, coracle man and watcher.

10th. Sunday. Went down stream, nil, too much water and old man can't manage the coracle, which it is no doubt very difficult to do. He made an error, saw small fall too late, and we went over it! Lucky not to go under, rapid water always dangerous. Coracle half full of water and we only just got to shore. Tackle box wet, took out everything and dried and vaselined it. Back to camp at 12.30.

Next day Siruvani a muddy flood: Bhavani high. Went up to above falls and fished down; fresh water coming down and river rising. From letting coracle over run my cast, the old man caused me to get hung up. Water too strong to work against and I had to break away. Killin trace, four swivels, treble hook, Hillman lead. This river never forgives any mistake!

12th. About 8 o/c I heard a lot of calling out and noise towards the village and this morning learn a cow had been killed by a tiger. Went to see, and found a nice cow had been killed, nothing eaten. A big hole in the throat, neck not broken. Seeing the tracks in loose sand I think this is work of a tigress not quite mature. Curious that there was no return to the kill; so it was a wanton slaughter of no use to any but the vultures which finished off the carcass by 10.30. I went to village and took photo of a group of women and children and dispensed a few bangles to the babies. I discovered the vultures didn't get the cow! They were driven off by the Chamars, of which there is a family in the village. Irulas won't eat flesh of killed cow, Chamars will, and paid owner of cow 5/- for the meat. Owner sent the skin to Mettupalayam and will get 1/8 only for it! So the poor cow did 6/8 of good to somebody and village dogs have some pickings, also the vultures a very little.

15th. Friday. Both rivers down in flood! Sunsets these past few evenings have been lovely. Just been told the cooly who carries coracle has lumps all over him and went to see: itch! sure it is. Anyhow another man will be engaged. Fortunately he has had no carrying of my kit to do. Hope old boatman hasn't caught it.

17th. Evening. Up stream; raining in hills at head of Valley and looks stormy. End of Falls Pool hooked a fish where I have always expected one, and only once got a small one. He was not to be denied and evidently lives in the deep pool below Grandfathers Run, for down he went; wrong side of a big rock and I thought he was gone. Then he started off; a lot of loose line as coracle overshot down the rapid. Then felt him on again, and he put up a dogged fight in heavy stream. Splendid sport: 22

1

2   3

CHAPTERS
25/26

1
Government House, Mahe,
Malabar, West Coast, 1934

2
Head tracker, Yala Sanctuary,
Ceylon

3
St. Hilda's, the Burton's
bungalow at Coonor, 1933

4
Bullock carts used for
transport

5

6

7

lbs, single treble, Punjab wire trace. Must not use Killin again in this river. He would no doubt have got off on a Killin trace, as did the one this morning.

Tomorrow the last day of this trip. Morning up stream; afternoon down to Sundapathy, so must move camp and go to the hut in case of rain. Mustn't have wet tents for coolies going up the Ghat.

Coonoor, 1933. On 15th October set out in hired car and was away until 15th November. We (H.G.& I) went a total of 1400 miles; and trip cost about Rs.750/-, or Rs.400/- more than cost of living a vegetable life at Clovelly. The car gave trouble for the first seven hundred miles owing to a blocked radiator. At Shimoga we had steam blown through it, and after that – no trouble.

On this sightseeing tour, Burton and his wife visited the famous temples of Belur and Halebid which are only one hundred and twenty five miles from Bangalore. They stayed overnight at Travellers Bungalows which could be found at most places, sometimes a meal was provided, sometimes there was just a caretaker. They admired the fascinating and intricate carving and sculpture of the temples at Belur and the particular beauty of the temple at Halebid, which is set in an open space with a palm-fringed, crescent-shaped lake in the foreground and wooded hills behind.

JOURNAL _____

The newly constructed Mettur Dam and the beautiful lake formed by it will be seen in future years by all travellers to the Nilgiri Hills, from the direction of Madras. The project will result in the irrigation of over a million acres of land, and supply electric power to a great part of South India. It has taken seven years to build and cost five and a half million pounds. On the way to the Gersoppa Falls we pass Chitaldroog Fort and crossing the Tunga River come to the town of Shimoga. The country around and beyond is most attractive. Avenues of shady trees, forests of teak and bamboo, wide expanses of ripening rice around the many sheets of water, and in the valleys, lotus covered lakes with a background of wooded hills, and in the distance the purple slopes and peaks of the Western Ghats.

The road descends the steep and winding Talguppa ghat to reach the ferry across the Sharavati River. Here the river flows placidly enough with but small indication of the tremendous Falls less than a mile below, where the river plunges in magnificent cascades into a huge chasm of over nine hundred feet in depth. No words can adequately describe these stupendous Falls, and perhaps it is best expressed by a simple entry in the Visitor's Book – 'The Falls is simply grand'. All visitors to the Falls should essay the descent to the bottom of the ravine, the difficulty of which is greatly exaggerated. Steamy it is no doubt, but with nails in boots there need be no fear of slipping on the spray-soaked rocks. At the end of the path, more than from any other point, can the grandeur and immensity of the cataracts be seen.

After seeing the gigantic stone statue of the Jain saint Gomatesvara at Sravana Belagola, we travelled on to Sivasamudrum and the Cauvery Falls. The volume of water of these Falls is greater than at Gersoppa, but the height is not much over two hundred feet. When the river is full the falls are spectacular, and turbulent whirlpools eddy and foam at the base of the rocks in the deep ravine. On the road back to Mysore, we stopped to see the exquisite Kesava temple at Somnathpur. This also is famous for its impressive carving and the rich adornment of its interiors. In the dark rooms there is an an arrangement of three candles on a tray which a caretaker will hoist up on a bamboo to enable the intricate ceiling carvings to be seen. The skill of the artists who carved the multitude of images of animals, gods and goddesses, make this temple a gem of its kind.

After this detour, on a 'parson's egg' sort of road, we jolt and bump along to the main road near Seringapatam and return to Mysore.

In December Burton ventured with friends into the unexplored jungle around the Peryar Lake to fish one of the small rivers which runs into it.

JOURNAL ——

Along the western border of the Travancore State, where the palm-fringed coast is washed by the Arabian Sea for over two hundred miles, the level country is almost as thickly populated as anywhere in the East; yet only forty miles inland, amongst the range of mountains which is seen from the coast are great areas of tropical forest rendered almost impenetrable by the dense vegetation which luxuriates in the humid atmosphere created by a tropical sun and an annual two hundred inches of rain.

This well drenched range of mountains receives the rain of both the south west and north east monsoons, so it is not until the cessation of the latter towards the end of November that one can comfortably venture into those wild forests. In 1933 the rains ceased earlier than usual, and it was on 1st December that three of us gathered to cross the wide and winding waters of the beautiful Peryar Lake, to land at the further end of Salt Creek, where commences the path to the back of beyond. The track leads up the valley of a stream, the waters of which are hidden from view by jungle trees and thickets of the 'etah' bamboo, beloved of elephants, and indispensable to the jungle people for the roofs and walls of their primitive habitations. Then comes a hillside of large shady trees, and beyond that is the catchment area of the river we were going to fish.

Leeches was the topic of conversation at the start. One of us said soap for stockings was the remedy, another had faith in a well salted solution of tobacco, while the third said kerosene. The coolies also had various ideas on the subject. Some had a rag in which was tied the astringent pulp of a jungle fruit and some had tobacco secured in a similar fashion. On the way, those who favoured tobacco juice and kerosene were jubilant, as runnels of gore showed that soap was no kind of preventative at all. But the decision was reached the next day when the advocate of kerosene proved to be absolutely protected under all conditions, such as wet to the hips when wading, struggling through mud and slush amid the 'etah' and forcing a way through the undergrowth, not a leech got above the spats, while he of the fragrant weed (who does not smoke it) was quite unprotected after the wading began. So this proved a certain preventive. A pair of woollen stockings over which cotton stockings and over the boots a felt spat well damped in kerosene – not too much however, as if it gets on to the skin the resulting blister will be worse than any leech.

Soon after crossing the divide which separates the catchment area of the lake from that of our river we dived into the undergrowth to gladly emerge into sunshine and the only grassy space we would cross during the march. After half an hour we again plunged into the forest from which we did not issue until we reached the banks of the river at four in the afternoon.

There were a few ground thrushes of brilliant hues creeping about in the undergrowth, the flight and call of imperial pigeons was heard and the deep notes of the Wanderoo monkey, but it was seldom that any living thing could be seen – always excepting the leeches. Tropical jungle is awesome in its immensity, yet the view is mostly limited to the circle of a few feet which accompanies ones perspiring progress. There is no hum of insects, no choir of frogs, no call of birds; well has it been said – 'Where is a desert to equal the forest desert?'

So it was with much relief that we extracted ourselves from the undergrowth to wade through the cooling waters of the knee-deep stream, and gain the further side where a great expanse of long grass clothes the slopes of the hills right to the skyline two thousand feet above. 'Paradise' this valley has been fitly named, for such indeed it is to the perspiring leech-bitten people who have fought for miles to gain it.

We discovered that a party of poaching meat hunters from the plains had been dynamiting the pools above camp for food. However they had not been upstream, and we found many mahseer there, the heaviest scaling 9lbs. In those upper waters we saw no human tracks, only the spoor of elephant, bison, sambur, tiger, panther, otter, and wild cats; and probably no people ever penetrate to that portion of the river.

The floor of this river in the pools where the fish mostly congregate is almost black with decayed vegetation, so the fish are consequently very dark, on the backs. The scenery along the river is tropical to a degree. Only along the elephant tracks can one go, and fortunately there are almost always such tracks within a few yards of the river bank. On one occasion an elephant trumpeted loudly on crossing our tracks, perhaps he also did not like the smell of kerosene.

The rain held off until after our return, so we were fortunate in that respect. We had once again enjoyed our sport and the mystery of the primaeval forest, and though we have the clammy memories of struggles through the undergrowth and the mud, yet there are also those mental pictures of the pools as of watered silk reflecting the giant trees and the feathery bamboos, the splash of rising fish, and many a tight line.

DIARY ———————————————————————————————

December. Went across lake in Travancore Government Launch; on the way saw elaborate bamboo and leaf camp being erected for Lord Ratendone – Viceroy's son (Lord Willingdon's). Such waste of money; much better put him in Rest House at Dam or at Thekady. Landed at Vincent's wharf up Salt Creek, and walked one and a half miles to his house on cardamom estate. Our party for fishing is: Self, M.W. Hoare – planter of Dymock Estate and H. Gibbon of Mount Estate. Hoare did all the arrangements, food and coolies. Started 7 a.m. on 2nd and got to camp 4 p.m., ten miles or less; but the path overgrown and we lost it three times. Much delay, many leeches. Realised how very easy to get lost in these forests as Vincent told us he was many years ago, although he had Mannans (aboriginal jungle men) with him as Guides. Whole lot of them lost for three days! Return journey took only half the time.

Next day to Lake and rowed as far as Dam; there picked up by Robinson in his launch and so to Thekady. Lord Ratendone had shot an elephant, murdered the poor brute. Three times he fell and got up and finally succumbed to about twenty shots fired into him; they also wounded two bison.

The Malabar coast
On his next fishing trip Burton went by bus to Kottyam and then by launch to begin an exploration of part of the West Coast, to discover what opportunities there might be for coastal sea fishing.

Malabar is the name given to the seaboard country, called by the Arabs from ancient times 'the Pepper Coast', extending from South Canara to Cape Cormorin. The origin of the word is possibly 'malai' the Tamil word for mountain and the Arabic word 'bar' signifying both a coast and a kingdom. The language spoken by ninety per cent of the people is Malayalam.

It was late in December when we arrived at Quilon, a town fast growing with the prosperity of the State and the ever increasing population. This port was once a famous one, called by the Arabs – Kaulam, and well known to the Chinese of the 7th Century. A mile north of the town on a rocky promontory known as Tangassary, the Portuguese constructed a Fort in 1519. The place was taken by the Dutch in 1662 and ceded to the British in 1795. The whole settlement is just one hundred yards in extent, and is British Territory, but there are rumours of its possible rendition to Travancore.

1934. On 2nd January went in boat and fished out to sea. A high wind and rough sea. Caught one fish, queer shaped one, of 6lbs. A great fighter, equal to twice his weight in mahseer. These sea fish are very strong and vigorous. His back fin after fashion of a murrel's and lovely purple colour, his spots indigo blue, his silver a sheeny golden yellow. Several names they give him and I don't know the right one. Poptos is one; or Kora, but I can't catch the initial letter very clearly.

We were blown a long way out to sea and too rough to sail so the men had a hard row to get to Nandikeri. There we found the sardine fishers still busy. They bang their boats to keep the fish within the net circle, and make a great din. Many gulls and kites hover and swoop on to the jumping fry. A boy in a boat had caught two small sting rays and a small shark. They all get sharks, small ones, both at sea and in this Channel. After giving the boatmen a seven anna drink of toddy, set sail for Quilon. Fitful breeze, poor fellows at managing a sailing boat, such a lot of talk and jabber. They must know this Coast most intimately and yet they three times got the boat on to submerged rocks. I could plainly see the Channel they should take, but they couldn't, or didn't. Might have been swamped, and lucky not to be.

4th January. Went to Mandagiri Bridge by 8 a.m. as arranged. No men to meet me, no boat, no prawns, no bridge watcher! I do hate these Travancore natives. Got a boat, two men, and an English speaking youth. Tried spinning from under the bridge as tide was running out very strongly, no offers: also tried dead bait with a heavy lead, nil. Then after one and a half hours of this, gave it up and went off to watch the fishing people. Men using cast nets, very good with them. Nets twelve feet long and big diameter on hitting the water. They catch a lot of bottom feeding fish, very like carp. Saw great heaps of sea shells collected for sending to make chuman. Went other side of channel to see the sardine fisher people. They are at it by night on moonlight nights as well as by day, and must make a lot of money. A big basketful for Rs.10/- and one trip out, a few hundred yards only, brings in Rs.20/-. Sometimes of course a man makes a bad haul and there is nothing doing during monsoon months at sea, but I expect they then do good business in the backwaters. They COUNT the fish into the baskets instead of weighing them, which seems very primitive and great waste of time.

8th. The car journey to Alleppey was same as on way to Quilon, and I much regret that we did not know, when we came from Alleppey that we could travel by motor launch. Cheaper, and we would have seen that sixty miles of waterways. Then we would have seen all the waterways – the direct ones that is – Cochin to Quilon.

Alleppey, properly 'Alappuzha' – the broad river – so named on account of the Pambiyar River which fills its waterways, is a busy minor port which has the advantage that even during the monsoon months, steamers are able to anchor and discharge cargo. This is due to the seven mile mud bank which has a calming effect on the tumultuous waters.

Passing over the Mendajon bridge, saw every post with an expectant gull sitting on it; and the men busy with casting nets. Fish don't have much peace along this coast. The scenery is pleasing; but a certain sameness about it: rice fields enclosed by palm trees, always beautiful, huts and houses amidst palm trees, an occasional canal or other waterway fringed with palm trees, and carrying on its placid reflected palm tree surface cargo boats and dug-outs of all sizes. Little brown babies and children toddling about, all fat and happy; no skinny ones such as in the drier, less favoured parts of India.

Bullock carts were seen along the roads; their matting roofs arched over in front to give the driver shade, and at the back also, to shelter the recumbent occupants from morning or evening sun, as in Ceylon. Here and there in the more spacious rice fields are islands of coconuts, The whole fifty three miles is one long village, not fifty yards without its hut among the palms. There had been rain in the night so the dust was well laid and the drive all one could wish. At one place half a dozen men were deftly raising water, there being all the time several buckets in the air passing from hand to hand. There were also the long pivot bamboos with lump of mud as counter-balance, a method to be seen in many parts of India, and of great antiquity.

We took the motor boat at 10.30; securing a whole cabin, open deck space and the fore part of the boat to ourselves. Very comfortable as to space, seats were but hard planks. There were laden barges with large matted sails, some of which were more holes than sails, coming up with the morning breeze. We passed the small lighthouse and entered the open waters of Lake Vembanad; and then came Tanirmukham where was the first halt. Night lines are used and big fish caught: there are similar lines of stakes at many other places – all, probably, just as good as at Tannir for fishing. At many places were the large deep nets, so largely used along this part of the Coast and said to have been introduced by Chinese in 18th Century. Very efficient they are and nothing that gets into them escapes be it large or small. The water was dotted in every direction with craft of all sizes.

A great fleet of cargo boats came along when we neared Ernakulam, as the evening breeze favoured their voyage to Alleppey and other places to the South. Our motor boat was not a race horse, but went quite fast enough; two and a half hours to Alleppey. Flocks of snowy egrets were seen against the green of the fields and coconuts, also many crows and paddy birds; hawks and kites also gulls and cormorants.

JOURNAL ⸻

Cochin is not now the 'Kochchi' – a small place – that it was in ancient times when it was known to the Hebrews in the days of Solomon, but it grew in importance with the discovery by the Romans of the monsoon winds. Since that time the sea has encroached upon the strip of land upon which the present settlement is built, for dredging operations in connection with the entrance channel to the modern harbour, have discovered fortifications some hundred yards out to sea. The future of Cochin is now assured, on account of the spacious harbour, which is now almost complete. It was interesting to cross over to Cochin with the sight of two big cargo steamers at inner harbour entrance. A very busy port even now, and in the future will be still more so. Native craft of all sizes and shapes were going busily about and a great number of coolies employed. Yet, judging by the clamour for a job with the luggage on landing, there are plenty of unemployed in Cochin.

Smells! There is no Eastern place which can do better than Cochin in this respect. Some little time ago, a leading Indian newspaper of Madras advocated the setting up of a Public Health Commission. Such a Commission could well commence its labours here, for it's members would gain much experience – if they survived! It will be interesting to pass, just once with handkerchief to nose, through the narrow streets of this congested town, where goats, diminutive cattle and mangy dogs dispute the path with yelling coolies and honking motors; and where are all the varied sights and smells of a busy hive of Eastern people gathered together from many lands.

Two rickshaws, clean and easy running, ran us through the narrow smelly streets of the native quarter. There were shops of every description; the artisans, as all through the East, working at their trades in the verandahs; a chinaman hawking the usual basket of cloth goods. Then we emerged from all the filth and varied smells to the cleaner air and more open spaces of the European quarter: yet here too, a few feet only behind the houses, are filthy lanes and stinking uncared for drains. Truly the East is unchanging in this one respect of attention to sanitation and the commonsense care as to surroundings of human dwellings; although it is doubtless changing in many other things that matter less and are not to the ultimate happiness of the millions of Indians. One reads that in the State of Cochin are to be found areas more thickly populated than anywhere else in the world; and I can well believe it!

DIARY ——

It was a delightful feeling to get into the clean and well appointed rooms of Club Quarters with the sea a short hundred yards away, and the interesting sight of the drop nets being worked by day, and by night with the aid of brilliant incandescent lamps. Not so pleasing to learn that the Club charges 9/- a day for each person + 1/- club subscription: so the double bedroom and all meals comes to 18/- a day; and with tips added one can call it 20/-! There is hope of a reduction in this and must be if we are to stay as 500/- to live on can't stretch to 600/- plus 5/- a day inclusive of boat and other expenses!

9th. Arranged with aid of Club Manager for boat to take me out to sea; smaller boat than those at Quilon and Alleppey. Agreed for four men and three turned up; arranged to start 4 a.m. and got off at 6.a.m! Such is the East. It was good to go out to sea in the dark, and to be four miles or near that from land when dawn appeared. Left the Dredger and the Lightship behind and at dawn began to spin on dead bait. Not nice shapely sardine, but one of the bottom feeders caught by the drop nets. Saw a sea snake, saw dolphins, saw many plaice, in the deeps of the green clear water. Found some eggs twined round a floating bamboo, and a device for attracting fish – a bamboo with a yard square of matting fastened to it; beneath it a number of small fish sheltering from the sun.

Then passed a fine native sailing craft, fully loaded, and bound for Bombay. Men wanted a drink, so we went to it, it hadn't got under sail as there was scarcely any wind, and I clambered on board. Very nice people, talked Hindustani, asked me if I had had any food; (a quick response – yes!), but I didn't want theirs! Interesting to see the curved deck, the great wooden pulleys of jack tree wood and poon masts. Fine expanse of sail, made in narrow strips of cloth, not the yard wide seams of English sails. Soon a breeze came and they began to get under weigh, so I got off and took photo, and with a loud 'Sulaam Sahib' from the ship and the same from me, off the beautiful craft – in appearance, pretty smelly inside I expect – went on her ten days voyage to Bombay. *Savatri* T.H.N. 10472, owner Jagari Krishna; and I promised to send a copy of photo. They showed me brass wire trace and big hook and small fish, dried, with which they catch big ones while on the move. Back at 3.30 p.m.; tired, as I hadn't slept since 2 a.m.

12th. Went to see Church; oldest church in India. Must take photo, which will be spoilt by electric wires. Inside the church a number of tombstones, both Dutch and Portuguese, are let into walls. Here also Portuguese fortifications and no doubt those at Quilon, Portuguese and not Dutch as we were told. Club rates reduced to 13/- plus 1/- , so can stay here ten days. Then ten days Tikkotti; ten days Mahe; ten days Cannanore, will finish up survey of Coast, and take us to Coonoor about 25th February.

15th. No reply yet to wire to Superintendent of Lighthouses Madras for permit to occupy Cotta Light Inspection Bungalow, which is very annoying. Ought to leave here 18th, and can make no arrangements.

JOURNAL ———————————————————————

Twenty miles north of Cochin at Cranganore there is an old Portuguese Fort dating from 1523, and Roman coins are frequently found along the Coast. So Cranganore was the first resort of Western shipping, and the earliest Settlement of Jew and Christian immigrants. Calicut was the scene of many brutal acts on the part of the early Portuguese, Vasco da Gama in particular being guilty of some terrible outrages which brought retribution in their train, as the pirates established on the Kotta River twenty five miles to the north, whenever they captured a Portuguese ship – and they took fifty in one year – slaughtered the entire crew. Vasco da Gama died at Cochin in 1524 and was buried in the church there, but his remains were later removed to Portugal and are interred at Lisbon.

Seven miles out to sea is Sacrifice Rock, called by the Malabar people 'Velliyan-kallu' (white rock), and all around this small island is excellent sea fishing. Twenty miles up the coast is Mahe, originally known by its Indian name of Maihi. In 1725 a French squadron took possession and changed the name to Mahe. The English Settlement at Tellicherry, four miles to the north passed through critical and troublous times between 1740 and 1760, but these ended with the surrender of Mahe in 1761; and the dangers threatening Tellicherry from the attacks of Hydar Ali of Mysore, were ended on 8th January 1782. However, it was not until the Treaty of Seringapatam in 1792 that British supremacy was finally established on the Coast. Those days are long past, and now the town has greatly increased in size. There is a large bazaar, motor cars honk through the streets, and the railway runs through the peaceful countryside.

DIARY ———————————————————————

19th. Fixed up boat with aid of Head Keeper of Light House: 5/- a day. First they asked 10/- and came to 5/- when they saw I couldn't pay more. Lighthouse R.H. (Inspection Bungalow) no rent. Very neat and clean: one bedroom and bathroom, wide verandah, store room, covered way to good kitchen. Canvas stretcher beds. Situation on rocky cleared space; very cool and all the breeze. Sea three hundred yards away through the palm trees. Sound of surf all day long, and the five minute flash all through night, overhead.

22nd. Fished at Sacrifice Rock, nil. Boats there caught four big fish; two covaloo, two pularmeen, one kwela meen. They fish by throwing hand lines, shrimp as bait, large single hook, very good at it they are and seldom miss a fish. Saw turtles, lots of long thin fish with long jaws and very sharp interlocking teeth; they eat the sardines and small fry. The hand line people use a spear and also a club. Great hammering with the club before a fish is hauled into the boat.

23rd. Went to Mahe, a quiet little place, no Europeans. All the people here and at Tellicherry wear a different pattern of hat, about two feet or more diameter on a stove pipe! Fishermen wear them too. Tree with mauve and cream flowers, very common hereabouts, and all along this coast. On 24th, fished at Sacrifice Rock, nil. Boatmen also caught very little; one shark only and some of the long billed fellows. Saw sea snakes, porpoises, sea urchins? — look like lump of tow with a mauve beret on top!

26th. To Sacrifice Rock: saw turtles, porpoises, sea snakes, WHALE! (close to the rock), used silex reel and dead bait and single hook and hooked several of the long snouted fish all of which got off. No breeze in morning so paddled out, big triangle paddle very effective.

28th. To Cannanore by train: two days at Tellicherry. Arrived Coonoor 6th February, and went into 'Kia Ora', house we have taken for a year at 100/- per month.

1st April. An idle life, and a dull one. No prospects of any fishing or shikar as can't go away and leave H. alone in house!

Attended meeting of Nilgiri Game Association on 14th February having been made an Hon. Member of Committee. Committee has too many members; seventeen sat at table plus President (Collector) and Hon. Secretary (D.F.O.); and everyone after his own personal interests! Am also Member of the newly formed 'Association for the Preservation of Wild Life in South India', and doubt if that is ever going to accomplish anything in way of practical results.

At Coonoor until 12th September. Not a word of any kind as yet from the South of India Wild Life Association in spite of my writing to Secretary to ask what is being done, or proposed to be done. Have joined U.P. Association, but doubt if they are any better. A U.P. Sanctuary has been proclaimed, two hundred square miles. It is apparently the Patti Dasu block which has always been kept a close preserve for U.P. Governors!

THE
LACCADIVES
ISLANDS
AND
OTHER
ADVENTURES
1935
TO
1936

Chapter 27

THE BHAVANI RIVER AND WEST COAST FISHING

The next trip to the Bhavani in September 1934 was cut short because Burton was suffering from severe sciatica, which was to trouble him for the next twelve months. His constant disregard of the elements probably contributed considerably to this, as well as there being a legacy from his earlier leg and hip injuries. His leg was causing him pain even at the start of the trip, and no doubt he shouldn't even have set out, but he was loath to forgo the fishing and took with him Pyramidun and Genaspirin tablets to keep the pain in check.

On arrival at the river he found the water was exceptionally low, as there had been no rain for weeks. Although he went out in the coracle on most days there were no fish to be seen, except a few small mahseer of under 2lbs. The coracle had to be carried quite often over the rocky channels. The heavy banks of cloud were not a sign of rain, but were caused by the drying up of the forest after the monsoon. By 24th September, the sciatica had become severe and as he had no pain killing tablets left, he felt obliged to return to Coonoor.

DIARY

25th. Instead of sending eight seater bus as ordered a five seater chevrolet car met me. At first sight it seemed impossible that all my tents and kit could be packed on to the car, but it was done! and the springs were more than flat. I didn't press the man to take such a weight; he was quite cheerful about it. So the car took – Self; servant; fish watcher; driver; driver's man; and fourteen coolie loads of tents and boxes. We dropped fish watcher and driver's man at Kolakambay, from where it was mostly down hill to Coonoor.

After a month at Coonoor, Burton was off on another fishing trip, this time back to the West Coast sea fishing for four weeks. At Cannanore it rained steadily for ten days which prevented him from going out to sea, and he found this very dull and frustrating. A move to Tellicherry proved no better and the only fishing he had was after moving to the bungalow at Cotta Point Lighthouse. With the same boat people as in January he was able to catch a few seer and gar fish, but his sciatica was bad and on 19th November he decided to go back home. He made arrangements to visit some of his friends over the next few weeks who had Estates in this area; and although his sciatica seemed to improve, he was perhaps unwise to embark on another fishing expedition; especially since this involved wading waist high through the river, and also a lot of walking.

DIARY

Cotta Point. All the time after leaving Coonoor on 10th October, in fact from mid

August, I had kept the sciatica in check by use of various medicines. Many a day I could with difficulty walk back from the boat. Then I took to Pyramidun on 16th November and seemed to get better. Left Cotta Point 19th and trained to Ernakulam. Thence by car to Kottyam where stayed the night and then on 21st by car seventy miles to Moorigalaar Estate, where we stayed with Mr. and Mrs. M.R. Coghlan. 'Mick' bull terrier, 'Lila' labrador, very companionable dogs. On 22nd walked two miles, and on 23rd four miles, no pain, so decided I could do the sixteen miles to Kakkiar.

On 23rd our party assembled at the small bungalow on Mount Estate: Self; M.R. Coghlan; A.N. How; David Bryson; Wallace Mackay; and fifty seven coolies plus four servants. Set off 4 a.m., down through tea, up through forest, over high downs, then through forest for five or six miles to Temple of Sabormalai, and thence two miles to Camp in river bed, below junction of Pambyar and Kokkiar. Leg gave very little trouble. Took photo of Temple and two of priests.

25th November. Up the Kakkiar. I waded across – up to the waist – (that did it!) and also had to be in and out of water on way up the river bed, about three miles to place where we camped. Leg all right. Bryson didn't think out the carriage of kit which had to be done in two trips, so when the first loads turned up at 3 p.m. it didn't look as if the remainder would fetch up at all! Wonderful to relate the coolies did turn up at 10 p.m! Marvellous how they managed to do the trip in the dark up that most difficult river bed. All had a peg of whisky on arrival! That day, 25th, Bryson and I remained at camp; and the others pushed on up stream. No big mahseer seen and evidently very few fish of any size in the river.

The evening of 26th, getting up out of chair after dinner I had bad sciatic pain; and next morning doubled up and very crippled. We were moving camp down to first camp, so I made my painful way, with two sticks, and aid of coracle along the pools, and went to bed at camp; in quite pain at any movement. Next day 28th, all five went fishing; I realised I couldn't possibly walk back the sixteen miles so rigged up one of Hoare's Rurkee chairs, with two poles, as a carrying chair.

29th. Morning, we set off: I had to walk short distances pretty often, quite doubled up. Photographed Temple again, and met the Head Priest and one other priest on slab of rock half a mile from Temple. He asked what was matter with me, and on being told remarked that – what could be expected, as I had walked along the top of Compound wall and had photographed the temple! Ramaswamy, my servant, learnt that the Temple exercised a very strong Curse! I gave him a rupee to put into the offertory bag, and when we were some miles up the hill he asked me 'Master much better now?' 'No', I said, 'and I wish I had given four annas instead of a rupee!' Ramaswamy has great faith in priests and temples.

On 3rd December went by car to Thekady where we met Vincent's launch, and crossed Periyar Lake in one and a half hours. From the landing place at Salt Creek it was three miles to Doonton Estate Bungalow where J.R. Vincent and his sister met us. With great pain and tribulation I struggled along, in twenty yards sprints! for one and a quarter miles and then the chair arrived and I was carried along. That amount of walking did much harm and from that night, until the 18th December at Coonoor, I had no sleep whatever during the night and very little by day. Terrible pain it was, and reduced me to tears on many occasions. I got myself dressed most days by 11 o/c and sat in Verandah until dark and then, after dinner, in drawing room until bed time, 9.30, when I went to bed to lie awake and watch the hands of the luminous clock until daylight and early tea! Twice or three times I saw bison in the hills opposite, but no elephant or sambur. Vincents were most kind and we stayed until the 14th when we recrossed the lake and went in car to Kottyam, and on next day to Ernakulam D.B.

Left D.B. at midnight and got into the train which left at 3 a.m. Went in rickshaws from D.B. to Station and was able, fortunately, to run the shafts into the carriage doorway and so step in direct without the great pain which I would have had in climbing up from the platform. Got to Shoranur Junction at 8.30 or so and was carried in chair across to the further platform and so into through carriage for Mettupalayiam, where we arrived found car waiting and got to Coonoor at 4.30. The journey on the whole was not so bad as I had feared it might be. No sleep on 16th, 17th, 18th; 30 grs. Bromide had NO effect! Then was introduced to a dope 'Nembutal' which put me to sleep – one capsule. 9.30 to 1 a.m., and on waking with great pain took another which put me to sleep till 7; and kept me drowsy to the afternoon! Very powerful stuff.

About the 25th December I began to be able to sleep on right side. Now, 5th February, sleep is normal and the sciatica really leaving me. I still get a good deal of pain on certain movements. Have had to cancel shooting blocks; since I anticipate that I will not be able to walk as in July last before this sciatica business, until quite next July: in fact I will have been crippled for a whole year.

12.3.35. Wrote to Hon. Secretary, South of India Society for Preservation of Wild Life to say that, as nothing appeared to be done, I remove my name from the Society and the Committee of the same. Have had no reply to my letters, or enquiries. Neither have R.C. Morris or Major Phythian Adams, who are also on the Committee! The Hon. Secretary is R.D. Richmond, who was Chief Conservator of Forests, Madras Presidency. Society inaugurated by Sir George Stanley at Government House, Ooty on 7.6.33.; and Committee formed, and subscriptions paid on 3rd November 1933. Nothing done and probably, for political reasons, nothing intended to be done, outside Government Reserved Forests. Phythian Adams has also resigned from Committee and Society, but neither he, nor I, have received any acknowledgement of letters! Marvellous Madras!

The native inhabitants of this vast country are entirely reckless and improvident of the needs of themselves and of posterity in the matter of fish (and wild life) conservation. Extensive lakes formed by the damming of rivers for purposes of irrigation and hydro-electric projects have much benefited the fish supply in many parts of India, for such lakes are safe breeding grounds and fish homes. Yet, even in these – as witness what is going on in the beautiful Periyar Lake in Travancore at the present time – dynamite, if constantly used, can do grievous damage to fish life, especially at the inlets of rivers and streams up which the carp run when the monsoons occur. 'We fish with dynamite', was the reply of a Periyar worthy when asked as to the best method of obtaining sport!

There are, in India and Burma, about sixty species of wild pheasant which are systematically shot, snared, and eaten; and of pigeons and doves about forty species known and valued. Quail are captured alive in great numbers and sold in the markets as food, with snipe, plover, partridge, florican and various wildfowl. Besides the enormous toll through the above, there was formerly the extremely lucrative plumage trade. It was due to Lord Curzon in 1902, that this was ended through legislation prohibiting exports. It is a marvel that any game birds have survived. In 1911, egret plumes were sold at £8 per ounce, or more than their weight in gold.

Let us hope that the Indian Administration of the New Constitution will devise and enforce the urgently needed measures necessary for the conservation of all forms of wild life before it is indeed too late.

27th June 1935. On 5th February I wrote 'sciatica now leaving me': but it is still with me! though much abated, and I can walk a couple of miles without much after effect. Tested out the home made sea rod and broke it in two in the process. The top joint 'Rans' wood of old khud stick stood the strain. It was the lower half of hard, but brittle wood of Travancore, which Gibbons got for me, which broke at lower end of splice. Now I will try and get one of bamboo; to tide me over Laccadive Islands trip in November.

After the disappointing trip to the Bhavani in 1934, Burton decided that he would go earlier the following year, probably in mid August, and hope for better weather. His sciatica was no longer troubling him, and he preferred to go fishing on his own. It was 9th August, 1935, when he left for three weeks by the Bhavani. At Sundapathy he found that the river was low, in spite of the heavy rain which had been falling at Coonoor.

JOURNAL —————————————————————————————————————

When one knows a river well, it is natural to name the various pools and runs, so we will start at Camp Pool, which is a stone's throw from the tent pitched a mile above Sirakadavu village. The coracle propelled by a squatting boatman with a single paddle takes me across the placid pool, through the shimmery reflections of the trees, and whirling down the rapid water comes to silent rest against the boulders of the near bank. With a short cast, as a fish might be lying where the heavy water begins to calm down from its turbulent entry into the pool, the light spinning rod is set bending. One has to be firm as there is a bad snag close by, but a spin from the reel results in a 10lb. mahseer being caught in a shorter time than usual.

Heavy Run, a bit further down, always raises hope, but has been mostly disappointing, due perhaps to the adjacent water not being deep enough for the big fellows, and 6lbs is the best from that place. Then comes Bathing Ghat where the Irula matrons come to fill the water vessels and for daily ablutions. It is about ten o'clock one gets there, so there is usually an interested bevy of spectators to witness the occasional extraction of a ten-pounder. We come next to Long Pool at the lower part of which is a barrier of rocks and some fine runs, only two fish have been taken there, but expectation is always high, and there should be better fortune. Then the water runs rapidly into Village Pool, always good for a fish and the last one taken here was 16lbs.

We now pass through lovely scenery down several miles of water. Here we negotiate shallow rapids and there paddle silently down long, deep pools. At a rocky barrier there is a mighty splash as a large mugger becomes aware of our craft. The final long stretch brings us to Varagaar Junction. Some good fish have been taken where the Varagaar stream flows into the pool, but there is no one hungry today, so we hurry down to camp which will be ready pitched at Koorapathy where the Siruvani comes in on the right bank. During this last three miles there is a considerable fall in the river, so several portages are necessary, as also the shooting of the rapids. After several days on the upper waters, it is nice to be at this camp where four miles of river may be searched for excellent fishing.

DIARY —————————————————————————————————————

10th August. Fished down; at 10 o/c caught an 8lb. mahseer in runs below the long pool; and 10.45 caught two more, 7 and 6lbs, further down. Went to head of long pool and walked back, about two miles. Leg painful so I was walking 'lame', and not done that for nearly a year. Took photos of the three fish at camp with the new boatman Sivalingam and two fish watchers.

12th. A flood down from the main river in the night. Coracle man says my casting net no good because the leads are flat, coast fashion, and so catch in the stones, also not heavy enough. Lucky he has his own to use! Matteswara malai looks very fine, slopes several shades of green, and fleecy clouds on top. There has been no tiger kill at Koorapathy since that one in 1933. I doubt if there are any game animals this side of the river, no game birds either, all killed off by the Irulas no doubt.

14th. Up stream till 10 o/c. Opposite village ghat got an 11lb. mahseer. Not many fish to be seen, I don't see the shoals of 3lb. to 1lb. which I saw in 1929. There were less in 1933, and still fewer – much fewer – now! No men here, they have all gone to the Estates to find work, as owing to two seasons of scanty rainfall they have sown but little ragi. The hill men of North India would have cut water channels and irrigated their fields. Evening: fished down, all bait except one too large. Moved no fish until I put on small bait which I had kept for the place where I have never yet caught a fish, Almost first cast was taken. Stream heavy so he felt bigger than the 10½lbs he proved to be.

17th. At Koorapathy. The two fish of yesterday were given to the villagers, at which they were pleased. This morning gave Ramaswamy 12 annas to give to children when passing through the village. Caught an 8lb. mahseer, very strong fish. River now very low and many portages necessary. Signs of rain, but it never rains! A Flood! My kingdom for a flood!

I don't expect to get many more fish without a flood, or rain. In all these long, deep, pools are muggers and they must eat a lot of fish. Will tell Fisheries Inspector he should see to the shooting of them. Quite easy to get them as river is narrow and cover all along the bank. Evening; started out and it came on to rain! and has rained for over an hour! If this rain is also up Avalanche way then perhaps a spate will come along. Had the first tackle loss today. Got hung up in a sunken tree below Varagaar and lost Hillman lead, trace, three swivels, one treble. Not so bad for seven days fishing. In Mali Hka one loses two or three traces a day. So one would here, perhaps, without a boat. River is full of snags.

JOURNAL ───

One afternoon we were upstream, sitting in the coracle and ready baited by 4 o'clock, which seems to be the mahseer's tea time. Top Pool is fed by a turbulent shallow rapid, in which you can hear the boulders being ground to the sand which they eventually become. All along the further bank is a fairly rapid run, so the pool can be thoroughly fished out as the coracle quietly floats down on the nearer side. Each cast is about twenty five yards, mostly with a backhanded swing. At the tail end of the pool the stream divides into two runs, which become rapids swirling into Lower Pool, where big fish lie. Any large fish hooked in the tail of Top Pool will be sure to race downstream, and it may be that the fish will select one rapid while the coracle is a bad second down the other. Then the line will be round the waving bush in midstream, and as much as two hundred yards of line out before you can say anything at all! The men cross the perilous passage of the near rapid and release the line from the bending twigs of the bush. Alas! on this occasion the treble hook came away and he sank out of sight, to the accompaniment of groans from the men at the loss of so much prospective curry.

That loss was partly compensated the same day by a fine 26lb. fish from Grandfather's Run a mile lower down, and by comparison it was evident that the lost fish was about 30 lbs. Lost? Not so; for as The Compleat Angler truly writes 'Nay, the trout is not lost; for pray take notice, no man can lose what he never had.'

At Mug's Corner is almost always an easily enticed seven pounder; easily, if the bait is just right. 'Turn nimbly' wrote the immortal Izaak two and a half centuries ago, 'for know, it is impossible that it should turn too quick'. Below Mug's Corner is Fall's Pool, where you get a soaking as the coracle whirls down, and here you can expect to find big fish; and in Grandfather's Run just below, many large fish have given exciting sport.

DIARY

19th. Started at same place as yesterday. In Mug's Pool caught a 10lb. fish after third cast. Then in Fall's pool got a small one, 2lb., which was hooked far down throat so couldn't be returned to water. Fish rising freely and gulping down flying white ants. Saw village women out gathering this harvest. They put the ants in a cloth, and each woman taking one end of it shake it about until all the wings are off. Then the mass of insects is put into a chatty. Fish rising and jumping all down the river. It would be good fun with a small fly rod, but I don't want to kill a lot of small fish. At 2 p.m. down comes Siruvani in a thick flood. 3 p.m. Bhavani also in a brown spate, not very high and will be clear by tomorrow.

20th. Siruvani very muddy: Bhavani almost clear. So I set off up river in great hopes; new flood coming down, so I was only just in time. Soon had two fish 12 and 11lbs: and an offer from another. Then water became too muddy, so I made my way fast down stream and back to camp at 11.30. A great hatch out of flying ants this morning, so birds and fish both very busy. Spiders too, for I saw several webs smothered with them. The cochineal insect also out. Now 1.30 and a thunderstorm with heavy rain. Probably won't affect the Bhavani as it is local in this Valley. Saw track of a sambur stag this morning, first seen for several years. In evening a thunderstorm again and looks very black up in Nilgiris to west.

24th. Now come the big ones! Fished down: at end of first part of the big river, a fish made reel scream. Had a tussle to keep him out of the broken water below, but managed to work him up stream, 11lbs. Mounted a fresh bait, then a few yards down, was taken at the very curl of the smooth water before it broke, by a big one which made a great splash and showed a back like a bullock as he tore off down stream; 100yds line out in a flash! The coracle raced down and I had hard work to keep in touch, at last felt him again and the fight was on.

He felt immovable. Had the water stoned below him as the bad water below none too safe for coracle. I always land for that bit and let coracle go down empty, man only, and he ships water! However, managed to get the fish to face the stream, or rather he wanted to! I could do little. First had to go to far side of river, then crossed over, then crossed to far side again. Took a long time to make any impression on him. He just stemmed the strong stream like a tug boat! Had to follow him down stream several times as when I made him turn he took out line. At last he began to tire, and soon the end came. Net no use for such a fish; signed the man to handle him out which he did. What a monster! Hooks had not penetrated beyond barb; points only of two of the hooks held him, and these in the bony part of throat. 10ft.6in. Hardy Greenheart rod did well and came out quite straight; a powerful rod. Had to cut fish in two at camp as spring bal. up to 40lbs only. His head 14lbs, remainder 37 = 51lbs! Biggest mahseer (also fish) I have ever caught! Hope photo will be good.

27th. Four days left. By 6 last evening Bhavani was higher and coloured: not fishable. I am knowing the moods of the fish now, in this river. When the floods have much subsided they are on the take. A heavy flood came down by 9 o/c p.m. and now, 6.30 a.m., river is bang full – a great flood and no fishing till tomorrow – so three days gone!

28th. I felt sure river would be just right for today. Skies were clear and all weather conditions seemed favourable. Some heavy clouds at head of Valley; but those probably condensed vapour from the steaming jungles and won't give rain for some days. Got to Top pool at few minutes past eight. Took an eight pounder and after him a bigger one which had to be followed down the rapid to Lower pool. A stubborn, strong fish; 17lbs. Took out coracle and went up stream no takers. Water a bit high and hard work for the coracle man. No takers in Lower pool until near the big snag. There a BLACK mahseer; the first in this river to me, took the bait after I had stopped spinning to move lower down! 4lbs.

29th. When out for a walk yesterday evening came across women picking green stuff, a small, dark leaved plant, for curries. Told Ramaswamy to get some and had it for breakfast; quite nice. There is really never any need, in jungles, to be without green food. Now a high wind and valley drying up.

Fished all the way down, not a sign of a fish anywhere. Can't think why. Men say it is too cloudy, but that is not the cause. Saw otters going down stream, and Ramaswamy says he saw a lot playing in the pool and on the rocks opposite camp. All that upper water fished for last time this trip. These last few days, Mugs pool only one fish and Grandfather's Run one fish.

30th August. Sun came out this morning so took opportunity to dry tents. Afternoon fished down, nil: rain came on and spoilt the fishing; so trip ends with a blank day.

31st. Left camp 7.15 a.m., crossed Kundah in coracle, water low, but thick yellow from recent rain. I gave all three men lift in cars to Ghat road where they took bus for Mettupulyam. Got to Pulp House 11.20. Paid up fourteen coolies 12as. and sent them off well pleased with pay and tobacco. Gave Fish Watchers tips at Sundapathy. Head Watcher 5/- plus 2/- for village children of Koorapathy, his village, and a coral necklace for his wife! Three watchers 4/- each and each a trinket, one watcher 3/- and trinket. Paid up coracle man: two days coming, two days going, twenty two days on river = 26 at 2/- plus 8as. plus 6as. = 2/14 a day: cooly and boy to cook food, and one days pay extra to all three; so everybody pleased. Cars loaded and started 12.10, and to 'Kia Ora', Coonoor, by 1.25.

Cost of Trip
Say 275/- near as may be 9 to 31 = twenty three days = 12/- approx. a day.

Cost of trip				Stores used			
Licence	25	0	0	3 × ½ butter	1	11	0
Coracle	77	8	0	1 × ½ curry powder		9	0
Watchers tips	20	0	0	2 × 1 coco	1	9	0
Village children	3	0	0	5 lb flour – wasted		12	0
Post coolies	5	0	0	2 lb jam		13	0
Sundries	1	3	0	1 × 4 marmite	1	3	0
Wood and water cooly	11	12	0	1 kilm	2	4	0
Baggage coolies	44	9	0	1 matches		6	0
K. oil, 1 gal.		13	6	1 Q. oats	1	1	0

1

2

3

4

5

6

CHAPTER
27

1
Walking up a coconut tree.
Kaup lighthouse can be seen
in the background

2
Chetlat, the Kutcheri
bungalow

3
Fishing boat and crew casting
their net

4
Bitra, parrot fish
(Pseudoscarus undulatus)

5
Kadai, 11lbs, caught at Kaup

6
Ambai, 8lbs, caught at Kaup

7
Cotta Point Lighthouse with
Hilda Burton

8
Cotta Point, with seers caught
by Burton weighing 12 and
16lbs

9
Fishing nets out drying at
Kaup

10
Fishing boat used by Burton

Cost of trip				Stores used			
Veg.	3	4	0	1 W. sauce		6	0
Atta	1		0	2 lb. sugar		6	0
Rice	1	0	0	½ lb. tea		9	0
Dal	1	0	0	1 chutney	1	0	0
Potatoes, 25lb	1	0	0				
Onion		5	6				
Tobacco, coolies	1	10	0				
Sundries	3	4	0				
1 cake	1	8	0				
Stores from Spencer	13	8	0				
Photo films	4	0	0				
Dried fruit	2	12	0				
Photo P & D	5	0	0				
Motor cars	42	0	0				
Rs.	270	1	6				

Say 275/- – near as may be 9 to 31 = 23 days = 12/- about a day.

This was to be the last fishing trip to the Bhavani for several years. In September 1935 he moved into a rented house at Coonoor, and was busy preparing his rods and tackle for sea fishing. In November he left for the West Coast, near Mangalore, and after some coastal fishing planned to take a boat to the Laccadive Islands – seldom visited (if ever) by Europeans, and try here for more adventurous fishing.

JOURNAL

It is not everywhere along the Coast that good rod and line sea fishing is to be had. There are a few well known places, but it is more adventurous and interesting to seek out new localities, and such a place was discovered in the autumn of 1935.

On 9th October I left Coonoor and took the train for Mangalore. The early hours of the day on the West Coast are very beautiful, the rice fields ripple like a many coloured sea under the gentle wind, the feathery leaves of the palms are sharp cut against the sky, and a golden light from the rising sun shines behind the dark and wavy line of the distant mountains.

It was very warm on the West Coast, as always, indeed. In the afternoon the temperature registered 93° in the verandah of the tent. All the world over the stranger is fair game to the local inhabitants, so an inquiry as to hire of a boat with four men, sail, bait, from dawn to three o'clock, was met with a firm demand of 'ten rupees'. 'Robbery', was the reply to that, 'Three will be correct.' After further withdrawal of the opposition and much haggling, the sum of four rupees eight annas was agreed.

Sail was set and in an hour or so the fishing ground was reached. It was not long before the reel screeched to the furious rush of a fish which went a full hundred yards without a check, the home-made rod bent to the strain, and after other lesser runs and wild cavortings, the long silvery form of a 35lb. seer was gaffed, not too skilfully, by one of the men, for to this game they were entirely new. This initial success had made the men exceedingly keen, for well they knew the sale value of the best eating fish on the coast.

Next morning we had to row all over the place in search of herrings as bait, and were again late at the fishing ground. However, an early start was not necessary as I soon realised to the relief of all concerned – it is not good to unduly hurry the East. Soon a fine mooloomeen of 28lbs, a dogged fighter, more powerful for his weight than even the seer, came to the gaff; also a 47lb. kandai, and a seer of 40lbs broke loose.

DIARY ——

15th. Found a boat with plenty of mackerel. Took a fine caranx, yellow belly, 24lbs, on way to rocks. Lost two or three seer fish, no hook hold. Altogether got nine fish – 132 lbs.
Three seer – 34, 32, 3; one pallameen – 24; two Gar – 3, 5; one ambai – 5; one kadai – 3; one moolloomeen – 17,   Total to date 336 lbs.
    16th. Out as usual. Could only get seven mackerel and all pretty high, from the boats which had been out all night. Moved no fish until 12 o/c. Then was taken by a fine fish, seer probably, which rushed out line, but no hook hold. A very big fish took the bait, trolling near Sacrifice Rock. The reel over ran and handle was bent, again no hook hold. Just as well! Even now the check is not strong enough for fierce rush of a big sea fish.

JOURNAL ——

One day a large sting ray was seen, its great tail swinging out of the water in a six feet circle, and several caranx of 60 to 70lbs displayed their fine proportions in parabolic leaps while pursuing shoals of small fish, which could be seen skimming in front of them. Generally speaking the bigger fish are to be found away out to sea, and it is necessary to go some seven to ten miles from land. One day we landed on a shell beach at Sacrifice Rock, the only place where a footing could be gained. Myriads of crabs scuttled in and out of crevices, small perch and other fish were cruising over the sand in the bays among the rocks, and large turtles frequently poke their heads above the surface. In weedy pools among the rocks the pipe fish and sea horses can be discovered among the sea weed, the tail of the latter prehensile for attachment to the sea-weed. Small rays and skates may also be seen amid the swirl of the waves beating on the rocks, and there are dolphins in the estuaries.

    Pigeons, gulls and herons were flying about, a few sandpipers and other small waders were balancing on the wave splashed pebbles. On the western side the water is deep; on one occasion an enormous whale, probably the Indian Fin-whale, upheaved his huge bulk within fifty yards of my anchored dug-out. These whales are not often seen; my boatman had never met with one before. The boatmen seem not to want to go out tomorrow, and after five days we all needed a rest. The men said their arms and legs ached which was not surprising for they row standing up, facing forward and pushing the oars instead of pulling in the ordinary way. This is not the custom all along the coast, but only off certain portions of it where the people seldom go more than three miles from the shore, for it is within that narrow limit the mackerel and sardine fishing is carried on.

    Between mid September and the following June the steady alternating land and sea breezes are very useful to the fishermen. A mile from the shore the land breeze fills the sails from dawn to noon, while almost precisely at that hour the sea breeze wafts vessels shorewards. About midday we were some miles out to sea when it became evident that something quite out of the ordinary was rapidly brewing along the mountain range fifty miles to the east. The crest of the hills changed from purple to pitch black, banks of racing black clouds came up from the south. Soon the wind came in fierce gusts, the boat heeled over almost gunwale under, and we all became tense and anxious. The men proved themselves reliant seamen, assisting with straining oars to counteract increasing leeway; but it was only just in time that we hit the beach with a bang, being pooped at the same time by a huge wave which filled it to overflowing. Fifty willing helpers quickly hauled the lifeless craft out of the clutching surf.

Thus began a notable storm of great intensity which originated in the Bay of Bengal, drove right across the Madras Presidency, and spread far into the Arabian Sea. A number of coasting vessels unable to make any port had to ride out the storm as best they could; and three of these, anchored some miles away opposite my camp, were seldom visible through the continuous smother of rain and spume. The unceasing roar of the tremendous surf upon the shore was most impressive. The sea ran mountains high and beat furiously upon the beach. Four whole days and nights the tempest drove the lashing rain against the back of my canvas prison, out of which it was scarcely possible to venture; and it was not until twelve days had elapsed that conditions became normal for further sport.

It was certain I should have come the first week in November for the fishermen said we had been fortunate to get any seer fish, these being not usually seen until the advent of the countless millions of herrings and sardines on their annual migration along the coast to the south. Whence they come and where they go is a mystery. The fishermen had suffered considerable loss and damage to nets and lines perforce abandoned in haste when they fled for shelter at the onset of the storm. Some nets had been wholly lost, others much torn by sharks; so the hard working community had much to do to get ready for the annual sea-harvest which means so much to them. This was the last great storm of the year, and there would be the certainty of fine weather until the following May, when the coming of the south west monsoon would put an end to all seafaring work for five months.

DIARY _____

25th. Storm over. Bought a hemp fishing line yesterday, very strong. It lifts a box of 60lbs; 103 yards for 3 rupees. The people sow hemp seed every year, spin lines out of the fibre for nets of all classes and hand lines. Waterproofed with crushed fruit of a jungle tree. Weather still uncertain; all this is a terrible waste of time and a dull business indeed. It seems likely I won't get any fishing until Tuesday 29th, almost a fortnight of doing nothing but sit in tent! It is noticeable that very few eagles or kites out over the sea now. When I again see these birds on the move I will know the weather is at last 'set fair'.

27th. Very calm morning. Dirvali Feast today, so no fishing. Ramaswamy produced a good pudding he calls Malabar Sago: sago, coconut milk, sugar, dried fruit. On 31st, heavy thunderstorm to north east. Bombay asks for sea snakes for Dr. Malcolm Smith of British Museum: deadly brutes and necessary to be very careful.

1st November. Out 6.15; but loitered for bait, at last having to start off with some very far gone mackerel. Fortunately found a boat with mackerel being hauled in on way to rocks. Made over the smelly ones which were promptly mixed with the fresh ones! Three miles or so beyond rocks, got two mooloomeen: 20lbs, 16lbs; great fighters. These fish must be of dog fish species; shark like skin, lower lobe of tail smaller than upper, ventral fin extends almost to tail: dorsal fin the same, large pectorals, big black eye with yellow ring round it. The men say they grow big 'big as three men' – so must get to near 400lbs. A terrible fight it would be to kill one of these, harness necessary. Even these made my arms ache. Rod much too stiff, scarcely any bend in it.

On the last day of the trip the surf rollers were unusually large, so it was quite a business to select the right one to start on. We had the example of several defeated boats to guide us to a successful effort. Nearing the rocks, hooked a seer fish; went a full hundred yards, then I thought he was off, reeled in and in and actually set reel running free in order to wind in faster. Then again felt the fish and he went off again, not very far. Great fighters are seer. At last brought him to gaff; 35lbs. The rod too stiff and so all the work is on one's arm, rod does nothing. After the seer, at north west corner of rocks hooked a kadai, very stubborn brute, boring down all the time; 11lbs – felt like 30. Then a perch – 8lbs; and a mooloo of 24lbs.

The last fish of the day – and of the trip, was a 34lb. mooloo, the capture of which afforded some excitement. The old man wielding the gaff forgot all his instructions, gaffed the fish near the shoulder as it was heading under the boat, did not secure the haft by the lanyard, and let go! Off went the fish with the gaff swinging from him, but was soon brought up by rod pressure. I saw the shaft far down in the translucent water, then it slipped loose to be seen no more, so the fish had to be played to a complete finish before it could be tailed with a clove hitch rope. With a last look at the rocks and the swirling tide-races, now so well known, we sailed back to camp, the men bemoaning the loss of the gaff and wondering how much it would affect the amount of 'baksheesh' to be received. Before the storm the bag had been a total of 399lbs, now it was twenty nine fish weighing 547lbs; not so bad for seven days sport. The sport in November should be quite above average, so a return visit is hoped for another year.

Going to Mangalore, Monday 4th, to get ready for Laccadives. Received a half anna H.E.I.Co. piece, date 1835, today in change from the Post Office.

3rd November. Struck camp: slept under palm tree.

Chapter 28

THE LACCADIVES — CORAL ISLANDS OF THE ARABIAN SEA

Chetlat and Bitra.

On 6th November, at Mangalore, found a Kavarathi island boat in and ready to sail on 7th; so fixed up at once to go with it. Rs.5/- per head, Rs.5/- per each 280lbs luggage; baggage stowed up by 4 p.m. Boat moved out to Channel entrance after dark, ready to cross bar at dawn on 8th. Servants with me, Ramaswamy and Sayed Abdullah, the latter a man of Ameni and talking Malayalam, island patois, also Hindustani. His pay agreed at R.38/- p.m. He should prove indispensable (note: and was very little use and not wanted). Ramaswamy Ayyangar from the Fisheries Department is to join me also.

JOURNAL _____

In the minds of most people a coral island consists of blue lagoons, feathery palms, coral reefs; and all these are to be found at Chetlat, the most northerly of the inhabited islands of the Laccadives.

    With a fair breeze from the land, the mountains of the Western Ghats were soon out of sight. With luck we might do the one hundred and fifty miles in three days, but with adverse winds or weather it might take thirteen. Such was the fate of one of these boats a year or so ago, which was driven ashore a hundred miles down the coast dismasted and rudderless. In view of this we carried forty gallons of water for our party of four, while the crew had their supply in a large earthenware vessel. This was encased in coir-rope netting and slung beneath the leaf-thatched platform amidships which served as living and sleeping quarters for the crew. Cabin accommodation on the boat was a space beneath the poop, nine feet wide and long, narrowing to three feet at the stern post, and two feet six inches high. When the vessel felt the first heave of the ocean, the smell of the bilge water was so nauseating that I spent the whole voyage lying in the open on the rice cargo. The course was kept by compass aided by the position of the sun and stars.

DIARY _____

All the people on the boat were very friendly. One passenger was the religious head of the Island. Much to my surprise ship was free from bugs and other vermin. Gear was in fair order; mainsail pretty new, but soon had a few holes by seams splitting when sail flapped about; after sail a mere rag; bowsprit sail of gunny. Boat was Island built of the wood of chirani which grows on the islands. Not a nail or bolt in the whole ship: all joints and fastenings secured by coir lashings, seams too. Lavatory accommodation a mere platform just behind the rudder. None too easy when ship rolls and dangerous in bad weather to one with stiff legs like myself. A rope frayed at mast head and it was a sight to see one of the men just walk up the mast and replace the rope by a new one! so also when it was necessary to see if land in sight on Sunday morning. The men ate rice and curry twice a day piled up on enamel ware plates; galley just a wood fire on mud floor. They say that fire never occurs: looks risky.

9th. A good wind during the night and fairly so during day, and at dawn on 10th a man went up to mast head and sighted land — Chetlat. Quite good navigation with compass and nothing else. Name of boat, ODAM as styled in Laccadives, is 'Valia Bukkari' of Kavarathi Island. Licensed to carry in fine weather twenty three tons, in rough weather seventeen tons. Sixty nine natives, fifty one Europeans in fine weather; in rough weather fifty one and thirty eight. I pity both the fifty one and thirty eight!

At Chetlat the Government boat *Chetlat*, built on the Island last year came out and took off all our gear and selves. Met the Monegar of Ameni, English speaking, Muhammadan, very helpful in every way. Saw a number of hermit crabs walking about with shells and empty coconuts as their dwellings. A great collection of these was got by Ramaswamy Ayyangar, who will arrange a numbered and named collection to go to the Bombay Natural History Society.

Went out fishing in morning. Large boat, six rowers, one steersman. I don't see prospect of getting many fish here; much water to cover and fish may be anywhere. Got a barracuda, 36lbs, at one hundred feet while lying to for a rest. Let the bait down and hauled it up a few feet and let down again and so on. Not as good a fighter as seer fish. In afternoon saw a rat hunt. Five rats were killed; it is difficult to judge, but they do not seem to be as great a pest as is said. Perhaps the regular Sunday rat hunts act as sufficient check. The rats live almost entirely in tops of coconut trees and are the common brown rat of the mainland. The evergreen Tulip tree with the two coloured flowers, yellow and orange-red, are plentiful; wood is used for boat building.

12th. In afternoon went out with R. Ayyangar on to outer reef. Water in lagoon during low tide quite shallow. Saw many curious corals and creatures. Many holotheriums which are the beche-de-mer of commerce — sea slugs they are, also hermit crabs, clams — these latter small ones of the Giant Clam which grows to 800lbs in weight in the seas of these islands. Deadly, absolutely, to a diver, or a man caught at low tide. Amputation the only course. Tested these little ones, and nothing short of a crow bar would open even a small one. There were several horrible centipede like sea worms, one of them with marvellous set of feathery feelers at his mouth; he progressed just like a snake. Men with us said these are very poisonous — may be. They look very nasty and are curiously sticky to the touch. Found several sea urchins, black, like porcupines as to quills. In pools were many brilliantly coloured fry of various species of Jew fish. Saw a heron, exactly merging with colour of the reef and almost invisible. Returned as sun set, a flaming sky with many clouds, heat clouds — not rain.

13th. Went to north reef, came back through palms and past houses of the Moopan of Chetlat. He is blind in one eye from cataract. Now the other eye is going and urged him to go to General Ophthalmic Hospital at Madras. Monegar said he would take him there. Will he go? In afternoon went out to sea. Three small fish for bait; one yellow with white longitudinal stripes; one dark green; one loach like with great array of teeth. No use staying here too long, so will arrange to go on 21st to Bitra if weather all right. Today, after three jabs by small fish and nothing hooked, old Ali Muhammad took the fish, poured sea water on it by way of ablution, and said prayers over it! No result! What a score for the old man if a fish had been hooked after the blessings!

14th. This morning went to east shore, on the way found bread fruit tree and also tulip tree and paratha, growing close together, Caught a few small fish and an eel. The lagoon is a beautiful colour, light emerald with shadows caused by dark corals below the surface, beyond is the deep blue and purple of the ocean. People of Chetlat row in European fashion, high rowlocks. Oars of coconut palm wood and blades of same, painted black and white. This black and white device is as far as their art goes – crescent of white and zig zag of white on black ground, so also is the decoration on their ships and boats. Houses are of coral stone, woodwork of coconut, roof of coconut thatch. The men are very noisy, shouting in unison on all sorts of occasions. Big vessels are berthed and launched by communal work, under order of the head man. The Karani is a Government appointed man for revenue. The Moopan is the domestic head man.

In afternoon 3 p.m. went out to sea. Nothing till almost dark; then caught a shark, 30 lbs. and a caranx, 20lbs. Men sang a song with a refrain to it, old Ali Muhammad joining in with the rest. He sits on stern platform and steers, but being so blind has to be told by the men which way helm is wanted. He is a fine old sailor, so Monegar told me, needs no compass to find his way to any of the islands or the mainland. The men tell me there are NO sea snakes in this part of the sea. Back at 9 p.m.; that is a drawback to night fishing, in this climate, one can't keep fish until the morning and besides that the people are hungry for fish meat and one doesn't like to not let them have it.

JOURNAL ————————————————————————————————

These island people are free, because not in prison, but man, woman and child from earliest years are doing the hard and unremitting labour of coir rope making, as a means of bare existence. Their mornings are spent in husking the coconuts, teasing and sorting the fibre, and beating it out with wooden mallets on stones. The sound of this beating is as incessant as the noise of the coppersmith. Tiny children assist in teasing the fibre and rolling it into short lengths which are twisted into ropes. In the afternoon the people take the material to the lagoon shore and bundles are made. Thence it goes to Mangalore to the Government Marine Yard, where it is exchanged for rice at a fixed rate. Without this labour they would starve as besides their coconut trees they have no other means of subsistence; for the fishing is unproductive commercially, and followed only as an additional means of food. The people make very good beds by stringing with coir twine.

Some of the men are fine looking people, and many of the women good looking and cheerful; in many ways a likeable people. There is much skin disease, ringworm, scabies. A travelling dispensary, going the rounds of the islands, would be a boon to them. There is a hospital at Ameni, but for ordinary ailments they won't go there. During the fair weather months, the Hospital Assistant could easily leave Ameni in charge of an Assistant and visit Kiltan and Chetlat. The people had few domestic animals; there were two or three cows, and a few chickens. There being no shops, money was not much in demand, but the children were insatiable for biscuits, and a ship load would not have sufficed as the adults wanted them as well. My own fare, which I had brought with me, was simple as always when in camp: dal, rice, atta, onions, potatoes, sugar, jam, tea, butter, and seasonings. The water came from wells on the island and had a very uninviting appearance; I made sure all the water for camp was carefully boiled.

The fishermen are marvellously adept in the use of the harpoon. Distance, pace, refraction, direction, all have to be judged in a split second. At night the beauty of the scene cannot be imagined; there is the reflecting mirror of the lagoon, the sparks flying from the torch, the dancing sparklets of the rippling water, the statuesque figure of the poised harpooner, the low echoing instructions to the oarsmen, the thud of the weapon and the resulting jubilation of the crew.

At night the sea was highly phosphorescent. At each movement of the oars, globules of light floated away, brilliant patches of jelly fish and other forms of marine life went past, and on several occasions large patches of phosphorescent light floated from below to remain a minute and then fade away; what this was the men could not explain.

All around were the quickly changing hues of the water, now cool and peaceful where just an hour ago it was glittering under a fierce sun, and along the horizon the enormous clouds form massive purple battlements. They look like castles in the air, an illusion of snow-topped mountains; then the silver changed to gold as the sinking sun shot great rays to the zenith and the dying day rapidly gave way to the wonder of the tropic night. This was the hour when one might expect to have the line torn off the reel; is it a seer, or a caranx, or perhaps a shark? One soon got to know the manner and feel of the various species. Some, like the red perch, would at once make for the floor and a coral retreat from which dislodgement would be difficult, so whenever the bait was seized it was well to allow as little liberty as possible, and tackle has to be strong.

DIARY

17th November. At 2.30 p.m. a coir boat from Agatti, bound for Mangalore, came here for shelter from the storm. Sound of the breakers on the Eastern reef is very loud and it has rained off and on a good deal. Very steamy now; thermometer at 7 p.m. in room is eighty two degrees. No hope of fishing for several days. Today saw shikra – light blue rollers, white heron, falcon, sandpipers.

18th. Storm completely gone! Went out from 7.0 to 9.30: saw a man harpoon a fine seer fish close to our boat, about 35lbs. Old Moopan did a lengthy prayer and ablutions of fish and a final spit, and launched the next bait to success! Caranx: number one; after that few misses and took six Caranx in all, average weight 9lbs; CARANX NIGRIPINNIS – Horse mackerel.

JOURNAL

When a hooked fish was reeled in to be gaffed, great lines and flares of phosphorescence were set up far below by it's wild gyrations, and all eyes would be out of the boat trying to judge the size. Many were the laughing comments on the lengthy business of playing with the rod a fish which would have been summarily hauled in by themselves using a hand line, and jerked into the boat. Old Muhammad Ali used to be doubled up with laughter at the idea; and when one evening the butterfly net with a small receptacle at the end of it was skimmed along the surface of the water as the boat moved quietly under the full moon, for the purpose of collecting plankton for scientific examination, he and the crew thinking this to be another method of the mad FERINGHI for catching fish, laughed so that tears streamed, the old man nearly fell off the boat! The merriment ceased only when the scream of the reel afforded other excitement. All that I had was strange. None of them had ever before seen a fishing reel. Said old Ali, with much emphasis, 'More than seventy years have I lived, and never have I seen such a TAMASHA as this!'

It was old Muhammad Ali, headman of Chetlat, who hired to me for the remainder of the trip the use of his boat with crew of eight men and himself as Tindal (or Captain), and a very excellent crew and craft it was. He was then blind in one eye, and later was to lose his sight in the other also from a cataract. The men lit leaf flares to attract fish, and in the blaze of this and sparks flying by, the old fellows cataract eye shone out, and there was indeed a funny scene and as much noise as in a rowdy pub!

Besides harpooning and hand-line fishing beyond the outer reef, nets of different sizes are used in the lagoon. The MULUVALA is of small mesh, worked from the shore by four men. The MUDUVALA is a circular casting net for catching small fish. The KADALIVALA is a much larger affair and is used in conjunction with the OLAVALA, this being a rope many hundred feet in length on which are tied lengths of palm leaves, the use of it being a holiday occasion. It is taken out about four hundred yards from the shore in two boats, the ends are joined together and the boats return in a wide semicircle paying out the rope as they go. When the semicircle has been reduced in size, the Kadalivala is payed out inside the leaf net and quickly brings the catch to the shore; among them on this occasion were several surgeon fish armed on either side of the waist with bone lancets of razor keenness.

DIARY _____

20th. Agatti boat left this morning for Mangalore. Gave Moopan 3/- to distribute to men working the net and it seems he thinks it not enough! Saw some of the fish split and drying in the shade covered with blow flies. Arranged we go Bitra tomorrow night to arrive there early on 22nd. Balance cash in hand is 257/- out of 650/- on leaving Coonoor! and I thought on starting that I would do whole trip on 500/-. R. Ayyangar very industrious at collecting.

Evening. Went out fishing. For a long time only a few tugs by small fish. Then took a caranx, 11lbs, and a red perch (Lutjanus) 13lbs. He went down to coral and when hauled out of that fouled the men's line, and there was a hell of a hooha, as we were nearly on the reef! Going out fouled the bottom with croc spinner and fortunate to get clear. Apart from the knife edged coral there are also poisonous sea creatures and clams infesting the reefs to catch the unwary, and on the frequent occasions when it was necessary to ease the boat over an obstruction there is the possibility of injury to bare feet. The fishermen seemed not to mind or take any particular care, while I was usually anticipating some mishap!

Men asked last night if the rod would stand up to big fish. Evidently they fear for my tackle, but with Sea Silex, this rod, and two hundred yards 72lbs olympian cuttyhunk, with fifty yards 36lbs hemp as backing, I should be able to compete with most fish I am likely to hook, and have plenty of spare line if the cuttyhunk is walked off with by some monster.

21st November. All packed up and ready to sail at 7 p.m. for Bitra. Glad to leave here. All night we sailed quietly along in the Poo Odam (the Flower Ship) to wake at dawn and look over the immensity of the grey of the sea. At day-break we saw the palm trees of Bitra Par seemingly floating in the water at the northern end of a great lagoon seven miles long encircled by a ring of creamy breakers. The main entrance is at the southern end, but before I realised what was being done we were inside the lagoon through a small high-tide gap known to the old man, and mighty proud he was to have found his way in!

22nd. Water of the lagoon shallow at south end and we progressed by poling along. After some time couldn't pole against the strong breeze and we began to 'kedge'. I told Ali Muhammad that he could sail up to island by tacking, but he said not and the kedge was put out and hauled up eighteen times, each one taking about twenty minutes. At 5.20 p.m. he put up sail and in one tack we got to anchorage. A man was kept at mast-head, two men either side with poles, one man with an oar, and lucky this was done, as only by speedy work of pole, oar, and rudder, following shout from mast head were several up-jutting coral rocks avoided. Wonderful how old Ali Muhammad with his cataract eye can get along, steer and navigate. The crew were wholly fed up after all this, besides having to row R.A. three miles to the island to shorten the miseries of a bad sailor, for the boat rolled much in the calm lagoon. I am fortunate not to suffer from seasickness, and slept on my six-by-two piece of deck, lulled by the unceasing surge of the sea on the reef.

The mate caught two fish; one caranx about 15lbs, one red perch 1½lbs: both these fish very WHITE, due no doubt to sandy bottom. Next morning tents and everything else landed and camp pitched among the palms. A party of people from Ameni have been here for about ten days and skinned the trees of all coconuts, also caught a great many fish. These are common property of all the islands; but not the coconuts. Night cool, no mosquitoes; rats didn't bother me, but Ramaswamy says they got into his bed.

25th. Monday. Only by 8 o/c was some bait obtained by means of adivala and my own circular casting net; and then the men go off to food! Walked around the island. Saw a falcon and a large blue grey heron with dark wings. The island has much coarse tussocky grass and is twenty six acres in extent. It is said to have altered in shape during last seventy five years and to be extending north and being washed away to south inside the lagoon.

Bitra is uninhabited except for one family from Chetlat who live there during the fair weather months to look after the coconut trees and make sugar from the palm juice. Soon after dawn a man, one of the four now on the island, climbed tree at my tent door, to get the unfermented juice collected during the night in the coconut gourds tied to the tree. His collecting buckets are of bamboo.

Went fishing at 9.30 over reef to north west and so to sea. Caught a GREEN perch, 5lbs, lovely colour: and a red one, 11lbs. On way back over reef, tide low and saw clam — gaping for an incautious toe! The men dived several times for big shells (*Pterocera lambis*); and at one place, where was a circular outcrop of coral of the striated type, there was much excitement. A man dived with a pole and poked about, then came up and took down a shark hook, very blunt and rusty, on a wire trace. After several efforts the men asked me for my big four inch hook which I gave, Sildur trace complete, fearing it would be all twisted and spoilt.

It seems they had seen a big fish go under the rock. There were now several men in the water breast deep. To the trace was attached a very thick cotton fishing line, my Mangalore made gaff was also taken; then there was more diving and at last a great shouting and pulling and out came a big blue fish (36lbs) with my hook in its mouth! Soon it was gaffed and lifted on board. Such a marvellous creature: a mouth like a mahseer, but with dog like canines projecting a bit forward; single row of teeth, broad tail. Linoleum pattern markings of dark rusty red on the blue scales and gill plates. A big hump like a zebu's on the shoulder. From Day's Fishes seems certain it is CHILENUS UNDULATUS. The men called it 'Chandi balavala'.

26th. Ali Muhammad brought some turtle eggs to show, both mature and immature, they dug up about one hundred. Some pieces of coral were brought to me, both round Fungoid corals, solitary and not reef building; also a piece of red-like coral, called Tubi-pora; and an oval Heart urchin of star fish group with shape of a star fish on its back. Went to see the net hauled. While waiting saw crab digging in sand and running to edge of water. His eyes fold down flat into his head but when he

1

2

3

4

CHAPTER
28

is in movement are carried upright like two periscopes. His name Ocypode (*ceratophth-alma*). Saw the olavala pulled in; the haul was about fifty fish, mostly big jew fish, PSEUDOSCARUS DUSSUMIERI (parrot or jew fish). Weight of many of them 11lbs, There was a green perch, not nearly so brilliant as the one caught yesterday among the coral, also a small fish black and white stripes, BALISTES ACULEPTUS (globe fish) which blow out like balloons when frightened and have very funny faces, and three box fish OSTRACION CUBICUS. which have a body square in shape and move only their two fins and a tail.

Went on reef in evening with R.A., quite dry in many parts and wide. Four feet difference between high and low water, stretches for miles as far as one can see to south west and south. Saw men extract an octopus, and squeeze it to make it discharge the inky fluid which coloured the whole 6ft. diameter pool. The man didn't mind the tentacles grasping his arm, but just detached them. They were about fourteen inches long and rough to the touch. Men collected a lot of cowrie shells. Found several star fish, one with six arms, big one. One has to walk very carefully, easy to fall and it isn't soft falling!

27th. At 12.30 set off for sand bank: tide went down at 4.30 and reefs were soon exposed. In the lagoon, west of sandbanks, a lot of fish, and clams and shells of various kinds. I only found one shell, a yellow cone shaped one, MITRA EPISCOPALIS, which R.A. begged off me, as it does not seem very common. I rather wished I had gone with the boat hunting about the lagoon. The men got two of the big blue fish and lost another one, and with it the hook I gave them; cotton line broke, they said. These two fish, 32lbs each. Dark before we got back; bumped many rocks. At first bump I called out 'chandi balala' at which great merriment. A lot of fish about which not seen before; very difficult to net them owing to the coral.

28th. Went out 4.30 p.m. The reef extends a long way out to east at an angle from south end. Caught one shark 90lbs, one shark 22lbs, and men got three caranx, and one gar. The smaller shark played well. The big one just a log, mostly, until it was stirred up by bad shots with the harpoon! At last the man struck it, close to boat, and in hauling it on board the men nearly upset the boat: and such a noise and all talking at once. The men say these sharks do not grow very large, so probably round about 100lbs is the maximum for them. These people are very primitive in many ways. The mate yesterday evening, to strip his hook of the morning's stinking bait still on it and tied on with cotton, didn't use my offered scissors but preferred his teeth. He just gnawed off the horrible thing!

29th. Yesterday was very calm and all the heavy clouds of 27th had gone. Today a good breeze. We want a breeze to take us to Ameni – Kadamath, rather, for we go there first. Saw the jayzang which these people make out of the unfermented palm tree liquid. It is boiled, with a piece of chalk stone in it. This extracts the acid and the sugar is left. It is quite good and one needn't fear running out of jam!

30th. Some birds are beginning to arrive. Today several whimbrel, an avocet beaked bird, a black billed stint of sorts, a sparrow hawk, a biggish white headed hawk with vulture pinions and looks a scavenger. Went out fishing, 3 p.m. Got two sharks, 40, 22; two caranx, 12, 7: one gar, 4lb; and two red perch, one balistes, these three small. Ali caught the three small fish by weighting the line with a stone tied on with grass stem just above hook. A jerk of line and stone is off while bait is where wanted. He fished at thirty five fathoms. Old Ali unwilling to sail for Kadamath unless he gets a good breeze from north east.

Kadamath and Ameni
2nd December. On board and up anchor at two o'clock, but waited for evening as old Ali doesn't want to pass Kadamath in the dark! We sailed over calm seas from Bitra and at

dawn were six miles from Kadamath. We made the entrance of the lagoon and came to anchor, to land amidst a gathering of islanders headed by the Muhammadan Hospital Assistant who had come across from Ameni on Inspection Duty. Soon we gathered all the local news, — a rice boat had just arrived from Mangalore, there were letters for me, and the Monegar at Ameni wishes to have early news of my arrival. Put up in the Cutchery (Court House), so quite comfortable. R.A. went into the school building. Found the Chetlat karani and peon here. From attentiveness of the new karani it is plain the Chetlat man has told him of tip to be expected!

The people are better off and better nourished than those of Chetlat. The houses are of the same description, coral stone walls, beams and rafters of coconut wood, palm leaf thatch. Several coral sandstone quarries were seen in use. This stone is of a beautiful whiteness when hewn and fairly soft, becoming hard when exposed to the air. Along the lagoon shore I picked up some pumice stone which had come from the great Krakatoa Eruption in 1883. I remember clearly hearing the news of the eruption when I was at school in England. Pumice stone drifted far and wide over the sea, and much used to be picked up on the shores of the Laccadives. A friend of mine who was on a plantation in Ceylon heard the noise of the eruption which was heard over a radius of two thousand miles.

As it is the fast of Ramzan I could not reasonably ask my crew to spend long hot hours out at sea. However, the first day I went out fishing I witnessed an unusual affair, probably seldom seen by white people.

3rd. A great tamasha. Men in some boats a long way off began to call out, and all the boats raced to them. An attempt was to be made to surround a shoal of porpoises. Some boats pursued and got the shoal encircled and gradually the boats, fourteen in all, were in a long half circle facing the reef. The porpoises were doing the usual graceful up and down dive and by degrees were herded towards the reef entrance to the lagoon. There was a great shouting and banging of water and boat, and thumping.

The boats closed in and the shoal was edged towards the island sands. Now the water shelved rapidly and was only thigh deep. The men dashed in with ready knives and in a few minutes the beautiful light green water of the lagoon was red with blood. Rapidly each poor wallowing beast was slashed across the spine behind the head and deep stabs given in the body. A brutal scene — horrible — such exultant shouts, such a shouting and babel and noise. The island man in my boat asked for the big gaff and dashed into the fray; soon he returned with it — broken, shaft broken and no wonder, as the Chetlat carpenter had half cut it through to fit the gaff! One porpoise, wounded, broke out to sea was pursued and harpooned, the boats, seven of them, were still out when I came away.

Eleven of them were slaughtered. I took photo of a long nose one, the only one of that kind, and of a big round headed one. A sole, both eyes on one side of its head, was put up out of the sand, pursued, and caught. I claimed it for my breakfast! Then the cutting up of the animals began and I came away. Left our boat to take a share of the spoil and walked back two and a half miles, with old Ali Muhammad. A nice walk through palm tree groves, high grass, plenty of green trees. Saw lantana, and some banyan and tamarind trees. Passed several wells and bathing places. All the water of these islands is very dirty. No care taken to have a clean supply.

In evening went fishing. The exit over the reef is by a somewhat difficult channel and outside we found a lot of fishing boats from Ameni, which is about five miles away. It was nearly dark by the time we started to fish and old Ali soon hooked a big fish. He wasn't ready, also line not well coiled, and there was a check, and he had two cuts round his little finger. The thick cotton line broke; only four of my best Alcock hooks left now out of eleven I had with me at the start. One of the boats had a sword fish, and we rowed over to see it. Lighting the lantern I was thrilled to see the lovely fish lying at the bottom of the boat. It was seven feet in length, including the sword of twenty two inches, the beautiful Prussian-blue back fin which gives it the local name of OLAMEEN (ola – meaning a palm leaf) was spread for my inspection. Came into lagoon at 10 o/c and back to camp.

5th. In evening went fishing with island boat. Out to sea over the bar at south end at 5 o/c. That bar a very tricky affair; lot of cross currents sweeping in over reef and around back and point of sandspit. The men, on the way back, sang a rowing song, the refrain of which – O! Bela, bela-la-la-bela, O! bela, bela, ila Kandai – couldn't get hold of the end of it. Many verses, to tune of which rowing varied. A different song to that of the Chetlat people with their refrain of – Hum Hai! All these islanders merry hearted and noisy.

The method when a fish is hooked is to row hard and pull him along, so giving him no chance to swim. He is just hauled along and half drowned in the process, and before he realises what is up a harpoon is on him. They all think my rod and reel business very funny tamasha. The fishermen caught a 14lb perch. No gaffing, just trace caught hold of and the fish lifted and dropped into the boat! We also caught one barracuda, and two caranx. I must get a list of names, written by R.A., as I can't catch their words at all for spelling purposes. Last night I asked name of the barracuda and couldn't catch it and said 'Abdul Kareem'?, for it sounded like that, at which much amusement.

It was seldom that the wind was too strong to permit fishing outside the lagoons. On the evening of 6th December it was blowing rather hard, but boatmen said it would be all right; once outside I rather wished myself back again! The white-crested waves looked enormous as the boat fell into the troughs between them where nothing but the angry onrushing water could be seen, as I faced the stern. Seated on the floor of the boat I could touch the water with my wrist resting on the gunwale. When a fish seized the trolling bait and tore the line screaming off the reel, I was quite glad it was not securely hooked! The setting sun lit up the heavy clouds to the west, and I was relieved when the men explained by signs that no rain would come and the sea would be more quiet to the south of the reef. Confident in their knowledge of the signs of the weather, the men were assured and happy in that desert of angry waves. On way back saw a lovely falling star, or rather a meteor, as is was very close. A lovely blaze of many colours: a great light, millions and millions of candlepower. Several big ones have been seen lately around these seas.

7th. Up at 5 and off at 6 to Ameni to pay visit there as asked by Monegar A.M. Khan. Took over two hours to row across with twelve rowers. Two influential men with the boat, one very stout, Muktesars of the Magistrate's Court who sit wit him during the trial of cases. Monegar very hospitable and put me up in the Cutchery. Accompanied by an interested crowd, we walked with the Monegar to see the principal mosque; then turned aside for coconut milk in house of young man who came across with us from Mangalore. Saw many fine bread fruit trees, and island very thickly planted with coconut trees. Houses were pitched in shade of trees and gave the impression of little farmsteads. Saw Monegar issue rice to poor people, out of the 4000/- fund, also some out of a Government grant of Rs.500, for the four islands! That doesn't go far.

In evening played tennis with Monegar and two of the islanders who have begun to play. I didn't do so badly considering I haven't played for thirty three years! My broken right wrist has almost fully recovered. Was told about Patti sandbank. The sea floor can be seen all the way from Ameni for over twenty five miles. This space is about ten miles wide in places, with depths of eight to twenty fathoms. A good many sword fish there; some caranx; seer in plenty; bonito; red perch, and sharks of all sizes. Monsoon rains fall in showers, and not heavy continuous rain of days and days.

8th. Went a long walk to south about five miles. Saw tortoise in sand. It was struggling on its back in a pit it had dug and don't think it would have got right side up; two boys with me turned it over. It was very exhausted. Then they took it by flippers and ran it down to sea and I saw it swim off after a short rest. Low tide and reef exposed. People here skim the reefs of all cowries, shells etc. to sell at Mangalore.

9th. Every morning I doctor old Ali's eye with permanganate and sulphate zinc lotion. Will give him some to use for himself when we part, with injunction not to use it every day! Fat man of Ameni, a Muktesar of the Monegar's Court, wanted to see the 'tamasha' of my rod and reel fishing, so we started off 3.30 p.m. with plenty of bait as I had told the Karani my troubles in that respect. Sailed down lagoon all along the island shore and were almost not able to get over the reef as today is a very low tide. We came over the tricky bar all right and so up the Lagoon, the fat man weighing down the stern and leading the song of 'O! Bela, Bela, ila, bela'; in fine style. A very noisy boat load we were. I joined in now and again with a hoarse croak. The song has endless variations, besides which the rowers sang rubbish, meaningless gabble, in a most joyous way. Wonderful rowers, marvelous energy on a diet of rice, fish, and coconut. They row the big 'Chetlat' boat taking Monegar there on duty, with all his kit and his followers, in six hours − thirty miles, twelve rowers. They sing all the way, and to a western mind, appear to uselessly waste energy that way, but they probably couldn't do it silent!

10th. Woke up feeling pretty bad as to throat, and about 1.30 decided to go over to Ameni with the fat Muktesar and get Doctor to make up the Blackheath bronchitis prescription. Necessary to go without delay as reef would be bare by 3 o/c. Arrived Ameni at 4.15. Doctor took over an hour to prepare prescription! His office and dispensary in a very dirty and untidy state. Poison cupboard all higgledy piggledy; no method, no arrangement. But what sort of eyes has the Collector who goes around 'inspecting'? Left Ameni 5.45 p.m. and got back, rowing all way as a head wind, by 8.15. Reef had very little water on it, so even fat man had to get out and wade a bit. Wind said to be very favourable for going to coast.

11th. All packed ready by 7.30. Monegar came over from Ameni to see us off. On to boat by ten o'clock. Head wind, so poled and towed up the lagoon, two hours later we were outside and under sail for Mangalore. I had temperature yesterday, and this morning; and now close on 100°. Wind seemed too much ahead and old Ali said 'Hawa karab'. Few Hindustani words has he; 'achha', 'barabar'. When I tell him the bait is 'Karab', and as often as not it is stinking, he says 'bar-r-rabar' rolling his Rs, and I say 'Hor-r-rible', and we laugh. We have been on these very good simple terms all the time, since he took me under his wing on 11th November. A bit grasping I expect as to cash. When I gave him 3/- to give to people working the olavala in Chetlat lagoon, he pouched the lot, none of which was intended for him, and the workers got none!

12th. We go along, but slowly I fear as wind still more in front than behind. My temperature went down on morning of 13th. R.A. dead to the sea and the world: can keep down nothing, not even water, and his whole body seems made of bile! By nightfall on 13th we were near the Coast as flash of some coast lighthouse was seen.

14th. All day we sailed up Coast, about ten miles out to sea, and were becalmed some of the time. During that the small boat came up close alongside and a fish was seen swimming about underneath it. It was a sucker fish, Echeneis, and travels mostly as an uninvited guest on a shark, or fish of suitable size, or a boat. Sucker is a ribbed affair, transverse ribs on top of head, a sort of extension of the dorsal fin, and the fish when attached will stand a pull of 17lbs: to detach it slides forward and is easily detached. It was about 2½lbs, shark like in appearance. By nightfall we were off Mangalore and anchored a couple of miles off the bar. Shortly before that lost my shikar topee overboard, a very annoying loss.

15th. Lay at anchor dawn to noon on account of land wind. The men rowed off to visit an Arab dhow from Korveit. I couldn't go being a prisoner in the rabbit hutch on account of loss of topee. A big dhow, with a cargo of dates, and pearls. EXACTLY at 12 o/c land breeze changed to sea breeze and we set off for the bar. Took a long time to pole and tow up the harbour and didn't lie up till 2.30. At once went off in julka and got a hat, horrid affair, two rupees, too big and no real sun protection. Returned to boat and paid off everyone. All seemed pleased. Old Ali sorry to see me go. I saw tears in the old fellow's eyes – one eye I should say. Gave him a letter to Civil Surgeon and hope to hear what prospects he has as to operation. Took a few minutes to get my eyes, so long focused on distant objects, to focus for shore objects. Ramaswamy Ayyangar very weak and emaciated, only my powdered 'klim' milk had kept him going, very small quantities at a time. He went off in two bullock carts; I in julka, my kit in two carts with Ramaswamy. Paid off the useless Sayed Abdullah and not sorry to see the last of him.   Went to Mudie's house, (Post Officer Mangalore), and had tea and a much needed tub, first for six days!

16th. Saw Collector, and told him that A.M. Khan, Monegar, a very good man at his job; and of lantana on Kadamath, and of poor plight of Chetlat people. R.A. came to station to see me off, he wants a rest badly and feeding up, got to Mettupalaiyam 5.30 a.m. So back to Coonoor at 12 o/c, after sixty eight days absence. Bronchitis still threatening; and Coonoor very cold. Total Expenses for trip – 761/13/0: say – 770/0/0

27th December. Foul weather still continues. Pretty well finished all sorting and packing of kit and making ready to leave in Lorry 7.30 a.m. 3rd January for Coimbatore jungles. First block – Gaddersol: second – Bailur. May be feverish so getting enough quinine to give 4 grs. a day to self, wife, two servants. 1935 ended and self quite fit again.

Chapter 29

SHIKAR IN THE NILGIRI HILLS

DIARY

3rd January 1936. Left Coonoor in a lorry loaded to full capacity with tents, and kit, for selves and Mr. and Mrs. Darcy McArthy. Ghat very steep and winding, twenty seven hairpin turns in six miles and 2500 feet. A letter came from Morris by hand telling us D.F.O. Darrington and family will be coming to this bungalow for ten days! At once sent a letter to D.F.O. to say we are in occupation. Feel sure Morris mistaken, as Forester knows nothing of it and has sent his staff away to get their pay at Satyamangala. Water all along the nala, and this is a bad block; no hope of any tiger in it. Three days later a notice came from Forest Ranger requiring us to vacate the bungalow by 10 a.m. 8th, as D.F.O. and family coming for ten days! So out we go, to Hassanur.

13th. Heard that panther had killed a calf, and found it in nala. Had it tied to a root, and made a shelter for McArthy in clump of dead bamboo. He had a Sholaga shikari sitting with him and I felt sure panther would spot him. He sat 2 p.m. to 8 p.m. and then came away. I couldn't go as my right eye very bad, throbbing, painful, red, and highly infected; dark room for three days.

18th. In the evening Mrs McArthy and H.G.B. took dogs, Scamp and Bunty, (airedales), up the road for a walk as usual. They chased some chital in the thick lantana jungle. Scamp came back to the road, and Bunty was heard barking in distance; she did not return and we all feared the worst. In the morning took the Sholaga trackers and went to search. It was like looking for the proverbial needle. Yet, one of the Sholagas, creeping about among the lantana found a tuft of hair showing the place where the dog was first seized: and tracked the hair up to where the carcass lay. The spiky collar hadn't saved her: spike bent. No doubt she had been seized by the body, or knocked over with a paw, and then the throat was gripped in the usual way.

21st–23rd. No shikar. Decided to stick to Bailur and wrote Morris for tents. As Conservator comes to Hassanur 26th to 30th, we have to clear out and go to Geddasal on 26th morning. A letter received from A.M. Khan of Ameni: very pleased with photos I sent to him, and with a 'Good Service' entry in his Record of Services. It is said that H.E. Governor of Madras (Lord Erskine) will shoot in Bailur Block in March: so perhaps we will not be allowed to comb out too many tiger and panther in February.

25th. McArthy's driver, Charlie, ill – remittent fever; so he stayed in camp. I went up the valley to work the country to west. Found McArthy disturbed at the driver's illness and the man, Charlie, 'playing up'. No doubt he is ill, but not very bad, not so bad as other servants in Central Provinces with the same kind of fever. McArthy been hinting at throwing up shoot and returning to Coonoor for some time and now he gets his opportunity for an excuse and suddenly decides to close down and be off tomorrow to Coonoor. Mrs. McArthy really sorry, I think, at this decision, but I am relieved as McA, no 'shikari', and I will be happier without him. He 'bosses' things too much and relegates me to back place.

28th. Up at 4.30 and off via the Settlement to hunt for bison. F.G. didn't want to start until daylight, talked of elephant. But I said we would go on, and no elephant! So up to top of the rise at dawn, followed a path and partly burnt fire line and tracked up a nala in which some water, – worked cat footed. Suddenly a tremendous snort ten yards to our right. We had come on a sleeping, or lying down, bull. Off he thundered. In course of tracking found remains, very little! – just a splintered bone or two and piece of jaw, of a barking deer killed by wild dogs. Signs of wild dog along every road and path, and no doubt they kill off much game.

29th. News by gawala of bullock killed near parao by a 'big tiger'. Had breakfast and then took machan chair, rope, and bamboo ladder, and went to see. Found the bullock on edge of dense cover: obviously a panther kill. Returned and seated, all quiet and well screened, by 5 p.m. At last glimmer of daylight, panther crept up and started to feed on ribs. Put on the torch and killed him dead, not a move, with .375 mag. 265 copper point bullet. It is McArthy's pet rifle which he has lent to me. A pity I didn't keep my .470 until end of this trip instead of selling it in July. McArthy's rifle has a very small foresight, no sling attachment, no 'moon' sight, and is an ejector, so it isn't my idea of a big game rifle. It is just what is made for deer stalkers, and McArthy gave Holland & Holland £200 for it!

Back to camp, had dinner, and then skinned the panther, two men holding lanterns. Had to do it all myself: no one able to skin. Many ticks began to leave the panther and crawl up arms of self and helpers, so we all had a good smear of Kerosene up to elbows, and no more ticks! Finished and to bed by 12.15. A long day.

2nd February. At Bailur. Wife has influenza, fever. News came of a tiger having killed two cows other side of Soondermara village. Found the kill beyond the village in a heavily wooded hollow up a ravine in the hills! Put up chair for right and left shoulder shots. Kakur up the hill notified tiger had heard us and come to have a look. He came close to machan and no doubt stood listening and I didn't hear him move away, but a sambur up the nala told me he had gone. He didn't return, a cunning brute. Got back to camp to find, so the Ranger says, that this tiger always kills two cows at a time and never returns to kill! It rained yesterday, a sharp shower, and today a big storm of rain drenched the camp. So lucky I didn't stay on and sit up as I half thought of doing: but didn't like to leave wife in camp, she still seedy, but fever going.

5th. Up at 4.30; and out on path to Soondermara village, by dawn. The solitary elephant which lives around here was close by and the men sheered off and went towards the hills. I don't see why one need be so afraid of him! keep clear of him to avoid trouble, but no bother otherwise: he hasn't killed anyone and is not proclaimed. Tracks and sign of several bears and they no doubt lie up in thick cover of bamboo and bushes. Found this mornings tracks of a tiger and by chance followed along the same way and eventually the tracks took us to within three hundred yards of the tents! It seems that the Forester saw the tiger at 8.30, calmly walking along up the broad 'ride' which runs from near the bungalow to the bed of valley. It is said emphatically by the Ranger that there is only this one tiger here; but I certainly saw tracks of tigress the first morning. Anyway the Valley would be pleased if the tiger could be killed.

The heavy rain of yesterday afternoon cracked the ridge pole of tent left by Morris and I spliced and bound that up. Today another storm and the pole has gone again in a different place, and must be mended at once when rain stops. Tent not safe otherwise and might come down in night. No end of troubles and mishaps this trip. Kicked out of Geddasal Bungalow for D.F.O. Kicked out of Hassanur for Conservator, and now this, and Bailur Bungalow won't be ready till 15th at earliest.

It is curious what an idea these people have of the size of a tiger. None illustrate its height, walking, by placing the hand lower than the shoulder (of a man). One of the Foresters, Gorinda, who saw the tiger near camp a few days ago, illustrated its height, walking along, by putting his hand above the level of his own head – he is a man of about 5ft.4in. So he put his hand at about sixty eight inches and the biggest tiger of these parts would not stand higher than forty four inches. All the banyan trees are now fruiting, hence plenty of green pigeons about. Along hedge rows are growing small tomatoes, size of a cherry, very nice to eat; but the people don't eat them. Yet in Satyamangala Bazaar I saw quantities of same fruit for sale. One cooly has fever, gave him 10 gr. phenacetin.

10th. Went out to foot of hills. People chopping wood and clearing ground for teak plantation. Signs and track of elephants all the way, about eight cows and calves. Heard them squealing in bamboo cover. Met forester on his way out to see the work, and remarked on the uselessness of these forests from timber and bamboo point of view. 'Yes', he said, 'they are merely for wild beasts for gentlemen to shoot'! I told him there were very few wild beasts for anyone to shoot, now, as natives have killed them all off. H.G. went with Mr. Morris to stay till 15th at Honnametti.

14th. Tiger was around but didn't show at kill. Machan quite excellent. Track of a panther coming down towards nala. Bullock might be tackled by a panther, in which case I would shoot to save it – the bullock, not the panther!

Supplies here easy as to green vegetables and limes (latter 5as. for 36). Fowls difficult to get, also eggs. Milk very difficult, even forest officials, cannot get it; now servants are getting buffalo milk.

21st. No tiger and no sounds during the night. Have purchased peace from the rat by leaving the tin open for him to lick clean, which he does! Elephants quiet for several days now: gone elsewhere. Heard from Morris that Marriott has made a mess over the rogue elephants. He wounded and lost them both, and then Van Ingen and he shot a third, which is the WRONG one! In view of fact that its tusks turn out to be SEVEN FEET LONG; whereas one rogue had one tusk of two feet; the other rogue had two tusks of two and a half feet, Morris thinks they will be fined: also its forefeet are much bigger than the proscribed animals too!

23rd. Tiger was after sambur around the conical hill at 1 a.m, but never came near the nala crossing; I had all places smoothed to show the tracks. So now I must own defeat and leave this brute; after sleeping for him nine whole nights in machan, besides that one night over carcass of old cow. Packed kit, making ready for going on 27th. Had a sleepless night, what with the rats and the tiger.

Shikar now ended. All kit packed and gun and rifle put away. A poor trip: went wrong all along. Great mistake to have joined up with McArthy. Trip has not cost very much: 400/ – including pay of servants and motor lorry out and back, with stores used to pay for. Mrs. Mc.Arthy's account 62/8: Total including servants pay, two months, under 500/-.

A heavy thunderstorm in the night. Mr. and Mrs. R.C. Morris of Honnametti had very kindly arranged their visit to Kotagiri for 27th in order to give us a lift home. They came after 12 o/c, having been delayed by necessity to hire extra labour for plucking coffee berries. Little white faced gibbon an engaging and affectionate little animal and took to me at once. He is two years old, and won't leave Morris for long.

1

2

3

CHAPTER
29

5

Four miles from Bailur a forest road goes to left and down a less steep ghat than Dhirban. We went by it in order to see new country and lucky we did; as lorry was up to axle in mud for some miles on the Geddasal road. The lorry got to Coonoor 4.30; and the axle broke and right front wheel came off just at foot of steps leading up to Clovelly! Very fortunate it happened just there, after ninety two miles run, and not at some place along the road. It was an old flaw and nothing to do with our use of the vehicle.

4th March 1936. Left Coonoor 4 p.m. Bibby Line, *Cheshire*. Very small cabins. Disembarked at Tilbury on 27th March, and were met by Phyllis and her husband with their car. They drove us to Blackheath, where we stayed until 24th April when we went to Jersey. While in London fixed up with New Zealand Tourist Department for passage to New Zealand by S.S. *Tainui* of Shaw Savill Line on 27 March.

On 15th July left Sheerness and, after some hours in London, went with Tiny to Ivinghoe, for Whipsnade. Spent all next day at Whipsnade. 17th morning, up Ivinghoe Beacon, and afternoon again at Whipsnade. Will write up account of Park for Bo.N.H.S. Journal. On 18th returned to Euston, and took train from Paddington for Rhyadur, Radnorshire, South Wales. There we stayed until 27th, taking walks all over lovely country.

15th August to Scotland. Had a comfortable train journey; arrived Edinburgh 7 a.m. On 18th was driven to Perth; passed Linlithgow Palace, Falkirk, Stirling Castle. I last saw it in 1889 when went there from Maryhill Barracks, Glasgow, with XX Regiment cricket team. On 20th, a bus tour to Glen Affric, along Loch Ness, up Glen Urquhart. Saw Urquhart Castle, over into Strath Glass; then up Glen Affric, pretty stream, wooded hilly scenery, very like some places seen in Kashmir. By train to Aberdeen on 21st. Next day, motor tour up Dee Valley to Balmoral Castle, Invergeldie, Braemar. Had a walk, fine moorland and hilly country.

November 3rd to 27th. Stayed Blackheath. Then to Southampton and on board Shaw Savill *Tainui* for Panama, Pitcairn, New Zealand.

WAR
YEARS
AND
THE
MAN-EATER
OF
SEETAGUNDY
1938
TO
1948

Chapter 30

FISHING IN THE BHAVANI AND OTHER RIVERS

After their New Zealand, Fiji, Australia, tour, Burton and his wife arrived at Cochin on 26th May 1938. Next day they travelled to Coonoor and made arrangements to stay at a boarding house until they could find a bungalow to rent for 1939. During the summer, Burton, Coghlan, and Phythian Adams went fishing on the Mukerti Lake, but it always seemed to be raining. The fishing wasn't very good, and he decided in August to make another trip to the Bhavani.

DIARY

Went with Phythian Adams to his house and saw his three labrador pups, one black, one brown, one piebald! May take the black one. Nice to have a dog, but really no use to me from shooting point of view, as I so seldom go out nowadays: can't afford to.

13th August. I may have missed the best time for the Bhavani this year, no rain since 7th, however, hope for the best! Found the main path from the coffee estate Pulp House much overgrown by lantana and high grass in many places. A pity such a well made, and permanent ghat road allowed to be obliterated. Will write to Collector of Nilgiris about it. Got to Kundah at one o'clock, and after lunch crossed the river to Sundapatti hut. A new masonry hut close to river bank, not at all nice to stay in as so hot. Coolies very late coming in because I had mentioned going on to Koorapatti! Paid the men 8as. each and gave them the usual chewing tobacco.

16th. Cut some jamun branches at big pool so that I can fish from shore at one good place. Coracle man misses much good water. I can't talk and explain that fish lie mainly in certain places and these must all be carefully covered. It is so often that a fish comes at the second or third cast and often he gives no time for more than one hurried cast; very different to way I used to work Berthon boat in the Kistna and Deema Rivers. Post in; Queen Victoria rupee is rejected by all in the Valley! Same all over India I believe. Servant put out waterproof sheet as usual for line to be dried on; in half an hour white ants were at it.

19th. Small yellow and white terrier bitch, cropped ears, very friendly, had lunch with me; belongs to the village. Found a herd of cattle fording the river and swimming the pool so now know why, at this state of the river water, I get no fish there as in former years. Got hung up in Fall's pool and lost lead, trace, mount. Fished on and in the swirl near the big rock ran another fish which would probably have been hooked had the boat man given me any time at all. As it was we were on top of the fish as it went for the bait, and I saw it turn over, a big fish, 20–30lbs. Went down Grandfathers Run and almost first cast there took a 6lb. fish. So fish were all on the take for some reason I can't make out. No apparent change in the weather or conditions of the water. Told off the coracle man for growling and swearing under his breath. Because one can't talk to them these Tamil people are not well mannered.

20th. Evening. Fished the Main Run: no sign of fish and it began to rain. So those Falls Pool fish knew there would be a change of weather. Forgot to note about the white ants and waterproof sheet. This sheet is waterproofed by the 'Nilga' process of Baily Bros., Ooty. Because the white ants came to it so quickly outside the tent I had it put down inside the tent where they have not attacked other things. Within quarter of an hour they were at it! Must be some ingredient in the waterproofing which attracts them by its scent.

22nd. Monday. Rain last night and this morning and a great gale. Feared tent wouldn't stand it, but it did. I was up several times in the night to see to ropes. Bhavani won't be now fishable until Wednesday. Little dog returned at 5 p.m. and slept in my tent all night, and is still here. Boatman has carelessly let the bait tin be carried away in flood, so I have had to make another one.

23rd. A great scare in the early morning, 4 a.m. Small dog barking excitedly, then a stampede of a beast through servant's tent which came down on top of him, upsetting his bed and throwing him out the further side. Was sure it was a panther which had got the dog. A hole in the tent wall through which the beast had gone and out the other side. Mourned for the small dog and thought that my having fed it and let it stay at camp had been the cause of its death. In the morning saw no panther tracks, but everyone had been walking about. Searching about the Fish Watcher pointed out track of a pig! and just then back came the dog! So all is well and camp cooly is sewing up rents in the tent walls.

Evening. Up to Mug's Pool. Took 'Koora' (short for Koorapati!) with me. When I was half across the river in the coracle, she jumped into the water and swam across; water very swift and strong and I though she would be swept far down. Not a bit! When she met the crested waves she trod water and so got into the slack and landed quite easily, very pleased with herself. Took some minutes to catch her and tie my coat belt round her neck. Then we took her across and handed her over to Watcher and coracle cooly. Fished down: water very high and strong. No sign of fish moving, and so back to camp.

26th. River came down about three feet in the night, and won't be fishable for several days, so decided to move up to Seerakadaon. Started 8 a.m. next morning with ten coolies. As no one knows anything about striking tents I had to do most of it. Coracle man very slow in getting along so I had to wait more than half an hour at Varagaar crossing. 'Koora' wouldn't go in coracle, swam across. I felt none too well and had no doubt fever coming along. Got to camping place about 11.45. Coolies arrived about 12.15, and I pitched camp. All done and men paid off by 2 p.m. and I had to lie down – couldn't keep down anything in way of food; felt sure I had a go of Remittent Fever (seven day fever) and so it was. A bad night.

28th. Fever still with me. River going down and would be perfect for fishing next few days. Quite impossible for me to fish, as I am very weak on legs. On 31st, sent camp down to Sundapatti; started 8 a.m. in coracle. Nothing in Camp Pool or the run below, at which coracle man covered the water too fast. Took an 18lb. fish opposite village ghat; and a 9lb. fish long way further down; both on 'Victor' 7ft. rod as other too big for me. Got to Sundapatti 3 p.m. and paid off coolies. Arranged for a pony to take me up the ghat, as I couldn't, I am sure, have walked up. Met an elephant resting in shade. Coolies were much perturbed! My invalid presence gave them courage when I caught them up, so their dumped loads were resumed.

1st September. Thursday. Paid up Coracle (42/-); man (10/8); cook (7/14); and tips (1/-); (12); (8)). Parted with 'Koora' at the village. Had to walk nearly a mile before getting the pony which had strayed. A wearisome ride up to Coffee Estate at Taimalai; where I arrived about 2.30 p.m. Back to Coonoor on 2nd, tired.

1938 Bhavani Trip 13th August to 2nd September

Fished only eight days and two half days. Got eight fish. Had I been able to fish from 28th to end of week I would very likely have done well and got plenty of fish.

Cost of Trip

Licence	25	0	0	Bt.fwrd.	198	6	0
Cars	42	0	0				
Tips, watchers	15	0	0	Servant	20	0	0
Coracle	42	0	0	Charity etc.	1	0	0
Man	10	8	0	Pony	4	0	0
Cook	7	12	0				
Tips	2	4	0	Stores			
Wood & w. cooly	9	0	0	3 butter 3/6			
Coolies	36	8	0	1Cy. Pr. 7/9			
Post Coolie	5	0	0	Salt 12/6			
Ragi	1	8	0	Sugar (3)	9	9	0
Fowls	1	14	0	Tea (11)			
				Marmite 1/9/6			
				Klim 2/4			
	198	6	0	Jam (12)			
				Bazaar	6	14	0
				Tobacco	2	0	0
				Veg.	2	9	0
				Total	245	0	0

for twenty days. Deduct 60 off Clovelly bill = 185. Rs.9/- a day, near as may be; say 10/- with all expenses in.

Looked up in Moore's Family Medicine – Remittent Fever: 'If taken in time may not prove fatal'! It can of course, be a very dangerous fever with complications and I am apparently well out of it.

20th September. Recovered from fever and now walk as before. Up to Coonoor Peak today in forty five minutes and down in thirty. Wrote Chief Marine Officer, Madras, for permit to pitch tent in Kaup Lighthouse compound. Post Officer, Mangalore, referred me to him instead of giving me sanction as Mudie did in 1935. Red tape! took nearly a month to get a reply.

Miss Marjoribanks very curious in manner since I told her we would leave Clovelly on 23rd November. Annoyed we don't stay to end of the year I suppose. We have stayed nearly six months and quite long enough! Never again, I hope. More rain all this year than I ever recollect before.

To Mettuppalaiyam by car and took the train for Mangalore, changing at Calicut. At Mangalore station collected the kit, all in one car! and to P.W.D. rest house at Kadra. Electric light, one anna per hour in slot. No linen, cooking pots, some furniture and a wire bed. Next day on to Kaup, crossing three ferries 1/8 each.

At Kaup, Burton and his wife were pleased to find the lighthouse keeper who had been there when they came last. He supplied them with eggs and firewood and lent them an easy chair and some useful boxes. The 5th November, Burton's 70th birthday, was spent confined to the tent which they had set up in the lighthouse compound. The gale which had blown up shortly after their arrival looked set to last another five days. The north-east monsoon was late and in this part of India the weather cannot be counted on from mid June to mid November. It wasn't until 16th November that Burton was able to take the boat out fishing. One of the fishermen's boats had caught a small dolphin, and these, when taken, are shared with the community and are not the property of the boat which makes the catch.

DIARY

16th. Went out in boat to the rocks. Half a mile out got a 10lb. kandai (garfish) nothing else until 11 o/c when got a mooloomeen, 28lbs, a great fighter. Lighthouse Keepers pleased to have fish; they selected the gar saying the other 'too tough'. It looks it! Mooloo are ugly fish, no big teeth, only file like patches of tiny teeth in places in lower and upper lips. Very heavy dew at night since Sunday. Old servant now has fever!

17th. Kaup. Very little wind, very hot sun, hottest yet. No sign of fish, not a single run of the reel. On way back, saw seer fish leaping out of the water in smother of spray and found the sea with dark patches, like reflections of clouds although the sky was clear, and these were large shoals of mackerel. A good many sandflies bit my legs yesterday evening, khaki cotton stockings too thin. Legs into a pillowcase!

I didn't feel too fit in evening and was running a temperature. Concluded it must be a return of the remittent fever, and took 15 grains quinine and a dose of camphorodyne. On 19th, packed fishing tackle. See that the Alcock sea rod has taken a bend where the tip goes into the cork. This because of the 28lb. mooloo! A poor rod; badly designed. My own Rans tip which I made in 1935 to use with butt of greenheart mahseer rod, a much better affair.

20th. Packed kit, tents, and paid up boatmen. Cost of this 'dud' trip – 262/9/0. 12/8 a day. Less 5/- a day which I would have paid at Clovelly = 7/8 a day for the trip.

Three days after returning to Coonoor from Mangalore, Hilda left by train to stay with her daughter Phyllis, who was living at Jhansi, while Burton went to stay with some friends who lived on Estates in the area around Lake Peryar.

DIARY

23rd November. Arrived Madura 10.10, where Vincent's car met me and took me to Thekadi, ninety seven miles. Madura streets and suburbs thronged with people on account of Ramzan. Much dirt, untidiness and squalor. Passed over roaring rapid of Peryar Lake water going to plains for irrigation. At Thekady into Vincent's launch which took me to Salt Creek. Walked up the path and was met halfway by Vincent at the place where are ruins of a former temple. Met by Miss Vincent at the house, a warm and kindly welcome. They now have bathroom and bath, walls beautifully tiled, and h.& c. water basin – most luxurious. A good deal done during past four years to improve house and surroundings, and water supply. The estate is five hundred acres now, all planted up, and cardamoms doing well. Vincent had a debt of seven and a half lacs during the slump and is now paying it off and will be clear in two and a half years. He has three estates of his own – cardamom, tea, rubber and large share in another rubber estate, and interests in others.

One evening Vincent and I went over the hill and a mile along the path to Pambyar River. Found many tracks of bison. A young bull elephant came from forest other side of the hill, going at a great pace; 'Spot' barked, and he turned and went away. Daily Miss Vincent sees a meal given to about forty children, under seven years of age. All look fat and well and very different to how they used to be. Evidently the parents are just on the border line and unable to give full feed to their children. NO malaria now, marvellous. This due to treating of streams and spraying of houses. Both Vincent and his sister have a full day's work, he looking after Estate and she after house and garden, and Estate children.

On 9th December, after a delightful stay of fifteen days! I left to walk to the launch, 'Spot' with me. Crossing the lake in one and a half hours I found Coghlan waiting for me at Thekady. We had tea and went off to Moongalaar to be warmly greeted by Molly Coghlan and old bull terrier 'Mick' now over ten years old. Walked all over the Estate with Coghlan and learnt a lot about tea pruning, as I had of cardamom. Herd of elephants in the valley often causes trouble; the animals walk nightly among the tea and do some damage. A short time ago a man in a tree dropped a cracker on an elephant's back to frighten it away from his crop, and on getting down from tree some time later was caught by the elephant and killed. Travancore Government on being asked to proclaim the animal, said it was the fault of the man – which cannot be denied!

Stayed until 14th with Coghlans and then Mrs. Gibbon came for me and took me to Tungamullay Estate. House being fitted with electric light. Already they have 'pull the plug' sanitation so will now be very up to date. House close to jungles: elephants visit the tea, panthers roam about, and tiger killed fifteen cattle one night a year or so ago.

On 18th, drove to Cochin and to Malabar Hotel. Leonard came to see me and I went to dine with them in the evening. Was astonished at amount of liquor they put away! I suppose that enervating climate is the cause. I would never drink like that. Probably it is liquid and not liquor which they really want. Liquor no doubt nicer!

19th December. Said farewell to Vincent at Hotel and took the 6.30 p.m. train for Mettuppalaiyam, arriving there 6.15 next day. On 1st January moved into 'St. Hilda's', rented for two years.

Having settled in at Coonoor, arrangements were soon made to go again to the Bhavani. This was to be the last trip to his favourite fishing haunt, although he didn't realise this at the time. The declaration of War on 3rd September 1939, meant that it was no longer possible to move easily about the country and this, plus the fact that both he and his wife were getting older, meant that his hunting and shooting trips were to become less frequent.

DIARY ————————————————————————————————
South West Monsoon much more than usual this year. All arrangements made to go to Bhavani river tomorrow, 21st August. Hope for a better trip than last time. Will take 'Flit' to keep tents clear of mosquitoes in evening.

21st August. Monday. Left Coonoor with the prospect of a World War breaking out any day during next three weeks. Stopped in bazaar for Sivalingam the Mettup-palaiyam coracle man who came yesterday in hopes of being taken on. I had arranged with Fisheries Department to have use of Government coracle and watchers, but Sivalingam wrote to say the watchers could not work the coracle properly and could not catch small fish for me. I wrote and told him I would send for him if needed. Now he has turned up! Gave him 5/- for supplies. The lorry was a very bone shaking affair. Got to Pulp House 10.15, and found coolies and watchers ready. At Kundah River coracle took kit and man across while I had lunch; Kundah in flood.

23rd. The coracle was not well made, too spread out, so Sivalingam took it to pieces and made a good job of it. Just as well I have him with me! People of the lower valley look thin and complain of 'no food'. Told Moopan of Koorapatti I would write to Collector of Malabar, Calicut.

24th. River fast going down. Fished below Camp Pool; one fish of 10lbs, this fish tore off second half of the bait, mounting must have been very bad. Have made another half and coloured it with iodine, ink, and varnish and it looks quite good! I have started making these baits which are expensive, Rs.42 each! and am mounting with one piece of wire passed end to end.

26th. Fish in this river seem to be getting less numerous each year: saw hornbills, and big blue kingfisher. Evening, fished down; in broken water above long deep pool ending at Village rock, struck a big fish which tore down stream quite 150 yards before stopping. Raced after him and eventually found line tight under some roots on left bank, just fifty yards of line out below that. Sivalingam dived with hand on line and released it. Fish went another hundred yards down stream and at last began to get on terms with him. Gaffed at 6 o/c. Hooked about 5 o/c. 41lbs. Spring balance 40 only; it was just more than that, and measurements check it correctly. Lucky to get this fish: it was very lightly hooked in roof of mouth and hooks not beyond the barb and came away at once.

30th. Sent off camp to Koorapatti. Started in coracle at 8.30. In Varagaar Pool at tail end, a fish 2lbs or so took the bait idly trolling close to the coracle. Let the boatman keep it for his curry. No sign of fish anywhere; not even among the boulders in shallow water. Forgot to note that remainder of the huge tree, half of which fell across Varagaar junction, has now fallen across and the outfall now completely blocked, and will remain so for very many years. No Varagaar flood can shift the huge trunk.

2nd September. Started at Mug's pool at 9 a.m. Thought of last time I started there when small 'Koora' swam the river. No sign of fish, not even little ones. Hooked a small mahseer 1½lb, in Temple pool, and put it back to disgust of Sivalingam. In the shallow water above first rapid saw a shoal of small mahseer; opposite camp a few small fish seen for the first time. Never before has the river been so devoid of life.

4th. Got letters yesterday evening. Foreign Mail news of 20–23 August and news of German Soviet Non-Aggression Pact about to be signed. That is what I have said all along: 'If we don't quickly conclude defensive alliance with Russia; Hitler will be gaining them over to his side.' And now this has come about, many changes in world politics may arise. Possibly whole world is even now at war!

Sent camp to Sundapatti. Started 8 a.m. and fished down. Nothing until about halfway, and there, in a place where I always hoped for a fish and never yet took one, got a 13lb mahseer. It took the bait by the tail as evidenced by the treble hook stuck in its lip and flattened. Can't understand how men like A. Macdonald, with experience, can have any doubt as to how mahseer flatten trebles, and spoons too on occasion. It happens when they get a 'square' grip at moment of seizing the bait.

6th. Up to Koorapatti. 7 a.m. Fished down and hooked one good fish. It ran up into the heavy water and there got snagged. Had to break away; lost eight yards line, trace, lead, mount. Many tackle losses this trip. On way back to camp saw two muggers. Packed kit and struck tents.

8th. On the whole a very poor trip. Have written fully to Inspector of Fisheries to say river seems to be deteriorating. On way up ghat saw a herd of bison, cows and calves, about a dozen animals. Coolies very pleased at 14as. annas each! and should be, plus tobacco.

Found War started on 3rd September. Likely to last three to four years. Anglo-Soviet Military Staff talks broke down because Russians wanted to send their troops through Poland and Poles wouldn't agree to this. Hitler has got the non-aggression pact with Russia which we should have had: but it may not make very much difference. Italy and all other countries, including Japan, have declared themselves neutral. Remains to be seen whether any of them come in for or against us, later on. If not, then the struggle is between England with France and Poland against Germany. We will win because of economic advantage and command of the seas; also because much dissatisfaction beneath the surface in Germany.

Have cancelled my trip to West Coast. Don't feel like going fishing and spending unnecessarily at this time. May go into camp if I find it won't be more expensive than living in Coonoor. Phyllis and family stay in Scotland.

Cost of Bhavani trip. Seventh trip – twenty days. Rs.214/4/9.

On 23rd December 1939 left for Erode Railway Rest House; and next morning went on to Hogainakkal. There found Brig. & Mrs. G.S. Palmer (Raichur days) installed in Forest Rest House, the D.B. being a mere native choultry and full of Indians. As no cooking pots etc. in the F.R.H., only tables and chairs and iron beds, the Palmers had been through a rough time. No plates, knives, forks, they had fed with fingers off bits of paper! Nothing in which to boil water, cook, make tea. Our tiffin box fitted for four people and provisions we brought hailed with glee. Even so we didn't fare too well. Got another iron bed from the choultry for wife, and I slept three nights in a chair. Fishing not much use, water too coloured. Falls not much of a spectacle, being confined between basaltic rocks in middle of river. I would not care to make a trip to fish and shoot at Hogainakkal. Very hot and the fishing not exciting, mostly sitting still with a bait in the water.

During this tour, car no trouble of any kind, except for the 'whistling' of the fan belt pump which I was warned to expect. Lucky I was told of this as it would otherwise have been rather alarming. It was as loud as a not too distant railway engine, which indeed we thought it was as we had just then come to a railway line. Down with fever, no doubt contracted at Hogainakkal. Cured it with Atebrin and Plassinogirin. Afterwards I was told that the latter a very dangerous drug which could affect the heart. Anyhow, the attack was killed.

At the beginning of January, Burton and his wife decided to move to Bangalore. They were able to exchange houses with an acquaintance who wished to move to Coonoor, and made arrangements for their kit and possessions to go by lorry, which was cheaper than sending it by rail. They took over some of the furniture which was already there, including two hundred and eight pots and plants! Burton later took a permanent home in Bangalore, and they stayed there until they left India in 1957 to return to England.

There was less opportunity now for long hunting and fishing trips, but one had been planned to an orange and coffee Estate in Wynaad, and Burton was loath to cancel this.

DIARY ——————————————————————————————————————

When passing through Cochin in December 1938, I met D.G. Leonard and his wife and heard from him of A.E. Lobb, a planter at Kartikolam, having caught – on paste – a 110lb mahseer in the Kabani River. Through Leonard I got into touch with Lobb; and in January 1940 took the opportunity on way to Bangalore, to look him up. Result of that short acquaintance was that I had a coracle skin made at Mettuppalaiyam and it was sent to Lobb by bus, with a man to build the basket work. Total cost to me Rs.30/-. Coracle completed and with Lobb for his use, that of his friends, and me when I go there.

Fishing Licence for Wynaad, Rs.5/- per annum. Shooting Rs.10/- and Rs.20 deposit – returnable. Bison and chital in forests around Lobb, also tiger and panther. February to June, elephants raid the Estate and can be shot if they do. Probably January would be good month for fishing and February, March to April for shooting. Lobb mentions having often caught mahseer, JET BLACK, dark red tail and fins.

ARMS LICENCE – A whole month to have it endorsed by Comm. Police, Bangalore for .500 Rifle. Another whole month to get reply from Calicut that endorsement for Malabar should be made by Comm. Police. Another whole month to get it eventually endorsed by Calicut! So, at last, 9th June; all set for an attempt to go Wynaad NEXT YEAR!

SHORT STEEL CASTING RODS and PLUG BAITS. Such an outfit, with Norka Reel taking 150 yds 15lb line would be a great asset for river banks overhung with vegetation, and for use in coracle at times. But I feel I don't get about so much now as to justify more acquisition of rod and tackle. Four and a half inch extra wide silex, spinning reel purchased from Hardy's £5.15.0. not sent owing to war, and is with Phyl to await a favourable opportunity should someone be coming out to India.

Burton had only one fishing trip to the East Coast near Nellore in September 1940. He went with three others, but found that he didn't care for 'party' fishing. The East Coast fishing couldn't compare with river fishing, nor even with the West Coast. The boatmen were undisciplined and unpunctual, in fact he considered them totally useless and felt it unlikely that he would return to this particular place. Total cost of the trip to each of three was just 100/-.

Chapter 31

A PANTHER AND A TIGER — WYNAAD ESTATE

DIARY

December 1940. To Wynaad for an outing. After much trouble, I obtained an Orange lorry, returning empty to Manantoddy, to take along all camp kit, and tents. Arranged for Rs.60, one hundred and fifty miles to bungalow of A.E. Lobb, Manager of an Orange and Coffee Estate, near Kartikolam, seven miles from Manantoddy.

23rd. All day at putting camp to rights. None of the three men know anything at all about tents and camp life. I have to do everything. One evening drove to Bhavali and up the new road into forest. Splendid jungle, and holds much game, but a swampy valley and would be very feverish just now. Much planting of teak is being done, acres of it every year, the bamboo and other forest being cleared away; so the teak forests around here should be valuable in about fifty years time. All is planted from germinated seed and in three years saplings are about nine feet high.

28th. Went fishing. Tried one hundred and fifty yards below the first big pool. Hooked and played a big fish. He went up stream, got among rocks and had difficulty getting him away from them; turned him down stream, great pressure kept him from going further down; showed tail above water, head boring to the bottom. Alas! he got off. Hook had not penetrated beyond barb, and I can't think why hook came away, no slack line. He was round about 60–70lbs, so Lobb thought and I also. I WAS TOO HARD ON HIM.

4th January 1941. Too cold now for spinning. No fish of any kind moving in the river. On 12th, shot a jungle cock on cart road to river. The first shot fired since February 1936. Have seen several racquet tailed drongos, and some scarlet minivets. Never saw more dense forest and grass than there is near there. Saw innumerable tracks of elephant, bison, sambur.

16th. I am not too confident that the Kurumbus are doing their work properly. From all I hear, they are very untrustworthy. Labour here very difficult. The Estate coolies do no work on Sundays and Mondays, and the Kurumbus won't work on Wednesdays! Labour Minister was at Kartikolam some time ago and had a meeting, and told the coolies not to work for less than 6 annas a day. Accepted wage is 5as., and after a short strike the people began to receive 5as. as before.

News of the buff having been killed by a panther. Into machan by 3.45. A good deal of the buff eaten. The men said very little was eaten when they left it, and COVERED IT UP. I think all they did was put one small branch over the part broken into. Fortunately scarcely any vultures in Wynaad. The panthers, two as it turned out, must have had a good feed after the men left. At 6.10 monkeys showed panther on move and by the 'swears' it came close to path and probably had a look to see if carcass still there. Nothing after that until Lobb came with lantern at eight o'clock. Told him to return to camp and I would stay all night: and an interesting night it was.

Moon rose about 9 o/c and shortly before that male panther came growling along from behind. I had seen by small tooth holes in throat and scratches in shoulders that the kill was probably by a small female. Lobb tells me that most of the Wynaad panthers hunt as a pair and that kill is usually by the female. Much growling and grumbling went on. After some time I heard eating at the kill and in the light of the torch saw a small panther. He dragged the hind quarters into a shady patch and was lying down, sideways to me. I put the light on to him and aimed at shoulder. Again forgot the 200yd leaf, as this is first time of using this rifle except for a few trial shots. It shoots about seven inches low at twenty yards if leaf not raised, and bullet struck three inches lower than intended. To the shot, after a short pause accounted for by a temporary 'knock out', the panther rushed off into tussocky grass of the 'park'.

In the morning looked for the male. Marri and Sobha tracked well, and we found it ninety yards behind machan. Shoulder smashed to pieces, several holes where bits of bone had been blown out. Seeing how the bullet had broken up on this small beast – 92lbs, though old and full size (Wynaad panthers all like this – dark, stocky, small, says Lobb) – I conclude this bullet made for the 'modified' cordite cartridges, is of some alloy mixture which makes it too brittle. Not at all like the solid soft lead bullet of the black powder cartridges. Not fair to the tiger, or myself, or the people working in the forest, and the forest villagers. I must get a .470 from Tibbets Aylmer, or give up idea of a tiger this trip.

18th. Petrol a difficulty here now. The pump at Manantoddy has been shut down, and sealed tins have to be got from Tellicherry: a great nuisance. Cook has fever, am giving him plenty of quinine, 10 gr. last night, 10 gr. this morning, 15 gr. tonight and again tomorrow morning; and hope he won't have much fever on Sunday. Vincent tells me of new drug – M & B 760 called Proseptacine; the troops, before going into action have an anti-tetanus injection which lasts them for several years, and also have this M & B 125 by which they are guarded against gangrene; and quite serious flesh wounds need only to be bound up and will heal. Another drug M & B 760 protects from pneumonia. Marvellous: everyone going into jungles should now have this protection.

Found a tiger had come night of 17th and dragged away the kill. Followed the drag and found the kill against a patch of lantana. Tiger not at home. Tibbets Aylmer came in the evening he has been made Game Warden and has the use of two elephants once a week, on Sundays. He left his 450/400 H.V. with me. I tried it by day at twenty yards with 200yd leaf and radium sight; also with torch after dark, both O.K. and he will bring me a .470 S.B. tomorrow. Now I feel sure of tiger, if he returns. He may be very cunning and wary. Quite possibly shot at and may have been hit some time or other. Many have tried for him. If he does not return to kill I may have to do a week's vigil as I have done on other occasions with success.

29th. A letter from Phythian Adams asking if he may put me forward for his 'welfare' job if he gets a 'lift up'. Wrote to say O.K. I would be a Major, and net pay about 1300 p.m., ex pension, which would lapse while holding the appointment. Doubt if I will be accepted. Age – seventy two, and no South Indian vernacular language. Lovely reflections in the river in the evening, forest trees of varying foliage and rushes.

1st February. Did what I should have done yesterday and had the kill dragged down just clear of the cover and put up chair in the big tree. Found last night's tracks of the tiger going up nala to the kill and up into the grass jungle where I had heard him: fear he won't return again. This is a very 'educated' tiger. He MAY detect I am in machan if he is cautious and scents all round before killing. He certainly cannot spot the machan and I must 'thorn' all round the foot of the tree each time I sit up. This tiger I am after is a notorious one, known to whole of Wynaad. Trip to Kaimaram off.

Next morning there were no tracks seen, and no sound of tiger during the night, so it had obviously moved on. Burton judged the tiger's circuit to be about ten days, so the only thing to do was to wait for eight days when the tiger might return and kill again. Burton spent some time fishing, but there was no sign of any fish little or big, so the fishing part of the trip was considered a failure.

DIARY _____

10th. To machan and settled in at five o'clock. A fine woodpecker, red crest, yellow on chest, came on to next tree and I had good look at him with glasses. Just at dark a flying squirrel ran up same tree and I watched him until he did a parachute to another tree. No alarm calls of sambur or chital and I had just decided to go to sleep, when came the swear of a tiger some twenty yards to right. I didn't dare to move the branch of leaves screening my loophole. After this 'swear', not a sound for one hour then there was the usual short rush and an unusually small choked sound from the buffalo. I instantly loaded the rifle, put aside the bunch of leaves and put on torch. The tiger lay square on to me, with one fore arm over the buff's neck, before its horn, and looking about, very alert, to his right. He didn't notice the light; it was nearly full moon. I aimed at centre of massive shoulder, a little high, for the plunging shot. Tiger instantly dead, saw his tail whack the ground a few times, the fatal sign. His forearm stayed as put, his head fell forward, he was killed. No other sounds during night, except one sambur which evidently scented the tiger.

Men came at 7.30 as usual. Sent driver to bring the car, a moplah skinner, some salt and scales. Car came back about 10.30. When separating the tiger from buffalo found that his opening and closing jaws had closed in death grip on the buffalo's nose, so it had to be cut off to enable the tiger to be dragged a few yards into shade for skinning. Removal of skin from body, leaving head and four paws, took two hours. The weighing took some time too, as carcass had to be cut up. Total – 415 lbs.

Paid Sobha and Marri, 15/- plus 2/- for the panther. So the rewards cover cost of kills. 40/- plus 12/- = 52/-: less 17/- = 35/- and a little over.

Decided to take the skin in car to Theobald at Mysore, but nearly four o'clock when I actually started. Now came a very lucky thing. Met the water cart on the estate road and stopped, and when tried to start again found the clutch cable broken! It had evidently worn through to very last strand of wire and might have parted any moment in the last forty eight hours. It might not have parted until we were some miles on way to Mysore; it might have parted on way to machan, and then no tiger; it might have parted coming away, or half way to Manantoddy – any hopeless place. Luck was with me and it parted half a mile from camp! I mended it by splicing a piece of tiger wire to it, and by passing end through a bit of a devon minnow and soldering it. Too late to go to Mysore, so had to skin head and paws – high time too! Head already smelling, made a 10% solution, carbolic acid and soaked this into hair side of skin of head. I ought to have just skinned the head at 2 p.m. and rubbed in alum and salt as usual. Theobald had written to rub salt only, but find on asking him, that he didn't mean to exclude alum.

To Mysore and back next day. Theobald says the skin will be all right; but didn't seem to try and test it: better not perhaps. Theobald gave me lunch and helped wash out

Seetagundy ESTATE
Sitharkunda P.O.
24th March, 19 47.

Lt. Col. R. W. Burton,(Indian Army Retired),
   3, Longford Jones Gardens, Bangalore.

Dear Sir,
        I have been directed by my Association to for-
-ward copies of Resolutions passed at a Meeting of this
Association held on the 27th February 1947 :-

Resolution No. 4.

    " It was unanimously resolved to place on record this
Association's high appreciation of Lt. Col. Burton's ex-
-tremely humanitarian motives which prompted him to under-
-take such a dangerous expedition with considerable incon-
-venience to Mrs. Burton and himself at their present old
age and unbounded gratitude to Lt. Col. R. W. Burton for
the immense sacrifice of his personal comforts and for the
indefatigable efforts he so cheerfully took in the matter
of hunting down the man-eater, who was a great terror to
the population in the whole district, to death.
        It was also resolved to present him with a suitable
souvenir towards the cost of which Mr. A. T. Rajam I.C.S.
Retd., Director of Chandramalai Estates promised to pay a
sum of Rs 100/- and Lt. Col. Arachard of Manalaroo Estate
promised to address his principals on the matter and get
a contribution from them. "
        I also take this opportunity to send you a
cheque on the Imperial Bank of India, Madras for a sum of
Rs 150/- (Rs 100/- from Mr. A.T.Rajam Esq., I.C.S.,(Retd)
and Rs 50/- from Manalaroo Estate) towards a souvenir
which you may purchase as you like best.

        Kindly acknowledge receipt of the cheque.

                    Yours faithfully,

                        Hon: Sec.,
                    Nel: Planters' Assn.
Encl: 1 Cheque.

THE PALACE.
MYSORE.

September 22, 1952.

My dear Colonel Burton,

I thank you for your letter of the 9th September 1952.
    I trust the lay-out will have reached you by now. As
suggested, a copy of the book prior to the final work of the
Press, may be sent to Shri G.S.Bajpai for purposes of writing
the Foreword. Expenditure on this account could be admitted
and will be paid by me.
    The distribution of the copies, when ready, could be
attended to at your end: I shall be glad to receive a bill
containing list of persons and institutions (indicating the
number of copies against each) to whom the copies of your work
have been sent.
    I shall be glad to meet you here any time convenient to
you, after the 29th September, so that we may have mutual discussion
on several matters concerning this subject and also to enable
me to avail myself of your vast and varied knowledge and
experience concerning Nature and its protection.
    Yes, I intend visiting East Africa, Belgian Congo & Angola,
and will be leaving India by the first week of December 1952: it
will be about 3/4 months before I return to Mysore.
    With regards,

                        Yours sincerely,
                        Jaya Chamaraja Wadiyar

Lt.Col. R.W. Burton,
The Bangalore Club,
Bangalore -1

I

CHAPTERS
30/32

1
Irala women and children,
Seerakadavu

2
Coracle shooting the rapids on
the Bhavani river

3
Irulas, 1939

4
Junction pool of the Bhavani
and Varagaar rivers

the car. Back to camp, and packed all my kit by sundown, a lovely RED moon. On 13th struck tents; lunched and dined at Lobb's and slept in verandah.

Total cost of trip: Rs.554/- about Rs.250/- p.m. I feel guilty in my mind as to this trip. I should not have gone and the money should have been applied to War. I scarcely realised the expense it would be.

At Bangalore. 22nd February. The clutch wire repair still O.K., waiting for a spare part to be got from Madras or Bombay. Theobald writes that skin appears certain to be all right, will know when the curing is completed. Have advertised gun and rifle for sale in Station Orders, and if sold will buy D.B. .470 of Packard, Norfolk, for sale at Bartons for 350/-. It is in good order, and quite new inside bore.

October. Not a word yet from Theobald's, taxidermists, as to the tiger skin being ready! Eight whole months gone. I haven't written him as no cash to pay his bill!

5th November. Since Wynaad outing have not done any fishing or shikar. No funds.

The tiger skin was raffled in Victoria Shoppe, South Parade, during July 1942. Rs.200 to War Fund, Rs.90/- to me, cost of curing the skin.

1.1.43. No use making War forecasts: I hope I am more sensible than many who are now BETTING that it will be over by July! Not much use thinking of going to Kaimaram now; War demands so much timber cutting in all forests.

27th April 1943. GUYUD ESTATE – Ochterlory Valley, Nilgiris. Left Bangalore 8.25 a.m., taking with us Betty Lobb aged five, daughter of Mr. and Mrs. Lobb, to go to Guyud for two months for change of air. Betty met us at City Station brought by Children's Matron (Miss Pyne) from Bishop Cotton's Girls' School. Arrived Mysore City 12.30 and met by Mrs. Lobb with their Austin 8 car, made all the heavy luggage over to the Bus Company. Got to Gudalur in the evening and up to Guyud without mishap. Bedding and our suitcases with us.

Ochterlory Valley used to have a bad reputation for malaria, now the upper portions at any rate are fairly clear: no mosquito nets used at Guyud. My two fox terriers, Ben and Jock, had great fun hunting all day and every day all over the Coffee Estates and in the jungle. Lucky they were not annexed by a panther, but all the time we were there, no panther about; as known by the fact that none of the many cooly line pi dogs were killed. Dogs were pretty well on starvation diet; no bones, no meat, just rice! They kept very lively, if a bit thin, and no doubt most domestic dogs, and their owners, have too much to eat.

Lobb tells me that when Bowring died in 1941, he left him his Fishing Diaries, and that he made these over at suggestion of Bowring's son, to G.O.C. Bangalore. I think Lobb should have attached some conditions to loan of the Diary; now it may be hard to get hold of it again. In spite of much effort it remains untraced. It may have been devoured by white ants; as was, I hear, much of Bowring's kit; a pity – record of thirty years gone. Among other things in it, says Lobb, was a Red Ink entry of a big mahseer, over 100lbs, being hooked and again, while being played a long way off, took bait of another angler fishing in the same pool, and so, hooked by both, was played by both. Which landed the fish is not known.

Some time after we left, a panther was about and Lobb lost his black labrador and a number of cooly line dogs disappeared also. That Ochterlory Valley is well known for black panthers, due no doubt, to the heavy evergreen jungles which clothe the slopes of the hills. The tigers too, are dark, though not black, as I saw from a skin of one shot by Lobb's game watcher before we went there. The man was watching, perched in a tree, for pig and sambur. After dusk he saw, a large animal coming along the path, fired his buck shot twelve-bore cartridge at it, and the animal went on. After a proper (?) interval he followed after and found a big tiger dead; but he didn't wait to see how much dead and fled for the cooly lines five hundred yards away. A male, about 9ft. deep black stripes, rich dark orange coat; a lovely skin.

In the early days of Planting, the whole of the Valley was leased on a nominal rent in perpetuity by the Raja of Nilambur to Sir David Ochterlory At that time proper shading for coffee was not understood and all the grevillea trees were allowed to grow to maturity; so now 1943, they are useless as shade and are being girdled to kill and cut out. Much damage is done to the coffee by the falling dead branches and trunks. At the time the coffee was in flower and a very pretty sight it was, also a cloying scent, this augured a good crop for the 1943 season; but owing to want of cooly labour, a good deal was not gathered. A scarlet erythrina, used as a shade tree, is conspicuous here and there. There were no fish of any size in any of the pools of the stream roaring down from the higher hills; and few sambur in the Valley. Now all the estates, tea and coffee, are owned and run by the Company, which makes about 30% profit yearly. Men of drive and capacity in business and control of labour, do well as Planters – tea, coffee, cardamom, rubber, oranges.

I left the writing up of this diary for a long time, and now, March 30th 1944, having a rest of two days from the making of rod, do this and a number of other things which have been neglected. I tied up for tiger for about a month with no result, until rain and a widespread cyclone came along which lasted several weeks. I went out two or three times in the early morning in the hopes of seeing sambur, pig or perhaps tiger, but never heard or saw any animal. Bird life was fairly plentiful; there were hill grackles nesting in holes in the trunks of grevillea trees. All along the road near the stream, the gadflies 'bit' savagely; a real pest, and no wonder the tiger did a non-stop journey to the higher hills and grassy open downs. Returned Bangalore 5/6th June. Luggage took nearly three weeks in transit due to Hill Exodus.

18th February 1946. Not been anywhere out of Bangalore since April/May 1943: no shikar, no fishing. Now the War is over one feels one can go on jaunts, but the food shortage all over the country is almost a complete bar to any outings; also difficulty as to transport would be great. Car can't be used as petrol is rationed; 16 gals. a quarter, about thirty two miles a week. Doubt if the petrol restriction will be lifted for another twelve months. I could get away in car, with wife, for ten days or so; but that also very difficult on account of all the robberies and theft going on all over the Station. Not safe to leave one's house at this time: also wife can't be left alone, must have someone with her if I go away, even for a few days. What a life! No sort of a life at all.

SEA ROD – not yet made. Have a piece of greenheart which may answer; but not much chance of using big game reel and rod, or indeed, any reel or rod!

5.11.1946. Still at Bangalore. Age seventy eight: well and hearty, but having a very dull life with little hope of any shikar. Only way to get out is to lock up house and leave present Mali, a trustworthy man I think, in charge – with a Police guaranteed Chokidar to help him. That way we could go away for a month at a time; but it wouldn't free me to do such jaunts as a trip to Bhavani, down Tungabadra, or to Mysore Forests, or North Kanara Forests, or to Central Provinces! I fear not a hope of anything at all of all these dreams.

I have been busy for several months putting together a 'Brochure' on 'Big Game Hunting in India', for Government of India, but have yet to hear that I am to go ahead and send in the typescript. Just as well, as a lot of material yet to fill in, and not done on account of delay in hearing from various officials.

From time to time, Burton was asked by the BNHSJ to review books on Big Game Hunting or similar subjects. One of these, which was published in 1945 was Jim Corbett's 'Man-eaters of Kumaon'. Burton's Review was polite. He acknowledges Corbett's skill with a gun, his bravery, and his unusual ability to imitate with accuracy the call of the tiger, and many other animals. The pencilled notes made while compiling his Review, however, show that he considered Corbett either extremely foolish, or inaccurate, or not well informed about wildlife in general.

He writes – 'In my Review I omitted some things that could have been commented upon, but felt it was not my business to call in question the foolish actions of the Author, or his veracity, especially in view of the distinguished sponsors of the book in the Introduction.' Corbett's practice of taking only three bullets with him when out after a tiger drew Burton's comment 'foolish!'; and on another occasion while waiting in a tree for a tiger, Corbett writes that he had tied his rifle securely to a branch – Burton's comment was 'so that in case of emergency it could not be used!' In another scene from the book Corbett puts himself into such a position that 'he could not direct the aim on to the oncoming tigress but had to hope that the animal would herself oblige him by coming into the prepared line of fire!'

These pencilled comments and other remarks indicate Burton's opinion, and other big game hunters amongst his contemporaries shared his views. When the B.N.H.S. Journal asked him to Review another book of Corbett's a few years later, he declined as he felt he could find nothing to say in its favour. Corbett's books were written from memory, and perhaps this obscured the facts, but to someone like Burton this inaccuracy was unacceptable.

There were men, like Dunbar Brander, Stuart Baker, and E.P. Gee, who wrote knowledgeable books about Wildlife in India. A. St.J. Macdonald's book on fishing – 'Circumventing the mahseer' was regarded as a classic. There was one other who helped especially to further the cause of wildlife preservation; F. Champion, a pioneer of wildlife photography in India. His two books 'With a Camera in Tiger land', and 'The Jungle in Sunlight and Shadow' were both enthusiastically reviewed for the BNHSJ by Colonel Burton.

The country of the Wynaad was well known to Colonel Burton's father. Perhaps Burton remembered reading the following extracts from his father's book. In any event, after his travels in Burma in 1930 and the Peryar fishing expeditions, jungle leeches and other insects were unlikely to be regarded as anything more than a tiresome nuisance.

Extract from *An Indian Olio* by E.F. Burton – p.335

'High over the summits of these mountains are the fertile hills and vales of the Wynaad and of Coorg, whence come thousands of bullock-loads of coffee for exportation, also of cardamoms and pepper.

Were it not for the dread of fever, which is seldom absent from the lower and more malarious parts of this mountain district, the Wynaad would be a perfect paradise. Its temperate climate, its beautiful scenery, where wood and water, hill and dale, are so justly mixed; its abundance of game, both large and small; and the interest of its cultivation of coffee and cinchona, all combine to give a charm to a life upon these highlands. I had nearly forgotten one drawback. The little jungle leech, which infests the hills up to about 4000 feet, is a most abominable nuisance.

The jungle leech is as thick as a small wheat straw, and about an inch long when empty and hungry; when full, as it speedily becomes when once it gets a hold upon man or beast, it swells up to the dimensions of a long grape. It lurks behind every leaf, and lies along every blade of grass in the ever-damp localities which it loves.

In such places, if the traveller sits down to rest, he very soon sees a host of little black objects converging on him, all, as they crawl up, pointing at him with affectionate interest. They come on with the peculiar motion which is affected by some caterpillars, drawing up their bodies in a hoop, and then standing on their tails with their heads lovingly turned to the 'piece de resistance' so invitingly reclining on the grassy bank.

In the meantime, if the traveller has, as is most likely, placed himself in the shade of some tree or bush overhanging the road, another cohort of bloodthirsty little villains will have mounted its branches and dropped from its smallest twig-ends into his coat collar. The first sensation – for the bite will probably be barely felt – is that of a cold clammy body, something like a long grape, rolling down his shuddering neck, or from his whisker into his lap, and which, on examination, proves to be a well-gorged leech. A strict search promptly instituted detects several more, perhaps only half gorged sticking to various parts of the traveller's body, and often he will find a dozen or two bloated insects hanging round his ankles. Sometimes, not having been wise enough to put on leech-gaiters, I have taken off my stockings after a trudge over the damp valleys and found them full of blood and remains of gorged leeches. The worst effect of the bite is afterwards, and lasts long, especially if the victim scratches the punctures to relieve the intolerable itching; then the bites fester, and painful ulcers are the result.'

Chapter 32

MAN-EATER OF A COCHIN COFFEE ESTATE

Burton's Diary was now filled with notes on big-game hunting, the proper use and care of equipment, and recipes for cockroach poison and ant bait. In 1946, he received from R.C. Morris, a copy of DFO Notification regarding a man-eating tiger which was roaming through the Seetagundy Estate, and decided to arrange an expedition in search of this tiger. Food supplies and petrol were still rationed and many arrangements had to be made before he was able to leave for the Nelliam-pathy Hills.

DIARY _____

16th January. We started 9 a.m. and intended to stay night in D.B. top of Gudalur Ghat, but found no accommodation there, so had to go on to Ootacamund where we got to Cecil Hotel at 6 p.m. A long drive of one hundred and ninety miles.

17th. Started 9.30. Got a big earthenware teapot from Spencer & Co., and a tin steak & kidney pudding. No camera films available at Bangalore or Ooty, so no photos of this trip. Famine in films, in torch batteries also. These latter I got from Military Canteen, and they were old stock as they did not last well.

Got down thirty two miles of ghat to Mettupalayam and twenty two on to Coimbatore; and thirty to Palghat. Most of the roads here from Bangalore were concrete or tarmac and dustless. Twenty two miles on from Palghat the hydraulic brake gave up. Decided to go on as it was uphill all the way to our destination. The car took the whole ghat on second gear except at a few turns. Driver had to use hand brake at times when foot brake would have been used, if in order. The bad road ate up a lot of petrol, but fortunately we got to Warne's place with a mile or so to spare. Road new to Joseph and he did very well to manage without any bumps or getting into side ditches on that narrow forest road. Later on Mrs. Warne told us that a wild elephant had been on the ghat road that night. Good thing we didn't see it as sometimes they give trouble.

Warnes loaned us two gallons of petrol and we left there 8 p.m. to do the remaining five miles to the Bungalow. Hoped to find cook and the luggage there, but caught up the lorry at Estate pulping house: cook ill with fever. Lorry led the way and we got to Bungalow at 8.30. We heard later that only five minutes after we passed over a bridge near the pulping house, a huge forest tree came down across the road! Our luck certainly in. (It took coolies three days to chop through the trunk!) I got to bed at 12.30 having kit to see to. Before we left Bangalore, cook had been drinking and I felt sure this was the 'fever', and it certainly seemed so, as cook was all right next morning! and remained so up to 23rd January. So we arrived safely – with luck, at the Bungalow on 17th as had been arranged.

18th January. I went to see the place (fifty minutes walk) where the maistri,

Muthu, was killed on 10th December. It seemed that the tiger had been watching the path, made a rapid stalk from behind a tree and seized him from behind by head and neck. The body had been dragged uphill among the coffee bushes and not eaten.

All these coolies talk Tamil and I don't, so I have to have one of the several English speaking subordinates with me when possible. However one can, as always in case of need, get on very well by signs. Difficulty is to make them understand that I want to shoot from left shoulder so chair must face half left of line from chair to the 'bait'. In spite of Manager explaining I found next day that it is tied almost facing the cow; however it will do. Had dry leaves strewn around where baits tethered and where necessary to give warning of approach of the tiger to 'kill'.

Not far from pulping house and Hospital I was shown place where a tiger killed a cow some time ago and returned to the kill on three nights and no one to shoot it. The Manager has an S.B. twelve gauge gun which could kill a tiger at short range with contractile or rotary bullet in expert hands. But I expect the Manager, a family man with six children, would not care to pot the tiger! I think there are several tigers in this area. Ben loves this place as he gets plenty of exercise and is not kept on leash as few dogs about. Manager has two bitches, Tiny a small red one, and Maggy a black and white, but Ben takes little notice of them, and he didn't want to fight the big male pariah we met near the coolie lines yesterday evening; just as well.

These Estates have passed with the changing times into the hands of Indians. They are known here as the Nelliampathy Group and this is the Seetagundy Estate of which Palagapandy is a Sub-Division. The Nelliampathy Hills are contiguous to the Travancore High Range. Height runs to around 5500ft., and while higher slopes and summits are bare, there are heavy jungles in folds of the hills and all along the bases. It is out of these heavy jungles the Coffee Estates have been made, and there are many pockets and strips of the original primaeval forest scattered among the coffee plantations. Outside the coffee and on the hills, bison, sambur, ibex, and the smaller deer said to be plentiful. All this part of the hills is owned by the Rajah of Kollengode. Very little shooting is done by outside sportsmen, both on account of difficulty of access and supplies, and because Kollengode preserves the shooting. I am told Viceroys have shot the area and Maharaja of Patiala also.

Just now the climate is delightful, day not too hot and nights quite cold. Has been cloudy for a day or two and heavy mist this morning. Rainfall about 200in. during south west and north east monsoons, and then the area would be much under clouds and very damp and there would be plenty of leeches and biting and stinging insects of all kinds. In the undergrowth, especially in ravines and damp places is a broad-leafed stinging plant – very virulent, called 'anaimaretti' in Tamil. The whole area densely wooded where not covered by coffee and cardamom.

This is a fine Bungalow and was the Residence of the European Manager. A sad thing to see it now lifeless and unoccupied. The Estates are traversed by made paths in every direction; must be hundreds of miles of paths and roads. Many giant trees, some of them embraced and being strangled by parasitic figs and banyans. Here, one is in complete quiet; no noises other than song of birds; but not many birds yet, all are quiet until the nesting season begins middle and end of February.

Elevation at Palagapandy is around 3000ft. To south east are the Anamalais with elevations to 8200ft. and more. Highest elevation in South India is 8540ft. near Ooty. I see few tracks of animals, and hear no deer call at night. Manager tells me there are both black and spotted panthers, and I know there is the small variety peculiar to the Nelliampathies which has a ground colour of dark ochre and a small, round, bullet head.

24th January. Am having a rest today, as yesterday was a hard day visiting all three machans and climbing rope ladder, two of them really hard work for me. Coming from machan I saw a big black snake, must have been a rat snake as cooly, by signs in answer to my signs, said it was not a hamadryad. I collared Ben just in time before he could see it.

26th. Cold wind last night, and now big clouds rolling up from the Gap. Cook still has a temperature, 20 grs. quinine yesterday and ten aspirin. Each of the servants need the extra blanket from the Estate Store. Petro Max lantern lent by Manager works well. I gave our 1924 lamp to Lobb last year as a present. Evening; cook's fever still on, must be remittent and not intermittent type.

28th. Cook 101° at 7 a.m., ten grs. quinine and seven aspirin last night also a mixture given by compounder; this morning 10 grs. quinine. No kill; tiger still about the jungles to east. Cook 103° so took him in car to Hospital where he had a quinine injection.

2nd February. No tracks of tiger. Wound in buff's forehead seems likely to yield to Dettol. Lint soaked with it and put into the wound; but I must treat it that way every day until healed, or it may get flyblown. Dettol a splendid disinfectant. If that, and sulphanilamide had been available fifty three years ago, I would have saved Sexton's life, feel sure of it. Carbolic not good for septic wounds of that kind and burning with caustic failed also.

4th. News of cow killed. Tiger had dragged carcass into the cardamom at edge of a small stream. No means on the sheet rock of tethering the kill; so I had to have kill hauled back to the sapling at edge of path. There I tethered it with the buffalo's wire rope. A case of shutting the stable door. I now only have two wire ropes, as no wire procurable at Bangalore to make others. One disadvantage of this place of tying bait is that it is too near the thick cardamom and cover from which tiger can watch his kill. All this is in Brochure and I should not have disregarded my own teachings.

I was all settled and quiet at 4 o/c. At 7.20 heard noise in the cardamom: the tiger, of course, and as there was sound of a hurried departure it was clear that he had crept up to the kill, found it gone, and cleared out. About day-break, a big hornbill flew over. From now on it will be increasingly dark during early hours of the night. No distant light available as no suitable battery procurable. No camera films, no torch batteries, no spotlight bulbs, no wire rope, all kinds of things one wants – not to be had.

10th. Note brought to camp to say tiger had killed the milking cow of Hospital compounder. This was naturally supposed to be the man-eater which killed Muthu on 10th December, and now kills the cow at same place on 9th February. It may have a round of a month for visiting this place. The cow had been dragged into a thickly wooded nala inside a large patch of dense forest. Neck broken, large fang holes. A tree was available on other side of the nala, so chair was tied on that and well screened. At latest daylight and the night fast shutting down, I heard the tiger coming and putting on the field glasses just made out a shape moving above the kill on the sloping bank. Could not, without knowing what it was, have said it was a tiger. It is against all experience and practice to put torch on in face of a tiger at that early stage of its appearance, so I waited until I heard cracking of rib bones and then put on torch. Nothing was to be seen! Not even the red raw ribs of the kill which had been on the rocky slope.

After more bone cracking, I again put on torch and after much search at last, high up, found the tiger's tail laid along the bank, all else entirely screened by high overhanging leafy boughs. No reflection of eyes could be seen. The eating ceased when light was turned on, and began again when turned off; and so for several hours. Looked several times and at last no tail to be seen, the tiger had gone. There had been, owing to the rocky bank, no means of tethering the hind part of the carcass. With one hook up of his paw he must have lifted the carcass, legs eaten the previous night, and lodged it behind a small sapling to prevent it slipping down.

11th. Sat up again in same machan having cleared away all the obstructing leaves and anchored the body to the small sapling. About 7.20 heard sounds and put on the torch but could not see the shape of the animal. After a while I saw eyes, and that they were not wide enough apart for a tiger. I waited a long time, but rightful owner of kill did not appear and push off the intruder, so I again put on light. I let the head turn to one side and then took careful aim and made a fortunate shot as bullet took the beast in side of neck and I saw by aid of torch that it was a panther – stone dead.

14th. Back to Bungalow and decided all hope of man-eater gone. Wife getting increasingly tired of this life at the bungalow. Seemed the best thing would be to return to Bangalore and be ready for instant return by train in case of need; so I began to pack up shikar kit. Had done much of this and put away rifle after oiling, when Warne's car hurriedly arrived with a note to say a cooly woman had been killed on the Chandramalai Estate.

Car came at 2.30 and I was off with all necessary kit at 3.15. The English speaking Estate Staff very helpful. I went some way in the car and was then taken up an open hillside, short rough grass and a few small boulders. One man, Ramaswamy, knew where the body had been dragged. All was very thick lantana between the tussocky grass and the evergreen tree forest having much bush undergrowth.

There were a dozen or so people behind and I signed to them to keep back. One man had a S.B. shot gun (learned afterwards he was the Estate Watcher) and he was not far behind me. I had made all ready opposite the tunnel in the lantana as the men said 'the Tiger is there, he has eaten her head'. Moon sight up, rifle loaded, two rounds in emergency pockets on coat, topee off, and was about to sit down and progress in the tunnel in that way, with Ramaswamy behind my right shoulder, when !!! off went the man's gun and away went the tiger with a frightened 'whoof'. A golden opportunity gone.

I found the brute had been lying a foot or two behind the woman's shoulders. He would have taken me to be one of the peepers who had evidently peered to see, as they knew the head had been eaten. I think I would have been able to kill him on the spot either before he quitted or while he was attacking. It was indeed fortunate that the gun didn't blow a hole in me. When I instinctively looked behind, I saw the barrel pointed quarter right away from me and slanting upwards, so as far as that went he was holding it in a safe position. The body was on its back, feet towards me and was in a narrow space clear of lantana growth. The tiger had crashed away through a kind of path in the lantana to my half left. The head had been chewed off and part of the upper surface of left side of body gnawed off. There was a deep claw gash in left side evidently caused by left paw thumb as the tiger hooked at the woman as she ran to escape. The body was lying straight, legs together and quite naked. Women of that class wear only two garments, a sari and a skirt fastened round the waist by tucking in as one does with a bath towel so her clothes were very soon torn off her when she was seized by the head and dragged off. She was a slim woman; age around thirty two they told me, with a daughter thirteen and a son of seven. I removed her silver anklet and bracelet from each wrist into keeping of Ramaswamy.

There was a good forest tree, a mango with many branches, and very suitable for tying of chair, which was soon in position. No screening necessary as except for the narrow space where the body lay, all in front and to either side was a mass of green lantana and behind was dense evergreen forest with much undergrowth. Just after the men left I had a bad moment as the torch refused to give a light! However I managed to get it going. My spotlight bulb had given out early in the month and the bulb in use threw a dark circle in centre of beam. I would have to try and make a fortunate shot as I had done for the panther.

The expected rustle came to my ears at 7.30 and putting on the light I saw the tiger's eyes brightly shining as he looked up. The torch light was not good, and batteries beginning to fail. I took several trial aims and thought I would be all right; I never fire head shots if they can be avoided. To the shot there was a groaning noise and I knew the shot had been a good one, but before I could make out his body and put in second barrel, he was up and lurched into the lantana. I saw the whirl of his forelegs as he went. After that no further sound up to the morning, except that an hour later I thought I heard a groan to my left and pictured to myself a dangerous crawl after him in the morning.

At day-break I couldn't see anything of the tiger. Men arrived 7.15. and I told them to cut a way through lantana to my right. This they did, but previously one or two of the more adventurous, or foolish, had peeped and peered until they could see the tiger's head moving to and fro, signalling this with their waving hands. That was a good moment for me as I knew I would not have to do the often considered and equally dreaded lantana crawl on track of a wounded tiger. The tiger was evidently pretty far gone, and he was only a few feet from where he was hit twelve hours after the shot.

I was still in the chair when I suddenly saw the tiger on his feet, but only his snarling head. I at once got in a shot over his head, into back of it at the neck and he went down for good. That was the finish, but when I had got down and circled round to the tunnel entrance I could see he was still breathing so put in a bullet above left elbow which finally killed him. It was necessary to be careful with such a crowd of men all over the place. So at last the man-eater was dead.

At first sight I thought him to be a young animal, coat staring, not silky, but soon saw his teeth and that he was a very old beast. Paws looked enormous owing to his emaciation. One canine tooth decayed away, other three mere stumps owing to decay and holes of decay down the centre of them. Two wounds, one at top of shoulder and other at top of spine at waist and a raw but healing wire noose scar all round the waist.

Cochin Police were present and said the body must wait there for the Inspector to arrive from the low country. I walked to car (jeep), waiting at foot of the hill, Joseph was there and produced a cup of tea provided by Manager. I had been ten nights in machan chairs, so would be glad of a rest and sleep, but I did not feel at all too tired. The tiger was taken amid shouts of the coolies, men, women and children, to the Factory, and there propped up to be viewed by all. After that he was placed on the Factory scale and weighed 316lbs – a hundred lbs short of what he should have been for his 9ft. 2in. curves measurement, (body 6ft. 2in. and tail 3ft.). All claws blunt, two missing from near fore paw. Bullet of the night had entered above and to right of left eye and blown a big hole at the cheek. Had I been able to see, I would have put in a fatal shot at top of shoulder and base of neck. A couple of inches to left and he would have been instantly dead; one more inch to right and there would have been a near miss and trouble. So I made a lucky shot.

Warnes came to see the tiger and wanted me to stay and have breakfast, but I went to Bungalow as wife would be anxious for my return. The tiger was put on a cart, propped up by packing cases, and so taken, well garlanded with flowers, by a team of twenty coolies amidst shouts and bang of drums along the five miles of road to Palagapandy. All coolies on the route were given a view of the dreaded monster and the cart got to bungalow at 11.20. Soon after, the Inspector of Police from Cochin Nemmara arrived in his jeep car to complete his report by actual sight of the tiger.

After measurements, I made the initial cuts for the skinning. The men who skinned the panther did well with the tiger under my supervision, and sewed up all the holes. No bullet found in the carcass except base of one of mine. I was fortunate to have these two coolies with some previous experience of skinning to help me, as all had to be done before dark. I skinned out head and part of paws myself, and the skin was pegged out in one of the godowns as had been done with the panther. One part finely powdered alum and two parts salt and it was well cured for the taxidermist.

17th. Paid 8/- for the tiger skinning and 5/- for the panther plus 4 annas to two children. Paid Ponnan 10/- and others in proportion for machan work, Rs.45/- in all. They get their full Estate pay of 8/- annas a day each in addition. So far as shikar goes, not an expensive trip, but however much one paid out the people would never be satisfied. I left two buffs with the Manager and he is to sell them at best price he can when they are fattened up a bit. Have not been asked to pay for the cow killed on 3rd February so am saying nothing about it. The Estate lorry none too safe to my mind so we take cook in our car. Also he is still in convalescent stage and forty five miles jolting in lorry would do him no good. A few days ago the lorry bumped into a rock at side of road and I see the two front wheels are of different sizes.

18th. Finishing packing and writing letters. Wrote Conservator Forest Cochin State, Trichur, to say tiger shot and giving some details. Same to R.C. Morris. Found he had sent copy of my letter to Van Ingen, and later received his acknowledgement of my letter and saying he would like to send account of the tiger to B.N.H.S.! Wrote him politely I could do that for myself.

Next day on arrival at Coonoor and Symons' house I went to bed and stayed put for three days. A very bad influenza cold and near bronchitis. After a couple of days H.G. got a temperature and went to bed. We were both of us a bit pulled down and glad to get away to warmer climate on 3rd March. I had to let Joseph have my lined waterproof coat, or he would have been ill.

3rd March. To Mysore. On the way, silencer pipe burst, Joseph tied it up and we had it repaired at Mysore next day. Hot at Mysore and the Hotel badly run as to food, many dishes scarcely eatable.

19th April. Sent a Note to the B.N.H.S. which will not appear till the August issue of the Journal. A Doctor here interested in dentition and decay of teeth will examine the skull, take X-ray photos, and write a scientific Note for me to add to my own Note to B.N.H.S. Skull sent to Curator, Bombay and I asked for it back, but not received yet and don't know if he got it. Hope it has not been lost in rail transit. Sent it 'To Pay' as some safeguard against loss.

The Nelliampathies Planters Association have sent me Rs.150/- with which to buy myself a souvenir. I couldn't very well refuse it. Sent a letter of thanks, and wrote that I take their Resolution etc. etc. as expressing the feelings of all Estates Staffs and Workers. Also told them the Souvenirs will be – gold mounted 'lucky' bone brooches, one each to PMST and SSM; a pair of silver anklet chains and pair silver anklets to Onnai, daughter of Meenachi who was killed by the tiger; some trifle which H.G. will select for herself, and a pen for myself. That comes to about 150/-.

Song of birds was heard a month earlier in Nelliampathies than here; also the flowering of several species of trees was early. A great cyclone has recently struck Madras and those hills, so am glad we are away. No rain or storm here, but much in the Nilgiris.

LETTER – from P.J.S., Chandramalai Estates Ltd. 16th April 1947.
    'Dear Col. Burton, Thanks for your letter of 9th inst. together with the silver leg chains and anklets for Meenachi's daughter.
    I am giving these to the girl with the instructions that theyshould be properly used. I hope she is very pleased with them.
    It is very good of you to have thought of her and sent the useful and valuable articles. The girl's name is Onnai. With kind regards,'

Last entries – hunting and fishing.

Colonel Burton was seventy nine when he shot the man-eating tiger of the Nelliam-pathy Hills. Another expedition later that year for a proscribed man-eater was hampered by appalling weather and the uncooperative and unreasonable attitude of the local shikaris and villagers.

Letters and Notifications

Notification – Rogue Elephant. (1) Copy
    'It is hereby notified for the information of all shooting license-holders that a rogue male elephant of the following description is reported to be roaming about from Gundimalam to filature coupe, and is invariably found to stay in the reserved forest near Eragabalu village near Mavathur in Kollegal Range, Kollegal Division and that it recently killed a Sholaga of Udhatti. It is solitary having separated itself from the herd. All shooting license- holders are encouraged to destroy the animal.
    Any person destroying this tusker with due authority will be permitted to retain both the tusks.
    Description:– Height: about 9ft. Diameter of foot print: 1½ft.
Tusks: two – about 3ft. long turning upwards clearly.
    This notification will be valid for one year from this date.
Dated 8.2.1947. A.V. Sundaram, District Forest Officer, Kollegal.

Notification – Rogue Elephant (2) Copy
    'It is hereby notified for the information of all shooting license-holders that a rogue elephant of the following description is roaming about in the vicinity of Thamarakarai etc. villages in Bargur Range of this Division and to be causing great damage to crops. It is also reported that it has killed 3 cows and is chasing men who frequent these parts. It has not killed any human being so far, but is proving a definite menace to many. All shooting license-holders are encouraged to destroy the animal.
    Any person destroying this animal with due authority will be permitted to retain both the tusks.

Description:– Height: about 10ft. Circumference of foot print 5¾ft.
Tail: unusually long and devoid of hair. Tusks: two – normal size, almost straight
and pointed downwards (without any interior or exterior curve).
Is found roaming about in the vicinity of Thamarakarai, Devarbetta, Eratty,
Vellimalai, and Ondonai, villages of Bargur Range.
    This notification will be valid for one year from this date.
dated. 7.10.1946. A.V. Sundaram, District Forest Officer, Kollegal.'

Notification Rogue Elephants
    It is hereby notified for the information of all shooting license holders that two
rogue elephants of the following description are reported to be roaming about in
the Forests adjoining Eratty and Thamarakerai and giving trouble to men, cattle
and property. All shooting license holders are encouraged to destroy them.
    Any person destroying them with proper authority will be permitted to retain
the tusks. This notification will be in force for one year from this date.
    Description No.1.
    Height about 9½ft.
Circumference of foot about 4½ft.
Length of tusks the tusks are cradle like about 3½ft. long each

    No.2.
    Height about 10ft.
Circumference of foot about 4½ft.
Length of tusks about 3ft. in length. There is a small bend in the tusks at the end.
    (signed) District Forest Officer.
Copy to – All shooting license holders.

N.B. Bargan Hills, Kollegal Division. Thamakerai is south of Thatakerai on the
Ramapuram – Bargam – Andirgar road. There is a Bungalow there.

(Copy of D.F.O. Kollegal's letter dated 12.11.48)
'It is hereby notified again for the information of all shooting license holders that a
man-eating tiger is residing in Sembakobai forest of Minniam Beat (Minna Valley) of
Ramapuram Range (Kollegal Taluk) and killing either the cowherds or the cows. All
shooting license holders are encouraged to destroy the animal. They are warned that
the animal should not be wounded and left alive. D.F.O. Kollegal.'

SHIKAR DIARY ————————————————————————————————
25 July 1947 to 25 August 1947. Received from R.C. Morris, copies of three D.F.O.
Kollegal Notifications regarding two Proscribed Male Elephants and one Tiger: the
latter said to kill cattle, also herdsmen tending the cattle that graze in the forests. Relying
on Morris telling me that very little rain in Minna Valley during south west Monsoon
(this perhaps not a normal year): I went 25th July to 25th August, FATAL. I should have
put it off until January, February. Wrote D.F.O. and Deputy Collector, Kollegal, as to
some preliminary arrangements, and got all shikar kit and supplies together.

At Kollegal I found D.F.O. and Deputy Collector away. D.B. full of babus, so I had to bed down under a tree beside the car. Next morning received Ration order from office of Deputy Collector (a month's supply) twelve Madras measures rice, 12 lbs sugar, six bottles Kerosene oil. Unable to get more than two gallons petrol at Kollegal, all sold out; so a little anxiety as to petrol for return journey.

Put up for the night at D.B. Ramapuram – almost bare of furniture. Arranged for three carts to go early next day, 27th Sunday, to Minnayam. A mile short of camp, the cart in which sat Tamby, upset in a sandy nala. Fortunately no one hurt: kerosene oil leaked on to the locked canvas sack of rations, and bundle of rice got a bit damped on one side. A woman and small girl had got a lift and made the narrow cart top heavy. The road very rocky in many places, so I had terrific jolts to suffer, although I was on my bedding roll, spread out. Ramshackle F.R.H., just a thatched cowshed affair, bath tub full of bandicoot droppings.

Had considerable trouble in getting tent pitched, a useless and obstructive village Head Man. Have been taking Paludrine tablets daily, also Tamby, as malaria preventive. All demands at this Village exorbitant: eggs 2 annas each, no fowls; F.G. away. Cart men demand Rs.12 each. I offered 6/- each, and as they refuse to accept must await decision of the Forester. F.G. of Mingam just arrived and says to pay 10/- each. Have told the Headman that if this is their attitude I had better go away, and let the tiger continue his killings. Rice will do for dinner if no egg curry possible.

29th July. Tuesday. Hills very stony, jungle thick in ravines, thorny everywhere. Got to camp at 3 p.m. just as thunderstorm came on with heavy rain. A herd of village cattle have just passed along, returning from the days grazing, all look in poor condition.

31st. News of a cow killed yesterday two miles to east. Went with shikari, kill by a panther and carcass picked almost clean by vultures. Took nearly two hours to go there and back. As the tiger and tigress were in the nala night of 28th, and left that night, they won't return until about night of 5th. Full moon is on 2nd August. Machan tree a good one, all others infested by red ants.

5th August. Kill by panther. Left camp 1.30, ladder to put up and screening and distant light to fix. A heavy thunderstorm came on and I, and all I had with me, got soaked. I expected panther to turn up about 4 o/c. It did: Alas! I had forgotten to have my head screened against the sky line and was spotted at the loophole (moon behind me), an error which should never have happened. I am more forgetful than I used to be. Can't blame the shikari, it is my job to see such technical details carried out. No single article of kit not soaked by the heavy rain. Minna nala in heavy flood. Six torch cells damaged, and only six left in stock and two in use in small torch.

Evening. A small tiger, (two years old?) but shikari says big tigers have small feet! went up the ravine, past the tethered cow some time after the night's storm. It has of course, seen the cow and may return and kill it tonight. Shikari was offended because I said the panther saw me at loophole, because there was not proper screening behind my head. He said he would return to his village! But eventually he became all right, as I said he was to blame and I was to blame as I should have reminded him about the back of head screening. I was foolish to have taken a survey through my loophole by leaning forward.

The men are saying 8 annas a day not enough. Headman and F.G. say Forester will be here soon and will settle all that. The villagers of this valley are industrious cultivators. The ground has to be cleared of trees and boulders, and these they build into walls, both protective and to bank up the red soil and prevent erosion. The herds of goats have the best of feed on the thorny trees and shrubs. All are sleek and fat, and nearly all are black: goat are priced up to 35/- each and sheep 65/-.

6th. Whole sky was black to south west and a great thunderstorm on. Water everywhere and tigers may be anywhere. Next morning found the cow had been attacked by a tiger, but not killed. Seems to be a fairly big tiger, and is the same that passed up the nala on 5th, and did not return that night as hoped. It seems that this tiger's teeth are bad and he can't kill a cow. Possibly it is the man-eater of this valley.

8th. Was in machan at 4 p.m. yesterday, and all quiet. At six o'clock, the tiger uttered several tremendous menacing growls; evidently to warn off all intruders. After the growls ceased a final lower growl and silence. He is evidently very old and experienced.

I was 7th, 8th, 9th, nights in machan and intended to rest on 10th, but men came to say a cow killed one mile east of my tethering place. Had machan chair put up in tree over the kill. Nil during the night. I have no doubt now that the tigers of this Valley don't return to kills made by them on grazing cattle as the people make such an uproar; AND, as in this case, skin the cow and remove all flesh and innards to the village to be eaten by chamars.

12th. Am told Forester sends word that I should pay shikari 2/- a day and all coolies 1/- a day. Sent for F.G. and he says this is to be the rate. Told him I can't afford it and will pack up and go. Sent shikari to fetch the chair and ropes; and by 2.30 most things sorted, listed and packed. Asking F.G. what would be payment to baggage coolies for the ten miles to Udhatti he asked shikari standing by, who at once in a curiously defiant manner said 2/12 each man. F.G. fixed loads at 50lbs. I said I would make them near that as possible, but could not guarantee it; may or may not be.

Heavy rain yesterday evening and again this afternoon. Only just had time to get kit dried for packing. Very little rice remains! and it was thirty days supply, and only fifteen days used! Tamby says 2½ seers, 5lbs, tainted by Kerosene oil and thrown away; anyway I will live on ragi and my rations. So I don't get this man-eater. As I have remarked in Brochure; it is very difficult to shikar when you don't know the language.

The jungles at top of the pass of Semba Kombai nala have a very 'farmy' appearance – plenty of grazing, and should be a number of sambur and the smaller deer. Not a sound during the night and the shikari said – so I understood – that there are no sambur there. I expect all this country is being continually and progressively denuded of game animals. Wrote several letters yesterday and all went today with F.G. to Ramapuram. I expect he has gone for 15th August 'Freedom of India' celebrations. He returns on 16th, and says will get seventeen coolies for early 17th.

Glad to have arranged with the Schoolmaster for all kit to be stored in School House Verandah. This relieves a great anxiety as to wet baggage before starting. Rain last night and a very heavy thunderstorm yesterday afternoon. Tent partly flooded; all dry now and very hot today, may rain tomorrow. Pray for none on 16th! Three miles here to Koppiam quite flat, so suggested to F.G. to have two carts to there and coolies from Koppiam on. However, let him do what he wants. On 16th moved tent into School House. Tiger killed a cow.

17th. Can get only one cart so left eight articles kit at School House, and engaged the one cart to take everything to Ramapuram in two trips; had to agree to pay 35/-, of which 20/- in advance. Started late, I walked ahead, about eight and a half miles; a good road, mostly; tracks of a few kakur and four-horn only. In former days these jungles must have held many game animals. At this time the scenery is pleasing, all green and some grass, later all will be dry and arid. Got to Ramapuram 6.30 p.m.

19th. Had intended leave here Friday for Hanur; but am now told can't get cart that day, only on Thursday. So must go Thursday, 21st, if kit arrives tomorrow from Minniam! Bad luck I did not get a shot at the man-eater. With better weather I might have tried further in spite of doubled rates for shikari and coolies. I should not have done this trip until January, but thought the people wanted the tiger killed, and they seemed not to care whether it was killed or not!!

Total cost of trip was around Rs.430/- which works out at usual average of 15/- a day. Neither I nor Tamby had fever. Paludrine seems to be an effective preventative and I have entered it as so in Brochure.

South west monsoon 1947. An unusually copious and long one; unceasing until 25th September and more rain every other day up to mid October! Unable to dry my tent until 26th September and other tents which should be pitched and aired must wait until January. No reply yet from Railway for claim R.50/- for loss of the tiger's skull in transit to Bombay on 25th March last. Panther skin not yet received from Van Ingen of Mysore, over seven months.

(Note: Entries shikar diary 8th to 12th August, show the change of attitude of people when Transfer of Power (15th August 1947) was imminent) RWB.

1948.
10th February. Heard from D.F.O. the tiger killed: the elephant not yet killed. Wrote to Schoolmaster asking for details.

5th April. Hear from R.C. Morris that tiger not killed, and a human kill has taken place since it was reported to have been killed. Elephant also not yet killed.

It wasn't until 1953 that Colonel Burton and his wife left India to return to England. Hilda was in poor health and they wanted to be nearer to their children and grandchildren. Hilda lived another two years, and Colonel Burton spent his days quietly in England until he died in 1963 aged ninety five.

His efforts to promote the work of the IUPN and towards the passing of the Indian Wildlife Preservation Act reflect his vision of the future, and particularly the future of wildlife in India. His main concern was the rapid destruction of the environment and the denudation of the forests for timber. In his travels, he had seen game diminishing from the jungle, and fish vanishing from the rivers, and realised the necessity for an official policy towards conservation before it was too late. After Independence, when many British officials had left the country, he redoubled his efforts, together with the BNHS of which Salim Ali was now Hon. Secretary, in attempts to arouse public and official awareness of the urgent need for conservation.

The tribute from the BNHS to his sixty years involvement with the Society, commented that his name had become a byword in Indian Wild Life Conservation, and that his persistent hammering on the gravity of the situation was largely responsible for the coming into being of the I.W.L. Board with H.H. the Raj-pramukh of Mysore as President.

The following entries dated February 1948 were the last in the Diaries, and it is characteristic of Colonel Burton that his last entry was not 'the end' but 'tomorrow'.

DIARY

1948. On Sunday 15th February went with H.A. Alderson, to Mekedatu to spy out the river. 7 a.m. to Sangama where the Arkavati River joins the Cauvery. Waded across the Arkavati, ten inches water, sandy; difficult crossing for car. Walked along good cart road, for two and a half miles to Mekedatu. River for about two miles, is a series of falls and deep pools cut through the rocks. Until the rapids fall into the first deep cut pool one could fish from coracle; the rest would be from the bank.

Two men here, say they SEE big fish in the rapids, Mekedatu way. Quite likely, may be some up river migration going on at this time. Before five years the Electric Power House of 15000 k.w. will be built at Mekedatu of which about 5000 k.w. will go to Madras Government on electrifying adjacent areas, and all this part of the river will become a long, deep lake. Am told there are lot of elephant, bison, tiger, on the east side of Arkavati River which joins Cauvery just here.

28th. Arrived Sangama 11 a.m. Pitched tent and all settled by 12.30. Fairly strong wind from down river, camp very sandy. I now have only twenty six iron tent pegs left – twenty stolen one way and another last few years. Alderson's car and driver stay with me until tuesday, then goes Bangalore to bring Alderson out on Friday. Sent a lad to tell coracle man to come. He sent word 'What pay?' I sent word 'Five rupees a day coracle and two men'. Reply came 'Ten rupees a day'. I said 'No'. Later news, the coracle and two men will be here at 6 a.m. May be, may be not! If Holder gets a rubber coracle for me then can tell the local sharks to go to hell! but have to be sure of getting man to work the rubber coracle and an extra helping man also.

29th Sunday. It was said yesterday evening that the coracle man and another would be here 6 a.m: they didn't arrive. At 8 a.m. I went down river with two men, walked on sand and boulders for about a mile or so. Then got to a very deep long straight channel, rocks both sides. Fished till a little after 10 o/c, then made way to the main road and by that back to camp. The high wind is a great nuisance, blowing up a lot of sand: everything in tent covered in sand.

1st March. Monday. Yesterday evening went up river. Saw the place where a big mugger lies on bank and roams about under trees. A lot of green riverside jungle on the other bank. One of the two Muhammadan men with me went back to Chennapatura yesterday; only have this one man now. He is a worker in lacquer, with a toy firm at Chennapatura, very fanatical look about him. It was at Chennapatura there was a riot last year, and a number of Hindus were killed. Head Master of local school was slain in the School House, his throat cut.

2nd. Tuesday: up and off by quarter to six, meant to start at five o'clock but can't get these people to be ready early. Went to Mekedatu, no small fish as bait. Tried all the lures I have, none taken. Found a place where there are rapids, also deep water, and all accessible from shores this side. One and a half hour's walk back to camp; hot sun on back all the way. Will take umbrella next time. If I ever come here again it will be to camp at Mekedatu. Could get car to here and a bullock cart to take kit onwards. A lot of mugger in this river but not at Mekedatu, no places for them to leave the water to get on to land. No tracks of tiger or panther.

4th. In evening went to Mekedatu in Jeep as far as the bad dip and walked the remaining half mile. When preparing a ¼lb. live bait for use with big float, the fish struggled and escaped and somehow one hook of one of the two trebles got me in outside edge of right hand. Had blades of my knife sharpened on rock and Mooriswamy cut very well, as I showed him, and I got out the hook quite easily. A big gash – plenty of blood. Tied up with hanky and in evening applied dettol and a proper bandage. No pain, no throbbing; wound will heal without trouble. Back to camp at seven o'clock.

Friday. Out in Jeep to Mekedatu, and crossed the V cut by use of two flat galvanised iron sheets. Used both spinning and live bait, no offers. Mooriswamy caught one CHARIAS – a cat fish. Never before seen one, very handsome, spotted like BARILIUS. In afternoon went with Alderson to Mekedatu; no offers to either of us using dead and live bait, and artificial spinners. Fished the live bait at depth 45 ft, just touching the bottom.

Saturday. We went to long pool in middle of river, a mile below camp, across the rocky bed of river and through several small water channels. No offers to either of us. I got hung up twice; lost trace, barrel lead, Hardy Leaded Spinner, and then No.5 spoon and trace and Hillman lead; too many rocks everywhere. Tomorrow morning to Mekedatu.

GLOSSARY

achha	O.K.
adha sher	half a tiger
Afridi	People from the area of the Khyber Pass, of Rajput or Aryan descent
Amin	Government Revenue or Judicial Officer
ankus	light goad for elephants
anna	currency – ⅟₁₆th of a rupee
asafoetida	resinous gum from plant, medicinal
arrack	alcoholic drink from distilled coco sap or rice
atta	flour of wheat
babu	Indian clerk, or similar profession
Bahadur	title of respect, champion
baksheesh	tip
Baluch/i	Islamic hill people of Baluchistan
baniah	moneylender
Banjara/Brinjara	nomadic grain carrier or gypsy
barbet	tropical bird
begar	forced labour
bhalu	bear
Bhils	bandit tribe of Malwar and Khandesh
bhisti	water bearer
bobbery pack	pack of dogs of different breeds used by Officers for hunting
boda	buffalo
bukarouts	goatherds
bund	raised embankment, causeway
burra	large
Canarese	language of people of Kanara
Cantonment	military station and living quarters
Chak	area or district
Chamars	workers in leather and skins
chandni balala	jew fish (chilenus undulatus)
Chanpans	native Indians of the Himalayas
chapatti	flat cake of unleavened bread
chapli	sandal
Chaprassi	Orderly, messenger
charpoy	wooden frame bed with webbing
chatty	earthenware water pot
chillum	Indian pipe
chinkara	Indian gazelle (deriv. from hindi 'chhink = sneeze' the alarm note of this animal)
chital	spotted or axis deer
chokidar	caretaker, night watchman

choultry	hut, shed, used as basic lodgings
chukor	partridge
chuman	a type of lime plaster
coolun	species of duck
cooly	porter, labourer
coppersmith	crimson breasted barbet
crore	ten million, 100 lakhs of rupees
Cutchery	Court house
dacoit	robber bandit
dah	large curved knife, Burma
dak/dhak	bungalow/house for travellers on relay route
dal/dhal	lentils, split pulse
Dashera	Hindu religious festival – October
dandi	open sedan chair used in Himalayas
dherzi	tailor
dhimar	fisherman
dhobies	washermen
dhow	large Arabian sailing ship
Diwali/Dhivali	Hindu festival of Light – October
dooly	covered sedan chair
drongo	Indian bird, similar to crow
Duffadar	Indian Army N.C.O., Cavalry
Durbar	Court, levee
feringhi	foreigner
florican	large bird of Indian plains
four-horn	antelope
francolin	pheasant
gawalla/gowala	cowman
ghat	mountain pass, landing place, or flight of steps leading to a river
ghee	clarified butter
girgaya	he is dead
godown	storeroom, warehouse
gond	swamp deer
goolar/goolu	wild fig
gooral	small goat/antelope
gram	chick pea, pulse
Gujars	ancient Indian tribe, mainly agricultural workers and in Kashmir people who graze flocks
Gurkhas	Inhabitants of Nepal, and renowned Army Regiments
hallal	killing of meat according to muslim law
hanuman	common langur or monkey
hawa	the wind
Holi	Hindu fertility festival, Spring
hoolock	whitebrowed gibbon
houbara	bird similar to bustard
Irulas	Native tribe of southern India living mainly in the jungles

jaghir	government assigned land
Jain	Indian religion
Jamadar	Native Officer, head of soldiers
jamun	wild plum
jayzang	syrup made from juice of palm tree
jharan	piece of cloth or duster
jheel	shallow natural lake, mere
jhula	seat on pulley of wire rope for crossing river in Himalayas
jowari	species of millet, grows 8 to 10ft
julka	transport
Kali	Black goddess of destruction and sacrifice
kalij	pheasant
kakur	barking deer, muntjac
Kamsidar/Kamavisdar	Revenue Officer of District, (similar to Amin of United Provinces)
karab	bad
Karani	Government Officer for Revenue, Laccadives
Karma	Buddhism and Hinduism, destiny, fate
kebab	pieces of mutton toasted on a stick
Khonds/Gonds	descended from barbarous inhabitants of the Eastern Vindhyan Mountains
khud	steep hillside
kilta	luggage pack
klim	dried milk
koklass	pheasant
Korku	tribe living in hills and forests of Central and Southern India
kulthi or khundi	crop like jowari, grown for cattle fodder
Kurumbus	Tamil low caste people, mainly shepherds
lac/lakh	one hundred thousand rupees
Lamburdar	Man appointed by village to pay the Government dues – Baluchistan
lammergeyer	bearded vulture of the Himalayas
lantana	spreading ground cover
lascar	Indian sailor
machan	shooting platform in a tree
Mahaut	elephant driver
mahseer	large Indian freshwater fish
maidan	open field, public land
Maistri	carpenter, foreman
Malayalam	language of people of Malabar
margaya	he is killed
maro	shoot to kill
maund	measure of weight, about 42lb.
minivet	small Indian bird
Monegar	Magistrate and Chief of Laccadives
moonal	pheasant

Muccadam	Head man of village
mugger	Indian crocodile
Muktana	Agent or Attorney in Court
Muktessor	Official/Commissioner of the Monegar's Court
Mullah	Muslim priest
murghi	chicken, fowls
Musjid	mosque
mythun	hybrid cattle
nala	stream, water course, ravine
Nirvana	Buddhism/Hinduism beatitude of release from earthly trials
nukta	species of duck
numdah	felt rug for horses
pan supari	special concoction of food containing betel nut and leaves
parao	courtyard
pastor	bird similar to starling but pink
Patel	head man of village
Pathans	People of Afghan descent settled mainly in Baluchistan
pavee	a look at
peon	messenger, orderly
pi dogs	ownerless mongrels
pice	smallest unit of Indian currency
Pindarus	originally plundering and marauding bands of rebels
Plantain	fruit similar to banana
poojah	Hindu worship
poojari	priest who performs poojah
pucca	correct, genuine
pucca road	tarred road
puggrie	turban
pullah	small bundle of grass
punkah	large fan suspended from ceiling
purdah	curtained seclusion for women
puttie	strip of cloth wound round leg from ankle to knee
Ramzan/Ramadan	Islamic period of fasting
Raj	Kingdom, British Rule in India
rupee	standard unit of currency
Sadhu	holy man
Sahib	Sir – European or indicate rank
salaam/sulaam	salutation, greeting
Seer	measure of weight approx 1 kilogram or liquid measure 1 litre
see-see	partridge
sepoy	Indian soldier, Infantry
serai	Inn with courtyard
sher	tiger
shikar	hunting
shikar/i	hunter
shikra	small hawk

Siana	head man in Himalayan village
Sircar	the Government
Siva	Hindu god
sholas	pockets of vegetation in hillsides
Sholegas/Soligars	native tribe of Southern India
sounder	herd of wild pig
Sowar	mounted Indian soldier or policeman
Subadar	equivalent of RSM, Indian Commissioned Officer, Infantry
Swaraj	Home Rule
syce	groom
tahsil	subdivision of territory for revenue
Tahsildar	local tax collector
takin	large goat/antelope
tamasha	spectacle
Tamils	race of Southern India and Ceylon
Telegu	language of Southern India
terai	plains country below Himalayas
Thadus	native Indian tribe
thamin	brow-antlered deer
Thanadar	Chief of Police Station
thar/tahr	wild goat
tiffin	light lunch
tonga	two wheeled horse drawn carriage
topee	pith or cork helmet
waler	small Australian horse
wallan	raft
yourt	large tent
Zemindian/dari	landowner
zemindar	estate

A. & N.S.	Army & Navy Stores
B.N.H.S.	Bombay Natural History Society
D.B.	District Bungalow
D.C.	District Commissioner
D.F.O.	District Forestry Officer
F.R.H.	Forest Rest House
G.I.P.	Great Indian Peninsula Railway
H.E.I.Co.	Hon. East India Company
H.G.V.R.	Hyderabad and Godavery Valley Railway
I.C.S.	Indian Civil Service
I.M.S.	Indian Medical Service
I.U.P.N.	International Union for the Protection of Nature
I.S.R.	Indian State Railways
N.G.S.R.	Nizam's Guaranteed State Railway
P.W.D.	Public Works Department
S.D.O.	Senior District Officer
S.F.O.	Senior Forestry Officer